GunDigest PRESENTS

The Illustrated History of Firearms

From the NRA Museums — SECOND EDITION

Jim Supica | Doug Wicklund | Philip Schreier

Copyright © 2020 National Rifle Association of America

All rights reserved. No portion of this publication may be reproduced or transmitted in any form or by any means, electronic or mechanical, including photocopy, recording, or any information storage and retrieval system, without permission in writing from the publisher, except by a reviewer who may quote brief passages in a critical article or review to be printed in a magazine or newspaper, or electronically transmitted on radio, television, or the Internet.

You can join the NRA by contacting them at:
The National Rifle Association of America, 11250 Waples Mill Road Fairfax, VA 22030 or by visiting their Web site, www.nra.org

And you can view the treasures of the NRA Museums at www.nramuseums.com.
The NRA National Firearms Museum in Fairfax, the NRA National Sporting Arms Museum at Bass Pro Shops in Springfield MO, and the Frank Brownell Museum of the Southwest at the NRA Whittington Center in Raton NM are open every day of the week with free admission.

Published by

Gun Digest® Books, an imprint of Caribou Media Group, LLC
Gun Digest Media
5600 W. Grande Market Drive, Suite 100
Appleton, WI 54913
www.gundigest.com

To order books or other products call 920.471.4522 ext. 104
or visit us online at **www.gundigeststore.com**

CAUTION: Technical data presented here, particularly technical data on handloading and on firearms adjustment and alteration, inevitably reflects individual experience with particular equipment and components under specific circumstances the reader cannot duplicate exactly. Such data presentations therefore should be used for guidance only and with caution. Caribou Media accepts no responsibility for results obtained using these data.

ISBN-13: 978-1-9511-1514-2

Designed by Jim Supica and Gene Coo
Cover Design by Gene Coo
Edited by Todd Woodard

Printed in China

10 9 8 7 6 5 4 3 2

CONTENTS

4 **Preface**

Introduction
6 A Brief History of Firearms

The Earliest Guns
22 Early Ignition Systems
29 Old World Artistry
32 Old Guns in the New World

The Flintlock Era
35 18th C. European Military Arms
37 Shot Heard Round the World
41 Blunderbusses & Flint Pistols
43 The American Long Rifle
48 Early 19th C, Military Arms
52 Oddities and Curiosa

New Technology I
54 Breechloaders
56 Percussion Ignition
58 Repeaters

A Prospering New Republic
68 The Lewis and Clark Air Rifle
69 The Plains Rifle
72 Beginning of Remington & Colt
74 H. Derringer & Perc. Handguns
76 Percussion Long Guns
78 Military Percussion Arms

A Nation Asunder
80 Union Arms
86 Arms of the Confederacy
89 Imported Arms

The American West
90 Sixguns
97 Pocket Pistols
100 Derringers and Curiosa
109 Lever-actions
114 Other Repeaters
115 Single Shots
119 Scatterguns
122 Native American Arms
124 The Army on the Frontier
126 Romance of the West
129 Golden Age of Engraving

New Technology II
134 Powder & Projectile, Bolt-Actions, Semi-Autos
135 Evolution of the Bolt-Action
138 John Moses Browning

A Bright New Century
140 Theodore Roosevelt
142 An Age of Elegance
150 A Splendid Little War

The World at War
152 Turn of the 20th C.Mil. Rifles
155 U.S. Military Pistol Trials
157 The Great War
170 Inter-War Arms Development
174 World War II

Modern Warfare
198 Post-war Dev. - AK47 & M16
200 Korea
202 Vietnam
204 General Officers Pistols
207 Military Arms Today
210 Military Sniper Rifles

To Serve and Protect
211 Police Firearms
215 In the Line of Duty
216 The Long Arms of the Law
218 Texas Rangers

Competition
219 Early Target Guns
224 Camp Perry & Others
230 Modern Competitive Shooting
232 The Olympics
236 Exhibition Shooters and Others

For the Fun of It
240 Plinking
244 Air Guns
248 Hollywood Guns

Modern Firearms
253 Innovations and Oddities
261 Handguns
266 Semi-Auto Rifles
270 Bolt-Action Rifles
274 Lever, Pump, & Other Rifles
277 Double-barrel Shotguns
281 Repeating Shotguns
284 Presidents & Royalty
286 Engraving Masterpieces

To Keep and Bear Arms
295 Guns of the NRA
298 The NRA Today
303 Join NRA

305 **Acknowledgements**

310 **Index**

PREFACE

NRA Headquarters, home of the NRA National Firearms Museum, 11250 Waples Mill, Fairfax VA 22030. Open every day of the week. Free admission.

At last count, there are 4,884 books in the NRA Museums Division Library. If you read them all, you'd have a decent understanding of the History of Firearms. Obviously, we have embarked on fool's errand to attempt to cram that information into a mere three hundred some odd pages. It's a journey we undertake joyously and with little trepidation.

No, you won't learn everything there is to know about guns here. However, we hope to provide you with a solid framework of the history of firearms development and technology, along with some insights into specific historic guns and the men and women who used them. You'll find the pivotal types and models you need to know about to understand firearms evolution, plus the guns that delight us for their history, their elegance, or… well, their weirdness.

The guns in this book are selected from more than 10,000 in the NRA Museums Collection.

Where did these guns come from?

The Museum Collection has been built since 1935 through the support of millions of NRA members, and the generosity of donors who share the vision of preserving our nation's firearms treasures, and educating future generations on the true story of Americans and their guns.

More than 99% of the guns in the Museum Collection have been donated. Guns come in one or two at a time, or in groups of hundreds or even thousands from large collections. They range from common specimens to pieces of great historic significance. Mamie Eisenhower brought in Ike's Winchester shotgun. Cornelius V.S. Roosevelt brought in his grandfather Theodore's engraved pistol (still loaded with a round in the chamber!)

In 2012, the estate of well-known publisher Robert E. Petersen made the largest donation in NRA history with the gift of 400 exceptional firearms, now displayed in The Petersen Gallery, which features the finest examples of engraved sporting arms and the largest collection of Gatling Guns on public display anywhere. A few years earlier, Dr. William L. and Collette N. Roberts' donation of their collection of hundreds of historical firearms made the museum a leading institution for the study and advancement of knowledge of firearms and their development and use.

Your guns and the NRA Museums

Substantial funding of the Museum comes from The NRA Foundation, which is a 501(c)(3) charitable nonprofit organization. This means that qualifying donations are tax deductible. Through the NRA Firearms For Freedom program, individuals can donate their firearms to benefit the Foundation or other NRA programs. These can be current gifts, or estate gifts from far-sighted individuals who would like to see their guns provide firearms education, support the shooting sports, or protect Second Amendment rights for future generations. All donated guns are reviewed for possible display in the National Firearms Museum. Interested parties may call (877) NRA-GIVE, or email nrafff@nrahq.org. Guns or collections with historical significance may be directed to the Museum Curator's attention by emailing nfmstaff@nrahq.org.

The First NRA Museums

In 1876, D. Barclay of the NRA won a L. D. Nimschke engraved Remington rolling block rifle during the international long-range rifle matches. This gun was the first of the NRA collection that eventually became the National Firearms Museum. The museum was formally started in 1935 when the Remington was put on exhibit in Washington DC's Barr Building, then the national headquarters of the NRA. It was displayed with many other firearms donated by firearms industry friends who sent them into the editorial offices of American Rifleman Magazine (est. 1923) for testing and evaluation.

In 1954, the NRA headquarters moved a few blocks up 16th Street to the venerable 1600 Rhode Island Avenue address. The NRA museum continued to grow with exhibits on the fourth floor and eventually on the first two floors off the main lobby. The guns were displayed on burlap-covered pegboard with hand-typed labels.

The NRA National Firearms Museum

In 1981, the NRA museum was christened the National Firearms Museum and by 1993, when the museum closed in preparation for the NRA move to Fairfax, Virginia, the collection had grown to 3,000 firearms.

In May 1998, the new National Firearms Museum opened at the NRA Headquarters

THE NRA MUSEUMS

NRA National Sporting Arms Museum at Bass Pro Shops, Springfield, MO. Open every day of the week. Free admission.

Fairfax location with a bold new look and design. In an effort to showcase the historic and valuable arms in the collection, museum staff designed 85 exhibit cases in 15 galleries that illustrate the museum theme of Firearms, Freedom, and the American Experience. With arms dating from 1350 to the present day, the collection traces in chronological order the history and development of firearms and their use in securing American liberty and in maintaining it ever since.

October 2010 was the opening of the Robert E. Petersen Gallery, which has been called "the finest single room of guns on display anywhere." While the collection is remarkable in its diversity, it is most noted for the spectacular examples of firearms engraving on display, especially on some of the world's finest double-barrel shotguns and double rifles.

The "Hollywood Guns" Gallery located in the William B. Ruger Gallery, features 120 actual guns used in movies and television over the past 80 years, from the first revolver John Wayne used on camera through guns from recent Academy Awards winners.

Brownell Museum of the Southwest

In 2008, Museum staff assisted in the development and design of the Frank Brownell Museum of the Southwest at the NRA's Whittington Center in Raton, New Mexico. Whittington is NRA's 30,000 acre shooting and hunting facility, and is located on the original Santa Fe Trail. With a theme of "Se Pasaron por Aqui" ("They Passed by Here"), this small jewel box of a museum features guns associated with centuries of history in this region, along with competition guns of the type used on Whittington's 17 active ranges.

Then NRA National Sporting Arms Museum at Bass Pro Shops

Since its opening in 2013 this museum has welcomed approximately a quarter million guests each year, making it the most visited firearms venue in the country. The Museum is a joint collaboration of NRA and Bass Pro Shops, as envisioned by Bass Pro's founder Johnny Morris, and is located in the very first Bass Pro store in Springfield Missouri. Its theme of "Hunting, Conservation, and Freedom" opens with a timeline of Sporting Arms in America, from the primitive muzzleloaders of the first explorers, settlers, and conquistadors through modern semi-auto sporting arms utilizing the latest in technology. It is the home of special displays, most notably the Remington Arms Factory Collection. The Theodore Roosevelt Conservation Gallery tells the story of wildlife conservation in America.

And Still More NRA Museums

At this writing, the NRA is in preliminary planning stages to develop an NRA Military Heritage Museum at Camp Atterbury Indiana, and to greatly expand the Brownell Museum of the Southwest.

NRA Museums Staff:

Jim Supica - Director
Doug Wicklund and Philip Schreier - Senior Curators
Erin Sabatini - Registrar
Ernie Lyles - Special Projects Coordinator
Katie Hoppe - Administrative Assistant
Bill Trible and Jerry Keathley - Curatorial Assistants

Photography by Terry Popkin. Additional photography by Michael Ives, Stoney Roberts, Ernie Lyles, Philip Schreier and Jason Connel.

Additional text from Museum projects by Harry Hunter. Additional material from current and former NRA Museums staff, NRA Publications staff, and NRA General Operations staff.

Dedication:

This edition of this book is dedicated to the late S. P. Fjestad, author and publisher, with our sincere gratitude for his never-ending support, encouragement and appreciation for NRA Museums and the National Rifle Association.

To join the NRA:

To join the millions of Americans who belong to the National Rifle Association call 877-672-2000 or join online at nra.org.

INTRODUCTION

A BRIEF HISTORY OF FIREARMS

Arms were some of the earliest tools. They have been used to provide food and protection since the formation of the earliest social units. From bone and wood through to bronze and iron, humans have made arms for hunting and self-defense—and the longer the accurate range, the better their effectiveness. Few of these arms have proved as effective as the firearm.

For centuries, and continuing through today, men and women have used firearms as the most effective arms individuals can wield. They have been used to implement both the highest and basest goals of humanity—to put food on the table, to provide personal protection, to enforce or defy the law, to defend or acquire territory and treasure, and to liberate or to enslave.

Handguns, rifles, and other firearms have also come to be used for a variety of recreational and competitive shooting, and millions of Americans exercise their constitutional right to own firearms simply for the pleasure of shooting in addition to more serious uses.

EARLIEST FIREARMS

The origin of gunpowder is unknown, but probably was developed in China where the earliest records are found. The first European references to gunpowder, which described the combination of charcoal, sulphur, and saltpeter to produce a rapidly burning or exploding powder, come from a coded writing by a Franciscan monk, Roger Bacon, shortly before 1250 A.D.

What is certainly true is that gunpowder firearms were in use in the Middle East by the 13th century. The Battle of Ain Jalut in 1260 A.D. between the Arab Mamluks and the Mongols is often cited as the first recorded instance of firearms being used—although it is unclear by which side. It is from the 13th century that the earliest physical example of a gunpowder arm is found: a bronze cannon in China dating to 1288. With a muzzle-bore diameter of an inch, this is almost certainly a hand-held firearm.

Firearms became more common at the end of the 13th and first half of the 14th century. Edward III of England used them against the Scots in the 1320s; they are recorded as being used in sieges in Spain at Alicante in 1331 and Algeciras in 1342. Early cannons—the word comes from the Latin *canna*, meaning tube—were developed as a thick metal tube with a closed end (the breech) and an open end (the muzzle). Loaded first with gunpowder and then with a projectile, the powder was ignited with a torch or smoldering ember through a small hole in the rear (the touchhole). The rapidly expanding gases from the exploding gunpowder threw the projectile from the barrel. This basic principle still applies today.

The effectiveness of early firearms is difficult to assess: initially they certainly scared more people than they killed. There is no doubt, however, that they quickly became an important part of the military inventory. Interesting research by engineers such as Ulrich Bretscher show how effective "hand cannons" or "hand gonnes"—essentially miniature cannons designed to be held by hand or attached to a pole for use by individual soldiers—could be. Using replicas of hand "gonnes" found in Germany—the Tannenberg and Danzig weapons of the late 14th century—Bretscher showed that they could pierce 1.5-2.00mm. steel and were surprisingly accurate. Larger cannon, often on wheeled carriages, were common on 15th century battlefields and played a significant role in one of the greatest events of the 15th century: the fall of Constantinople to the Turks in 1453—the end of the Eastern Roman Empire that was created in the early years of the 4th century A.D.

FROM MATCHLOCK TO FLINTLOCK

The evolution of firearms from the cannon of the 14th century to the accurate, reliable guns of the 19th makes a fascinating record of the progress of engineering and chemistry in the period. Key to this evolution were the search for more reliable methods of igniting the gunpowder—as well as improvements to the gunpowder itself—and design advances allowing rapid repeat shots and better accuracy.

The term "lock, stock, and barrel" comes from firearms design and represents the three major components of early guns. The barrel is self-explanatory. The stock is the wooden holder in which the barrel is mounted, allowing the gun to be fired from the shoulder or from one hand. The lock is the mechanical contrivance that is used to ignite the charge of gunpowder in the chamber of the barrel.

The first gun to combine all three components was the matchlock, in the early 1400s. Many early hand cannons were ignited with a slow match—a length of slender rope or cord that had been chemically treated so that an end could be ignited and would continue to burn or smolder, much like a 4th of July punk used to shoot fireworks. Obviously it was awkward to hold both gun and slow match while trying to dip the match to the touch hole of the hand cannon.

The matchlock solved this problem by using an arm called a serpentine on the gun to hold the slow match. By mechanical linkage, a trigger mounted on the bottom of the lock could be pressed to lower the match to the touch hole, which now included a small pan of fine gunpowder that would be ignited first, transmitting the fire through the hole to ignite the main charge in the barrel.

This increased firing—and, therefore, aiming—efficiency, but lighted matches were not the best accompaniment to powder-fired weapons. Keeping the match lit in poor weather—and keeping it away from the powder at all times—was a continuous problem and an accident waiting to happen.

This simple system was followed by a much safer—but more complicated—approach: the wheellock first seen in the early 1500s. It was the first ignition system to take advantage of the fact that sparks

A BRIEF HISTORY OF FIREARMS

Manual of arms for a matchlock.

could be produced by striking flint or other substances against steel. The lock contained a wheel with a serrated edge, attached to a spring that could be wound with a separate key called a spanner, much like early clocks, and held under tension. A hammer-like piece called the dog or dogshead held a piece of pyrite rock. To fire a wheellock, the dogshead was lowered onto the edge of the wheel, which was released by a pull of the trigger causing a shower of sparks to fall into the pan igniting the charge. The principle is much the same as a cigarette lighter.

This was an improvement in reliability over the matchlock, primarily because the shooter did not have to constantly attend to the smoldering slow match to ensure that it remained lit. It also avoided the problem of an enemy seeing or of game smelling the smoke of the match before the gun was fired. It took highly skilled craftsmen to build the clock-like mechanism of the wheellock, making it an extremely expensive piece, primarily available to royalty and the like for hunting. Although wheellocks saw some military use, the matchlock remained the most common military firearm during the wheellock era.

Improvements using flint against steel to provide the igniting spark continued in the second half of the 16th century, with two early examples being the snaphaunce, the first flintlock-type gun, circa 1560, and the Miquelet, which followed a couple of decades later.

The snaphaunce held a piece of flint in the hammer-like cock, with a pan of priming powder mounted on the outside of the barrel over the touchhole as with the matchlock system. When ready to fire, a steel striking plate ("battery") would be manually swiveled into place above the pan, and the cock pulled back until it was caught by a sear. Pulling the trigger would release the cock to swing rapidly forward striking the battery, and showering sparks into the pan, hopefully firing the gun.

As with all flintlock-type systems, sometimes the priming powder in the pan would ignite but fail to transmit the fire to the powder in the barrel, resulting in a failure to fire and giving us a colorful phrase still used today—"a flash in the pan."

Of course, it as also vital to "keep your powder dry," and accordingly, many early firearms of this era had a sliding pan cover to hold the powder in place and give it some protection against the elements. The pan cover would have to be manually swiveled out of the way before firing.

Around 1580, the Miquelet system improved on and simplified the snaphaunce by combining the battery and pan cover into a single piece called the frizzen. This L-shaped spring-loaded piece would be pivoted down to cover the pan after it had been primed with powder. When the cock was released by the trigger, it would swing forward striking the frizzen, producing sparks at the same time it pushed the frizzen up and forward to expose the powder in the pan to the igniting sparks.

In the early 1600s, the basic design of the flintlock, originally known as the French lock, was perfected. The major improvement over the Miquelet consisted

INTRODUCTION

of moving the mechanical components for the lock mechanism from their previous position on the outside of the lockplate, where they were exposed to elements and damage, to the interior of the lock.

At around the time flintlock systems were first being developed, two improvements were introduced that dramatically increased the accuracy of firearms.

Archers had found that if the fletching feathers on the rear of their arrow were at a slight angle, causing the arrow to rotate in flight, their ability to hit the target was improved. This concept was applied to gun barrels by cutting slowly twisting grooves down the interior length of the barrel, imparting a spin to the bullet as it left the muzzle. These grooves were called rifling, and "rifled muskets" or "rifles" so equipped were found to be much better at hitting their mark over further distances than "smoothbore" muskets.

With the improved accuracy offered by rifled firearms, a system of aiming them other than pointing became more important, and early forms of sights became more widely used. A common system, still used in many guns today, was a notch of some type at the rear of the barrel and a post on the front. With this type of open sight, the top of the front sight post is aligned with the target, and the post is centered by eye between the edges of the rear sight notch, with the top of the post level with the tops of the sides of the notch. When the sights themselves are properly physically aligned with the axis of the bore, this system still provides all the accuracy required for most practical shooting needs.

EARLY GUNS IN AMERICA

Despite imaginative pictures of Pilgrims bearing flared-muzzle flintlock blunderbusses, the earliest firearms in America were doubtless matchlocks and the occasional wheellock.

However, during the colonial years, a distinctly American type of gun would be developed, by first dozens and then hundreds of gunsmiths scattered through the new land. In the late 17th and 18th centuries, colonists coming to America brought their indigenous European firearms and gun design concepts with them. The gun was a necessary and treasured tool when pioneering a frontier wilderness far from civilization, and gun makers were valued and essential members of the small settlements.

The American long rifle, variously known as the Kentucky, Pennsylvania, or Ohio rifle, is most likely the descendant of the German *Jaeger*-type (translated "hunter") flintlock, a practical classic European hunting rifle. In the New World, it slowly evolved into a longer-barreled firearm with wooden stock extending the full length of the barrel, while the rear of stock developed a graceful downward curve. Eventually, deluxe versions would come to be decorated with colorful brass or pewter inlays in the stock, with stars,

First Blow for Liberty by Alexander Hay Ritchie. The central figure is priming the pan of his flintlock at the battle of Lexington.

A BRIEF HISTORY OF FIREARMS

hearts, and simple animal silhouettes being popular motifs. The brass-covered patchbox in the rear of the stock would become more elaborate and decorative over time.

This is a gun that fed and defended early pioneer families. Marksmanship was a valued, necessary, and common skill.

European military doctrine of the time called for the use of smoothbore muskets as the primary martial firearm. Although less accurate than rifled arms, the smoothbore allowed for faster reloading, because a lead ball slightly smaller than bore diameter could be rammed down the barrel with wadding quite quickly, even as the barrel became fouled with gunpowder residue from previous shots. By contrast, to be effective, the lead bullet for a rifled arm must fit the bore tightly to engage the rifling, and takes more time and effort to ram home.

European armies would meet on a field of battle in massed formations and exchange volleys of fire from their smoothbore muskets, more pointing the weapons at the clustered line of enemies across the field than precisely aiming, and relying on volleys of multiple lead balls to strike down some opponents before closing for combat with saber and bayonet. The classic British Brown Bess and French Charleville Musket were sturdy smoothbore flintlock designs, well suited for this type of combat.

The ways and rules were changing, however, and in the French and Indian War, the Revolutionary War, and the War of 1812, American marksmen used their rifled "squirrel guns" and well-honed shooting skills to good effect on selected targets from longer distances and from behind cover in wilderness areas.

After securing independence, the new country rapidly sought its own means of mass-producing military arms, establishing government arsenals in 1794 with the manufacture of firearms beginning at Springfield in 1795 and Harper's Ferry in 1800. Many of their early products were indeed smoothbore muskets, still a useful military arm. But the age of the rifle as an essential arm for the marksman in combat had arrived. In addition to arsenal-made firearms, the federal government and some states contracted with numerous small individual gun-making firms to produce military firearms or parts based on sample patterns provided by the government. America's oldest continuing gunmaker traces its lineage to this era, with Eliphalet Remington producing barrels as early as 1826. The Remington firm remains one of America's premier gun manufacturers today. The famous Henry Deringer, whose name later would become synonymous with small concealable handguns, produced flintlock rifles for the U.S. government as early as 1810, as did Eli Whitney's Whitney Arms nearly a decade earlier.

THE PERCUSSION SYSTEM

Although the flintlock had dominated firearm production for nearly two centuries, it still had major defects as an ignition system. To begin with, a shooter often had to carry two types of powder—fine grained for priming and coarse for the main charge—which complicated reloading and kept down shots per minutes. Second, the system was unreliable in wet weather, and it was difficult to store a gun loaded ready for use.

In 1807, a Scottish clergyman, Rev. Forsyth, is credited with developing an ignition system based on the principle that certain chemicals would ignite with a spark when struck a sharp blow, a concept which can be observed in toy cap pistols or "pop rock"-type fireworks today. Various methods to utilize this approach were tried, and in 1822 the percussion cap was invented.

The percussion cap contains a small charge of chemical in a small copper cup-like holder which can be quickly pressed

This gunsmith will walk about 20 miles back and forth to cut the rifling in the barrel with this rifling lathe. Diorama at the NRA National Firearm Museum..

INTRODUCTION

onto a nipple mounted in the rear of a gun barrel. When the trigger is pulled, the hammer strikes the cap and ignites the chemical, which sparks through a hole in the nipple into the main charge in the barrel, and fires the gun. This system offered such obvious advantages to the flintlock method that gunmakers around the world rapidly adapted their existing designs to percussion ignition.

The introduction of the percussion system marks the beginning of a dramatically rapid era of firearm advancements, coinciding with the Industrial Revolution and including the era of the American Civil War, through the turn of the century. During this relatively brief time, guns would go from primitive flintlocks to the basic systems that still dominate firearm designs today—and the percussion cap would be obsolete within 50 years of its introduction.

Development of effective breechloading systems was another significant step. From the matchlock through the early percussion era, the vast majority of guns had been "muzzleloaders;" that is, the powder and projectile had to be dropped down the muzzle at the front of the barrel and rammed to the rear before firing. This made reloading awkward, especially when shooting a long gun from a prone position or behind cover or concealment and, as noted earlier, it became more difficult after a few shots when barrel fouling made the job more strenuous. This led to many attempts to develop a gun that loaded from the rear of the barrel, although most early efforts were not effective due to weakness of materials and the leakage of hot gases from the breech seal when the gun was fired.

In the early 19th century, various breechloading designs were finally produced in quantity. A notable example is the U.S. military Hall North system, which in 1833 marked both the first U.S. percussion arm, and the Army's first breechloader. In 1841, the breechloading Dreyse needle gun, which packed the projectile and powder together in a combustible cartridge, was adopted in Germany as the first military bolt-action gun.

The Civil War saw the adoption of a wide variety of breechloading systems, including those made by Sharps, Maynard, Burnside, and many others.

BIRTH OF THE REVOLVER

From the start, firearms manufacturers tried to address the problem of slow-repeat shots and reloading. Multiple barrels (and usually multiple locks) loaded onto the same stock was a sensible basic concept and—in the form of double-barrel shotguns—this type of gun is still produced by some of the finest gun makers in the world today, including firms such as Browning, Franchi, Beretta, Remington, Ruger, and Charles Daly, and is a system preferred by many discriminating hunters and competitive shooters.

But with more than two barrels, the system begins to become heavy and cumbersome. Other systems were tried, including manually rotated groups of barrels mounted to a single lock, multiple superposed charges within a single barrel, and cylindrical or rectangular clusters of chambers that could be manually repositioned to align with a firing mechanism and barrel.

The most successful solution was invented by one of the great names of gun manufacturing, Samuel Colt. He developed a handgun design with a rotating cylinder and multiple chambers, each of which could contain a charge of powder topped by the bullet, loaded from the front of the cylinder. The rear of the cylinder was closed, with a nipple for a percussion cap installed at the back of each chamber. When the hammer is cocked, a fresh chamber rotates into alignment with the rear of the barrel, and when the trigger is pulled, the hammer drops, firing the load in that chamber. This is the basis of the mechanical system still used in all revolvers today.

Colt's first manufacturing venture was based in Paterson, NJ, and produced percussion revolvers with folding triggers and revolving shotguns and rifles. These are called Colt Paterson models by modern collectors. Few were produced, and the firm folded, having been in business only from 1837 to 1841. In 1847, however, Colt was back with a new, heavier, and more powerful revolver, this time with a traditional bow-type trigger guard. Prompted by an initial order from Captain Samuel Walker to equip his troops in the Mexican war, the new model tipped the scales at nearly five pounds, and remained the most powerful repeating handgun until the introduction of the .357 magnum nearly 90 years later. Called the Walker

This Union "Sharps-shooter" is using a telescopic sight on a breech loading Sharps rifle in the Civil War.

A BRIEF HISTORY OF FIREARMS

Model after the young captain, Colt's revolvers were initially manufactured by Eli Whitney, but Colt soon had his own plant in Hartford, CT.

Colt had patented his revolving cylinder design, and therefore held a monopoly on revolver manufacture for a number of years. The only serious competition for a repeating handgun was the pepperbox design, in which a cluster of barrels, each with a percussion nipple on the rear, rotated around an axis by the pull of a ring trigger, which also cocked the hammer and released it to fire the chamber that had rotated into position. Pepperboxes were made by a number of European and American firms, the foremost probably being the succession of companies founded by Ethan Allen, including Allen & Thurber and Allen & Wheelock.

The Colt pattern cap-and-ball revolver rapidly came to dominate the repeating firearms market. Colt also offered revolving shotguns and rifles as well as handguns. Among his most successful designs were the little 1849 Pocket Model in .31 caliber, the mid-sized 1851 Navy Model in .36 caliber, and the 1860 Army Model, offering .44 caliber chambering in a much smaller and handier package than his earlier Walker and Dragoon models. After the expiration of Colt's patent in the mid-1850s, other firms jumped into the revolver business, with major manufacturers being Remington, Starr, Whitney, and Manhattan. Manufactured by these and other makers, the percussion revolver became the major sidearm of the Civil War.

THE SELF-CONTAINED CARTRIDGE

The cap-and-ball revolver offered an effective repeating firearm, with five or six shots available as fast as the hammer could be cocked and the trigger pulled. After the gun was shot dry, however, reloading was a slow and cumbersome process that involved loading each chamber with loose gun powder and a lead bullet, ramming the loads home, and placing a percussion cap on the nipple of each chamber. What was needed was a self-contained cartridge with the primer, powder, and bullet all in one neat and weatherproof unit.

An early attempt at this was the pinfire system, first introduced around 1846, in which a firing pin was mounted on each copper-cased cartridge, igniting an internal primer when struck by the gun's hammer. Although it gained a good deal of popularity in Europe, it never caught on much in the U.S. because the external pin on each round was cumbersome and hazardous.

Among the firms eagerly waiting for the expiration of the Colt revolver patent was the partnership of an inventor named Daniel Wesson and an older businessman, Horace Smith. A few years earlier, in a previous partnership, they had entered the race for an effective repeating firearm that shot self-contained cartridges with a lever-action pistol. This pistol had a tubular magazine mounted under and parallel to the barrel, and shot "rocket balls"—hollow-based lead bullets, with the powder and primer mounted in the base of the projectile itself.

Wesson and Smith pursued production of their lever-action pistols only a few years, and the design was acquired by a shirt manufacturer, who carried it further. His name was Oliver Winchester, and his famous lever-action rifles, based in large part on the design of the first Smith & Wesson partnership, eventually became the most popular repeating rifles of the second half of the 19th century.

The second Smith & Wesson partnership had designed a tiny .22 revolver. Perhaps more important than the revolver was the cartridge it fired. It consisted of a copper casing, with a hollow rim at the bottom that held a priming compound. The case was then filled with gunpowder and capped with a lead bullet mounted in its mouth. When the firing pin of the revolver's hammer struck the rim

Eliphalet Remington

Samuel Colt

Horace Smith

Daniel Wesson

Oliver Winchester

INTRODUCTION

of the cartridge, the priming ignited the powder, firing the bullet, leaving the empty copper casing in the chamber.

The cartridge was essentially identical to the modern .22 Short rimfire, and was the grand-daddy of all our traditional ammunition today.

Colt had patented his revolver, so Smith & Wesson acquired the patent to their innovation of the revolver, and held a fairly complete monopoly on the production of effective cartridge revolvers through the patent's expiration in 1869. There were a number of infringements and evasions of the patent as the market rapidly recognized the superiority of metallic cartridge ammunition.

THE AMERICAN WEST

The military has sometimes been slow to embrace firearms innovation, preferring tried and true technology over the new and untested. This was certainly true during the Civil War and Indian Wars eras. Winchester had abandoned the rocket ball system in favor of a .44 rimfire cartridge in its famous brass-framed Henry rifle in 1860, but only a few were purchased and used during the Civil War. The Spencer Repeating Rifle Company had also patented an effective lever-action repeater that fired metallic cartridges by the beginning of the Civil War, but its adoption by the U.S. Army was resisted until it was demonstrated to President Lincoln, who promptly personally championed its purchase.

Although the Spencer was the most widely used repeating long gun of the Civil War, and breechloading single-shot Sharps rifles in the hands of expert "Sharps-shooter" marksmen took a toll, the vast majority of the soldiers on both sides were armed with muzzleloading percussion muskets.

With the post-war westward expansion, the civilian demand was for the new repeating metallic cartridge firearms. Winchester responded, first with an improved brass frame rimfire Model 1866 lever-action, followed by a centerfire Model 1873, and then by Models 1876 and 1886, made strong enough to handle true big-game cartridges in the .45-70 class. Marlin was Winchester's strongest competitor in the field, with Whitney Kennedy and Evans also producing lever-action repeaters. Despite the development of repeaters, single-shot rifles remained a popular option, and in the early years of metallic cartridges, they could handle stronger rounds than the more complicated repeaters.

The tradition of powerful, big-bore rifles for the large game of the American West, such as bison, wapiti, and grizzly bear, certainly predates the Civil War. As trappers and mountain men and then settlers and farmers pushed into the Great Plains and Rocky Mountain west, a new type of American rifle was developed to meet their needs.

The percussion "Plains Rifle" tended to be shorter than its long, slender Kentucky rifle predecessor and to be easier to handle on horseback and in brush. It took a heavier, larger-diameter ball appropriate to the larger game, which necessitated a heavier barrel, the weight of which was another factor that dictated a shorter length. The Plains Rifle tended to have a half-stock, with the wood only cradling the rear half of the barrel, contrasted to the full-stock Kentuckies. As befits a working gun, decoration tended to be minimal or nonexistent.

In the years preceding the Civil War, Plains Rifles by prominent makers such as Hawken and Gemmer, both of St. Louis, were eagerly sought after by long hunters and pilgrims heeding Horace Greeley's advice of "Go West, young man."

After the war, Sharps began producing its well-respected breechloading single-shots for centerfire metallic cartridges, and with a half-inch diameter projectile, the Sharps "Big 50" was perhaps the quintessential buffalo rifle. Other popular single-shots included the Winchester Model 1885 High Wall and Low Wall rifles, Stevens Ideal rifles, and the sturdy Remington Rolling Block rifles. Most were offered in a variety of frame sizes, barrel lengths and weights, and calibers ranging from .22 rimfire to the .40 to .50 caliber rounds favored by commercial hunters. Various types of sights were available, from simple to elaborate, and various stocking options could be had, from fairly straightforward to the ornate buttplates and trigger guard configuration favored for Scheutzen-style target competitions. The single-shot was generally considered to be more accurate than early repeaters, and thus was favored for target competition and other precision work.

The American West of 1865 to 1900 is perhaps one of the most romanticized eras of American history, with the lore of cowboy and Indian, lawman and outlaw, figuring large in our collective imagination. The handguns of this era also have a special fascination.

The most famous handgun is undoubtedly the Colt Single Action Army, introduced in 1873, and also known as the Peacemaker. Its sturdy reliable design and effective cartridges made it a favorite with Westerners on both sides of the law.

It is little recognized, however, that Smith & Wesson large frame top-break revolvers and their foreign copies represented the most prolific full size handgun pattern of the early cartridge era. All were based on the "Model 3" frame. The first was the American model in 1870, followed rapidly by the Russian model. The Schofield model was made for the American military in the 1870s, followed by the New Model Number Three and Double Action models.

The S&W design was much faster to load and unload than the Colt. When a latch in front of the hammer was released, the S&W barrel and cylinder pivoted forward, automatically ejecting empties and exposing all six chambers for reloading. To reload the Colt, each individual chamber had to be aligned with a barrel-mounted ejector rod, and the single empty brass case punched out and replaced with a fresh cartridge before rotating the cylinder to the next chamber, repeating the operation a total of six times to fully load the revolver. Smiths were also generally held to have an edge in accuracy, although the Colts were simpler, sturdier, and less liable to malfunction in extreme environments. A large portion of S&W's early production went to foreign military contracts.

Other revolvers of the era included the Remington 1875, similar to the Colt pattern, and the unusual but exceptionally well made twist-open Merwin Hulbert revolvers.

The military's resistance to new concepts continued into the Indian War years of the late 19th century. As a good example, when repeating rifles with sixteen or more rounds available as fast as you could work the lever were on the market, the U.S. Army chose to stay with a single-shot as its primary issue long arm. One concern cited was that soldiers armed with repeaters might expend ammunition too rapidly in the heat of battle.

Economic factors also undoubtedly influenced the decision. Vast quantities of now-obsolete muzzleloaders remained in inventory from the Civil War. A method was developed to convert these to breechloading cartridge rifles by cutting open the rear of the barrel and installing a breechblock that could be flipped open to load cartridges and remove empty brass like a trapdoor. When manufacture of new rifles resumed, they were based on the same system, and the "Trapdoor Springfield" single-shot became the standard military rifle from 1873 through the beginning of the Spanish American War in the late 1890s. In defense of the Army's decision, the trapdoor's .45-70 cartridge was significantly more powerful, with longer effective range, than anything available in a repeater in the early 1870s.

A similar thought process led the military to initially select a Remington single-shot in 50 caliber as its first cartridge handgun. By the mid-1870s, however, the Colt Single Action Army and the Smith & Wesson Schofield six-shot revolvers became the Army's primary sidearms for the Indian Wars era.

After the Custer rout at Little Bighorn, there was a vigorous debate over the military's choice of weapons. Some of the Indian victors had been using repeating rifles. One school of thought contended that if Custer's men had been armed with lever-action rifles instead of trapdoors, and fast-loading Schofields instead of the slower Single Action Army, the outcome might have been different, although that conclusion is hard to support in light of the vastly outnumbered 7th Cavalry's forces and strategic choices.

Although the big six guns of the Old West are those that capture the public's fancy, their production quantities were significantly less than smaller-frame revolvers. S&W offered tip-up spur-triggers and top-breaks in single or double-action; Colt produced a series of single-shot derringers and spur-trigger revolvers; and Remington offered spur-trigger revolvers and its famous double derringers, in addition to other designs.

The late 19th century saw a proliferation of small manufacturers churning out cheap, small single-action spur-trigger revolvers, sometimes derisively referred to as "Suicide Specials." Other firms such as Harrington and Richardson, Iver Johnson, and Hopkins and Allen produced millions of inexpensive, but generally serviceable small top-break and solid-frame double-action revolvers. These companies have been referred to as the "armorers to the nation's nightstands," accurately reflecting the fact that even persons of moderate means could afford their products as a handy means of home and personal protection.

THE SWING-OUT REVOLVER

Just before the turn of the 20th century, a new type of revolver was developed,

Details from Custer's Last Stand by Samuel Paxon. At left two troopers reloading their breech-loading Springfield Trapdoor Carbines. At right, a cavalry scout fires his single-shot trapdoor at a Sioux warrior carrying a lever-action repeater.

INTRODUCTION

first by Colt in 1889, followed by S&W in 1896. This revolver used a solid frame, like the Single Action Army, but the cylinder swung to the side to load and unload. Empty cases were simultaneously ejected by pushing a plunger-like ejector rod at the front of the open cylinder. S&W called their versions hand ejectors to differentiate the method of operation from their top-break automatic ejecting products.

These swing-out cylinder revolvers were also double-action (DA), a term describing the ways in which the gun could be fired. Early revolvers were usually single-action—the hammer had to be manually cocked before the trigger pull performed the single action of dropping the hammer to fire the round. On the DA revolvers, the gun could be fired in the traditional single-action (SA) mode. Alternatively, the DA could be fired by a longer, heavier pull on the trigger, beginning with the hammer in the down, uncocked position. In this mode, the trigger would perform the double action of first cocking and then dropping the hammer to fire the weapon.

This type of revolver rapidly caught on, and would become the dominant handgun design for most of the 20th century in America.

In its early revolvers of this type, Colt offered frame sizes ranging from its massive New Service to handy compact pocket-sized revolvers with short two-inch "snub nose" barrels. When the New York City Police got a brash new young commissioner just before the close of the 19th century, he selected the little .32 Colt New Police as the department's first standard-issue handgun. He also instituted the first formal police marksmanship training under the guidance of Sgt. William Petty, who happened to be a national shooting champion. The commissioner's name was Theodore Roosevelt, and a few years later he carried another swing-out cylinder Colt, a New Army model, when he led the First Volunteer Cavalry up San Juan Hill in 1898.

The early S&W hand ejectors ranged from the large N-frame, the first of which was the famous Triple-Lock, which introduced the .44 Special cartridge, through the tiny .22 Ladysmith, which was far smaller than any swing-out revolver being made today.

Smith & Wesson found the workhorse of their product line in 1899 when it made its first medium-sized K-frame "Military & Police" (M&P) revolver, chambered for their new .38 Special cartridge. Although Colt & S&W shared the police market in the first half of the century, the S&W K-frame .38 Special was probably carried by a majority of law enforcement officers in America after World War II through the 1970s.

The same cartridge was also popular in the smaller short-barrel five-shot J-frame "Chiefs Special," which served both the police backup gun and the civilian concealed carry market. Colt's competing Detective Special packed six rounds in a package that was only slightly larger. The little J-frame was also the platform for S&W's "Kit Gun," a handy .22 revolver that would easily fit in a hunter's, camper's, or fisherman's kit.

Continuing to the present day, the .38 Special is a well-made double-action revolver like those made by S&W, Ruger, Colt, and Taurus. It is considered by many to be the best choice for a first-time shooter's home-defense handgun. The small J-frame size is also the first choice of many experienced shooters for their personal concealed carry. In a gun that is small enough to carry easily, yet large enough to be manageable, the combination of safety, reliability, simplicity, and effectiveness is still hard to beat.

EUROPEAN BOLT-ACTION RIFLES

The double-action system for revolvers had caught on faster in Europe than in the U.S. It was used for early pinfires and for military handguns, such as Britain's ugly but reliable and hell-for-stout Webley top-breaks in .455 caliber.

While the U.S. market was well satisfied with lever-action repeating rifles, a different repeating mechanism gained favor with the armies of Europe. When the switch to metallic cartridges began, many of Europe's early single-shot rifles used a

bolt-action breechloading system. In bolt-action rifles, a bolt handle extending from the breechblock is lifted up to unlock the breechblock and pulled to the rear, which slides the block back to allow a cartridge to be loaded into the chamber in the rear of the barrel. The bolt handle is pushed forward and then down, engaging locking lugs to hold the breechblock in place while the rifle is fired. Single-shot bolt-action rifles adopted by European military units included the Chassepot (France 1866), Vetterli (Switzerland 1869), Berdan (Russia 1870), Beaumont (Netherlands 1871), and the Mauser (Germany 1871). Of these, the seeds of greatness lay in the last, in the invention of brothers Peter and Paul Mauser.

The earliest military bolt-action repeating rifles used tubular magazines under the barrel, similar to the system on most American lever-actions. The Portuguese Kropatschek in 1878 was among the first of this type. Mauser's tube mag repeater was first produced in 1884 as the German Model 1871/84. Most of these early military cartridge rifles chambered cartridges similar to the U.S. .45-70—a large, heavy, round-nosed bullet in a metallic case filled with a healthy charge of black powder. In 1885, smokeless powder was invented and would lead to dramatic changes in firearms and ammunition design.

SMOKELESS POWDER

Smokeless powder, as the name implies, had the military advantage of not generating a cloud of smoke when fired. Black powder smoke would reveal a shooter's position and, after a few rounds, develop a haze that could begin to obscure his vision. Another advantage was that smokeless powder produced far less fouling after shots than black powder, meaning that more shots could be fired before cleaning, and that powder debris was less likely to clog an action.

Its most important quality, however, was that when ignited, its gases would expand more rapidly, creating higher pressures and driving the bullet to a higher velocity when it left the muzzle. As a bullet approaches 1,100 ft./sec. (about the speed of sound), its wounding capacity increases dramatically, allowing a lighter, smaller-diameter projectile to have the same "stopping power" as a larger, heavier round at a slower speed.

The faster, smaller-diameter bullet also has a further range and a flatter trajectory. A bullet leaving the muzzle of a gun does not fly straight. From the instant it departs the barrel, it is "falling" toward the ground due to the effect of gravity. A gun's sights are adjusted so the barrel is actually pointed very slightly up, giving a slight rainbow-like curve to the bullet's path. A faster, lighter bullet will travel further before gravity pulls it to earth, and a smaller-diameter bullet has less wind resistance. The flatter trajectory means it will be on target over a longer distance.

In general terms, the caliber of a bullet refers to a rough measurement of its diameter, expressed either in decimal fractions of an inch or millimeters. For example, a .45 caliber cartridge takes a bullet approximately 45/100 inch in diameter, which would also be very roughly 11mm in diameter.

Firearms designers took advantage of the new smokeless powder, using a smaller bullet, closer to 1/3 inch in diameter (8mm is the most popular, but they range from under 7mm to 9mm). Heavy lead was still used to form the core of the bullet, but it was encased in a harder copper or brass metal jacket, so it would not quickly foul the rifling in the bore with soft lead that rubbed off at the higher velocities.

The first such bolt-action repeating rifle and smokeless smaller-caliber ammunition combination to be adopted by a military was the 8mm French Lebel bolt-action in 1886.

The pointed "spitzer" bullet design is much more aerodynamically efficient than a round-nose design, offering better accuracy at longer ranges. But when such cartridges are loaded nose to tail in a tube magazine, there is a danger that the pointed nose of one bullet will ignite the primer of the cartridge in front of it when the rifle recoils. Use of a box-type magazine, in which the cartridges are stacked parallel, one on top of the other, overcomes this obstacle to spitzer bullets. The British Lee Metford bolt-action, generally based on the Mauser concept, in .303 caliber used such a box mag in 1888, and in 1889 Mauser produced its own 8mm box magazine rifle.

Another early box magazine repeater was the Mauser & Mannlicher-influenced German 1888 Commission rifle in 8mm, which rapidly became a staple design. Meanwhile, the Austrians adopted a straight-pull bolt-action Steyr Mannlicher repeater in 8mm the same year. Mid-bore bolt-action box magazine designs rapidly followed, such as the Danish Krag Jorgensen in 1889 (with the U.S. adopting a Krag-based design in 1892) and the Swiss straight-pull Schmidt Rubin in the same year. The year 1891 saw the adoption of the Lebel-pattern Mosin Nagant by Russia, the 6.5mm Italian Carcano, and the 8mm French Berthier.

INTRODUCTION

During this period, military bolt-actions were often modified to incorporate the new advances, and numerous military rifles from the turn of the century or slightly later are bolt-action single-shots converted to magazine-fed repeaters, or had large-bore barrels relined to smaller calibers.

The perfection of the bolt-action design is believed by many to be the Mauser 98, introduced in 1898. Improvements include cocking on opening of the bolt rather than on closing, an added safety lug, and a larger chamber ring. This basic design became the basis of many, if not all, subsequent bolt-action military and sporting rifles, and variations served as primary rifles for many countries through World War II. The tried-and-true U.S. Model 1903, which served with distinction through two world wars, with its "thirty ought six" (.30-06) chambering is basically a modified Mauser 1898 design. Current-production sporting rifles, such as the classic Winchester Model 70 and bolt-actions by Remington, Ruger, and others, can trace their lineage to the Gewehr 98.

AUTO-LOADERS

Another firearms design trend in Europe given a boost by the introduction of smokeless powder was the attempt to make automatic-loading firearms. In general, gun designs to this point had relied on some mechanical action by the shooter to load a fresh cartridge into the firing chamber after the initial round had been fired, whether it was swiveling a lever or lifting, pulling, and pushing a bolt or cocking the hammer or pulling the trigger to advance a revolver cylinder to the next chamber. Inventors sought a method whereby the loading of the next round would be accomplished automatically.

The first auto-loading pistol designs to see limited production were the German-made Schoenberger and Borchardt designs in 1893 and 1894, respectively. A couple of years later, in 1896, the Mauser firm began to manufacture the first auto pistol that gained widespread acceptance, the Model 1896, nicknamed the Broomhandle for its slender oval cross-sectioned grip.

Germany continued its dominance in European firearms design when Georg Luger introduced his classic pistol in 1900. Whereas early automatics had used fixed box magazines, the Luger magazine was mounted in the pistol's grip frame, was quickly detachable, and was easily replaced with a fresh magazine for a quick reload. Originally manufactured in 7.63mm (.30 cal.), in 1909 it was adapted to a new, larger-diameter cartridge, and the 9mm Luger (or 9mm Parabellum) round was destined to become possibly the most widely used centerfire pistol ammunition of the 20th century. The Luger was widely adopted as a military pistol by many countries, including Germany where it was designated the "Pistole 09" (P-09) for the year it was first purchased, being used through both World Wars. Its distinctive profile is widely recognized and may be identified as "graceful" or "sinister," depending on the eye of the beholder and how many Grade B war movies he or she has seen.

Probably the greatest of U.S. firearms inventors, John Moses Browning, played a significant role in the development of automatics. One of Browning's earliest designs was the Winchester 1885 single-shot rifle. Others brought the Winchester lever-action repeaters into the smokeless powder era, first with the slim and handy Model 1892; followed by the Model 1894, which with its "thutty-thutty" (.30-30) cartridge became America's classic deer rifle; and the Model 1895 whose box magazine allowed the chambering of true high-power smokeless rifle cartridges with spitzer bullets in a lever-action repeater.

Browning was also responsible for some of the first repeating shotguns. Revolver-based shotguns had been around since the Colt Paterson models of the 1840s, but had never caught on (probably because of the tendency of hot gases escaping from the cylinder gap to pepper the supporting hand with powder grains). Spencer Arms (of Civil War lever-action rifle fame) had manufactured a moderately successful repeating pump or slide-action shotgun as early as 1882. As would befit the Winchester legacy, Browning's first design for a repeating shotgun for the firm was a lever-action, the Model 1887. This was followed by a pump-action Model 1893, which would be modified to become highly successful Model 1897.

With a pump or slide-action firearm, the shooter pulls back on the wooden forearm and then pushes it forward to eject the empty shell and replace it with a loaded one. Browning had earlier applied the principle to a handy little .22 rifle for Winchester, the classic Model 1890, which remained popular for decades, happily

Yukon Trouble by Lynn Hunt Bogue from the Remington Factory Colleciton displayed at the NRA National Sporting Arms Museum at Bass Pro Shops illustrates the use of semi-auto rifles in early 20th century outdoor adventure scenes.

A BRIEF HISTORY OF FIREARMS

employed in shooting galleries, by squirrel and rabbit hunters, and for all around "plinking."

It was in the area of automatic firearms, however, that Browning probably made his greatest advances. Auto-loaders use the part of the force of the firing cartridge to eject the empty casing and load a fresh round into the chamber. This may occur by direct or delayed blowback of the breechblock, by utilizing the recoil of the gun, or by redirecting some of the expanding gases of the burning gunpowder from the barrel to operate the action.

In 1900, the same year the Luger was introduced, Colt first offered a Browning-designed auto-loading pistol, the .38 caliber Model 1900 Automatic. Variations and improvements followed in rapid succession, with a smaller Hammerless .32 Pocket model in 1903, and a tiny "vest pocket"-sized .25 caliber pistol in 1908. Colt introduced the .45 ACP (Automatic Colt Pistol) cartridge in the Browning-designed Model 1905.

This is the cartridge that would be chambered in the famous Model 1911. The 1911 was rapidly adopted by the U.S. military, and, only slightly modified over time, remained the primary U.S. issue sidearm through the Vietnam War. Colt and many other firms continue production of 1911 pattern pistols today, and they still serve military, law enforcement, and personal protection duty on a regular basis. It is the handgun of choice for many shooting sports that seek to simulate combat-type shooting and, in accurized forms, is dominant in many traditional target-shooting sports. Its mastery requires effort, training, and practice, but in the right hands many would argue that it is the finest combat handgun of all time.

Whereas the 1911 may have been Browning's finest handgun design, his contributions did not end there. His final pistol design, the Model 1935, took advantage of the Luger's smaller-diameter 9mm cartridge "double-stacked" in two parallel columns in the detachable magazine for a total magazine capacity of 13 rounds (compared to 7 rounds in a 1911 mag). The 1935 is also known as the Browning High Power.

It's worth mentioning that most detachable magazine auto-loading pistols present a potential hazard for untrained individuals. It's easy to check whether most double-action revolvers are loaded simply by swinging open the cylinder and looking. However, a person who is not familiar with firearms may assume that an auto-loading firearm is unloaded once the magazine has been removed. This is a potentially lethal mistake. An auto-loading pistol may still have a live round in the chamber after the magazine has been taken out. In most designs, this round will fire if the trigger is pulled, with the potential for tragic consequences.

Browning's auto-loading designs were not limited to handguns. His "humpback" Auto 5 shotgun was a tremendous success, popular still today, and has been made by Fabrique Nationale, Remington, and Browning. He made many military firearms as well, especially machine guns.

Today, the term "semi-automatic" or "semi-auto" is used to refer to the auto-loading guns that fire only one round for each pull of the trigger. Although Colt originally called the Browning pistols "automatic pistols," in modern usage the term "automatic firearm" is used to describe a gun that fires multiple rounds for a single pull of the trigger.

These "full-auto" firearms, popularly called "machine guns," will usually continue rapidly firing until the trigger is released or the magazine is empty. Those that will fire a set number of rounds, usually three, with a single pull of the trigger are called "burst fire," and those that can be set to fire either a single shot per trigger pull or to fire full-auto are called "select fire."

The concept of a firearm that will "spray" a stream of bullets is hardly a recent one. Most famous of the early rapid-fire guns was the Gatling gun, which fired steadily through a cluster of rotating barrels so long as the gunner was turning its crank and his assistant was feeding ammunition. It was first demonstrated in 1861 and was a successful military design.

The first successful true full-auto machine gun, which would fire continuously while the trigger was held back, was perfected by Hiram Maxim in the 1880s and adopted by several armies in the 1890s. John Moses Browning invented a number of successful machine gun designs, beginning in the 1890s. His most remarkable achievements were probably his water-cooled .30 caliber Model 1917 and the .50 caliber M2 "Ma Deuce," which is still in use today.

The machine guns just briefly described fall into the category of fixed-position, crew-served weapons and their continued

The Scarecrow by G. Ryder.

INTRODUCTION

evolution is outside the scope of this work. Browning's famous BAR was a traditionally stocked box magazine full-auto rifle in .30-06 caliber. While it served decades as an effective military arm, it was generally fired from a bipod.

SUBMACHINE GUNS, BATTLE RIFLES, and ASSAULT RIFLES

While cartridges in the .30-06 class are readily aimed and controlled in single-shot fire, including semi-automatic fire, they tend to be less controllable and thus less effective when fired full-auto offhand due to the recoil and cumulative muzzle climb with each round to leave the barrel.

This limitation of full-auto fire from a personal arm was first addressed by the development of "submachine guns." Generally, these are full-auto capable weapons designed to be fired from the shoulder like a rifle, but chambered for a lower-powered pistol cartridge instead of a full-power rifle cartridge. The resulting gun was controllable and could be effectively aimed in short-range full-auto fire. The stubby pistol cartridges used by the gun could efficiently burn all their powder in a shorter barrel than required for a high-powered rifle round, resulting in a lighter gun with a shorter and handier overall length. The trade-off was that their effective range is much shorter than a traditional rifle, and an individual round hits with less power. The submachine gun is considered more effective when encounters are likely to be fast and at short range, such as trench warfare, inside buildings, or in heavy jungle. They are less effective for precision shooting or over long ranges.

The first Submachine gun was the 9mm Italian Viller Persoa in 1915 but the first one to see widespread production and use was the Bergmann M18 in 1918. One of the best, and certainly the most famous, was the Thompson submachine gun, or "Tommy Gun," introduced at the end of WWI in .45 ACP. Used by both law enforcement and gangsters, it has been called "the gun the made the 20s roar" and the "Chicago typewriter." It went on to serve honorably in WWII and beyond. Other WWII sub-guns included the German MP38 and MP40, the British Sten gun, the Russian PPS series, and the U.S. M3 "grease gun."

A milestone in post-war submachine gun design was the 9mm Uzi, designed by Israeli officer Uziel Gal, first produced in 1951. Although still popular, it has since been replaced as the first choice submachine gun for military and law enforcement by the MP-5 in the same caliber, produced by the German firm of Heckler & Koch (H&K).

Most countries entered WWII with a bolt-action as their primary battle rifle. Germany had its latest Mauser, the 8mm Kar 98; Britain, the Short Magazine Lee Enfield (SMLE) in .303 caliber; Japan, the Arisaka; and so forth. The Springfield '03 was still widely issued to American forces, but in the decade preceding the outbreak of hostilities, the U.S. Army had been testing competing designs of semi-auto rifles, then proceeding to manufacture and issue the pattern deemed best.

The U.S. M1 Garand in .30-06 caliber was without question the finest full-power rifle fielded in WWII. Instead of a fixed or detachable box magazine, it was loaded with eight rounds held in a metal clip. When the last round was fired, the clip was automatically ejected with the action remaining open for quick insertion of another loaded clip. It was rugged, reliable, and powerful.

It was also heavy. The Army sought a firearm that was more accurate and powerful, and had a longer range than a pistol, but which was lighter and handier than the full-sized rifle, intended primarily as a secondary weapon for tankers, artillery crews, and personnel who were not in a primary combat role. This role was ably filled by the M1 Carbine, a semi-auto accepting a 15-round detachable box magazine. It fired a new straight-wall cartridge, midway in power between the pistol and the full-sized rifle.

Germany also was developing a mid-range shoulder weapon, but with a different intent. They sought a detachable magazine rifle that would fire a reduced-power cartridge and would be controllable and effective in full-auto firing mode, with more range and power than a submachine gun. The resulting MP-43 filled the bill, but was developed late in the war. The concept was one that would survive the conflict—the Germans called the gun a Sturmgewehr, loosely translated as "assault rifle."

Most military establishments hesitated to "downsize" the power and range of their primary rifles in the early Cold War years. The semi-auto detachable magazine concept was an obvious success, and there was something to be said for full-auto capability. A series of full-power "battle rifles" was introduced to meet this need—the FN-FAL and the Heckler & Koch G3 being two patterns that were widely adopted. The U.S. developed a Garand look-alike with detachable magazine and full-auto capability, the M14.

But the assault rifle concept wouldn't go away. The Soviet Union accepted the lower-power round idea in its fixed-magazine semi-auto chambered for an intermediate power 7.62x39mm round in 1945, the SKS, which saw wide distribution and production in Soviet client states and enjoys popularity in the post-Cold War U.S. as an inexpensive semi-auto military surplus rifle.

They followed two years later with what would become probably the most widely produced military long arm design in history, and the quintessential assault rifle—the Kalashnikov-designed AK-47 in the same caliber.

The AK-47 is a select fire (semi-auto or full-auto) carbine-size weapon with a detachable 20- or 30-round box magazine. It has a well-deserved reputation for relatively cheap production and for reliability, even in the most adverse environments or when used by undertrained forces who may neglect maintenance. It makes extensive use of sheet metal stampings in its construction, with a simple wooden buttstock with pistol grip.

The U.S. version of the assault-rifle configuration was introduced in 1963, originally known as the AR-15 and XM16 designed by Eugene Stoner. It was ultimately adopted as the M16 manufactured by Colt. It is chambered for the 5.56mm NATO round, a military twin of the .223 Remington cartridge, and takes a detachable box magazine of 20 or 30 rounds. The rear sight is mounted on a distinctive integral carrying handle, and the stock and handguard are made of black synthetic material.

Initial reviews of the M16 were mixed. A combination of an improper type of powder used in the manufacture of the cartridge and a mistaken belief that maintenance could be neglected resulted in some early failures in the field. Some in the military establishment resisted a .22 caliber round for combat, dismissing it as a "poodle shooter."

This concern may be understood by reviewing a statistic commonly used to summarize a cartridge's power level—the muzzle energy. Muzzle energy is a product of the weight of the bullet and the velocity at the moment it leaves the barrel, expressed in foot pounds (ft./lb.). The WWII and early post-war battle rifles chambered for .30-06 and 8mm Mauser-class cartridges typically develop 2,000 to 2,600 ft./lb. of muzzle energy. By contrast, the .45 ACP and 9mm Luger rounds, commonly used in military pistols and submachine guns, run in the 300 to 400 ft./lb. range. That's nothing to sneeze at by the way… the common .22 Long Rifle cartridge, which can certainly be lethal, runs in the 90 to 125 ft./lb. range.

The intermediate "assault rifle" cartridges, such as the 7.62x39mm and 5.56mm NATO, average in the 1,200 to 1,600 ft./lb. range. The designers of these were effective in "splitting the difference" between the high-power rifle and pistol-cartridge-power ranges, but many old soldiers were not sold on the compromise.

Yet, both M16 rifle and ammunition were significantly lighter than either the old battle rifles or the AK system, allowing an infantryman to carry more ammunition or other load. With tuning and evolution, the M16 pattern proved to be highly accurate out to distances reached by the earlier full-sized battle rifles.

The evolutionary descendants of the AK-47 and M16 have become the dominant military rifle patterns as the world enters the 21st century. Both have proven to be effective in combat.

Semi-automatic versions of both designs have become highly popular with civilian shooters in recent decades, with the AR-15 (semi-auto version of the M16) coming to dominate many types of target competition.

In the 1970s, anti-gun forces incorrectly applied the "assault rifle" terminology to these semi-auto sporting versions. The function of the sporters is identical to other semi-auto sporting guns—it takes a separate pull of the trigger to fire each round. They lack the full-auto capability that originally defined "assault rifles."

The terminology redefinition stuck, however, leading to ill-conceived legislation that temporarily banned the production of certain types of guns, based solely on cosmetic appearances. Fortunately, the Clinton semi-auto ban has since sunset, so that these popular semi-auto rifles are again available in their original configuration at affordable prices.

Eugene Stoner holding M16 and Mikhail Kalashnikov holdking AK47. USMC photo.

INTRODUCTION

MODERN GUN MILESTONES

Recent decades have witnessed the continuing evolution and development of other types of sporting firearms, with several recurring trends.

Handguns, and revolvers in particular, have seen the development of more and more powerful ammunition. In 1935, Smith & Wesson rocked the handgun world with the introduction of the .357 Magnum cartridge and their prestigious Registered Magnum revolver to fire it. At a time when full power "big bore" handgun rounds ran in the 300 to 350 ft./lb. muzzle-energy range, S&W upped the ante to over 500 ft./lb. Results of actual law enforcement

shootings suggest that the .357 magnum round, with 125 grain hollowpoint loads, may be the most effective "stopper" still today. The fact that revolvers chambered for the .357 Magnum can also shoot the milder .38 Special has contributed to their continuing popularity.

S&W followed this with the .44 Magnum in 1955. With muzzle energy approaching 1,000 ft./lb., the .44 Mag changed handgun big game hunting from a "stunt" to a serious and common sporting pursuit. When the Dirty Harry movies hit the theaters, lots of folks with more imagination than experience decided they needed "the world's most powerful handgun," not understanding how to manage the considerable recoil. It was not uncommon to find a S&W .44 Magnum advertised for sale in "as new" condition, with 6 cartridges missing from the 50-round box. Once around the cylinder was enough for many would-be Harry Callahans!

In 2003, Smith & Wesson raised the bar to a previously unimaginable level with the introduction of their X-frame .500 Magnum revolver. Developing an incredible 2,500 ft./lb. of muzzle energy,

NRA Law Enforcement competition shooting

the 500 readily surpasses the power level of many high-power rifles.

Auto-pistol evolution took a leap forward in 1971 when the Smith & Wesson Model 59 was the first weapon to combine the high-capacity double-stack magazine of the Browning High Power with the double-action mechanism of the German WWII era Walther P.38. A number of firms followed suit, and the genre, known as "wonder nines" for their usual 9mm chambering, began to make inroads into a police market that previously had been dominated by double-action revolvers. The Swiss-based firm of SIG Sauer developed a strong reputation for quality and reliability in this type of pistol, and the Beretta Model 92 in the wonder nine configuration replaced the old warhorse 1911A1 pistol as the U.S. Army standard issue.

In 1982, the semi-auto pistol market was turned upside-down by a new Austrian manufacturer offering a radically different design. The frame was made from plastic-like polymer. Traditionalists initially scoffed at the 17-round design with no external manual safeties other than a lever on the face of trigger and an operating system that was neither SA nor DA, but was instead called a "safe action" by the maker. Beauty is as beauty does, however, and the Glock did nothing but perform. It combined reliability, simplicity, affordability, and functional accuracy. Today, it is likely that more Glocks ride in police holsters than any other make.

The trend to new materials other than traditional blue steel and wood had begun years before. Smith & Wesson used lightweight alloys to make lightweight guns easier to carry, beginning with aluminum-frame Airweight Chiefs Specials in 1952 and continuing through scandium and titanium alloys today that get .38 revolver weights down to the 10-ounce range.

Smith & Wesson and Charter Arms led the way in using rust-resistant stainless steel for small revolvers likely to be carried in sweaty environments close to the body, beginning in the mid-1960s. Since then, stainless steel has nearly replaced blued carbon steel in revolver designs and has made major inroads in long gun and semi-auto pistol production.

Many major handgun makers have followed Glock's lead in offering synthetic-framed auto-pistols. For long gun stocks, synthetic stocks have been found to be more lightweight and less affected by environmental extremes than wood. Rubber has replaced wood as the most likely handgun grip material.

In the repeating shotgun field, the Winchester Model 12 was probably the standard for pump shotguns in the mid-20th century and was perhaps replaced by the Remington Model 870 in more recent years. Semi-auto shotguns have overcome their reputation for finicky performance, first with Remington 1100, and then with the Benelli Model 90, and have enjoyed an outstanding reputation for reliability in recent years.

Probably the last of the great firearms inventor/entrepreneurs in the tradition of Sam Colt and D.B. Wesson was Bill Ruger. His Sturm Ruger firm developed a reputation for improving classic sporting

A BRIEF HISTORY OF FIREARMS

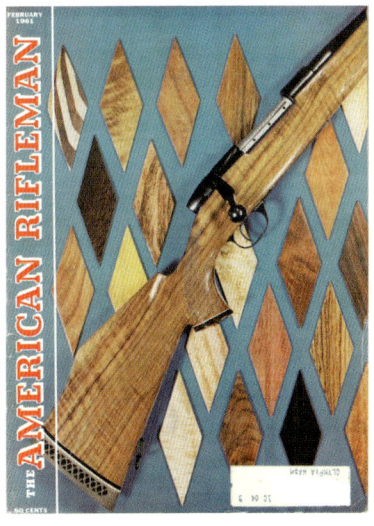

gun designs, and turning out a broad line of well-made and reasonably priced firearms, from revolvers and rifles through auto-pistols and over/under shotguns.

Other new firms sprang up to challenge the old line makers with improved or cheaper versions of the classic designs. Springfield Armory has become a major maker of military pattern sporting arms based on classic military designs such as the 1911 and the Garand patterns. Taurus began to offer serious competition to S&W in the revolver field. Firms such as Bushmaster and others began to develop a reputation for quality AR-15 semi-auto rifles, a market once belonging to Colt. Other makers such as Uberti and Navy Arms saw the strong nostalgia market for 19th century designs and began to produce quality versions of early percussion revolvers, Single Action Armies, Winchester lever guns, and other arms appealing to Old West buffs and participants in the fun new sport of Cowboy Action Shooting.

Options for aiming a firearm have expanded dramatically over the past 50 years. Telescopic sights for precision rifle shooting were used as early as the Civil War. It wasn't until after WWII, however, that it became a standard practice to mount a scope on most serious hunting rifles. The technology of these optics has continually evolved and improved. In the 1970s and 1980s, scopes came to be used on hunting handguns. New forms of sighting equipment, such as electronic red dot sights, glow in the dark night sights, ultra-compact laser aiming systems, and even night vision scopes, have come on the market and met with acceptance. They have been incorporated on firearms from concealed-carry handguns to target competition arms and military issue rifles.

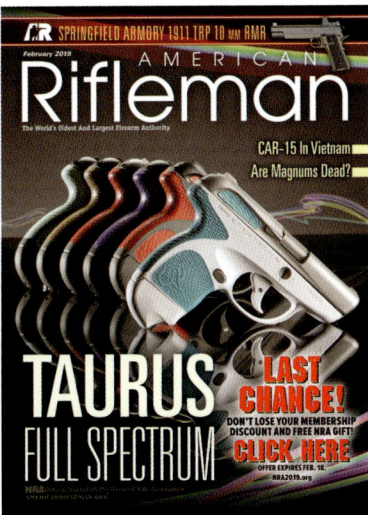
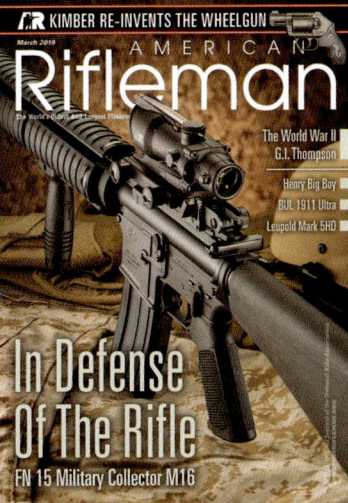

THE EARLIEST GUNS

European Hand Cannon - 1-inch-diameter bore - circa 1350 - This early hand cannon was found in a ruined fortress that fell in the mid-14th century, and was once part of the Archduke Eugen collection at Salzburg Castle. It is the oldest gun at the National Firearms Museum and may be the oldest gun on display in America. The piece projecting down near the muzzle was hooked over a wall or branch to help absorb recoil.

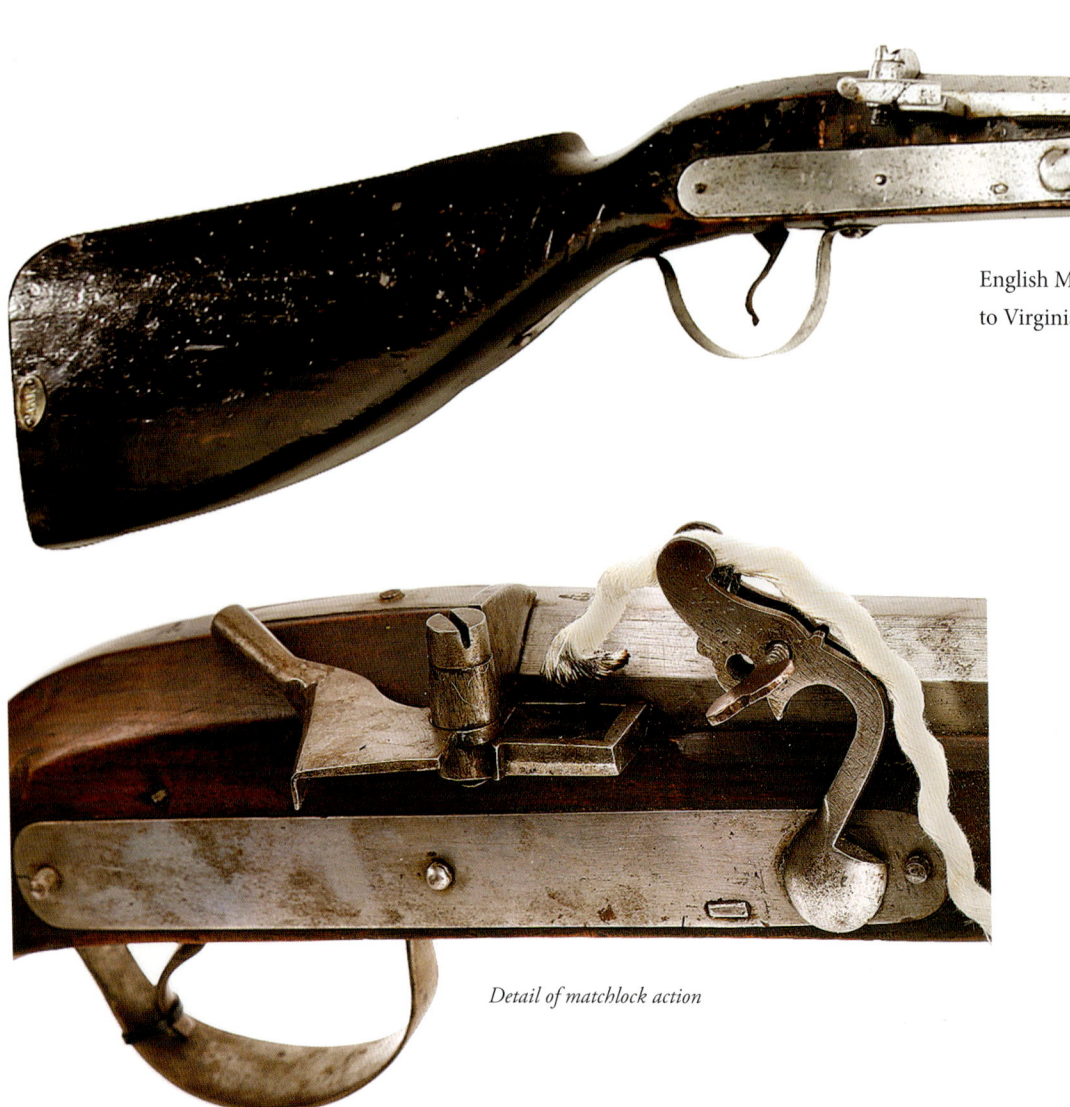

English Matchlock Musket - .82 caliber - circa 1575. Style common to Virginia and Bay Colony Militia units of the 1600s.

Detail of matchlock action

Hand Cannon circa 1350

The earliest and simplest guns are called hand cannons, used from 1350 into the 1500s. These are essentially metal tubes, closed on one end, with a touch hole for manually lighting the powder charge. Handcannons were the first projectile arms that relied on blackpowder as a propulsive force. Loaded with an assortment of lead shot, nails, small rocks, or other material, a handcannon could deliver a devastating blast at close range. Many examples exhibit a protruding flange or spike extending from the barrel to serve as a retaining point against a wall or tree branch during firing.

The handcannon and matchlock were followed by a series of advancements in mechanical locks that did not rely on a burnng ember for ignition, including some elaborate examples as pictured at right.

EARLY IGNITION SYSTEMS

1. German Matchlock Musket - .80 caliber - circa 1580-1600.
2. Japanese Matchlock Temple Gun - .50 caliber - circa 1750 - Gold and silver barrel inlays. Temple guns were fired to open religious ceremonies.
3. Indian Matchlock Gun - .63 caliber - circa 1760 - This modified Indian pattern gun is decorated with gold damascene.

Matchlock circa 1450 A.D.

The matchlock was the earliest type of lock for firing a gun. The "slow match" was a length of cord treated with chemicals to help it burn slowly, presenting a glowing tip on the end that was mechanically lowered into a pan of gunpowder adjoining the touch hole in the rear of the barrel to ignite the charge in the barrel. The "serpentine" is the device that holds and lowers the slow match. Matchlocks were used in India, Japan, and elsewhere in Asia well into the 19th century.

THE EARLIEST GUNS

Saxon Wheellock Musket - .72 caliber - circa 1600 - The winding spindle is concealed and protected by hemispherical cover.

German Brescian Fishtail Wheellock Pistol - .54 cal - circa 1650.

Italian Wheellock Pistol - .56 caliber - circa 1660-1690.

Wheellock circa 1500 A.D.

The wheellock was a mechanically complex ignition system, but less susceptible to wind and rain than the matchlock. The lock contains a vertical metal wheel with a serrated edge attached to a spring. The spring is wound like a clock with a spanner. The dogshead holds a piece of iron pyrite or flint which is lowered onto the edge of the wheel prior to firing. The trigger released the spring-driven wheel to spin creating a shower of sparks to ignite the powder in the pan, much in the way that a Zippo lighter works. Since it did not require a burning ember for ignition, the wheellock was the first firearm that could be carried concealed on the person, ready for use. Wheellock guns were expensive to make, limiting their military application. Beautifully decorated specimens served as hunting arms for royalty. The concept is sometimes attributed to Leonardo da Vinci.

EARLY IGNITION SYSTEMS

French Wheellock Rifle - .45 caliber - circa 1560.

Austrian Wheellock Rifle by Caspar Zelner with spanner - .59 caliber - circa 1770 - Zelner was a famed gunmaker in Vienna and Bebenhouse, Austria. He served as Imperial Arquebusier to Holy Roman Emperors Joseph I and Karl VI at the Hapsburg Court. Note spanner used to wind the internal spring that drives the serrated wheel.

16th Century Sixteen Shooter

German Multi-shot Wheellock/matchlock - .67 caliber - circa 1580. This three-lock firearm can be loaded with up to 16 superposed charges, loading powder and ball for the first charge, and repeating that process down the same barrel fifteen more times. It used slightly oval bullets with a hole drilled longitudinally through most of them, containing combustible fusing material. Firing the front wheellock ignites the topmost charge, and then the fire commutes through the fused hole of each successive bullet to fire the next charge in line. In this way, multiple charges are fired successively with a single pull of the trigger, roman candle fashion. It could be loaded for several firing patterns by using solid bullets with no longitudinal hole drilled through them at certain points in the firing chain. One example would be the front wheellock firing the top nine rounds, the second wheellock firing the next five rounds, with one last round held in reserve to be fired by the rearmost matchlock.

THE EARLIEST GUNS

Spanish Snaphaunce Fowler - .72 caliber.

Giovanni Beretta Italian Folding Stock Snaphaunce Pistol - .56 caliber - circa 1590 - This pistol features a folding stock to enable its owner to carry it under a cloak, providing cover from inclement weather or concealment.

Persian Miquelet - .58 caliber - circa 1770 - Decorated with gold damascene and an ivory buttplate.

Spanish Miquelet - 16 gauge - circa 1750 - Gold overlaid brass scrollwork

Spanish Miquelet Pistol - .70 caliber - circa 1800-1820.

Snaphaunce circa 1550 A.D.

The snaphaunce is the earliest form of flintlock, where a cock holds a piece of flint that is released by the trigger to strike a metal frizzen creating sparks to ignite the gunpowder in the pan. The name snaphaunce was derived from the Dutch word *snaphaan* meaning snapping hen, a reference to the snapping or pecking action of the hammer against the steel battery. The snaphaunce is identified by having a separate frizzen and pan cover. Later flintlocks consolidated these functions into a single piece.

Beretta

Fabbrica d'Armi Pietro Beretta S.p.A., is not only the world's oldest existing gunmaker, it is the world's oldest industrial firm in continuous operation. Beretta has been producing firearms in northern Italy since the days of Leonardo da Vinci and Christopher Columbus. Bartolomeo Beretta, a master barrel maker, operated an iron forge in the Val Trompia Valley as early as 1500. Beretta-manufactured arms were used by the Venetian Republic in its war with the Ottoman Turks in 1570. Over the past four hundred years, the company has produced every type of firearm from arquebusses to wheellock and flintlock pistols to modern automatic rifles, semi-automatic pistols, and fine sporting arms, as well as machinery used in the manufacture of guns.

Miquelet circa 1580 A.D.

The Spanish-developed miquelet type of flintlock was the first to use a frizzen that also served as a pan cover. The main spring is mounted on the exterior of the lockplate, distinguishing it from later flintlock designs. Rugged design was especially popular in Spain and Spanish colonies, and was used well into the flintlock era.

EARLY IGNITION SYSTEMS

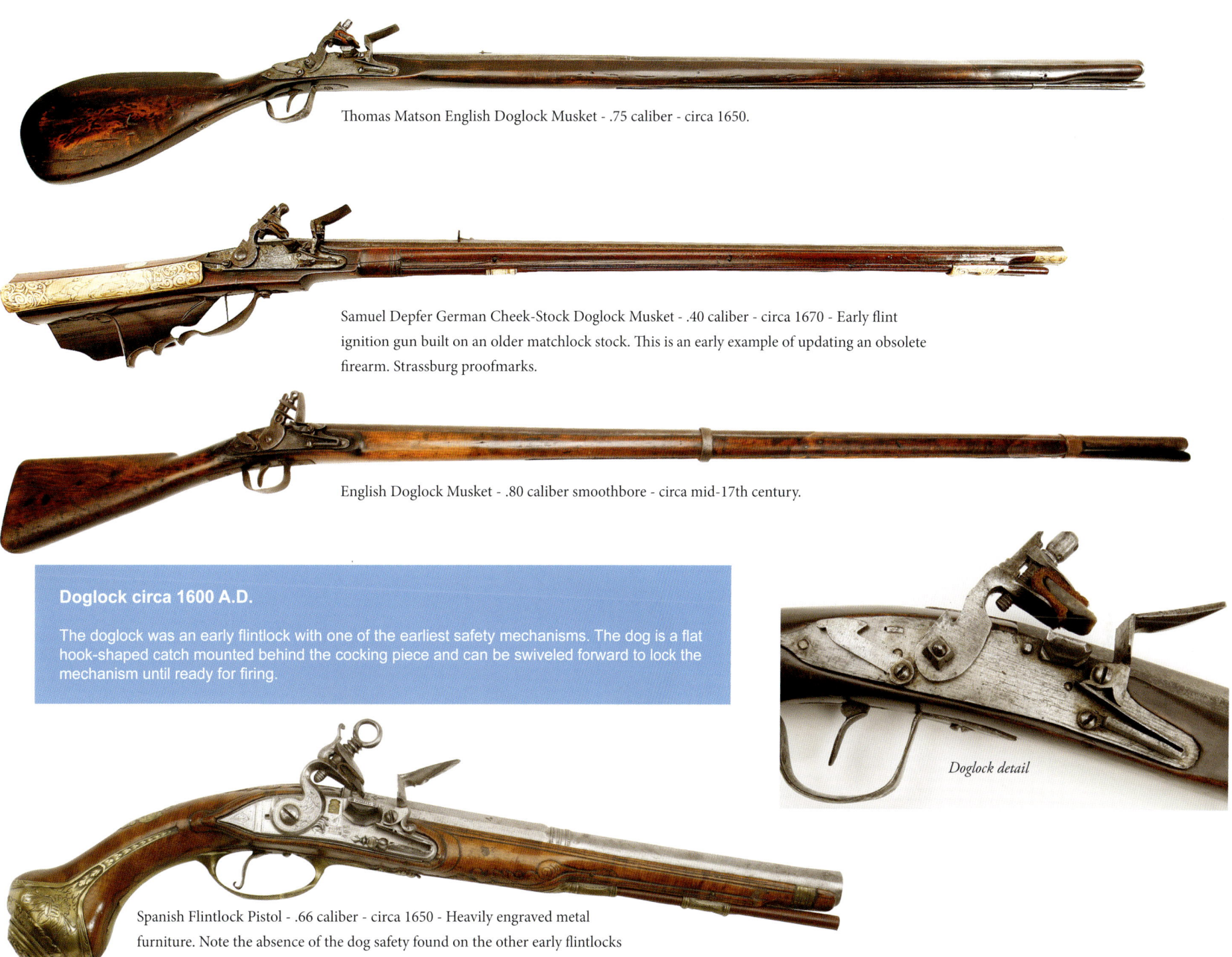

Thomas Matson English Doglock Musket - .75 caliber - circa 1650.

Samuel Depfer German Cheek-Stock Doglock Musket - .40 caliber - circa 1670 - Early flint ignition gun built on an older matchlock stock. This is an early example of updating an obsolete firearm. Strassburg proofmarks.

English Doglock Musket - .80 caliber smoothbore - circa mid-17th century.

Doglock circa 1600 A.D.

The doglock was an early flintlock with one of the earliest safety mechanisms. The dog is a flat hook-shaped catch mounted behind the cocking piece and can be swiveled forward to lock the mechanism until ready for firing.

Doglock detail

Spanish Flintlock Pistol - .66 caliber - circa 1650 - Heavily engraved metal furniture. Note the absence of the dog safety found on the other early flintlocks on this page.

THE EARLIEST GUNS

Pair of Perkins English Flintlock Pistols - .77 caliber - circa 1790.

A. B. Weston English Flintlock Turn-barrel Pistol - .45 caliber - circa 1830-1845 - Barrel can be twisted off for loading or cleaning.

Fabrica Reale Italian Flintlock Pistol - .69 caliber - circa 1810 - Damascus barrel with goldschmeltz (goldplated silver) furniture.

John Manton English Flintlock Duelling Pistol - .57 caliber - circa 1820.

Spanish Model 1803 Flintlock Musket - .69 caliber - Smoothbore flintlock.

A & E Weston British Side-by-Side Flintlock Fowler - 12 gauge - circa 1790.

Flintlock

Flintlock - circa 1630 A.D. - The flintlock mechanism, used until the advent of the percussion system, was developed in France during the early part of the 17th century and spread throughout western Europe. It was a combination, with refinements, of the snaphaunce and the miquelet. It embodied the interior mainspring and lock mechanism of the snaphaunce and the combination flash pan cover and frizzen, or battery, used in the miquelet. The interior mechanism was improved by notching the tumbler for both half- and full-cock positions. (The half-cock was a safety feature.) The flintlock action, with its internal safety and simpler manufacturing process, quickly replaced the snaphaunce and miquelet as the most popular ignition system.

OLD WORLD ARTISTRY

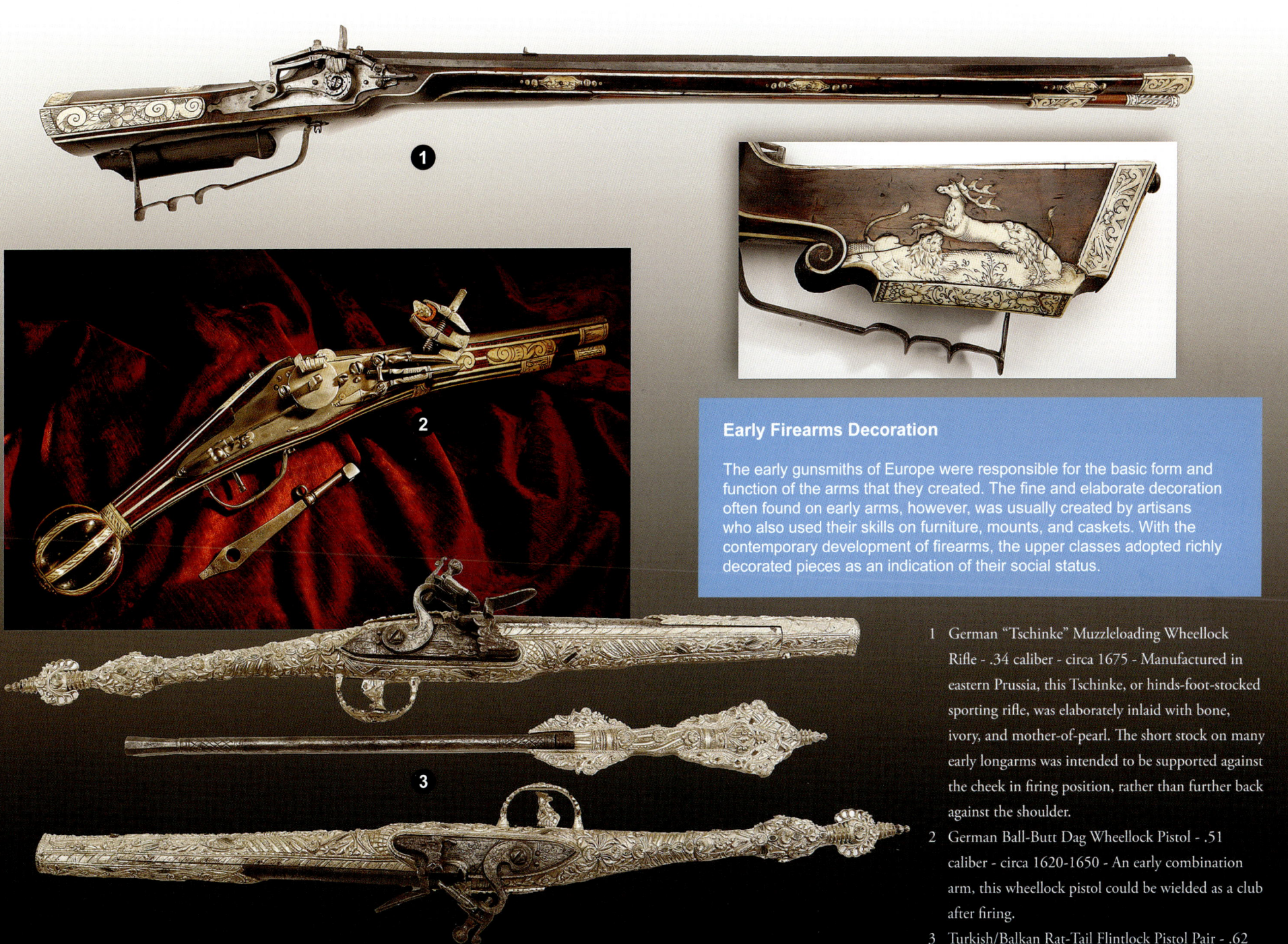

Early Firearms Decoration

The early gunsmiths of Europe were responsible for the basic form and function of the arms that they created. The fine and elaborate decoration often found on early arms, however, was usually created by artisans who also used their skills on furniture, mounts, and caskets. With the contemporary development of firearms, the upper classes adopted richly decorated pieces as an indication of their social status.

1. German "Tschinke" Muzzleloading Wheellock Rifle - .34 caliber - circa 1675 - Manufactured in eastern Prussia, this Tschinke, or hinds-foot-stocked sporting rifle, was elaborately inlaid with bone, ivory, and mother-of-pearl. The short stock on many early longarms was intended to be supported against the cheek in firing position, rather than further back against the shoulder.

2. German Ball-Butt Dag Wheellock Pistol - .51 caliber - circa 1620-1650 - An early combination arm, this wheellock pistol could be wielded as a club after firing.

3. Turkish/Balkan Rat-Tail Flintlock Pistol Pair - .62 caliber - circa 1800 - Ornate cast silver stocks.

THE EARLIEST GUNS

Sardinian Miquelet - .44 caliber - circa 1625 - Decorative silver fretwork reinforces the slender stock.

Swedish Cheek-Stock Snaphaunce Musket - .60 caliber - circa 1650 - Unusual forward-acting Baltic lock; ivory inlaid patchbox.

King James II's Flintlock Fowler by John Cosens - 10 gauge - circa 1688 - A well-worn flintlock fowler bearing the crest of King James II, the last of the Stuart line to hold the throne of Great Britain, Ireland, and Scotland. This piece was reportedly taken from the royal baggage train after James fled England in 1688.

The Duke of York's Flintlock Fowler by John Manton - 16 gauge - circa 1795-1800 - This John Manton flintlock fowler was once owned by Frederick Augustus, Duke of York and son of King George III of England.

Cassiano Zanotti Italian Snaphaunce Pistol - .60 caliber - circa 1690.

OLD WORLD ARTISTRY

Napoleon Bonaparte's Flintlock Double Fowler - 20 gauge - circa 1804-1815 - Crafted by Fatou of Paris, this double flintlock fowler, inlaid with gold, silver, and platinum and fitted with a purple velvet cheekpiece, was presented by Napoleon Bonaparte to Marquis Faulte de Vanteaux of Limoges, a general in Napoleon's army.

THE EARLIEST GUNS

Spanish Matchlock Musket - .78 caliber - circa 1530-1550 - Matchlocks were favored by many European explorers in the New World because they were cheaper to obtain and easier to maintain than mechanically complex wheellock arms. This musket was likely made in Madrid and was intended to be used with a forked rest.

"The Mayflower Gun" - Wheellock Carbine - .66 caliber - circa 17th century - Dutch or Italian. Oral tradition among early Museum staff held that this carbine was brought over on the Mayflower by pilgrim John Alden. It was reportedly recovered from his cabin during a 20th century restoration and donated by an Alden descendant. However, no documentation exists, and some experts who have examined the gun believe it was likely made decades after the pilgrims set sail for the New World.

OLD GUNS IN THE NEW WORLD

European Firearms in North America

The explorers and settlers who crossed the ocean to the New World brought firearms that had been crafted in their Old World. These early firearms protected the explorers and colonists against man and beast, and aided them in their unending quest for food. Relationships between the European settlers and the Native Americans were tenuous at best. English, French, and Spanish colonists, although friendly and peaceful at times, showed little hesitation in attacking them for economic gain. As tobacco, gold, and other spoils of the New World gained demand in Europe, the competition and greed for land and resources often resulted in war.

As settlements in America were established, protection from attack became a primary concern. Although the colonists' firearms were inaccurate, heavy, and slow to load and fire, these arms had a tremendous effect on the American Indian. James Rosier reported that when the native inhabitants of the Maine coast witnessed in 1605 the firing of the English musket, *"they were most fearful and would fall flat down at the sound of them."*

European colonists formed an alliance with some tribes by procuring valuable furs, food, and other goods through trade. Desirous of European trinkets and articles, the Indians traded beaver pelts to the colonists. The beaver pelts brought high prices in Europe.

After witnessing the value of the firearm for hunting, war, and protection, the American Indians wanted to obtain guns for themselves. However, most colonists regarded the possession of firearms by the native population as a threat to life and security. Proclamations, laws, and ordinances were enacted prohibiting firearms trade with natives. By the end of the 17th century, the illegal trade of guns and munitions became so prevalent that the colonies began to establish a legal arms trade which included licensing and taxation.

1. Spanish Miquelet Blunderbuss - 1.25 inch bore - circa 1670 - It is believed that this Spanish arm was reworked and restocked in Mexico in the 17th or 18th century. Spaniards had taught Mestizos in the area around Mexico City to repair and refurbish firearms. The decoration on this gun shows a fascinating mix of European and Mesoamerican symbols.
2. Francisco Targarona Spanish Miquelet Escopeta - .72 caliber - circa 1775 - Spanish military carbine typical of the arms carried in Mexico and Spanish colonial America.
3. Spanish Model 1803 Flintlock Musket - .69 caliber - circa 1800-1830 - Typical of those used by Spanish soldiers in the New Mexico area.

THE FLINTLOCK ERA

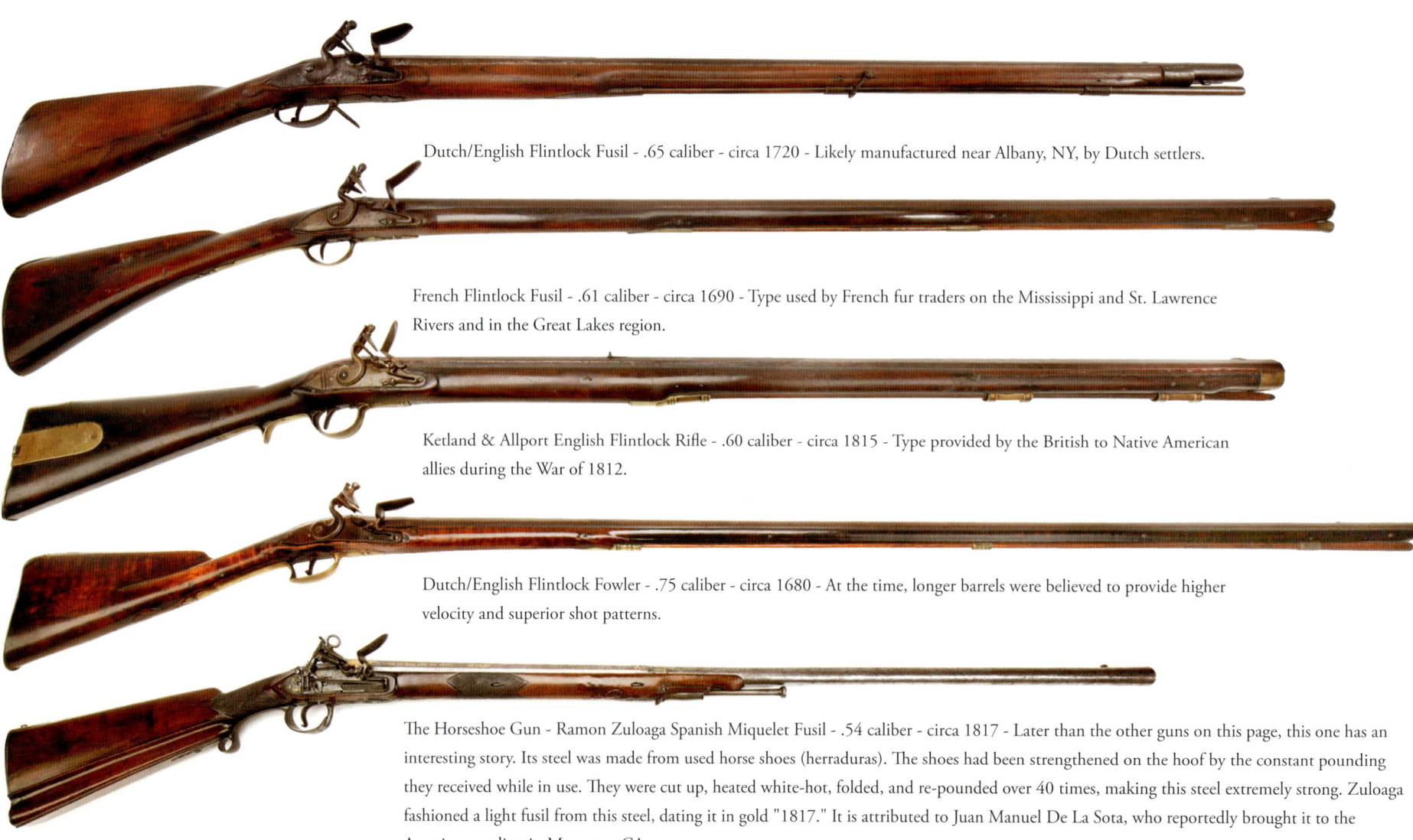

Dutch/English Flintlock Fusil - .65 caliber - circa 1720 - Likely manufactured near Albany, NY, by Dutch settlers.

French Flintlock Fusil - .61 caliber - circa 1690 - Type used by French fur traders on the Mississippi and St. Lawrence Rivers and in the Great Lakes region.

Ketland & Allport English Flintlock Rifle - .60 caliber - circa 1815 - Type provided by the British to Native American allies during the War of 1812.

Dutch/English Flintlock Fowler - .75 caliber - circa 1680 - At the time, longer barrels were believed to provide higher velocity and superior shot patterns.

The Horseshoe Gun - Ramon Zuloaga Spanish Miquelet Fusil - .54 caliber - circa 1817 - Later than the other guns on this page, this one has an interesting story. Its steel was made from used horse shoes (herraduras). The shoes had been strengthened on the hoof by the constant pounding they received while in use. They were cut up, heated white-hot, folded, and re-pounded over 40 times, making this steel extremely strong. Zuloaga fashioned a light fusil from this steel, dating it in gold "1817." It is attributed to Juan Manuel De La Sota, who reportedly brought it to the Americas, settling in Monterey, CA.

Musket, Fusil, Rifle, Fowler

Musket: From the Spanish word *mosquette*, denoting a heavy military firearm. The earliest muskets were matchlocks weighing as much as 20 pounds and having a bore of nearly 8 gauge. By the colonial period in America, standardization of firearms had begun and the term *musket* was applied to any smoothbore military firearm of large caliber.

Fusil: A lightweight flintlock smooth bore, as distinguished from the heavier military musket.

Rifle: From the German word *riffeln,* meaning to cut or groove. The process of rifling a gun barrel was developed by either Gaspard Kollner of Vienna or August Kotter of Nuremberg in the late 15th or early 16th century. In the rifling process, a series of spiral grooves are cut into the inside (or bore) of the barrel. The areas between the grooves are called lands. This rifling imparts a spiral motion to the projectile that aids in accuracy and increases its effective range.

Fowler: By the late 15th century, it had been discovered that when a large number of small lead projectiles (called shot) were loaded into a gun and fired, the projectiles would scatter or spread increasing the chance of success when hunting fowl and small game. The English pioneered the manufacture of shot, and subsequently developed a very long barreled firearm with a large smooth bore, called a fowler.

18TH CENTURY EUROPEAN MILITARY ARMS

Swedish Flintlock Fusil - .63 caliber - circa 1700.

British Pattern 1777 Short Land Pattern Flintlock Musket - .76 caliber - circa 1780 - Regimentally marked, with the Royal Cypher of George III.

British Long Land Pattern "First Brown Bess" Flintlock Musket - .78 caliber - circa 1780 - Contract musket by London gunsmith William Predden.

Spanish Model 1752 Flintlock Musket - .70 caliber.

French Model 1765 Cassagnard Flintlock Fusil - .78 caliber.

French St. Etienne Model 1777 Flintlock Musketoon .69 caliber.

French Model 1768 Flintlock Cavalry Carbine - .80 caliber.

THE FLINTLOCK ERA

British Pattern 1769 Short Land Pattern Musket - .80 caliber - circa 1780 - Family attribution to use in conjunction with the battles of Lexington and Concord.

Committee of Safety Musket - .80 caliber - circa 1770 - Converted from a British musket salvaged for issue by a colonial Committee of Safety.

Captain Moses Bouton's British Militia Pattern 1760 Light Infantry Flintlock Carbine - .75 caliber - circa 1773-1780 - Captain Bouton served in several militia units in the American Revolution with this arm. With powder and priming horns, U.S. marked bayonet, and combination pick, brush, and chain tool.

THE SHOT HEARD ROUND THE WORLD

Shot Heard Round the World

By 1775, relations between England and her American Colonies had suffered greatly. British military occupation and rule, and the excesses and abuses inflicted by the British upon the Americans, greatly angered the colonists. For example, under the revised Quartering Act of 1765, an officer of the King's Army could knock on the door of any private residence and demand lodging for his men.

Young British officers, spoiling for a fight, regularly took parties of soldiers on short military exercises through the Massachusetts towns of Waltham, Dedham, and Cambridge. The sight of Americans drilling in the fields greatly amused them. Their superiors, however, saw these drills as an omen of future armed resistance. In Cambridge, the British troops seized powder and arms belonging to the townspeople. Private houses were entered and arms were seized. In Charlestown, more arms were seized. These acts sent an alarm throughout New England. In response, the men of Massachusetts formed Committees and exercised the right to call out colonial troops should the occasion arise.

To provide for defense, special groups of men were established who could answer the call to arms immediately. These citizen-soldiers were called Minutemen.

In Boston, British General Thomas Gage commanded 4,000 troops who were called Redcoats by the native Bostonians. These soldiers had been given the task of enforcing British ordinances and keeping peace in the City of Boston. General Gage's exercises through the countryside and his recent confiscation of civilian firearms had aggravated the local population to the point of armed insurrection.

In April of 1775, Gage ordered the confiscation of all privately owned arms, gun (cannon) powder, and shot held by the local militia units that dotted the countryside between Boston, Lexington, and Concord. Hearing of this plan, residents devised a system of signal lamps hung in Boston's Old North Church to signal the approach of British soldiers by land or sea. Paul Revere made his famous midnight ride to alert the citizenry of the British approach.

On April 19, 1775, under the direction of Colonel Francis Smith and Royal Marine Major John Pitcairn, Gage's troops clashed with the colonial Minutemen and patriot troops at the North Bridge located between Lexington and Concord. With the first shot upon the King's troops, the American Revolution had begun.

As in previous wars, the American Revolution was, for the most part, fought and won by the infantryman. His firearm was the flintlock musket with bayonet. This large bore musket had a maximum effective range between 80 and 100 yards.

The typical inaccuracy of these firearms led to the development of tactics known as volley firing in which the massed infantry of one unit fired in unison at their enemy. Troops were trained to load and fire with accuracy, three times per minute. Rifles, which provided excellent accuracy at long ranges, were used by the Americans in guerilla warfare, but were ineffective on the battlefield due to their small numbers. The American rifle, with no provision for a bayonet and a lengthy loading procedure, gained notoriety only in the hands of the sharpshooter.

THE FLINTLOCK ERA

British Long Land Pattern First Model Brown Bess Musket - .79 caliber - circa 1740-1793 - Marked "5/4."

British Short Land Pattern Second Model Brown Bess Musket - .79 caliber - circa 1740-1768.

Hession Musket - .79 caliber - circa 1770-1800.

Committee of Safety Musket - .78 caliber.

French Model 1746 Charleville Musket - .69 caliber - circa 1746-62 -captured and remodeled by the English Colonial Militia.

French Model 1766 Charleville Musket - .69 caliber - circa 1766-1780.

Dutch Musket - .79 caliber - circa 1760-1854 - Marked "Maastristch," "CORBAU," and "CAPT VAN DYK NO 13."

Yeomanry Carbine by Henry Nock (London, England) - .75 caliber.

THE SHOT HEARD ROUND THE WORLD

American Flintlock Long Rifle - .60 caliber - circa 1770-1780 - In the Revolutionary War, many colonists were armed with their traditional hunting arms. Such rifles were slower loading but allowed better accuracy than military muskets.

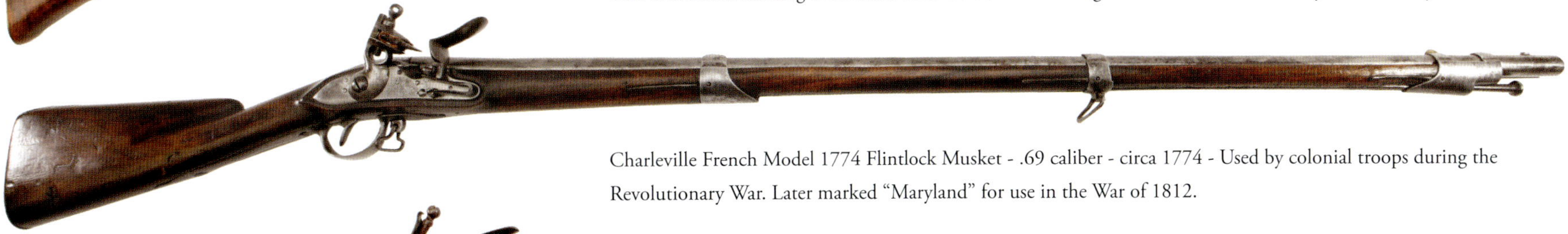

Charleville French Model 1774 Flintlock Musket - .69 caliber - circa 1774 - Used by colonial troops during the Revolutionary War. Later marked "Maryland" for use in the War of 1812.

Committee of Safety Flintlock Musket - .80 caliber - circa 1775.

Brown Bess, Charleville, and Committee of Safety

The prevalent longarms of the American Revolution were smoothbore large caliber flintlock muskets of the type used by the British and French military. The British Army Land Pattern musket was nicknamed The Brown Bess. The French pattern muskets were called Charlevilles.

Committees of Safety were established in the thirteen colonies to organize and equip their respective militias for military action against the British. Committee of Safety muskets were produced by local gunsmiths, usually patterned on the British Brown Bess. The muskets did not include any sort of manufacturer's markings lest the makers be charged with treason by British authorities.

Simeon North Flintlock Pistols - This pair of .53 caliber dueling pistols are typical of the type of privately owned arms that might have been carried during the Revolutionary War. North later became the first contract maker of U.S. military pistols.

membership.NRA.org | 39

THE FLINTLOCK ERA

T. Henshaw British Sea Service Flintlock Blunderbuss - 1.00 caliber - circa 1750 - Sea service arms generally lack sling swivels.

Blunderbusses

Blunderbusses feature flared muzzles. They were close-combat arms, loaded with lead shot. The flared muzzle served the dual function of spreading the shot charge wider than a cylinder bore and of serving as a built-in funnel for reloading. These were used as naval boarding weapons and coach guns, requiring reloading on a pitching ship's deck or a rocking coach.

Oval Bore Percussion Blunderbuss, made by Briel in Belgium, mid 19th century

Pape & Christian Flintlock Blunderbuss - .80 caliber - circa 1790s - Brass barrel. Spring loaded bayonet.

Alexander Wilson British Muzzleloading Flintlock Blunderbuss Pistol, 1.00 caliber - circa 1790.

BLUNDERBUSSES AND FLINTLOCK PISTOLS

Flintlock Pistols

Full size flintlock pistols such as the British Tower pistol (top) were popular with officers and cavalrymen. Large-bored and short-barreled, they were effective only at close range. Officers' pistols were seldom used in combat, and were primarily decorative accessories symbolic of status and rank.

Civilian flintlocks were made and used in a variety of sizes, from full-size traveler's or duelling pistols to easily concealable pocket pistols Through the 18th and into the 19th century they were carried and used for personal defense.

Traditional style flintlocks in the left column include, top to bottom, a miquelet, a British Adams pistol with safety latch, and a Queen Anne style pocket pistol

More unusual and later variations in the right column include a twist-barrel pocket flintlock, and double-barrel flint pistols, the lower one with a folding bayonet.

Royet French Flintlock Pistol - .59 caliber - circa 1780-1800 - From a cased pair of antique pistols presented to Gen. Solomon Lowe, U.S. Army, by his staff officers after WWII.

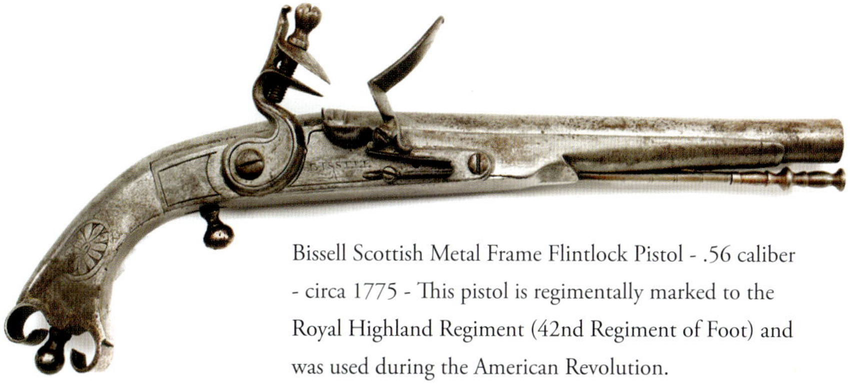

Bissell Scottish Metal Frame Flintlock Pistol - .56 caliber - circa 1775 - This pistol is regimentally marked to the Royal Highland Regiment (42nd Regiment of Foot) and was used during the American Revolution.

THE FLINTLOCK ERA

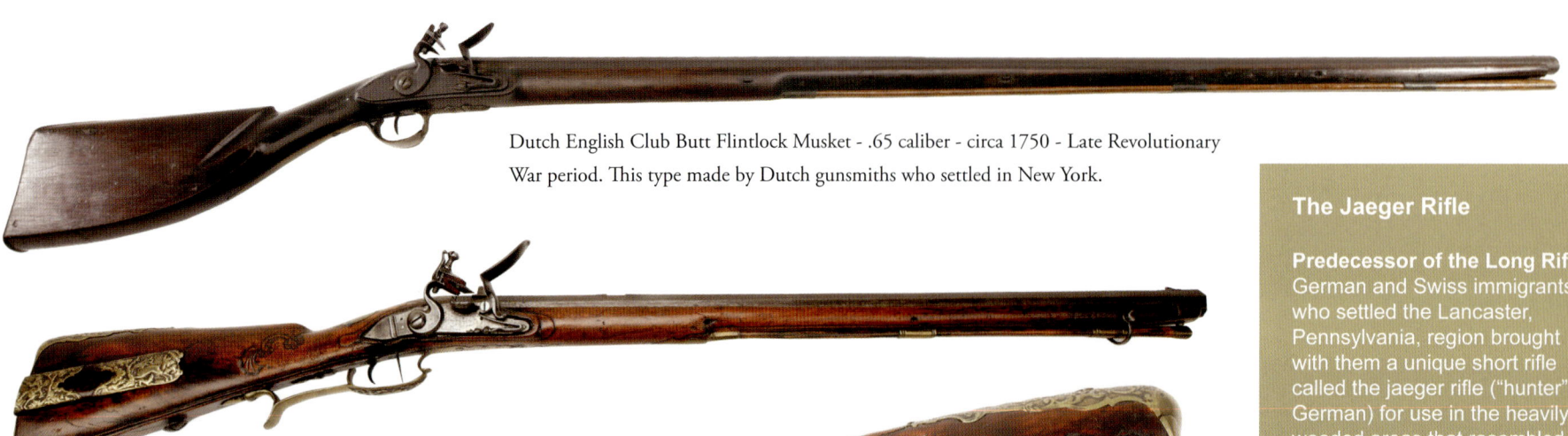

Dutch English Club Butt Flintlock Musket - .65 caliber - circa 1750 - Late Revolutionary War period. This type made by Dutch gunsmiths who settled in New York.

Ambrose Frelig German Flintlock Jaeger Rifle - .52 caliber - circa 1780-1800 - Swamped barrel (thinner in the middle than at breech and muzzle).

German/English Flintlock Jaeger Rifle - .50 caliber - circa 1730.

The Jaeger Rifle

Predecessor of the Long Rifle
German and Swiss immigrants who settled the Lancaster, Pennsylvania, region brought with them a unique short rifle called the jaeger rifle ("hunter" in German) for use in the heavily wooded areas that resembled their homelands. This rifle was a short, heavy, octagon-barreled gun in large caliber and was used not only for hunting big game, but also for sporting and target competition. In *The Last of the Mohicans*, a classic work of American literature by James Fenimore Cooper, a jaeger rifle is used by the hero Hawkeye.

Short in barrel, the jaeger offered greatly enhanced accuracy for hunting or military applications at a time when smoothbore muskets were considered "cutting edge" technology. In the closely packed forests of Europe, a short rifle could be carried and quickly brought to bear on a target. But with the arrival of Europeans in the New World, longer hunting distances became common with the open meadows and river valleys of North America. The short-sighted jaeger was updated with a lengthened barrel to provide a better sight radius and higher muzzle velocity, yielding in time the "Kentucky" rifle, a long rifle well-suited for frontier hunting.

THE AMERICAN LONG RIFLE

The American Long Rifle

The American long rifle, sometimes called the Kentucky or Pennsylvania rifle, was actually made in almost every colony and state from the mid-1700s until shortly before the Civil War.

During the first decades of the 18th century, immigrant German gunsmiths began to redesign the jaeger rifle into a firearm that was better suited to the wilderness of America. During the transition period, the barrel was lengthened to 40 inches or more for greater accuracy. Patchboxes were fitted with sliding wood covers and later with hinged metal covers. Rifles of this early period were relatively plain, although some arms had a few simple embellishments.

Why "Kentucky Rifle"?

At the close of the War of 1812, some 2,000 frontiersmen soldiers under General Andrew Jackson defeated the British at New Orleans in 1815. Carrying long rifles, these pioneers turned the tide of battle and won an American victory. A popular ballad *The Hunters of Kentucky* or *The Battle of New Orleans* memorialized the frontier riflemen, and did much to add the term Kentucky rifle to the common vocabulary:

> But Jackson he was wide awake,
> And was not scared at trifles,
> For well he knew what aim we take
> With our Kentucky rifles.

The generic name "Kentucky rifle" is recognized the world over. It is truly one of the very few indigenous American arms. Their use in the early wilderness, the American Revolution, and the War of 1812, plus their role in opening the American West to settlement, has indelibly linked this gun to many of America's beloved pioneers and frontier heroes.

The long rifle was a practical, graceful, and highly accurate arm that originally was used primarily for hunting and protection. However, it soon became a source of recreation and competition in frontier America. By the late 18th century, the legendary skill of riflemen prompted challenges between competitors for prizes such as livestock, fowl, and purses of money. Offhand shooting was the rule in the early days. Later, the bench rifle would dominate competitive shooting. Competitive shooting often attracted riflemen from long distances, and the sport became a major cultural and social event for many localities.

Comparative types of sporting arms from the late 18th and early 19th centuries, *top to bottom:*

English Flintlock Fowler - .72 caliber - circa 1730-1750 - Most arms of the early colonists came from their home countries. Fowlers are smooth bore for bird hunting.

Fordney American Long Rifle - .54 caliber - circa 1810-1820 - Classic "Kentucky" rifle by Melchior Fordney of Lancaster, PA.

Southern Percussion Rifle - .45 caliber - circa 1840-1850 - Less ornate than the American Long Rifle, the so-called "Southern" or "Mountain" rifle was a more affordable hunting arm.

THE FLINTLOCK ERA

Mathias Miller Flintlock Long Rifle - .50 caliber - circa 1780 - Eagle & flag patriotic engraving on patchbox, unusual on a civilian firearm.

Jacob Albright Long Rifle - .50 caliber - circa 1788-1800 - Exceptional rifle. Ketland & Co. lock, relief-carved maple stock, silver star and wire inlays, engraved patchbox.

John Palm #192 Swivel-Breech Flintlock Double Rifle - .45 caliber - circa 1800-1820 - Over-and-under flintlock rifles were a rarity in the day and this silver-mounted example rotates barrels with a squeeze of the trigger guard.

THE AMERICAN LONG RIFLE

membership.NRA.org | 45

THE FLINTLOCK ERA

London-made copy of Lancaster Flintlock Rifle - .60 caliber - circa 1800-1809.

P. Quattlebuw Flintlock Rifle - .36 caliber - circa 1800-1820 - Likely made in the Shenandoah Valley of Virginia; two bone inlays; elaborate pierced patchbox.

Percussion Long Rifle with G. Goulcher lock - .35 caliber - circa 1840 - Goulcher made components, such as locks, that were used by other gunsmiths to build guns. This rifle was likely made in what is now West Virginia.

D. Christ Long Rifle (reconverted to flint ignition) - .45 caliber - circa 1780-1810 - Many flintlock arms were converted to percussion ignition in the mid to late 19th century. Collectors sometimes convert these back to original flintlock, a somewhat controversial modern modification.

Anstate Long Rifle (reconverted to flint ignition) - .45 caliber - circa 1800 - Curly maple stock, Drepperd-marked lockplate, Fordney-style engraving.

J. Cooper Left-Handed Flintlock Long Rifle - .50 caliber - circa 1795-1815 - Left-handed long rifles are rare. Horsehead patchbox.

THE AMERICAN LONG RIFLE

The Golden Age of the Long rifle

During the period 1790-1830, the design and manufacture of the long rifle went through a golden age of manufacture. Exquisite examples of gunsmithing artistry exist from this period. Fine grades of curly or tiger-stripe maple were used, and the engraved metal parts and carving of the wooden stocks achieved the status of a high art form.

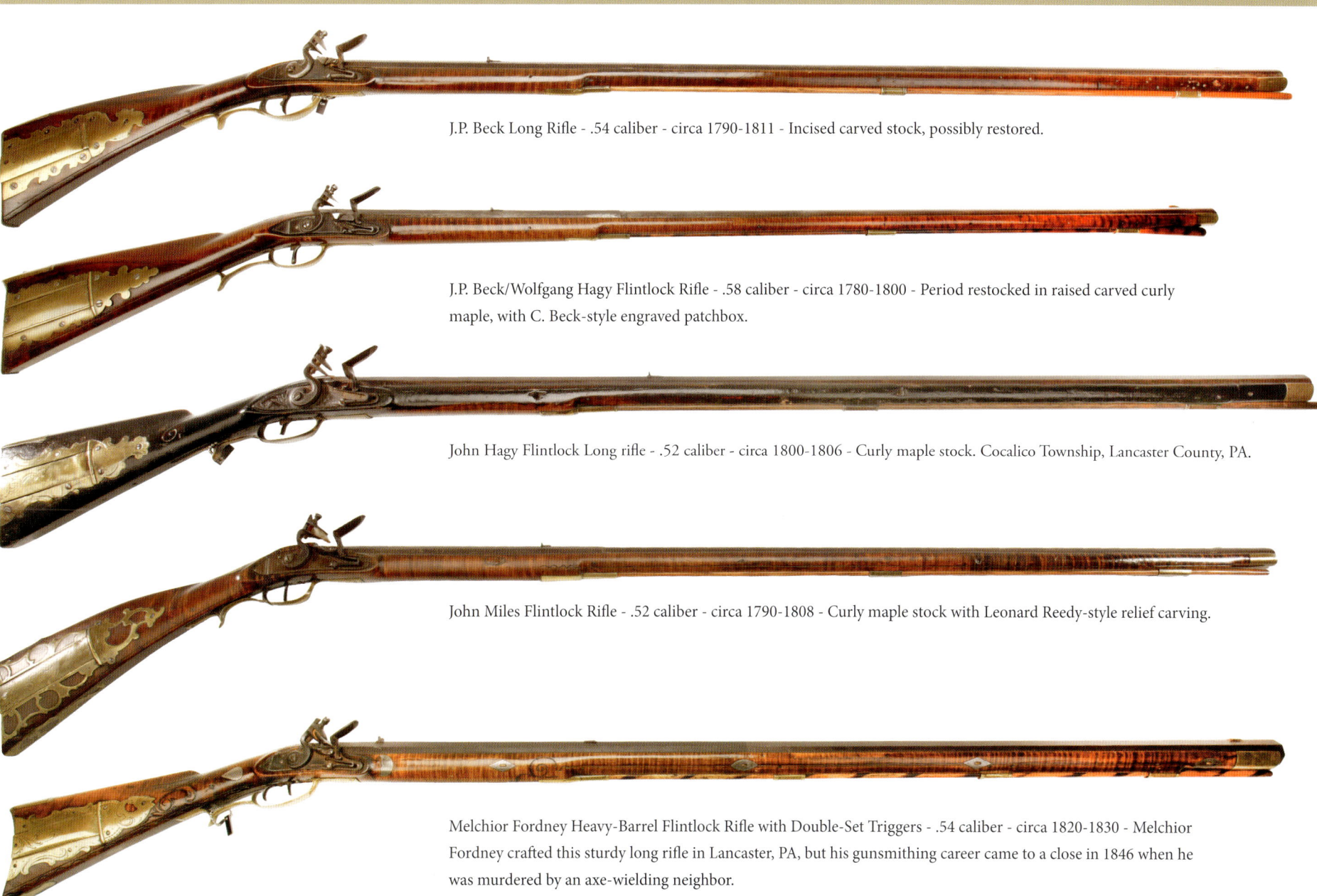

J.P. Beck Long Rifle - .54 caliber - circa 1790-1811 - Incised carved stock, possibly restored.

J.P. Beck/Wolfgang Hagy Flintlock Rifle - .58 caliber - circa 1780-1800 - Period restocked in raised carved curly maple, with C. Beck-style engraved patchbox.

John Hagy Flintlock Long rifle - .52 caliber - circa 1800-1806 - Curly maple stock. Cocalico Township, Lancaster County, PA.

John Miles Flintlock Rifle - .52 caliber - circa 1790-1808 - Curly maple stock with Leonard Reedy-style relief carving.

Melchior Fordney Heavy-Barrel Flintlock Rifle with Double-Set Triggers - .54 caliber - circa 1820-1830 - Melchior Fordney crafted this sturdy long rifle in Lancaster, PA, but his gunsmithing career came to a close in 1846 when he was murdered by an axe-wielding neighbor.

THE FLINTLOCK ERA

U.S. Springfield Model 1795 Flintlock Musket, Type I - .69 caliber - circa 1805 - The first model produced by an American National Armory.

U.S. Eli Whitney Model 1798 Contract Flintlock Musket - .69 caliber - circa 1798.

U.S. Harpers Ferry Model 1803 Flintlock Rifle, Late Production - .54 caliber - circa 1814-1820.

National Armories

In 1792, Congress authorized two National Arsenals for the storage, maintenance, and repair of military arms. By the end of 1794, Congress also authorized the construction of two National Armories for the manufacture of service arms. President George Washington personally selected the sites of Springfield, Massachusetts, and Harpers Ferry, West Virginia (then part of Virginia), as the locations for the two armories. In 1795, production began at Springfield, and by 1800, arms were being produced at Harpers Ferry. The new armories at Springfield and Harpers Ferry began production of the U.S. Model 1795 Musket, the first standard pattern arm made for the United States military.

Based on the French Model 1768 Charleville used during the Revolution, the Model 1795 did not have the aesthetic beauty of the British Brown Bess, but it utilized barrel bands with retaining springs instead of pins, a double-bridled lock mechanism, and a reinforced cock, giving it great strength and utility.

The U.S. Model 1795 was produced at Springfield until 1814 and at Harpers Ferry until 1816. Total production at the two National Armories was approximately 168,000 muskets.

Eli Whitney Revolutionizes Manufacturing

In 1798, Congress authorized the purchase of muskets from private contractors in order to supplement those firearms being made at the national armories. Eli Whitney of New Haven, Connecticut (who achieved fame at an early age with his invention of the cotton gin), was awarded a government arms contract for 10,000 U.S. Model 1795 muskets on June 14, 1798. Whitney's contract contained a unique idea: "to make the same parts of different guns, as much like each other as the successive impressions of a copper-plate engraving." With this idea, Whitney articulated the industrial concept of parts interchangeability.

Whitney devised tools and machines for manufacturing separate components and proved that workmen with little or no experience could operate machinery and turn out large quantities of gun parts with amazing precision. By developing special machinery, jigs, and other devices, Whitney turned a complex manufacturing process into a series of simple operations - a concept that revolutionized all manufacturing in America!

Model 1803 Flintlock Rifle

Patterned after the popular Kentucky rifle, this rifle was an accurate, well-made firearm that was practical for protection and for hunting in the wilderness. Made only at the Armory at Harpers Ferry, Virginia, it was the first and only muzzleloading flintlock rifle to be produced at a government armory. A total of 4,015 of these rifles was produced at Harpers Ferry Armory between 1804 and 1807. Additional rifles were needed by the military for the War of 1812, and production of the Model 1803 (Type II) was restarted in 1812. This production run lasted until 1820, resulting in a total of 15,703 Type II rifles.

EARLY 19TH CENTURY MILITARY ARMS

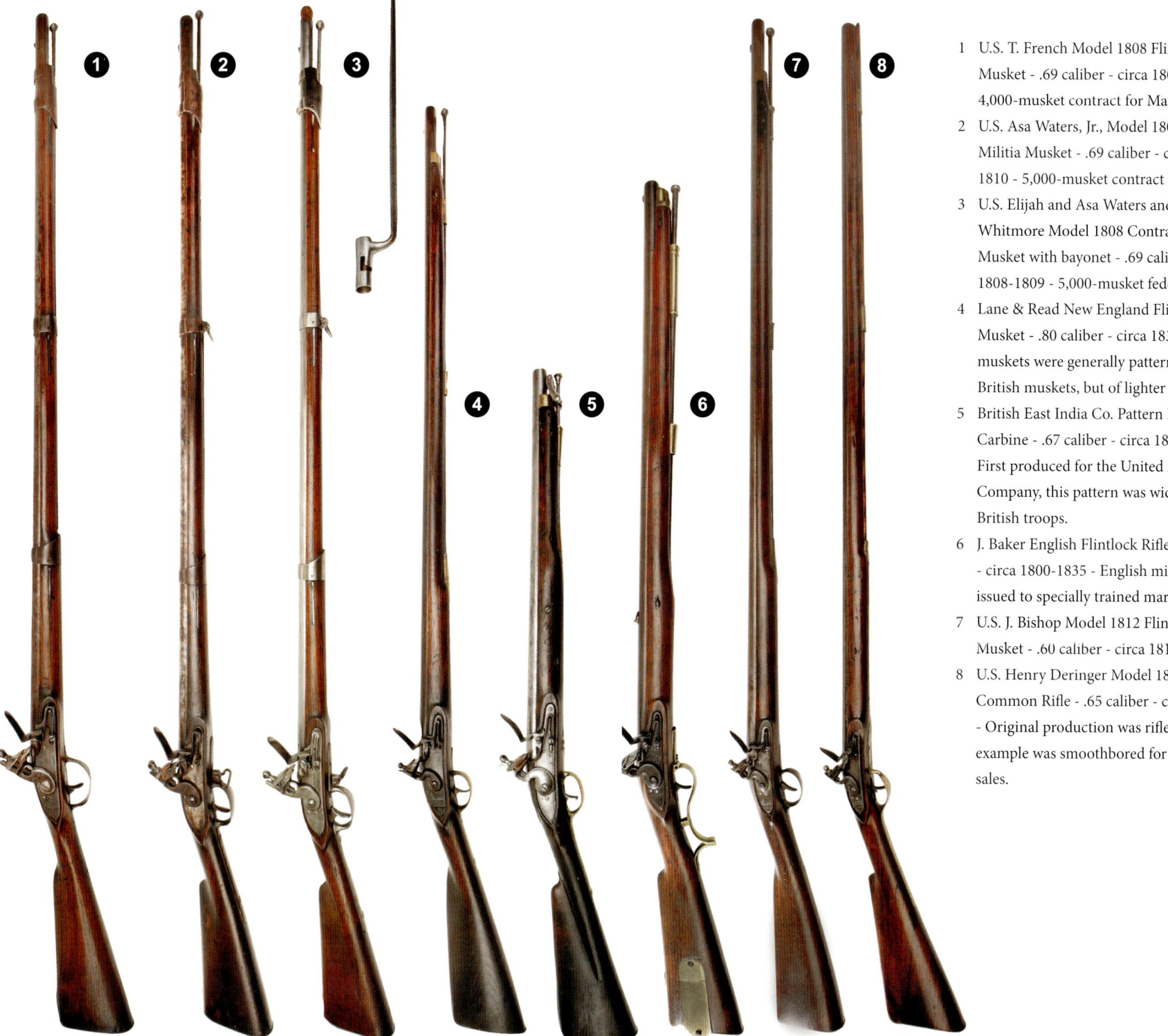

1. U.S. T. French Model 1808 Flintlock Militia Musket - .69 caliber - circa 1808-1812 - 4,000-musket contract for Massachusetts.
2. U.S. Asa Waters, Jr., Model 1808 Flintlock Militia Musket - .69 caliber - circa 1808-1810 - 5,000-musket contract for Maryland.
3. U.S. Elijah and Asa Waters and Nathaniel Whitmore Model 1808 Contract Flintlock Musket with bayonet - .69 caliber - circa 1808-1809 - 5,000-musket federal contract.
4. Lane & Read New England Flintlock Militia Musket - .80 caliber - circa 1835 - Militia muskets were generally patterned after British muskets, but of lighter design.
5. British East India Co. Pattern Flintlock Carbine - .67 caliber - circa 1800-1830 - First produced for the United East India Company, this pattern was widely issued to British troops.
6. J. Baker English Flintlock Rifle - .69 caliber - circa 1800-1835 - English military rifle issued to specially trained marksmen.
7. U.S. J. Bishop Model 1812 Flintlock Militia Musket - .60 caliber - circa 1814.
8. U.S. Henry Deringer Model 1814 Flintlock Common Rifle - .65 caliber - circa 1814 - Original production was rifled, but this example was smoothbored for Indian treaty sales.

THE FLINTLOCK ERA

Model 1816 Flintlock Musket

Model 1816 muskets were the first standard U.S. military longarm to be produced at both Springfield and Harpers Ferry Armories. Nearly 700,000 of these muskets were manufactured at Springfield Armory and Harpers Ferry over a 28-year period, making this the largest production total of any U.S. flintlock musket.

1. U.S. Harpers Ferry Model 1816 Musket, Type II - .69 caliber - circa 1822-1831 - Originally finished in "National Armory Brown."
2. U.S. Springfield Model 1816 Musket - .69 caliber - circa 1818 - Dated 1818; originally finished "National Armory Bright."
3. U.S. Harpers Ferry Model 1816 (Type II) Musket - .69 caliber - circa 1816-1840.
4. U.S. M. T. Wickham Model 1816 Contract Musket - .69 caliber - circa 1822-1837 - In addition to the national armories, Wickham and other contractors produced the Model 1816.
5. U.S. Waters Model 1816 Type III Contract Musket - .60 caliber - circa 1816-1832. Stamped "UXBRIDGE GRENADIERS."
6. U.S. Robert & J. D. Johnson Model 1817 "Common" Rifle - .54 caliber - circa 1817.

Model 1817 Common Rifle

The "Common Rifle" designation distinguishes this muzzleloader from the contemporary Hall breechloading rifle. Four contractors made 38,200 between 1823 and the early 1840s.

Arming the Militia

On May 8, 1792, Congress passed the Militia Act which provided a general guideline for states to arm and equip militia units. The bill provided that every free, white, able-bodied male between 18 and 45 years could be enrolled in the state militia. The idea was that each state would have a free-standing and independent army that could supplement the regular U.S. Army if needed. Composed entirely of volunteers, the militia units of the 1800s became very social organizations and chose such colorful names as the Fencibles, Washington Greys, Lafayette Troop, Palmetto Guards, and American Highlanders. State governments faced the same problem as the federal government in securing arms for their troops. Some states established contracts with local arms makers. Virginia erected its own arms manufactory and arsenal - the only state to do so. The General Assembly of Virginia authorized the establishment of the manufactory on January 23, 1798. More than 58,000 muskets, 4,200 pistols, 2,100 rifles, and thousands of swords, bayonets, and accoutrements were produced at the Virginia Manufactory of Arms until it ceased operations in 1818.

EARLY 19TH CENTURY MILITARY ARMS & FLINTLOCK PISTOLS

Virginia Manufactory of Arms 2nd Model Rifle (reconverted to flint) - .54 caliber - circa 1815 - Similar features to the Harpers Ferry Model 1803. Approx. 1,700 made, 1812 to 1821.

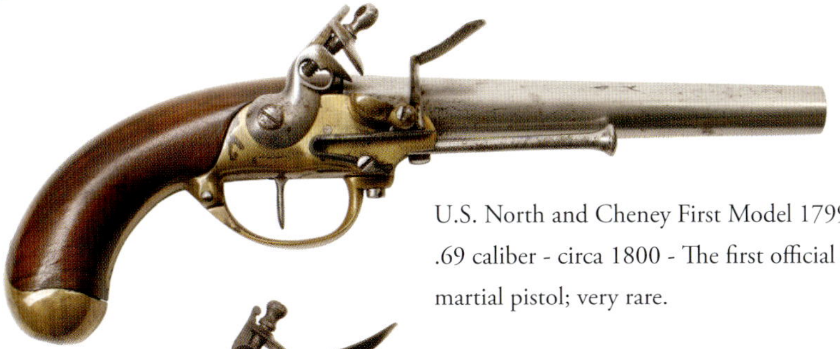

U.S. North and Cheney First Model 1799 - .69 caliber - circa 1800 - The first official U.S. martial pistol; very rare.

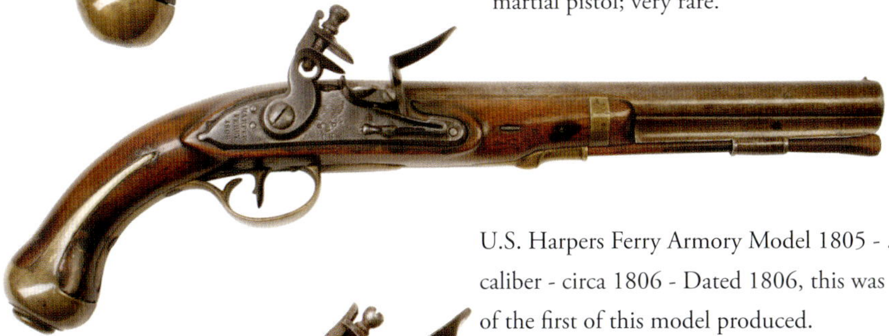

U.S. Harpers Ferry Armory Model 1805 - .54 caliber - circa 1806 - Dated 1806, this was one of the first of this model produced.

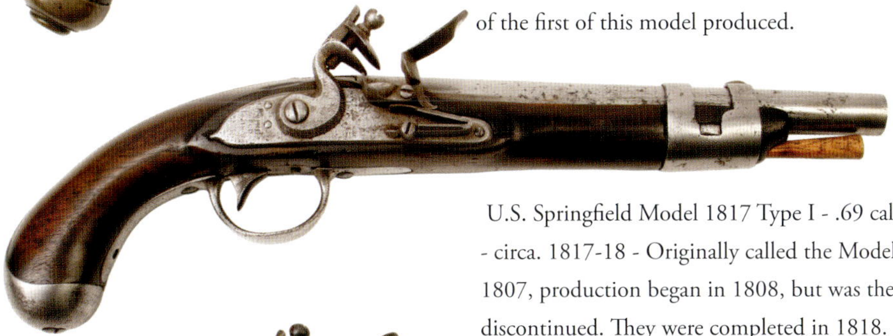

U.S. Springfield Model 1817 Type I - .69 caliber - circa. 1817-18 - Originally called the Model 1807, production began in 1808, but was then discontinued. They were completed in 1818.

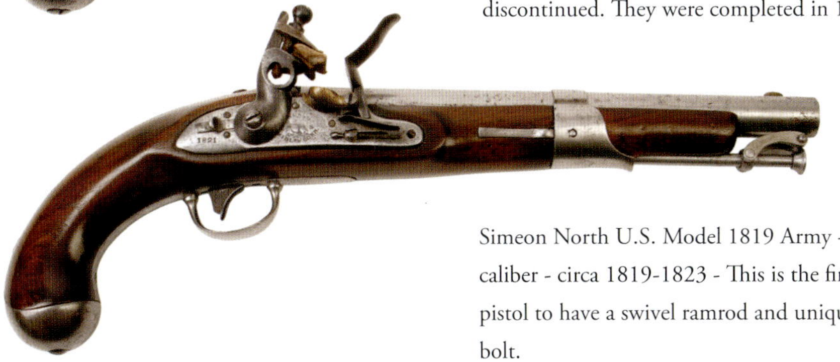

Simeon North U.S. Model 1819 Army - .54 caliber - circa 1819-1823 - This is the first U.S. pistol to have a swivel ramrod and unique safety bolt.

Commercial flintlock pistols were often sold in pairs, and might include elaborate decoration such as grotesque mask buttcaps. Above, J. Richards cannon barrel English pistols - .63 caliber - circa 1780. Below, French Officer's Pistols - .64 caliber - circa 1780

THE FLINTLOCK ERA

Oddities and Curiosa

Arms on this page combine a muzzleloading firearm with a blade for a weapon with multiple capabilities.

The facing page shows non-firearm uses of flintlock mechanisms, along with a very bizarre booby-trap gun.

Left column: Knife pistols. The top double-barrel percussion pistol is ornately engraved, gold plated, and has an ivory handle. Below it is a fixed-blade flintlock and two folding knife flintlock pistols.

Top right: Three flintlock sword pistols. This type was used in Europe for hunting wild boars for sport, with the pistol for the coup de gras.

Below: Battle-axe incorporating a wheel-lock pistol.

ODDITIES & CURIOSA

The sundial alarm clock gun at right uses a miniature cannon barrel to hold a powder charge that ignites when the magnifying glass focuses the sun's rays on the touchhole at a predetermined time.

Cemetery gun - This type of flintlock trap gun had a macabre use during the late 18th and early 19th centuries in England. "Anatomical theatres" performed autopsies to train physicians, and wealthy individuals could purchase access to watch the grisly procedure. Only the corpses of executed criminals could legally be used for this purpose. Since demand was greater than supply, a black market arose in corpses stolen from fresh graves by "resurrectionists." To prevent such indignity, the family of the departed could rent a cemetery gun to protect the burial site until the body had aged enough to be unmarketable. Tripwires attached to the three rings at the front end of the trigger rod were stretched across the grave. When a grave-robber stumbled on the wire, the gun would swivel towards them and fire.

Below it, the tinder lighter uses a flintlock mechanism to ignite tinder, which can then be used to light a candle in the holder - very handy in the days before matches or lighters.

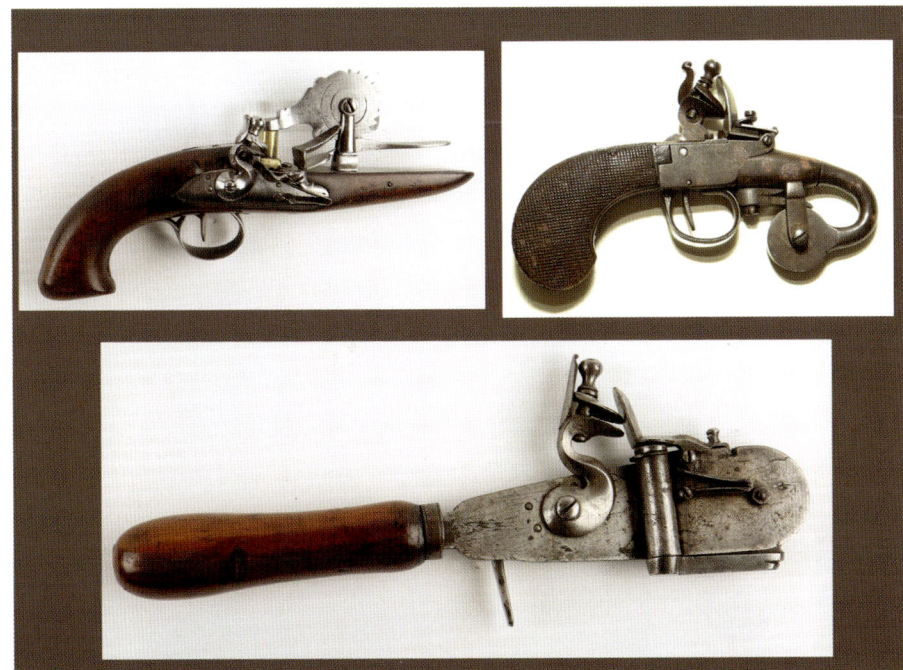

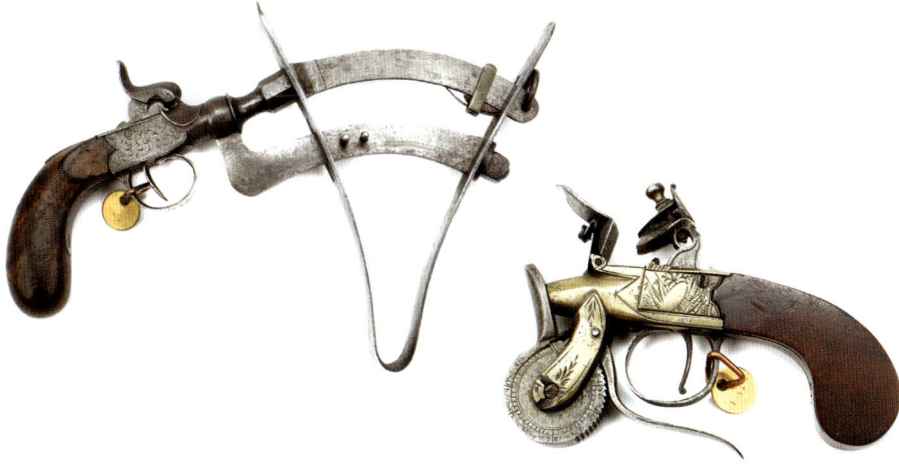

Eprouvettes

These powder testers were used by shooters that wanted to determine the potency of their gunpowder charges. A chamber is loaded with powder and the percussion or flintlock mechanism ignites the charge, moving a dial or gauge that indicates whether the powder is over-powered, under-powered, or a goldilocks blend - just right. Designs varied, as illustrated by the five examples shown here.

NEW TECHNOLOGY I

Pendrill English Flintlock Breechloading Rifle - .67 caliber - circa 1760 - Pendrill's design allowed loading via a screw-plugged hole in the top rear of the barrel.

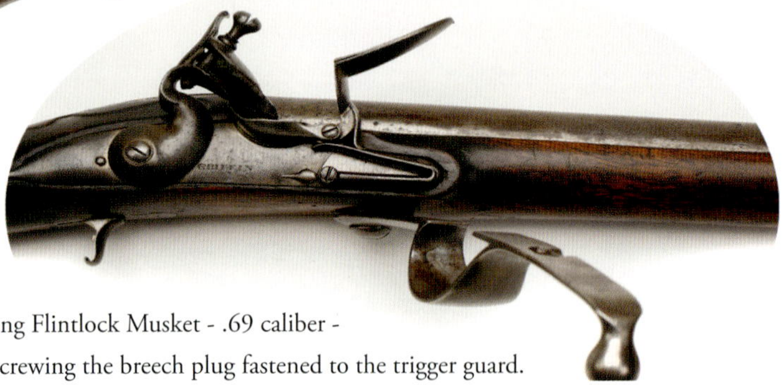

Griffin English Breechloading Flintlock Musket - .69 caliber - circa 1760 - Loaded by unscrewing the breech plug fastened to the trigger guard. Forerunner of the Ferguson breechloading rifle used by British troops in the American Revolution.

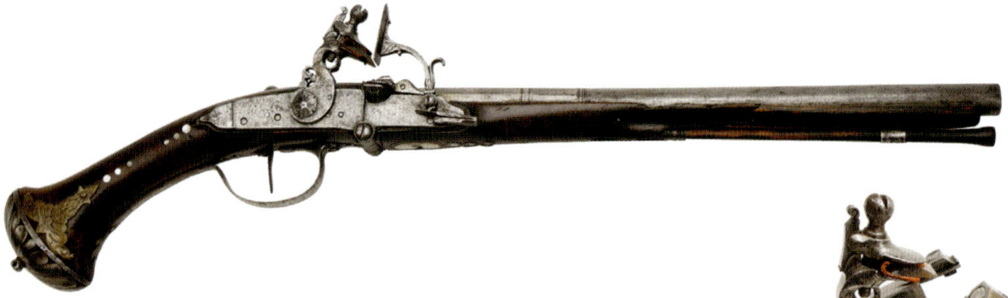

Italian Breechloading Snaphaunce Pistol - .60 caliber - circa 1650 - This pistol's break-open design allowed for quick reloading with removable chambers, each fitted with an integral flash pan.

Breechloaders

Traditional early military arms were smoothbore muzzleloaders. This allowed quicker reloads in combat, since a round ball slightly smaller than the bore could be rammed home with little effort, even if the barrel was fouled with residue from previous shots. To be effective, a rifled arm required a bullet that had to fit tightly to the rifling, and took additional effort to ram home, especially as fouling built up. However, a rifled arm that could load from the rear allowed the faster reload with the accuracy and additional effective range afforded by rifling. Breechloading arms also offered the advantage of reloading while in a reclined position behind cover, and the access at the rear of the bore provided for better cleaning capability.

The early breechloading systems shown here saw only limited production.

BREECHLOADERS

NEW TECHNOLOGY

After 200 years of the flint ignition muzzleloader being the dominant firearms system, the first half of the 19th century saw rapid improvements in technology, including:
* BREECHLOADING
* PERCUSSION IGNITION
* EFFECTIVE REPEATERS
* SELF-CONTAINED CARTRIDGES

Although some of these concepts had been experimented with much earlier, their perfection coincided with America's westward expansion and the Civil War.

Hall's Breechloader

John H. Hall of Portland, Maine, patented a breechloading rifle in 1811 that became a landmark in the arms industry. The breechblock tips up for loading, and the entire lock is easily removed. The rear sight is offset to clear the centrally mounted hammer. Following the War of 1812, Hall successfully petitioned the government to test his breechloader.

This firearm was found to be superior to muzzleloaders in every respect, and on March 19, 1819, Hall furnished an additional 1,000 rifles to the government. All of these arms were made at Hall's factory in Harpers Ferry. Hall adopted Whitney's idea of interchangeable parts and installed machinery in his factory to produce standard, interchangeable parts. A series of rifles and carbines utilizing the Hall breechloading system were produced in the United States from 1823 to 1853, both in flintlock and percussion configurations.

U.S. Hall Model 1819 Breechloading Flintlock Rifle - .52 caliber - circa 1817-1840.

U.S. Hall Model 1819 Breechloading Percussion Rifle - .52 caliber - circa 1841-1842 - One of the Hall flintlocks that was later converted to percussion by the military.

U.S. Hall Model 1836 Breechloading Percussion Carbine - .64 caliber - circa 1836 - This model was issued to the 2nd U.S. Dragoons during their service in Florida.

NEW TECHNOLOGY I

Forsyth Scent-bottle Priming Fowler - circa 1808-1821 - This system dispensed fulminate pellets from a scent-bottle shaped container to be ignited by a blow of the hammer. It could hold enough fulminate to prime up to 25 shots. It provided quicker and more reliable ignition than the flintlock system, without the pan flash that could startle game.

Austrian Tube-Primed Percussion Military Pistol - circa 1853 - By 1818 Joseph Manton had developed a percussion primer consisting of a fulminate-filled copper tube open on one end. The open end was inserted through a hole in the side of the lock, and when crushed by the hammer created a spark to ignite the charge. The tube primer enjoyed limited success and was soon replaced by the percussion cap such as is still used in blackpowder muzzleloading percussion guns today.

Joseph Manton English Tube-Lock Percussion Double-Barrel Fowler - 14 gauge - circa 1820.

Joseph Manton English Tube-Lock Percussion Double-Barrel Fowler - 14 gauge - ca 1820.

Ferdi Furwith Austrian Tube-Lock Percussion Rifle - .75 caliber - circa 1835-1840.

PERCUSSION IGNITION

The Percussion System

In 1807, Dr. Alexander Forsyth, a Scottish Presbyterian minister, patented a gun lock that eliminated the priming powder charge, flash pan, and frizzen. Forsyth's design instead used a modified hammer to deliver a sharp blow that ignited a small, pill-shaped, impact-sensitive chemical compound placed upon a metal part called a striker. This design, also known as a pill-lock, resulted in the invention of a wide variety of detonating-type locks. Another was the tube-lock, which employed a primer-filled cylinder open at one end, ignited by the force of the hammer. These eventually led to the development of a percussion cap-lock system patented by Joshua Shaw in 1822. The percussion cap was a small, copper cap containing an impact-sensitive chemical compound (usually fulminate). This new percussion system became the principal means of discharging firearms until the perfection of the metallic cartridge used today.

The percussion system revolutionized the design and use of firearms. It eliminated the flint and priming pan, and was less susceptible to dampness. But the new system did not immediately replace the old. Although percussion arms were in general use by civilians as early as 1830, the military did not accept them until about 1840. Once the percussion system caught on, both military and civilian flintlock arms were often converted to the more modern system. Conversion from flintlock to percussion ignition was a common way to update older firearms, both military and civilian.

U.S. Model 1836 Flintlock Pistol by Asa Waters.- .54 caliber - circa 1836-1844.

U.S. Model 1836 Percussion Conversion Pistol - .54 caliber - circa - 1847-1850 - Bolster style conversion from flintlock to percussion.

S.H. Staudenmeyer English Pistols - .59 caliber - The upper pistol is an original flintlock, circa 1800. The lower pistol is the same model converted from flint to percussion, circa 1830. This was a common modification to adapt old guns to the new system.

Massachusetts Arms Co. Double-barrel Fowler - 12 gauge - circa 1858 - Maynard tape primer system.

The Maynard Tape-Priming System

Dr. Edward Maynard, a dental surgeon from Washington, D.C., patented an automatic tape-priming system for percussion firearms in 1845. Dr. Maynard had spent a single semester at West Point. Combining this brief introduction to the military with his knowledge of chemicals, he invented a successful, but short-lived, priming system. Maynard's system used a narrow paper tape that had small quantities of impact-sensitive fulminate placed in a single row down the middle of the tape. The tape was sealed with shellac or varnish and resembled a roll of the paper caps used for modern toy pistols. During the period 1848-1860, hundreds of thousands of government and contract arms utilized the Maynard Tape-Priming System. In 1861, the government replaced the tape system because the tape failed to hold up to the rigors of foul weather and moisture. The 1855 Pistol Carbine on the next page is an example of a gun made to use this tape-priming system.

NEW TECHNOLOGY I

Of course the simplest method to get repeat shots was to carry multiple guns, or add additional barrels.

Cased Pair of W. R. Pape Double-Barrel Percussion Pistols - .50 caliber - circa 1858. With both guns fully loaded, the owner has a total of four shots before reloading. Gold plated with ivory grips and accessory handles and fine scroll engraving.

British Four-Barrel Flintlock Pistol - .36 caliber - circa 1800 - The barrel cluster is rotated by hand to fire the second pair of shots. Each barrel has its own frizzen, which when closed keeps the priming charge from spilling.

H. V. Perry Three-Barrel Percussion Rifle - .45 caliber - circa 1845-1850 - The multiple-barrel concept begins to become heavy and cumbersome as additional barrels are added. Guns with more than two barrels in this era are scarce.

Left - Brackley Double-Barrel Tap-action Flintlock Pistol - .40 caliber - circa 1800 - A lever on the side adds a priming charge to the pan for the second shot. Spring-loaded bayonet.

Right - Charles Lancaster Over/under Double-barrel Percussion Pistol - .52 caliber - circa 1850 - Cased with accessories including bullet mold, primer tin, powder flask, ramrod and nipple wrench.

REPEATERS

Repeaters

The muzzleloading system was slow for repeat shots. After a round was fired, a fresh charge of black powder had to be poured down the barrel, a lead projectile rammed down on top of it, and either the priming pan filled with powder on a flintlock or a cap placed on the nipple on a percussion arm. In the early 19th century, experimentation in firearms design was often focused on development of guns that could fire multiple times without reloading. The earliest form of repeater—a gun with multiple barrels—is still popular today. Double-barrel shotguns are used for bird hunting and clay target shooting, and double rifles for heavy game.

Not every multi-barrel gun is a repeater. The firearms on the bottom half of this page fire all their barrels at the same time.

Kentucky Style Combination Gun - .44 rifled / .45 smoothbore caliber - circa 1800 - With one barrel rifled and one smoothbore, a combination gun makes a versatile hunting arm.

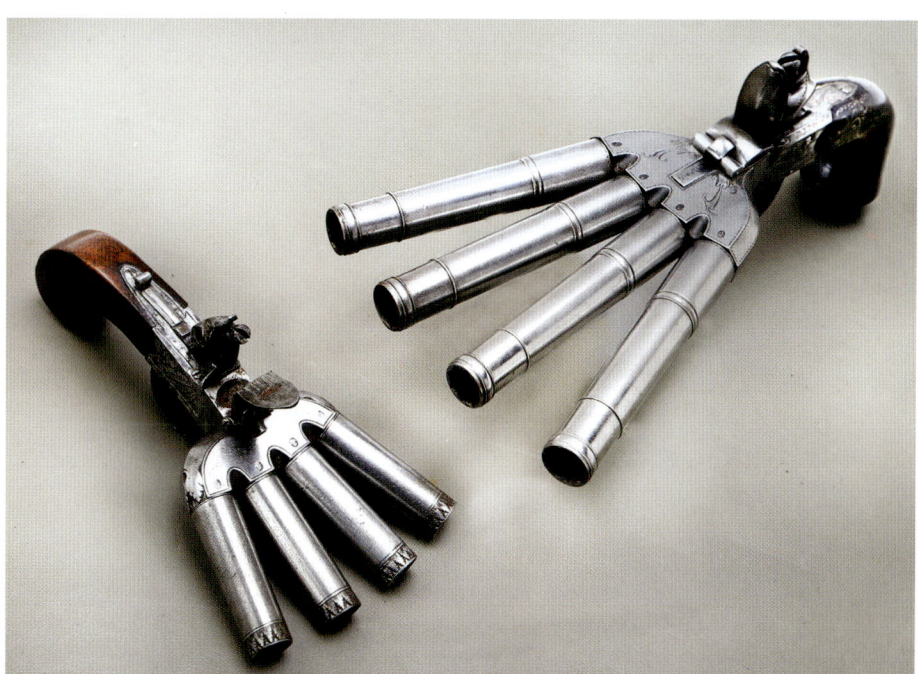

Above: Duckfoot pistols feature an array of splayed barrels which fired simultaneously, spreading the shots. Intended users were sea captains who might have to face down a mutinous crew, or bank guards and prison wardens where one man might have to face down multiple attackers. These two British examples are .60 and .50 caliber, circa 1800.

At left: The Nock Volley Gun was adopted by the British Navy in 1779 for repelling boarders. All seven .52 caliber barrels fired simultaneously. Only 500 were made, and the brutal recoil combined with a propensity to ignite the ship's rigging limited their utility.

NEW TECHNOLOGY I

Early superposed repeaters

One method of creating a repeating firearm was to stack multiple charges in the same barrel. Various methods were used to provide sequential shots, while some were designed to fire mutliple rounds with a single trigger pull.

DeWalle Freres Superposed Charge Shotgun. 12 gauge - circa 1844-1862 - This Belgian-proofed shotgun was fitted with four hammers and the two forward hammers were intended to fire the upper loads first, then the lower loads would be discharged by the second set of hammers.

Isaiah Jennings Multi-Shot Flintlock Rifle - circa 1821 - This "Roman candle rifle" took superposed charges to extreme levels, accommodating 12 charges of powder and ball loaded one on top of the other in the barrel breech. A self-priming flintlock was slid back from the front charge to the next behind it as each was fired. Other innovative features include detachable barrel and detachable buttstock.

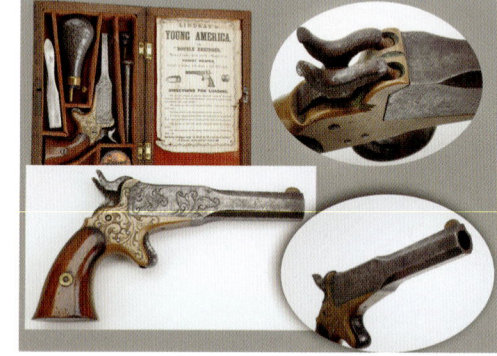

Lindsay "Young America" Superposed Charge Pistol - .41 caliber - circa 1860s - This handgun counterpart to the Lindsay double musket stacked two loads in a single barrel with two hammers.

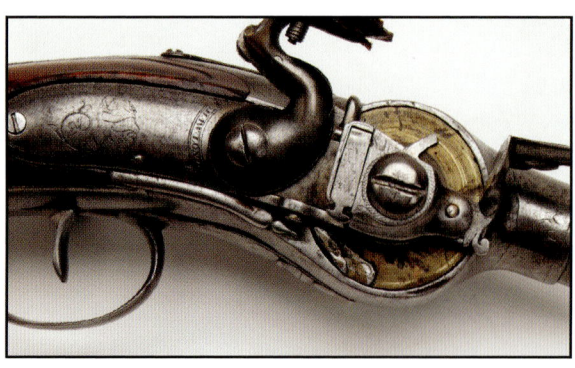

John Shaw Cookson-Type Flintlock Repeating Rifle - .57 caliber - circa 1690-1720 - This Cookson pattern repeater had a powder magazine and a magazine for seven lead balls inside the buttstock. A turn of the crank on the left side of the frame loads the chamber, cocks the hammer, primes the pan, and lowers the frizzen for firing, making for a very early seven-shot repeater. The original concept was developed by Lorenzoni of Italy about 1680.

REPEATERS

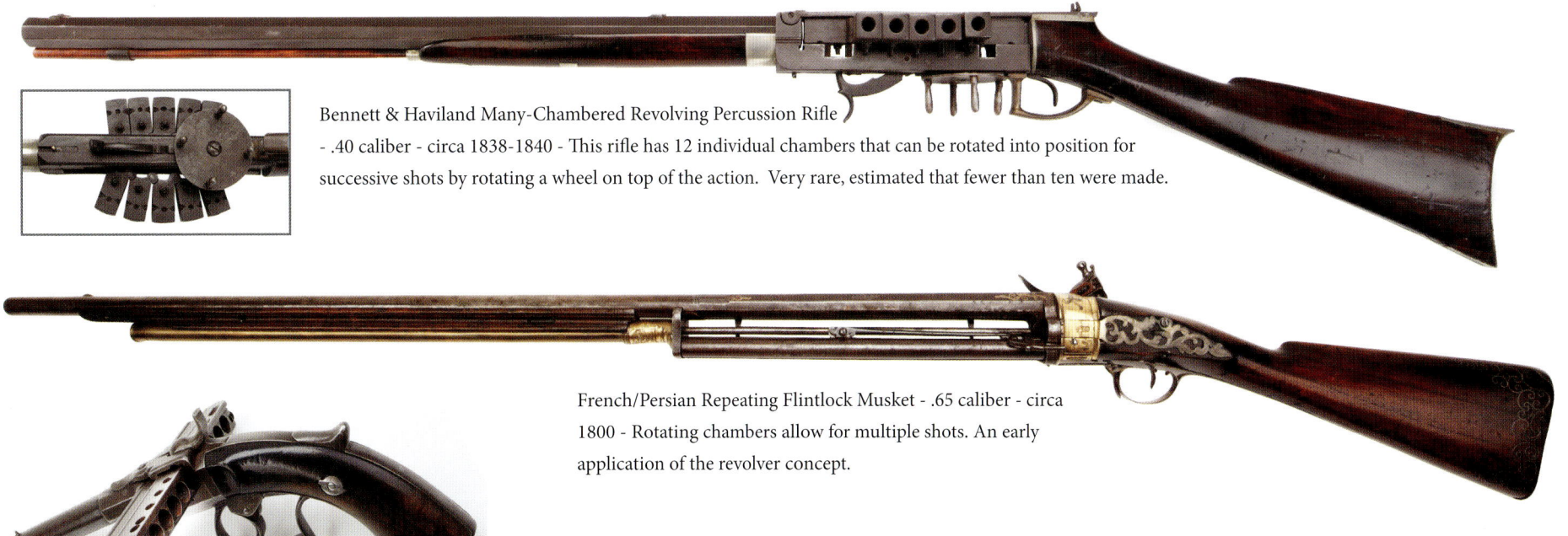

Bennett & Haviland Many-Chambered Revolving Percussion Rifle - .40 caliber - circa 1838-1840 - This rifle has 12 individual chambers that can be rotated into position for successive shots by rotating a wheel on top of the action. Very rare, estimated that fewer than ten were made.

French/Persian Repeating Flintlock Musket - .65 caliber - circa 1800 - Rotating chambers allow for multiple shots. An early application of the revolver concept.

European Bar Magazine Harmonica Pistol - 9mm pinfire - circa 1880 - This ten-shot handgun requires manual advancing of the horizontal magazine for each shot.

Treeby Chain Repeating Rifle - caliber .52 percussion - circa 1855 - Incorporating a 14-chamber chain that is advanced in a loop through the action by unbolting and re-attaching the barrel, this design was patented in England in 1855. A folding hand rest under the barrel is a surprisingly modern feature. Caliber: .52 percussion.

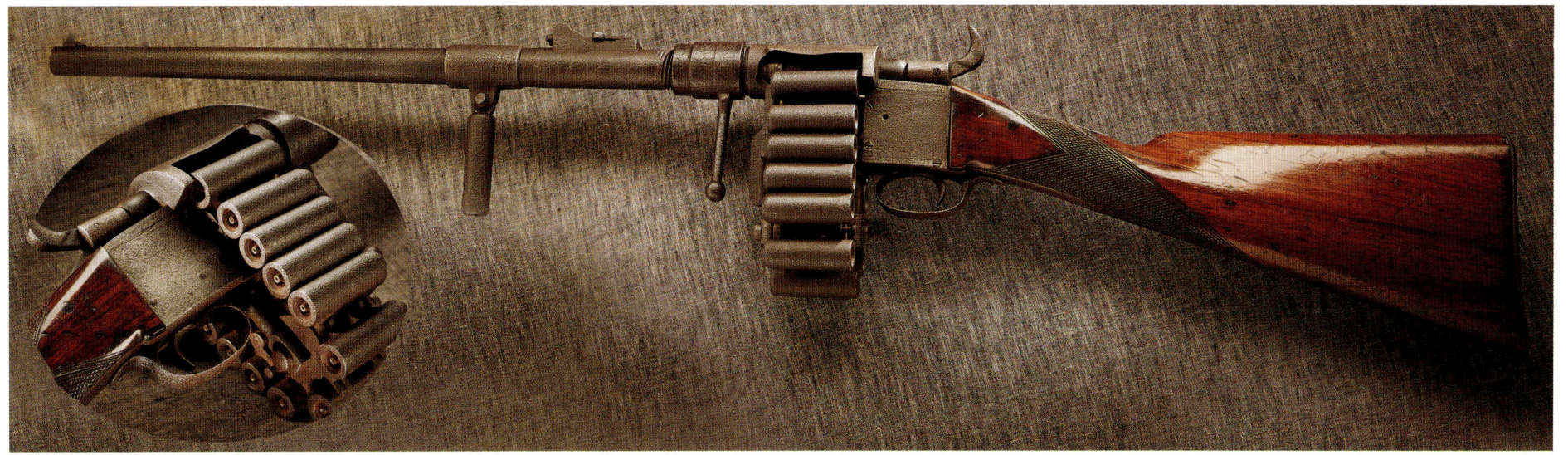

NEW TECHNOLOGY I

While most pepperboxes were five or six shot, other configurations existed, such as the manually rotated four shot all brass British single action above, circa 1840, and the eighteen shot ring trigger double-action Belgian pepperbox below, circa 1850.

Above, left to right:
Allen & Thurber Double-Barrel Single-Trigger Pistol - .34 cal. - circa 1850s - A 2-shot predecessor to pepperboxes.
British Pepperbox - .32 caliber - circa 1830s-1850s - six shot.
Manhattan Firearms Pepperbox - .28 caliber - circa 1850s - six shot.

Pepperboxes

The earliest widely successful repeating handgun, the pepperbox used a rotating cluster of barrels. Introduced around 1830, most were manufactured in England, the U.S., and Belgium. They remained popular through the 1850s. However, they soon lost ground to Colt style percussion revolvers which were lighter, more compact, and more accurate.

Collier's repeating flintlock design is one of the first true revolvers. Elisha Collier's invention in America of a manually rotated cylinder holding five chambers that was primed separately was manufactured in England by John Evans & Son, beginning in 1819. The .40 caliber Collier was seen by a young Sam Colt during his travels aboard the brig Corvo and it has been speculated that Colt's later Paterson revolver design was in part due to his exposure to the Collier. This example is believed to be a well-made reproduction.

REPEATERS

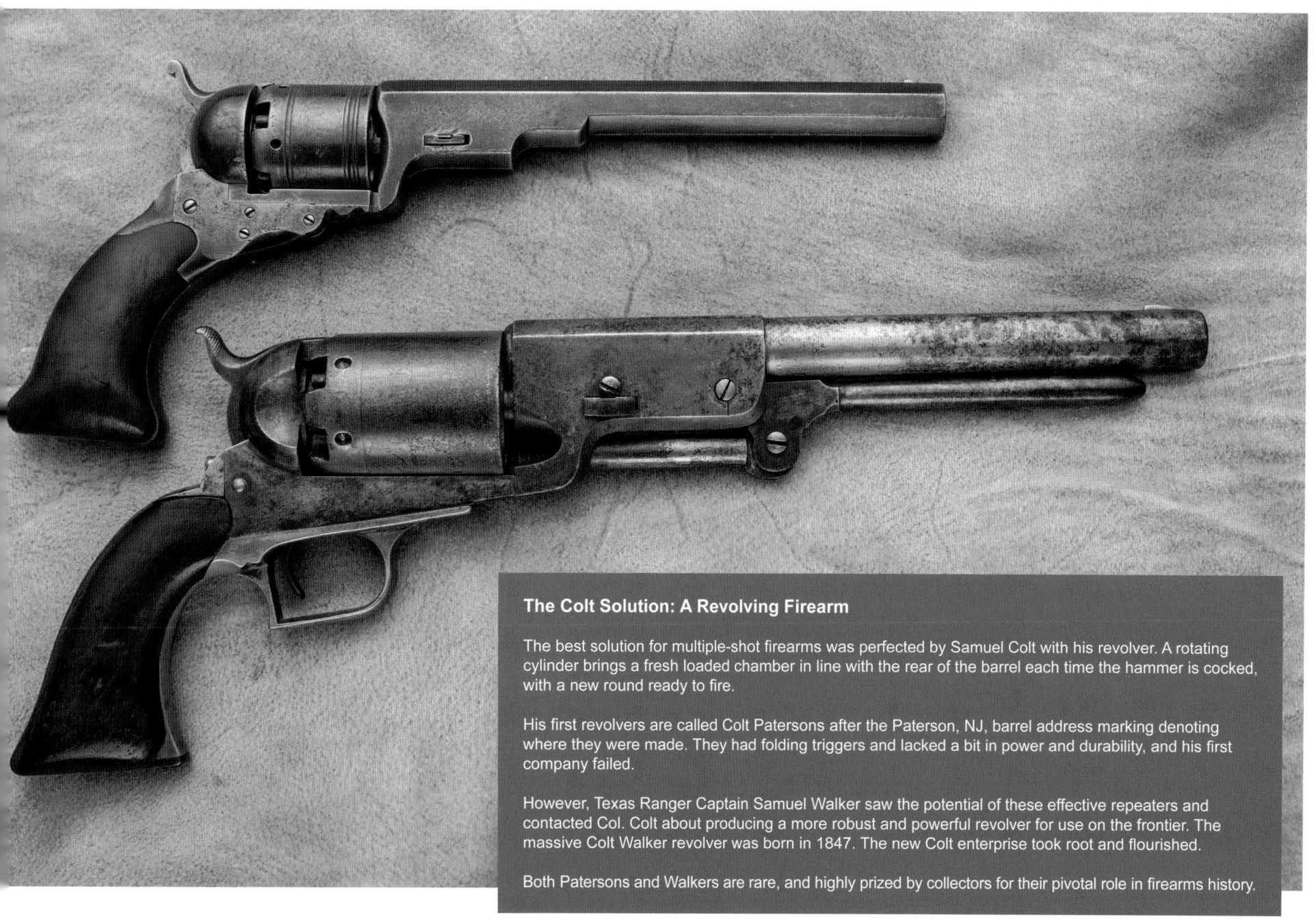

The Colt Solution: A Revolving Firearm

The best solution for multiple-shot firearms was perfected by Samuel Colt with his revolver. A rotating cylinder brings a fresh loaded chamber in line with the rear of the barrel each time the hammer is cocked, with a new round ready to fire.

His first revolvers are called Colt Patersons after the Paterson, NJ, barrel address marking denoting where they were made. They had folding triggers and lacked a bit in power and durability, and his first company failed.

However, Texas Ranger Captain Samuel Walker saw the potential of these effective repeaters and contacted Col. Colt about producing a more robust and powerful revolver for use on the frontier. The massive Colt Walker revolver was born in 1847. The new Colt enterprise took root and flourished.

Both Patersons and Walkers are rare, and highly prized by collectors for their pivotal role in firearms history.

Top: Colt Paterson Holster Model No. 5 Revolver - .36 caliber - circa 1838-1840 - Texas Rangers immortalized the fast-shooting Paterson Colt revolver in a series of frontier encounters with Comanche Indians where the five-shot capability of the new handgun provided overwhelming firepower.
Bottom: Colt Walker Revolver - .44 caliber - circa 1847 - A massive revolver weighing nearly five pounds. In total, 1,000 were made for the U.S. Mounted Rifles and 100 for the civilian market.

NEW TECHNOLOGY I

Why not a revolving rifle?

Although there were numerous attempts to create a repeating revolving rifle, there was a serious problem with the concept in the percussion and flintlock era. Unless each chamber was well sealed with grease, fire from the discharging round could ignite adjoined chambers which were not aligned with the barrel, resulting in a "chain-fire." This was especially hazardous in long guns, where the non-trigger hand might be supporting the barrel forward of the chamber and in the path of the emerging bullets.

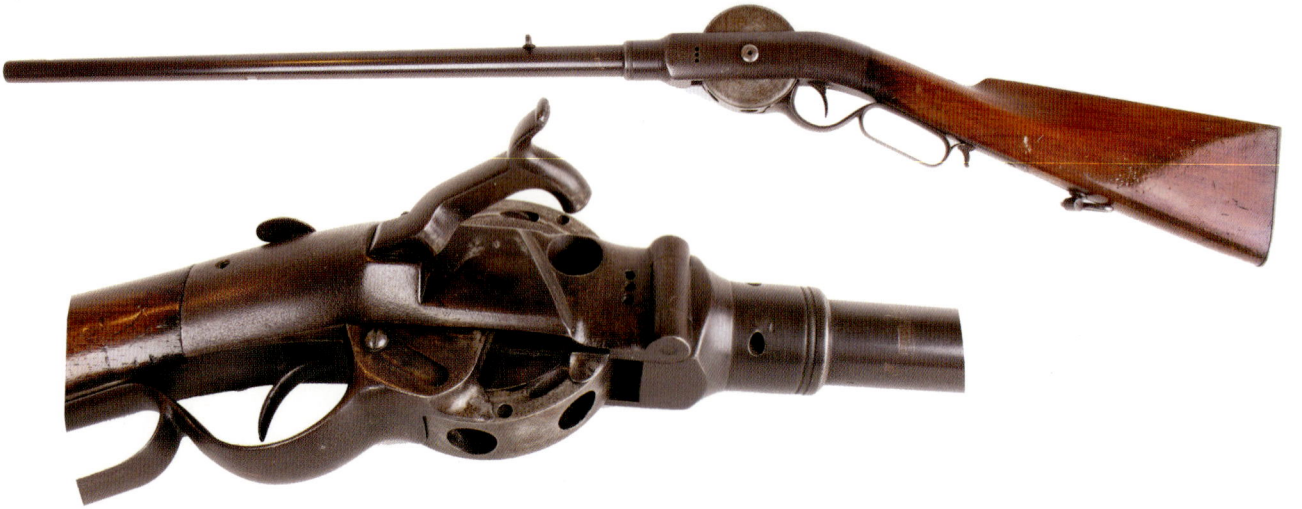

Pictured at left, top to bottom:

Cochran Revolving Turret Rifle - .45 caliber - circa 1840 - John Cochran began with revolving cannon, but found turret rifles sold better. To moderate issues with multiple discharges, he offered a half-turret design that limited the potential for shooter injury.

P.W. Porter Revolving Turret Military Carbine - .44 caliber - circa 1850s - Employing a vertical cylinder, Porter arms were fitted with an iron turret cover that most users elected to remove.

Alexander Hall Revolving Rifle - .38 caliber - circa mid-1850s - New Yorker Hall's design utilized a suspended cylinder mounted to a hinged frame with a fifteen shot capacity.

REPEATERS

The Smith & Wesson Solution:
The Metallic Cartridge

Just as Colt was founded on the perfection of the repeating handgun, so Smith & Wesson was established by perfecting the marriage of revolver to self-contained metallic cartridge. And like Colt, the first S&W enterprise failed.

The lever-action S&W Repeating Magazine Pistol, later nicknamed "The Volcanic," used hollow-based bullets with powder packed in the hollow and a primer affixed to the base, carried in a tubular magazine mounted under the barrel. The underpowered design did not flourish, and was eventually sold to a shirt manufacturer named Oliver Winchester who saw promise in the lever-action mechanism and built a firearms empire on the lever-action rifle.

The second S&W partnership introduced a little seven-shot .22 revolver, the Model One, that used a self-contained metallic cartridge with priming compound in the rim of the base. This basic cartridge is still made today as the .22 Short.

Smith & Wesson also purchased Rollin White's patent on a revolver cylinder bored through end to end, and thus secured a monopoly on effective cartridge revolver production through 1869. Colt had been offered the Rollin White design, but had passed.

The self-contained metallic cartridge offered tremendous advantages over the percussion system for speed and ease of loading and durability of ammunition, and introduced the modern era of firearms.

Above: "Volcanic" lever-action repeating magazine pistols, left to right - Smith & Wesson .31 caliber circa 1854; New Haven .42 caliber circa 1857-1860; and New Haven .41 caliber, same era.
At right: Smith & Wesson Model No. 1 - .22 rimfire - circa 1857 to 1860.

membership.NRA.org | 65

NEW TECHNOLOGY I

B. Tyler Henry, working for Oliver Winchester, took the lever-action design of the Volcanic and improved it, creating the 16-shot Henry rifle, chambered for a .44 rimfire cartridge fed from a tubular magazine mounted under the barrel *(top)*.

The Spencer was another early lever-action repeater *(lower gun in the photo above)*. The tubular magazine was inserted into the rear of the buttstock. It carried seven rounds of the .56-56 Spencer rimfire cartridge.

The Henry and Spencer marked the beginning of lever-action rifles as the state of the art repeater. Both were used by the Union Army. 14,000 Henrys were made 1860-1866, and 200,000 Spencers 1860-1869. Spencer was ultimately acquired by Winchester.

The double-barrel LeMat system of a revolver cylinder rotating around a shotgun barrel was also applied to long guns. This LeMat carbine used 12mm and 28 gauge pinfire cartridges, circa 1867. The use of metallic cartridges in a revolving long gun minimized the danger of chain-fires. However, on most revolving firearms, bits of burning powder and small shavings of lead can escape the gap between the front of the cylinder and the rear of the barrel when fired. With a revolving cartridge rifle, this debris could painfully pepper the non-shooting hand if it is being used to support the barrel forward of the cylinder.

REPEATERS

CARTRIDGE TECHNOLOGY

The Combustible Cartridge
The development of the conical, hollow-based bullet by Francois Minie of France led to experimentation with a variety of cartridge designs. In the combustible cartridge, a percussion cap was combined with a flammable, or combustible, wrapper and a bullet to produce a self-contained cartridge. Heavily nitrated cloth or paper was used to produce highly flammable wrappers. These types of cartridges were used with the Sharps, Starr, and Merrill breechloading carbines.

The Separately Primed Cartridge
The first successful use of a metal cartridge case occurred during the Civil War period. Rubber and cardboard cases were also used for some cartridges. In this type of cartridge, a small hole in the base of the cartridge case allowed sparks from a percussion cap to enter the case and ignite the powder charge contained in the cartridge. The Maynard and Burnside breechloading carbines used metal cases, and the Smith carbine used rubber cases.

The Pinfire System
One of the earliest self-contained metallic cartridges was the pinfire.

In this system, the firing pin was mounted on the cartridge itself instead of on the face of the gun's hammer. When the pin was struck by the flat face of the hammer, it ignited a priming charge inside the cartridge.

Cardboard pinfire cartridges were introduced in 1835 and metallic cartridges about 10 years later. The pinfire system was much more popular in Europe than in America, although pinfire revolvers did see use during the Civil War.

The Rimfire Cartridge
Invented by Nicolas Flobert, a noted French gunmaker, this metallic cartridge was developed just prior to the Civil War. It is a self-contained metallic cartridge that consists of four basic components: the case, the primer, the powder charge, and the projectile (or bullet).
The primer in a rimfire cartridge is an impact-sensitive chemical compound that is contained in the inside rim of the case's base. When the cartridge is struck on the rim, the primer ignites, and the flame from the primer in turn ignites the powder charge.

Smith & Wesson was the first firearm manufacturer in America to successfully use the rimfire cartridge, and B. Tyler Henry used a .44 caliber rimfire cartridge in his famous Henry Repeating Rifle. Rimfire cartridges have changed little in design over the years and this type of cartridge is widely available today in .22 caliber ammunition that is used in a variety of modern handguns and rifles.

The Centerfire Cartridge
Great strides in ammunition technology took place between 1860 and 1875 with the development of a cartridge that contained a primer located in the center of the base of the cartridge. The Frankfort Arsenal in Philadelphia had begun experiments based on this idea as early as 1858, and other experimenters continued developing this concept until the cartridge evolved into its present form. Other types of cartridges, such as the pinfire and the teatfire cartridges, offered little competition to this new centerfire concept. Today, the centerfire cartridge is used universally.

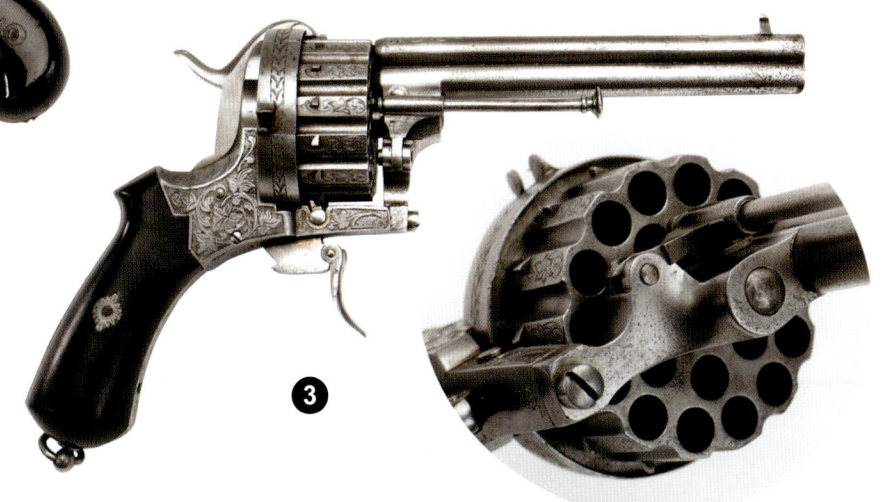

1. Rollin White Arms Co. Single-Action Pocket Revolver - .22 rimfire - circa 1861 - White licensed his patent for a bored through cylinder to Smith & Wesson. When S&W couldn't keep up with the demand during the Civil War, he manufactured solid frame spur-trigger revolvers under his own name.
2. Moore's Patent Firearms Co. Front-Loading Single-Action Revolver - .32 teatfire - circa 1864 - 1870 - S&W's Rollin White patent on a bored-through cylinder resulted in other manufacturers looking for ways to circumvent it. Moore used an unusual proprietary cartridge with a small priming compound-filled teat poking through a small hole in the rear of the cylinder to be struck by the hammer.
3. Belgian Pinfire Revolver - 7mm pinfire - circa 1870-1880 - This unusual high-capacity 21-shot revolver uses two rows of chambers in the cylinder and over/under barrels with a folding trigger.

A PROSPERING NEW REPUBLIC

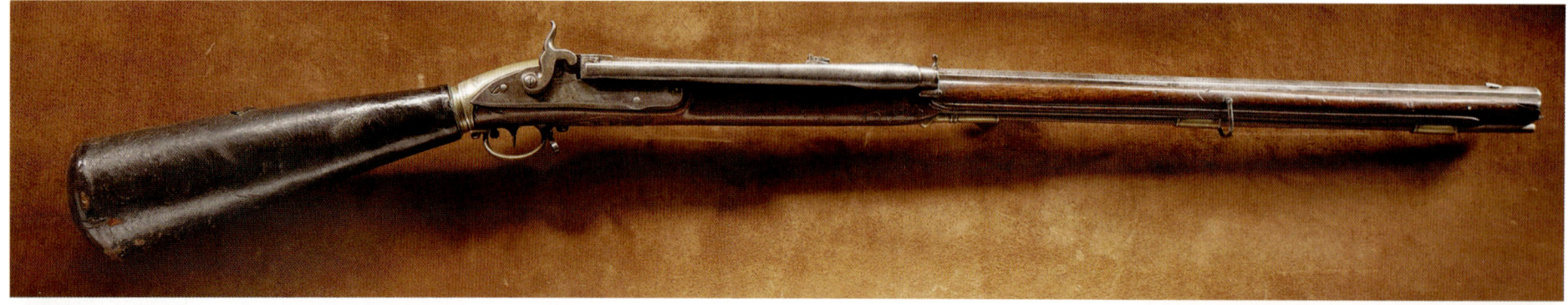

Girardoni Repeating Air Rifle - .46 caliber - circa 1795 - 20-shot repeating air rifle, built by Bartolomeo Girardoni, who originally supplied similar air rifles to the Austrian army around 1790. As originally issued, each Girardoni air rifle had three detachable air reservoirs, each requiring about 1,500 strokes of a separate pump to completely pressurize the reservoir. Once filled to operating pressure (about 800 psi), the air rifle could fire up to 70 shots before the reservoir needed to be replaced. A hollow metal tube on the side of the barrel held up to 20 lead balls that could be fed one at a time to the firing chamber by a simple sideways push of a plunger. At a distance of 50 feet, this rifle is capable of placing 10 shots into a group the size of a quarter, and could penetrate a 1-inch wood plank or bring down an elk.

Lewis & Clark and their Air Gun

The Louisiana Purchase in 1803 doubled the size of the United States. Meriwether Lewis and William Clark were chosen to lead an expedition across the new territory.

Their objectives were to find the source of the Missouri River and to discover an overland route to the Pacific Ocean. Lewis and Clark brought a selection of firearms. One of the most unusual was a Girardoni air rifle. The principle of the air gun is propulsion of a projectile by compressed air. This type of gun is thought to have been invented in Germany as early as the 15th century. By the 18th century, air guns were used in Europe for hunting, sporting, and military purposes.

In *The Lewis and Clark Expedition Into The American Northwest in 1804-5 and 6* (published in Philadelphia in 1814), the following account is given:

They [the American Indians] had indeed abundant sources of surprise in all they saw, the appearance of the men, their arms, their clothing, the canoes ... all in turn shared their admiration, which was turned to astonishment by a shot from the air gun; this operation was instantly considered as a great medicine, by which they as well as the other Indians mean something emanating from the Great Spirit, or produced by his invisible and incomprehensible agency.

THE LEWIS AND CLARK AIR RIFLE & THE PLAINS RIFLE

St. Louis made guns, top to bottom: Schaerff Buffalo Rifle - .58 caliber - circa 1850.   S. Hawken Gemmer Rifle - .50 caliber - circa 1849-50.   Wilmont Percussion Double Shotgun - 12 gauge - circa 1850.

The Plains Rifle

As America moved West, the old long rifle, with its slender barrel, small caliber, figured wood, and fine ornamentation began to give way to a new type of firearm. Although the long rifle was fit for the forest, the new breed of people who crossed the Appalachians needed to travel vast prairies, ride long distances on horses, and shoot large game such as bison and elk. These activities required a rifle that was shorter, of larger caliber with a heavier barrel, less decorative, and more utilitarian. The development of the short, heavy-barreled, half-stocked plains rifle was the result of these needs.

The Hawken Rifle

The plains rifle was developed in St. Louis, Missouri. Christian Hawken, Sr., a notable riflesmith from Hagerstown, Maryland, taught the skills of gunsmithing to his sons George, John, Jacob, Samuel, and William. Jacob and Samuel Hawken moved to St. Louis in the first decade of the 19th century. The earliest development of the plains rifle and its distinctive form can be traced to these brothers, and their design became known as the Hawken Rifle. Also called a mountain rifle and buffalo rifle, the name Hawken Rifle has become a generic name for the plains rifle style.

The typical form is a short, heavy-barreled rifle with a half-stock and little, if any, decoration. A pair of barrel wedges with oval escutcheons was often used to fasten the barrel to the forestock. A patchbox, if present, was normally of simple design, and was circular or oval in shape. Trigger guards were usually rounded and scrolled in order to avoid snagging on clothing or saddles. Delicacy was not a design consideration, and these rifles were made for hard, rough use. Barrel length was between 36 and 38 inches, and stocks were fashioned of plain maple or walnut.

Other Makers

Plains rifles became so popular that many other riflesmiths began to produce them. Henry Leman of Lancaster and James Henry of Philadelphia joined St. Louis makers, such as H.E. Dimmick, in the production of the plains rifle.

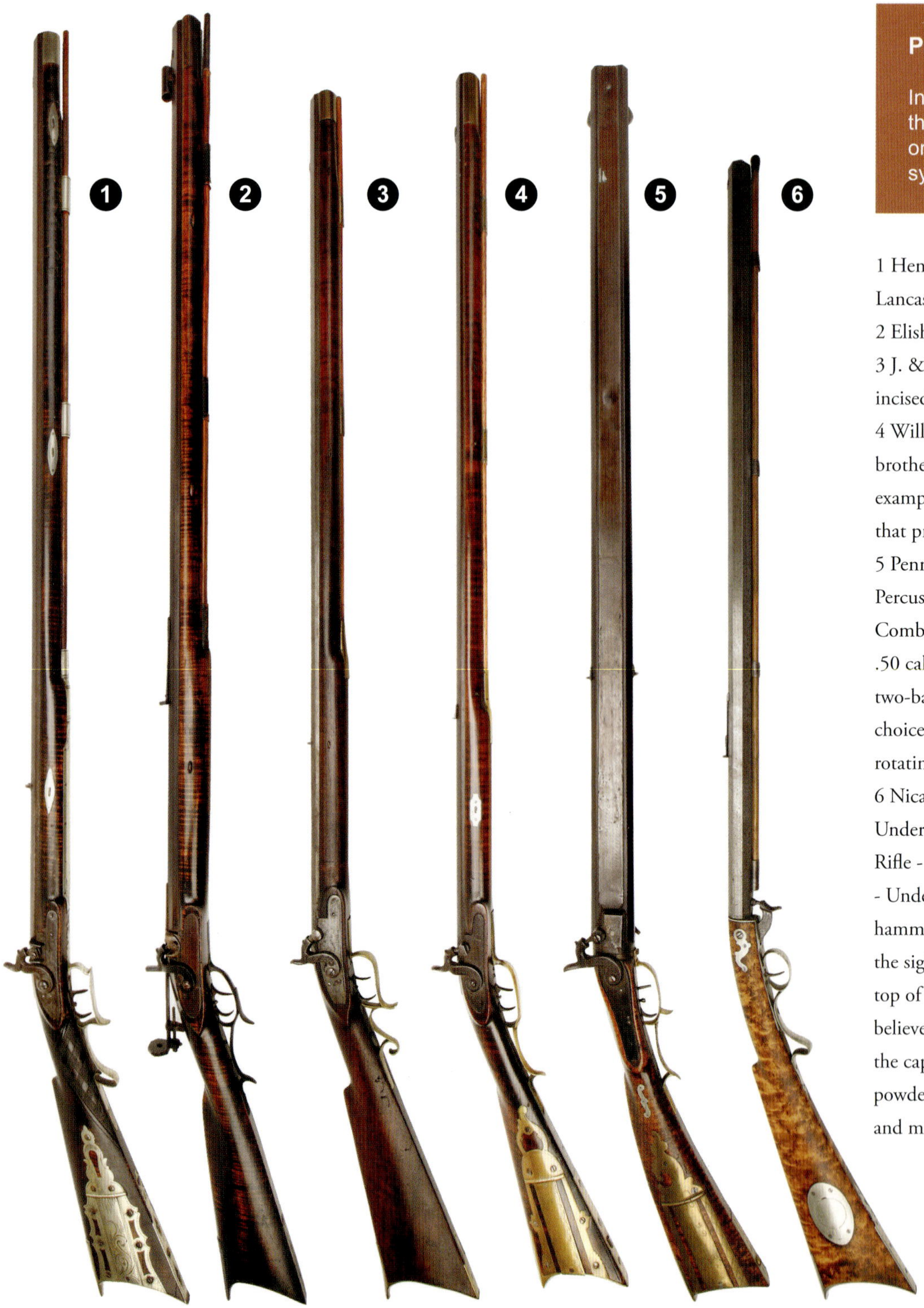

A PROSPERING NEW REPUBLIC

Percussion Long Rifles

In the mid-19th century, the percussion cap rapidly replaced the flintlock as the preferred ignition system for muzzleloading arms. Some long rifles were originally made as percussion arms, while others were converted to the new system.

1 Henry Drepperd Percussion Long Rifle - .54 caliber - circa 1840-1850 - From the Lancaster, PA, area. Converted to percussion from flintlock.

2 Elisha Pancost Percussion Long Rifle - .40 caliber - circa 1838.

3 J. & W. H. Moll Percussion Long Rifle - .36 caliber - circa 1840 - Plain maple stock with incised wrist.

4 William Hawken Percussion Rifle - .43 caliber - circa 1850 - The youngest of the Hawken brothers, William Hawken stayed in Hagerstown, MD, and built full-stocked rifles like this example, while Jacob and Samuel Hawken went West and established a St. Louis business that produced the half-stock plains rifles revered by mountain men.

5 Pennsylvania Rifle Works Percussion Over/Under Combination Gun - .45 over .50 caliber - circa 1870 - This two-barrel gun allowed a choice of calibers by simply rotating the barrels.

6 Nicanor Kendall Underhammer Percussion Rifle - .50 caliber - circa 1848 - Underhammer guns kept the hammer from interfering with the sight picture along the top of the barrel. It was also believed that the spark from the cap rising from below the powder charge enabled quicker and more reliable ignition.

Wagon Train - Robert Wesley Amick

THE PLAINS RIFLE

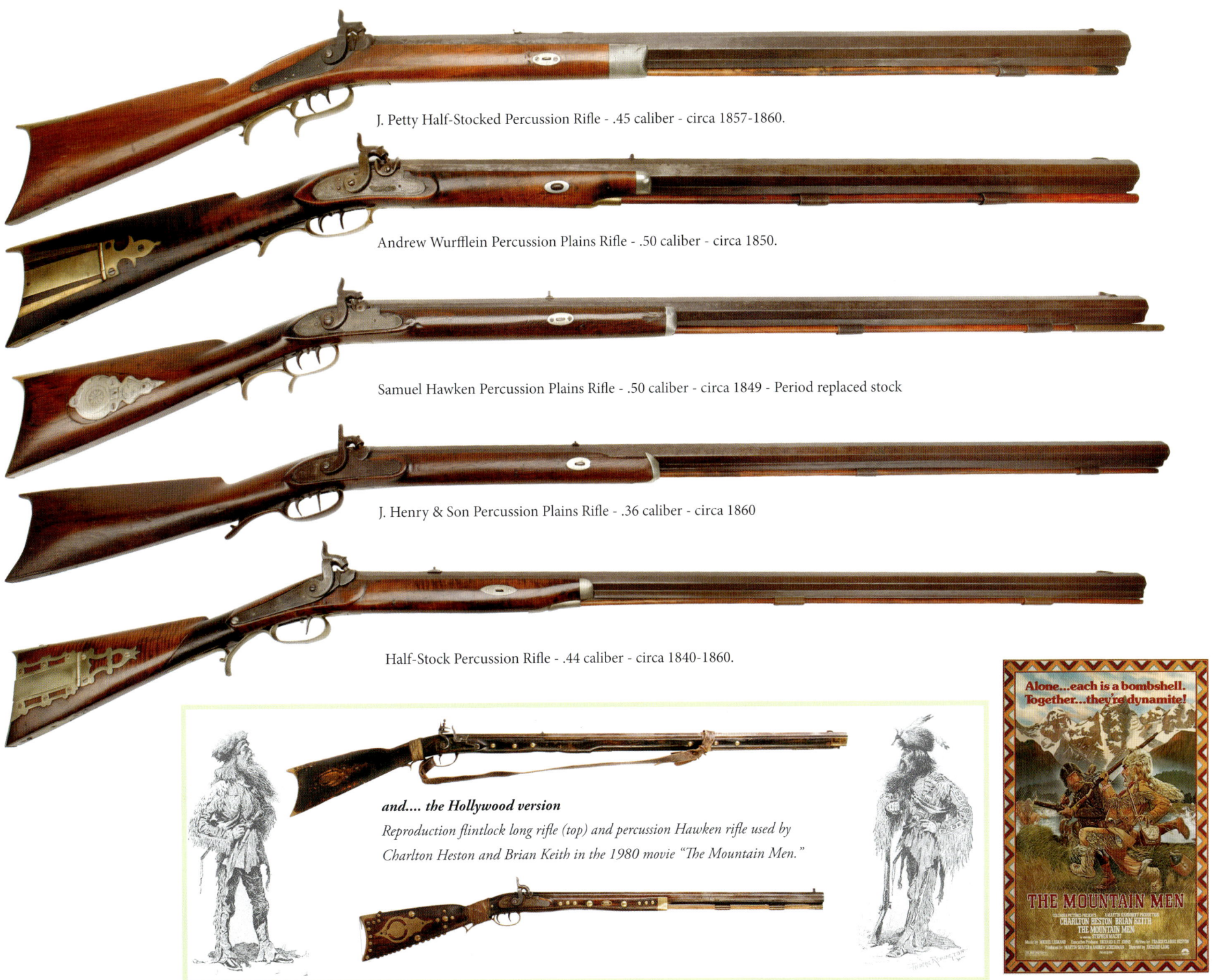

J. Petty Half-Stocked Percussion Rifle - .45 caliber - circa 1857-1860.

Andrew Wurfflein Percussion Plains Rifle - .50 caliber - circa 1850.

Samuel Hawken Percussion Plains Rifle - .50 caliber - circa 1849 - Period replaced stock

J. Henry & Son Percussion Plains Rifle - .36 caliber - circa 1860

Half-Stock Percussion Rifle - .44 caliber - circa 1840-1860.

and.... the Hollywood version
Reproduction flintlock long rifle (top) and percussion Hawken rifle used by Charlton Heston and Brian Keith in the 1980 movie "The Mountain Men."

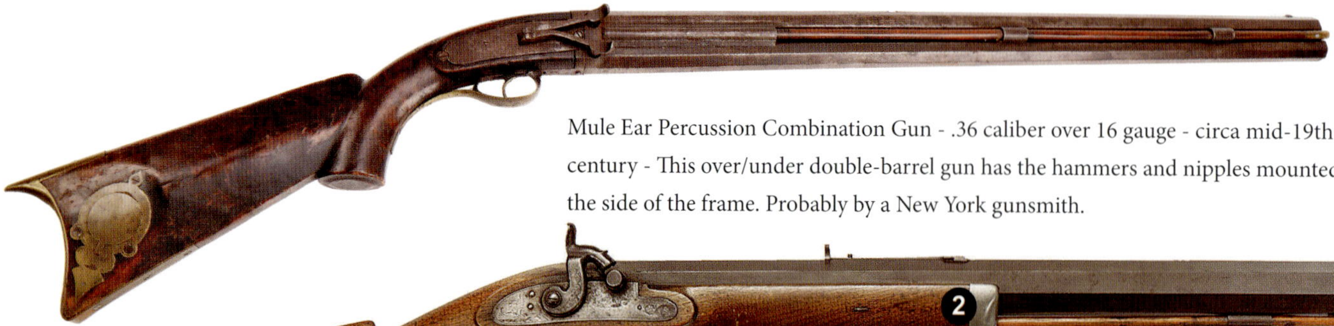

A PROSPERING NEW REPUBLIC

Mule Ear Percussion Combination Gun - .36 caliber over 16 gauge - circa mid-19th century - This over/under double-barrel gun has the hammers and nipples mounted on the side of the frame. Probably by a New York gunsmith.

Early Remington Percussion Target Rifle - .42 caliber - circa 1845-50 - Fewer than 100 heavy barrel rifles were made.

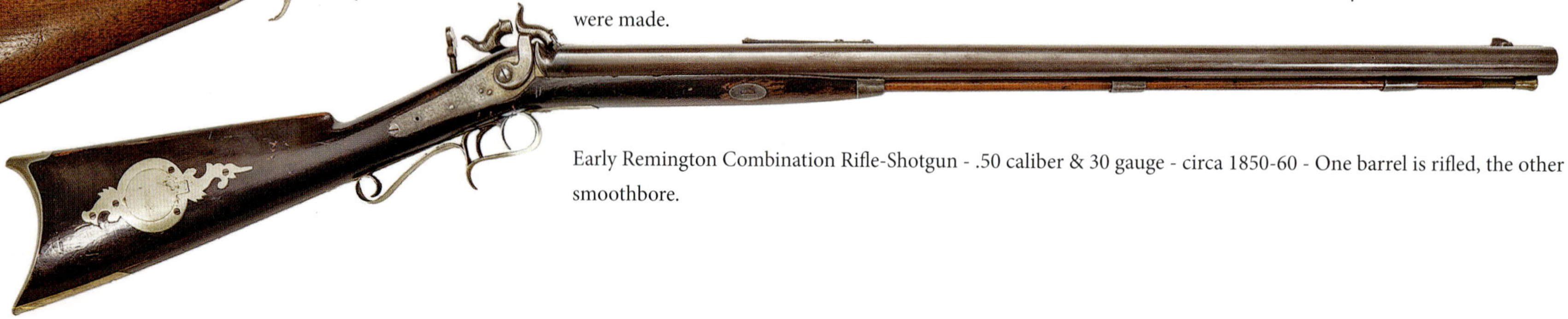

Early Remington Combination Rifle-Shotgun - .50 caliber & 30 gauge - circa 1850-60 - One barrel is rifled, the other is smoothbore.

Remington

Eliphalet Remington II made his first gun in 1816, and promptly began the regular manufacture of gun barrels. In 1828, he established his own forge in Ilion, NY, manufacturing up to 8,000 barrels a year. Other gunsmiths would add these Remington-marked barrels to lock and stock to produce their wares. In 1848, Remington began to manufacture completed firearms, beginning with a contract for Jenks breechloading carbines for the U.S. military. By the mid-1850s, three sons had joined the firm, and it became E. Remington and Sons.

These two and many other historic guns from the Remington Factory Collection are on display at the NRA National Sporting Arms Museum at Bass Pro Shops in Springfield, MO. Part of the exhibit is pictured at right.

THE BEGINNINGS OF REMINGTON & COLT FIREARMS

U.S. Colt Model 1839 Percussion Revolving Carbine - .52 caliber - circa 1838-1841 - This was the first Colt model used by the U.S. military.

Early Colts

Colt revolving firearms were state of the art in the years leading up to the Civil War. In addition to handguns, Colt also made revolving long guns, both with the first Paterson, New Jersey, company and the later Hartford, Connecticut, company.

The large-frame .44 Walker Model was modified slightly to become the Dragoon Model. In 1848, a small .31 caliber revolver was introduced and was perfected the following year as the Model 1849 Pocket Revolver, destined to become the most widely produced Colt percussion revolver.

Colt Paterson Revolvers - In addition to the larger #5 Holster or "Texas Model," the Colt Paterson, New Jersey, factory produced a mid-size #2 in .31 caliber and a #1 "Baby" mode in .28 caliber. The folding trigger drops down from the frame when the hammer is cocked. Approximately. 2,850 revolving handguns were produced at the Paterson plant between 1836 and 1847.

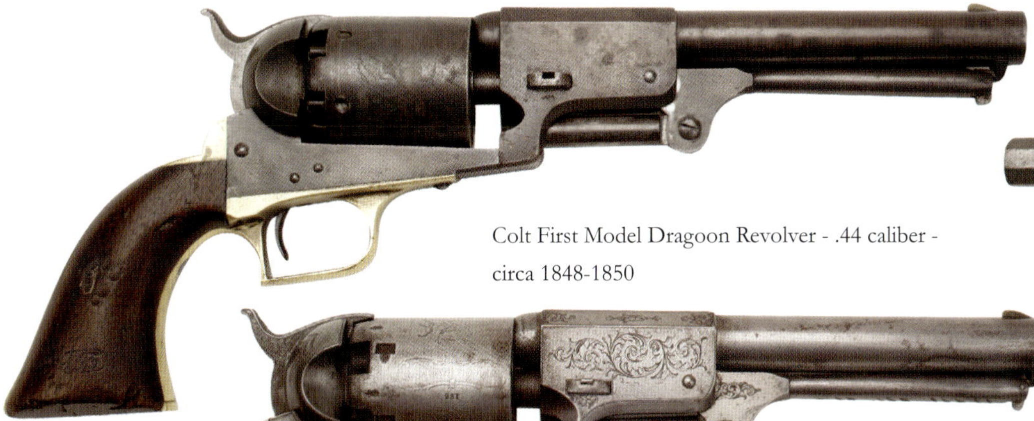

Colt First Model Dragoon Revolver - .44 caliber - circa 1848-1850

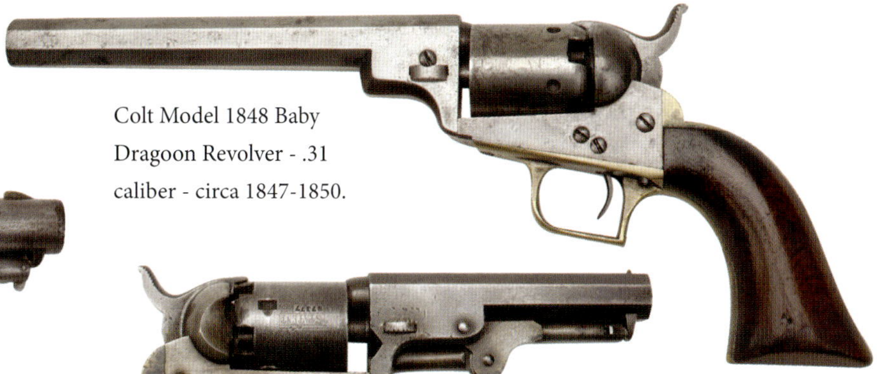

Colt Model 1848 Baby Dragoon Revolver - .31 caliber - circa 1847-1850.

Colt Third Model English Dragoon Percussion Revolver - .44 caliber - circa 1853-1857,

Colt Model 1849 Pocket Percussion Revolver - .31 caliber - circa 1850-1873.

A PROSPERING NEW REPUBLIC

Henry Deringer of Philadelphia, PA, was already well known for his rifles and larger handguns when he turned his efforts toward manufacturing smaller pocket pistols. Beginning around 1852, these compact percussion arms—sold in pairs or individually—became the favorite personal protection choice of riverboat travelers and those bound for California's Gold Country. Some of Deringer's pistols were marked by the factory for his sole agents on the West Coast—Charles Curry and Nathaniel Curry & Bro. of San Francisco. But Deringer copyists abounded; and the generic term "derringer" was, in time, applied to both Deringer's own product as well as to other, similar small-scale handguns.

The Gold Rush

In the wake of the Mexican War, America acquired the former Spanish territory of California. Prior to 1848, California, as a generally undeveloped frontier area, had attracted mountain men and a few enterprising merchants who established trading posts. But the discovery of a few gleaming nuggets in a sawmill's tailrace waters on January 24, 1848, changed California forever. Gold had been found and the world rushed in! Traveling to California involved a long sea voyage around South America or a faster, but more hazardous, overland route across the Great Plains. Thousands of 49ers seeking their fortunes in California brought an incredible variety of handguns and longarms for personal protection during the arduous trip and at the lawless mining camps.

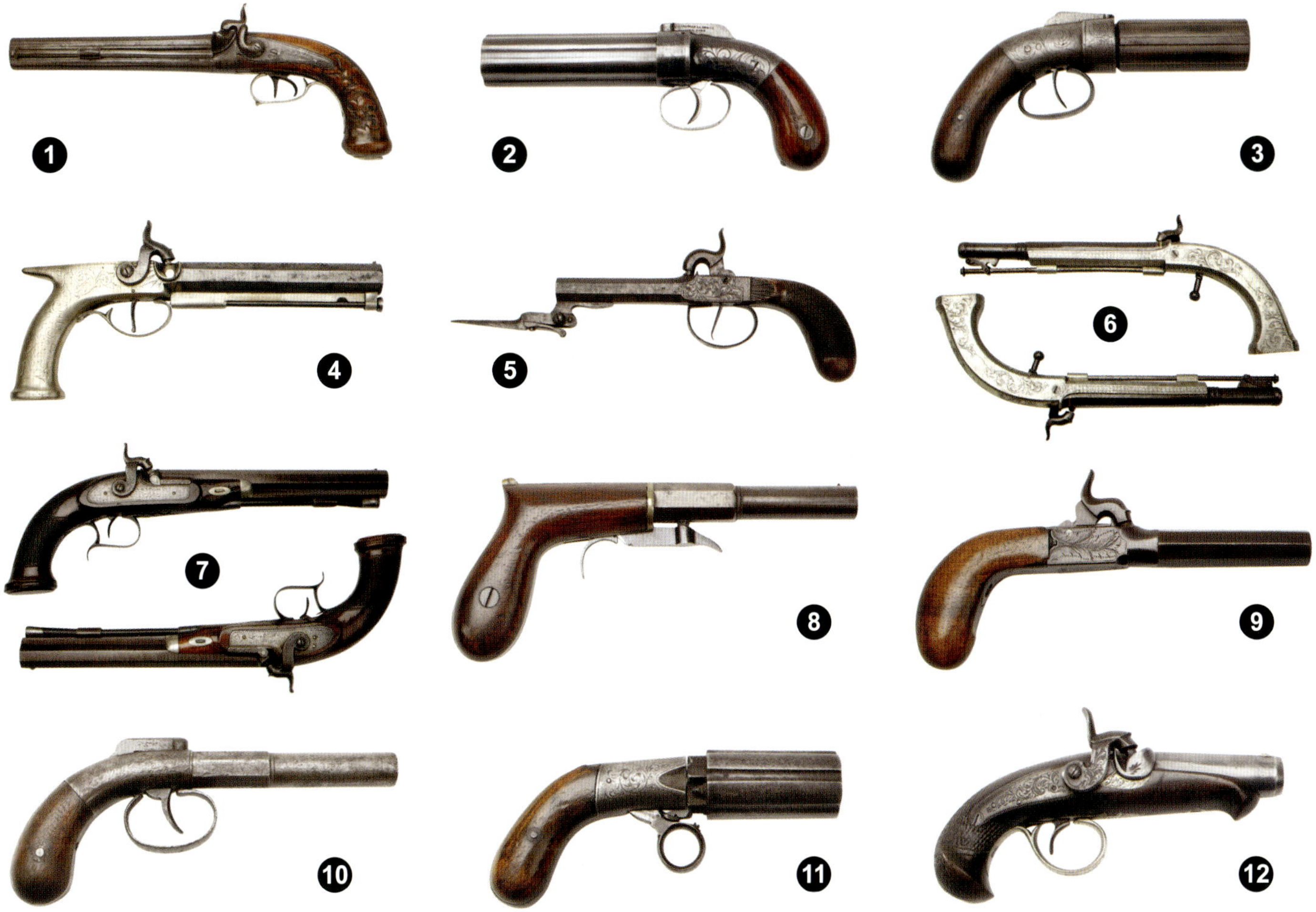

HENRY DERINGER & PERCUSSION HANDGUNS

1. Belgian Double-Barrel Percussion Pistol - .58 caliber - circa 1840-1855.
2. Manhattan Pepperbox Revolver - .31 caliber - circa 1855-1860 - The pepperbox was the primary rival of Colt revolvers in the repeating handgun market in the 1850s.
3. Sprague & Marston Double-Action Pepperbox Pistol - .31 caliber - circa 1850-1860.
4. English Saw-Handle Single-Shot Percussion Pistol - .52 caliber - circa 1840-1860.
5. Belgian Dagger Pistol - .48 caliber - circa 1850-1860.
6. Pair of C & G Abbott English All-Metal Percussion Pistols - .45 caliber - circa 1850.
7. Pair of William Hollis English Percussion Pistols - .50 caliber - circa 1820.
8. W. Ashton Underhammer Percussion Pistol - .28 caliber - circa 1835-1860.
9. Belgian Screw-barrel Percussion Pistol - .46 caliber - circa 1840-1860.
10. Allen & Wheelock Double-Action Bar Hammer Pistol - .44 caliber - circa 1857-1863.
11. J. P. Cooper's Patent English Pepperbox Pistol - .44 caliber - circa 1840-1860.
12. J. E. Evans Pocket Percussion Pistol - .44 caliber - circa 1850-1860.
13. Turlock English Officer's Pistol - .69 caliber - circa 1850-1870 - Converted to percussion from flintlock.
14. Rigby English Percussion Pistol - .54 caliber - circa 1840-1855.

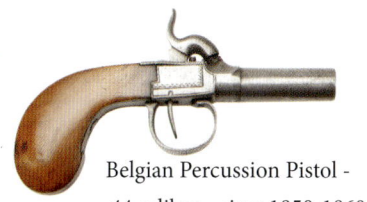

Belgian Percussion Pistol - .44 caliber - circa 1850-1860.

Agent markings on Henry Deringer pistols.

A PROSPERING NEW REPUBLIC

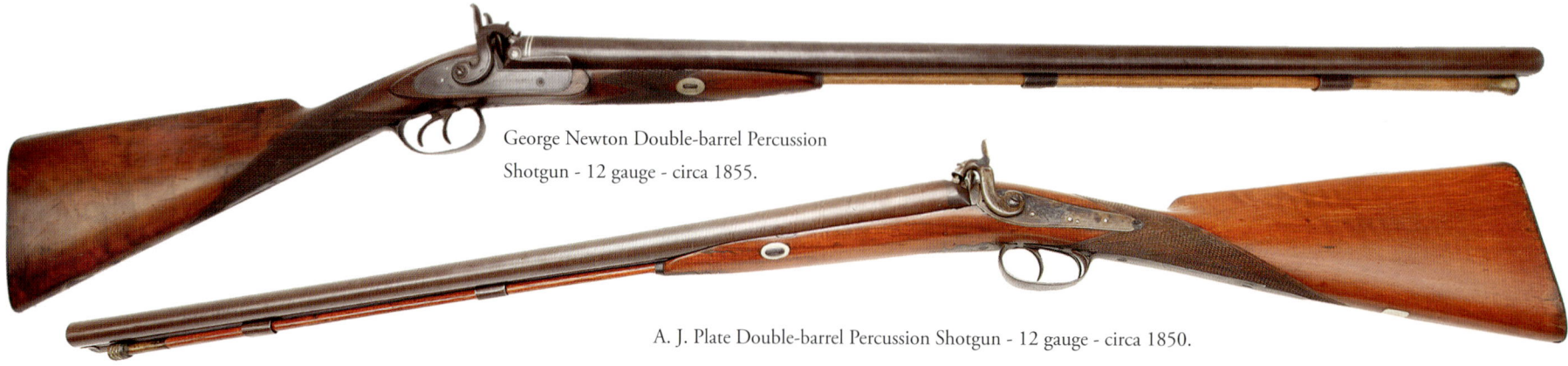

Joseph Egg English Percussion Shotgun with case and accoutrements - 12 gauge - circa 1840-1860 - Englishman Joseph Egg was known as a maker of high-grade firearms. His son, Durs, was appointed gunmaker to several British monarchs and his dueling pistol sets are among the finest ever produced.

George Newton Double-barrel Percussion Shotgun - 12 gauge - circa 1855.

A. J. Plate Double-barrel Percussion Shotgun - 12 gauge - circa 1850.

PERCUSSION LONG GUNS

1. Brevete Colt Dragoon Revolving Rifle - .44 caliber - circa 1870 - Copies of Colt revolving arms were produced in Belgium for the European arms market. While many of these were not sanctioned, Colt did license certain firms to make copies to market in regions where Colt products were not well represented.

2. Ann Patrick English Percussion Double Rifle - .70 caliber - circa 1838 - Female gunsmith Ann Patrick regulated the two barrels of this double rifle to shoot to the same point of impact, an exacting task that would have taken nearly three times as long to finish as a single-barreled rifle.

3. Bentley English Percussion Plains Rifle - .44 caliber - circa 1849 - This type of rifle was sold in Canada during the Gold Rush period.

4. A. J. Plate Percussion Side-by-Side Shotgun - 10 gauge - circa 1850 - Made in San Francisco.

5. James & Ferris Half-Stock Percussion Target Rifle - .36 caliber - circa 1855-1865 - Both U.S. and Confederate armies employed sharpshooters armed with rifles of this type for long-range shooting, including fire against enemy officers.

6. Percussion Benchrest Rifle - .50 caliber - circa 1850-1860 - This type of percussion rifle, originally designed for competition, weighed 40 lbs. and had an effective range of more than 1,000 yards.

7. Russia America Fur Co. (Tula Arsenal, Russia) Model 1838 Percussion Musket - .70 caliber - circa 1838 - Obsolete military muskets frequently were reissued as trade goods on the California frontier.

8. British Model 1838 Land Pattern Percussion Musket - .72 caliber - circa 1838-1844 - Typical of the imported arms issued to Mexican forces in the Mexican War.

A PROSPERING NEW REPUBLIC

U.S. Harpers Ferry Model 1841 "Mississippi" Percussion Rifle - .58 caliber - circa 1846-1855.

U.S. Springfield Model 1842 Percussion Musket - .69 caliber - circa 1844-1855.

U.S. Springfield Model 1855 Percussion Rifle-Musket - .58 caliber - circa 1857-1861.

Elgin Cutlass Pistol - .53 cal. - circa 1838. 150 of these were made for the US Navy to outfit the South Sea exploring expedition.

Henry Deringer Model 1842 Navy - .54 caliber - circa 1847 - Rifled barrel. Note the small rear sight is on the tang.

Henry Aston Model 1842 Army - .54 caliber - circa 1845-1852 - This was considered to be the best military pistol of its time.

The Mississippi Rifle

This rifle was developed and approved for manufacture by the U.S. government in 1841. An accurate and attractive brass-mounted rifle, it was admired by the men who used it. The U.S. Model 1841 Rifle was first used during the Mexican War at the Battle of Buena Vista in February 1847. The successful use of this rifle by the First Mississippi Volunteer Infantry, under the command of Colonel Jefferson Davis (later to become President of the Confederacy), won the rifle its common name - the Mississippi rifle.

These rifles were manufactured by the government at Harpers Ferry and by five other contractors (including Remington, Whitney, and Tryon). Over 70,000 of these rifles were produced between 1846 and 1855. On July 5, 1855, the Secretary of War ordered that the standard caliber of U.S. arms be changed from .54 to .58 caliber. Accordingly, many of the Model 1841 Rifles were altered to .58 caliber prior to and during the Civil War.

Model 1842 Musket

This was the first regulation musket with a percussion lock to be made at both Springfield and Harpers Ferry Armories, and the first with fully interchangeable locks. About 275,000 were made from 1844 to 1855. They were also made by contract makers and South Carolina's Palmetto Armory.

MILITARY PERCUSSION ARMS

Sharps Model 1853 Percussion Carbine - .52 caliber - circa 1854-1857 - This Sharps carbine's serial number falls into the range of carbines that were used by abolitionist John Brown in his ill-fated raid on Harpers Ferry Armory in 1859.

U.S. Springfield Model 1855 Percussion Pistol/Carbine - .58 caliber - circa 1855-1857 - Intended to be used with the shoulder stock in carbine configuration by mounted troops or as a pistol when dismounted. Note Maynard tape-priming system.

Colt Model 1855 Revolving Percussion Military Rifle - .44 caliber - circa 1856-1864 - This specimen is attributed to Col. Hiram Berdan's U.S. Sharpshooters.

U.S. Lemuel Pomeroy Model 1840 Contract Conversion - .69 caliber - circa 1840-1846 - Converted from a flintlock smoothbore.

U.S. Sharps New Model 1859 Breechloading Percussion Rifle - .52 caliber - circa 1859-1863 - A falling-block design, Sharps breechloaders were manufactured in great numbers throughout the American Civil War in both rifle and carbine configurations.

A NATION ASUNDER

Union Longarms

On December 20, 1860, the legislature of the state of South Carolina, exercising the powers granted to it by the 10th Amendment of the Constitution of the United States, passed an ordinance of secession and separated itself from the United States as a free and sovereign government.

Within the next six months, 11 other states adopted similar resolutions and formed the Confederate States of America. After the Battle of Ft. Sumter in April of 1861, the federal government refused to recognize the independence of the Southern states and declared that open rebellion existed, calling 100,000 men to arms to suppress the revolt. At the beginning of the Civil War, the bulk of the North's longarms were safe in the hands of their regular infantry units or were secured in federal arsenals and armories. Previous U.S. Pattern arms such as the Model 1841 rifle, the Model 1842 musket, and the Model 1855 rifled musket were quickly readied and issued to waiting troops. Changes in the standard service arm resulted in the adoption of the Model 1861 rifled musket, the Colt Contract Model of 1861, and eventually the Model 1863 rifled musket. Over 1.5 million .58 caliber arms were turned out by the Springfield Armory and 32 private contractors during the course of the war.

The age of steam ushered in an industrial revolution, and thousands of advances were made in manufacturing processes. Factories were located to make the best use of water, or hydraulic, power that was sometimes referred to as white coal.

In New England, the Merrimac, Concord, Connecticut, and Chicopee rivers flow through a fertile valley creating a region known as Gun Valley due to the numerous arms manufacturers who set up factories along these valuable water sources.

On April 9, 1865, the war ended after 650,000 deaths, the most costly conflict in American history.

U.S. Whitney Arms Co. Model 1861 Navy Percussion Rifle - .69 caliber - circa 1861-1864 - Nicknamed the "Plymouth Rifle" for service aboard the *U.S.S. Plymouth*, a test vessel for naval ordnance, where it was developed. 10,000 made during the war, most for naval service.

U.S. Alfred P. Jenks & Son Model 1861 Percussion Rifle-Musket - .58 caliber - circa 1861-1865 - With total production of over 98,000, Jenks was the largest of 21 private contractors making 1861 Rifle Muskets for the Union.

U.S. Springfield Model 1863 Type II Rifle Musket - .58 caliber - circa 1863-1865 - Note the "tampion" barrel plug that was used to provide protection from the elements during carry.

U.S. Colt Model 1861 Special Musket - .58 caliber - circa 1861-1865 - Approximately 100,000 produced during the war.

UNION ARMS

1. U.S. Greene Breechloading Underhammer Percussion Rifle - .53 caliber - circa 1859-1860 - Underhammer design with unusual oval-shaped bore. The first U.S. martial bolt-action, with 900 purchased by the Army
2. U.S. Remington Model 1863 Percussion Contract (Zouave) Rifle - .58 caliber - circa 1862-1865.
3. U.S. Spencer Model 1860 Army Repeating Rifle - .56 rimfire - circa 1863-1864.
4. U.S. Lindsay Model 1863 Double Rifle Musket - .58 caliber - circa 1863 - Two-shot capacity was achieved by loading one charge on top of the other in the same barrel, resulting in a superposed charge. 1,000 of these were manufactured in 1863-1864. Their combat usage was unsatisfactory, with reports of simultaneous firing of both charges.
5. U.S. New Haven Arms Co. Henry Lever-Action Repeating Rifle - .44 rimfire - circa 1860-1866 - Although this lever-action 15-round repeater offered a tremendous firepower advantage over the single-shot muzzleloaders commonly fielded at the time, only about 1,700 were actually purchased and saw use during the Civil War.
6. U.S. Burnside Rifle Company 5th Model Breechloading Lever-Action Percussion Carbine - .54 caliber - circa 1862-1865 - The third-most numerous cavalry carbine of the war.
7. U.S. Spencer Lever-Action Repeating Carbine - .56 rimfire - circa 1860-1862.

A NATION ASUNDER

Union Carbines

Cavalry was far more effective with a gun that was light, short, and easily reloaded in the saddle. The Federal government contracted for the maximum output of guns from such primary manufacturers as Sharps and Spencer. However, the tremendous demand for arms was still not met, and the government was forced to purchase arms from manufacturers who, although their products were not up to government standards, could make deliveries of shootable firearms on schedule.

1. U.S. E. G. Lamson & Co. Ball Repeating Carbine - .50 rimfire - circa 1865 - 1,000 ordered but not received until after the war ended.

2. U.S. Richardson & Overman Gallager Percussion Carbine - .50 caliber - circa 1860 - 23,000 made with extensive use by Union cavalry. Made in both metallic cartridge and percussion configurations.

3. U.S. Massachusetts Arms Co. Maynard Second Model Breechloading Carbine - .50 caliber - circa 1863-1865 - 20,000 produced

4. U.S. N.P. Ames Jenks "Mule Ear" Carbine - .54 caliber - circa 1843-1846 - Sidehammer breechloader, nicknamed the Mule Ear Carbine. Naval usage.

5. U.S. Amoskeag Mfg. Co. Lindner Percussion Breechloading Carbine, Second Type - .58 caliber - circa 1859 - Some used by 1st Michigan cavalry.

6. Colt Model 1855 Percussion Revolving Carbine - .56 caliber - circa 1856-1864.

7. U.S. American Machine Works Smith Breechloading Percussion Carbine - .50 caliber - circa 1861-1865 - 30,000 Smith carbines were purchased by federal government.

8. U.S. Sharps New Model 1859 Percussion Carbine - .52 caliber - circa 1859-1866.

9. U.S. Sharps & Hankins Model 1862 Single-Shot Breechloading Percussion Carbine - .52 rimfire - circa 1862 - Leather-covered barrel to protect from salt water for naval usage.

UNION ARMS

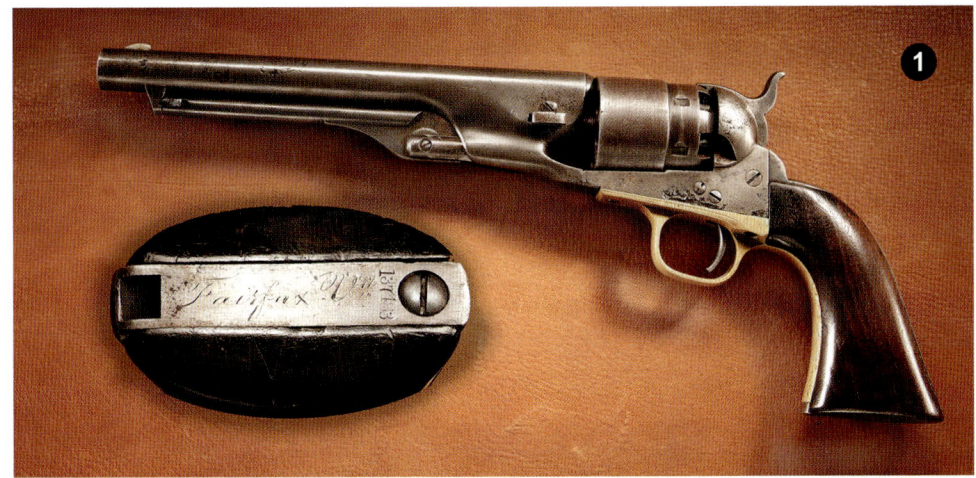

Union Handguns

Federal quartermasters struggled to overcome a severe shortage of firearms that were needed to equip the Union troops. With the age of sword, saber, and lance giving way to the revolver and carbine, pistols were desperately needed by the Union army.

Colt and Remington made revolvers at record levels, but could not produce the quantities that procurement officers needed. As a result, a dozen or more additional revolver companies and manufacturers began supplying their entire production output to the government, even though their arms had not been received favorably by the military or the public prior to the war.

1. Colt Model 1860 Percussion Revolver associated with Mosby Fairfax Courthouse Raid - .44 caliber - circa 1863 - On March 9, 1863, Confederate guerilla Mosby and 29 men evaded sentries, capturing General Edwin Stoughton, other officers, and many horses. This revolver was found, left by Mosby's men and it was presented to Lt. Joseph LeBeff, a wounded officer leaving military service. Inscribed "Fairfax, Virginia" on the butt.

2. Lt. C.H. Peirce's Cased Pair of Colt Model 1851 Percussion Revolvers - .36 caliber - circa 1860 - Peirce served for 25 years in the U.S. Army during the Mexican War and Civil War and followed that with 15 years in the Lighthouse Service at Western postings in California, Washington, and Alaska.

3. Mad Harry's Smith & Wesson Model Number One, 1st Issue Revolver - .22 rimfire - circa 1858 - Presented by "Charlotte" to Lt. Col. H.D. Townsend of the 1st Cavalry on the eve of First Manassas.

4. General W. T. Sherman's Smith & Wesson Model Number Two Revolver - .32 rimfire, circa 1865 - This factory cased and inscribed "Old Model Army Revolver" was resented to Sherman by his staff after the Civil War.

A NATION ASUNDER

Army and Navy Revolvers

In the terminology of the era, an "Army" revolver was .44 caliber and a "Navy" revolver was .36.

Remington Beals Army Revolver and Remington Beals Navy Revolver - 1861-1862.

Remington revolvers were widely used by Union forces, especially the New Model Army.

Remington Model 1861 Army ("Old Model Army") and Model 1861 Navy Revolvers - circa 1862.

U.S. Starr Arms Co. Model 1863 Single Action Army Revolver - .44 caliber - circa 1863-1865 - About 33,000 made, with 25,000 going to the U.S. government. After Colts and Remingtons, Starrs were the Union's third-most widely used handguns.

U.S. Starr Arms Co. Model 1858 Army Double-Action Percussion Revolver - .44 caliber - circa 1858-1862 - 23,000 manufactured, with most going to the U.S. military. One of the earliest American double-action revolvers.

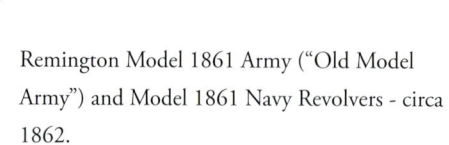

Whitney Navy & Eagle Co. Percussion Revolver, 1st Model, 2nd Type - .36 caliber - circa 1858-1862 - When Colt's patent on revolving cylinder arms expired in 1857, Whitney introduced the first solid frame percussion revolver and became a significant competitor, producing about 33,000 units. This is a rare 1st Model, 2nd Type, with only about 200 produced.

Remington New Model Army and New Model Navy Revolvers - circa 1863-1875.

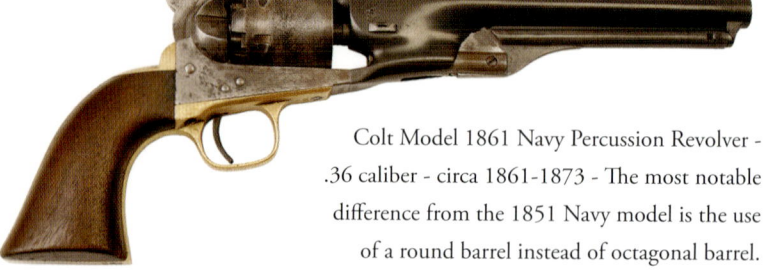

Colt Model 1861 Navy Percussion Revolver - .36 caliber - circa 1861-1873 - The most notable difference from the 1851 Navy model is the use of a round barrel instead of octagonal barrel.

UNION ARMS & PRIVATE PURCHASE HANDGUNS

Unusual action large frame Union revolvers:

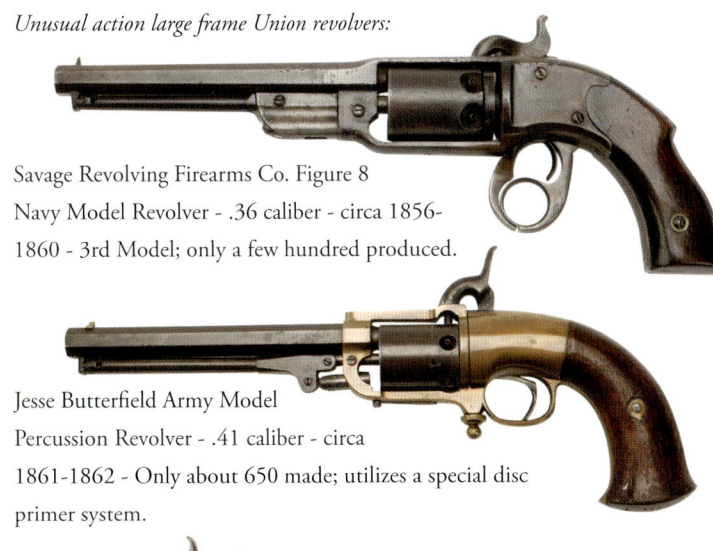

Savage Revolving Firearms Co. Figure 8 Navy Model Revolver - .36 caliber - circa 1856-1860 - 3rd Model; only a few hundred produced.

Jesse Butterfield Army Model Percussion Revolver - .41 caliber - circa 1861-1862 - Only about 650 made; utilizes a special disc primer system.

Savage & North Figure 8 Percussion Revolver, Second Model - .36 caliber - circa 1858 - Only about 100 2nd Models were made. Unusual two-trigger system in which the lower trigger rotates the cylinder and cocks the hammer, while the upper trigger drops the hammer to fire the gun.

C. S. Pettengill Army Percussion Revolver - .44 caliber - circa 1858-1863 - Double-action only. Manufactured by Rogers & Spencer.

Savage & North Percussion Revolver - .44 caliber - circa 1856-1859 - Lower ring trigger operates action; upper trigger fires the gun.

Private Purchase & Patent Infringement

Although not military issue, many small revolvers were privately purchased by Civil War soldiers. Some of the cartridge models infringed on or avoided the S&W Rollin White patent for a cylinder with chambers bored through end to end.

1. Colt Model 1855 Root Sidehammer Pocket Percussion Revolver, Model 2 - .28 caliber - circa 1855-1870 - 40,000 produced.
2. Plant's Mfg. Co. Eagle Arms Front Loading Revolver - .30 cup fire - circa 1863-1866 - Cup-primed cartridges circumvented the S&W Rollin White patent.
3. Allen & Wheelock Sidehammer Rimfire Single-Action Revolver, 2nd Model - .32 short rimfire - circa 1860 - Production halted due to infringement.
4. Lucius W. Pond Single-Action Belt Revolver - .32 rimfire - circa 1861-1870 - Another S&W Rollin White patent infringement.
5. John Walch Pocket Model Percussion Revolver - .31 caliber - circa 1860-1862 - John Walch's 10-shot revolver design relied on superposed cylinder charges, with two rounds loaded into each chamber.
6. Moore's Patent Single-Action Belt Revolver - .32 rimfire - circa 1861-1863 - Seven shot. Another S&W patent infringement,
7. Lucius W. Pond Front-Loading Revolver - .32 rimfire - circa 1862-1864 - This Pond model circumvented the S&W patent by using separate removable chambers for each round.
8. W.W. Marston Union Pocket Model Revolver - .31 caliber - circa 1858-1862.
9. Manhattan Pocket Model Percussion Revolver - .31 caliber - circa 1858-1862 - After the expiration of Colt's revolver patent in 1857, Manhattan became a significant competitor, with many of their models closely resembling Colts.

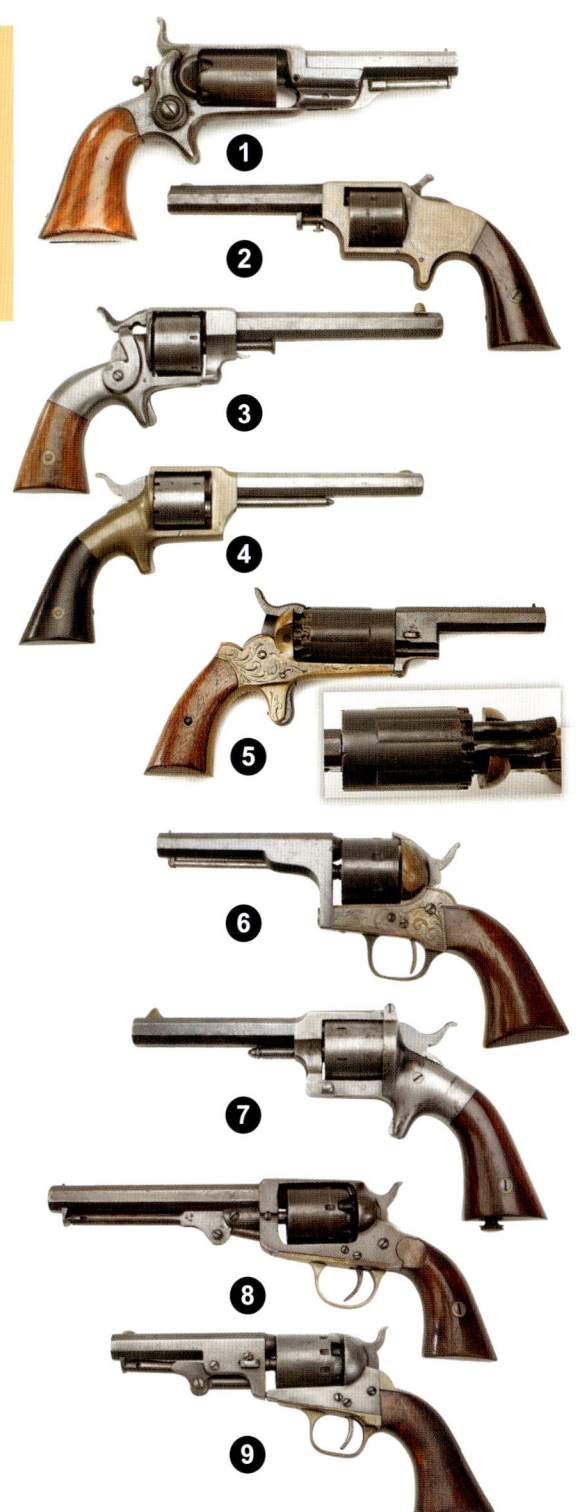

A NATION ASUNDER

Top: Griswold and Gunnison Navy Model Percussion Revolver - .36 caliber - circa 1862-1864. Copied from the Colt Navy with a bronze frame for expediency, manufactured by a transplanted Yankee, Samuel Griswold. The factory in Georgia was destroyed by Union forces in 1864. This had the largest production of any Confederate revolver although only 3,600 were made.

Bottom: Spiller and Burr Navy Percussion Revolver - .36 caliber - circa 1862-1864 - Patterned after the Whitney Navy revolver, but manufactured in Richmond, VA, and later Atlanta, GA; about 1,500 were made.

Columbus Firearms Manufacturing Company Confederate Revolver - .36 caliber - circa 1863 - Possibly the rarest of CSA made revolvers. It is a copy of the Colt 1851 Navy, and it's reported that Columbus used some Colt parts in assembling these. There are only 3 other known surviving examples, and the company name stamping of this one varies from at least two of the others. It is unknown whether this one is a variation or spurious.

Arms of the Confederacy

The sudden rush by both the North and the South to arm and equip their armies resulted in a boom in the arms industry. The Confederacy had the greatest difficulties to overcome in equipping their troops. Primarily an agrarian society, the South did not possess the manufacturing capabilities of the North.

The Confederacy used arms from a variety of sources, including the former federal arsenals, state militia arms, and personal weapons of individual soldiers. The South was able to augment these arms with imports until the Union Navy effectively blockaded Southern ports. For the most part, the Confederacy fought with weapons that had been captured on the battlefields and with a relatively small number of weapons made at armories that were established in the South after the start of the war.

ARMS OF THE CONFEDERACY

Top right - Jefferson Davis Presentation Kerr Revolver - .44 caliber - During his escape from Richmond in 1865, CSA President Davis gave this revolver to his bodyguard, Givern Campbell. Davis was captured on May 10 in Georgia. Shown with Campbell's diary, Kerr holster and a cased Great Seal of the Confederacy.

Bottom right - LeMat First Model Percussion Revolver - .42 caliber cylinder over 20 gauge central barrel - circa 1862-1864 - The "Grapeshot revolver" featured nine rounds in the cylinder, which rotated around a 20-gauge shotgun barrel; favored by Confederate officers such as Gen. J.E.B. Stuart and Gen. Beauregard.

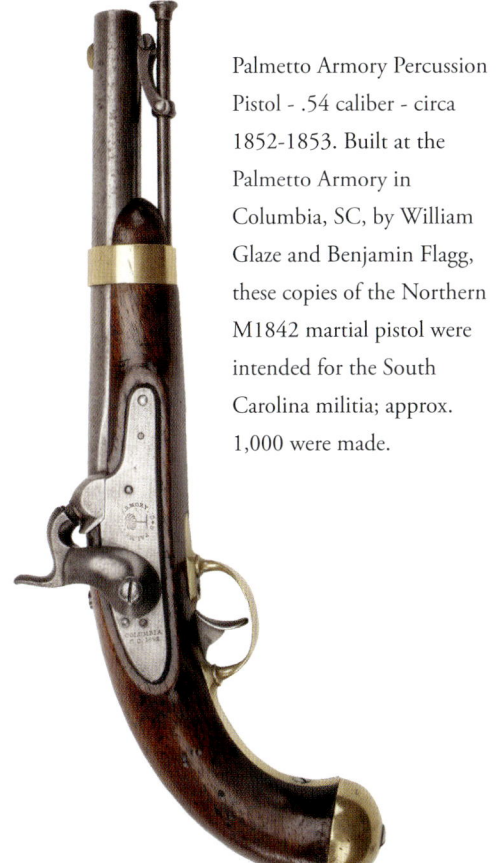

Palmetto Armory Percussion Pistol - .54 caliber - circa 1852-1853. Built at the Palmetto Armory in Columbia, SC, by William Glaze and Benjamin Flagg, these copies of the Northern M1842 martial pistol were intended for the South Carolina militia; approx. 1,000 were made.

A NATION ASUNDER

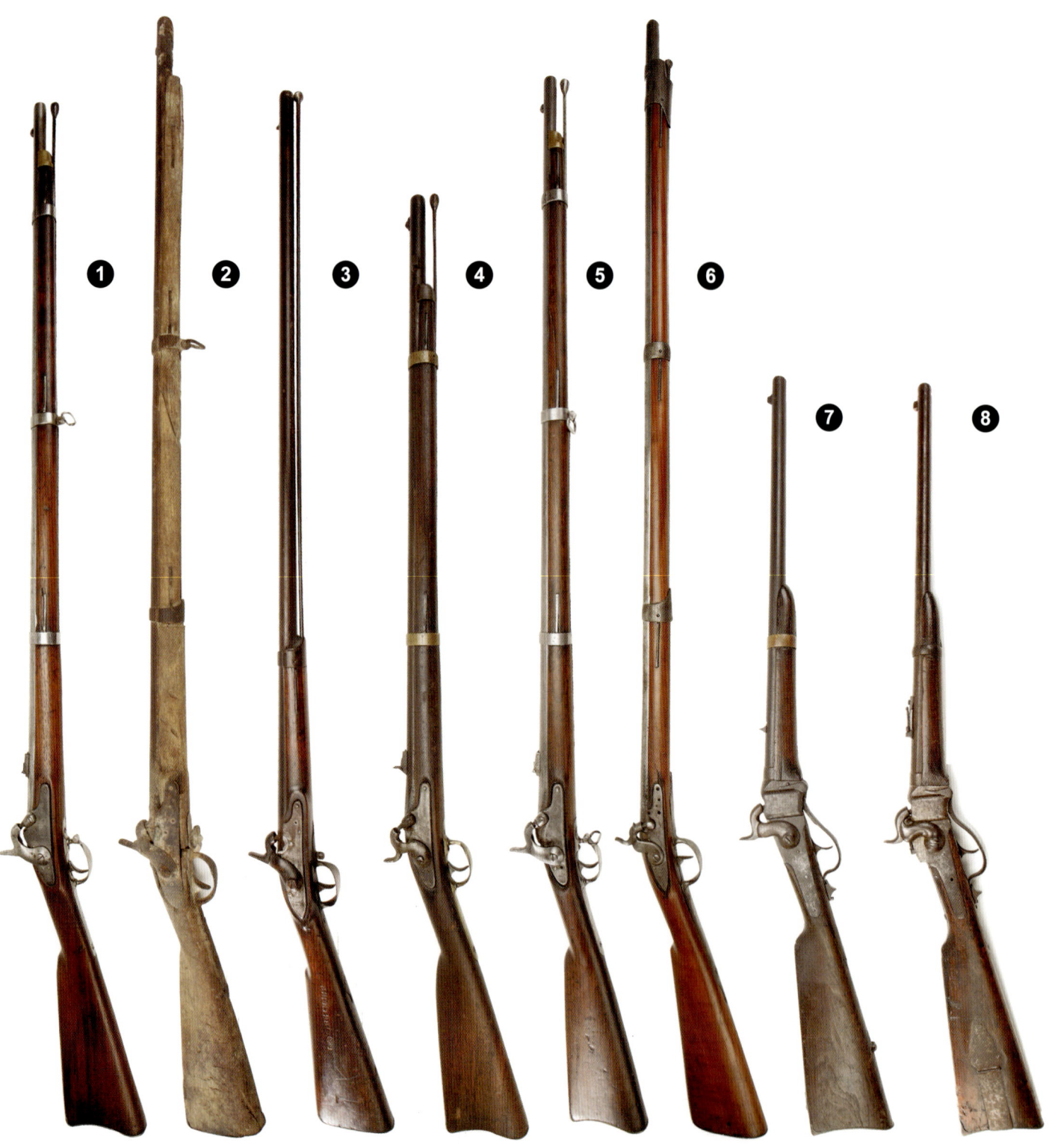

1. C.S.A. Richmond Armory Percussion Rifle-Musket, Type II - .58 caliber - circa 1862 - Carried by James M. Rosser of the 7th Virginia Regiment.
2. Model 1816 Percussion Conversion Musket - .69 caliber - Percussion conversion, recovered near Gettysburg in "battlefield dug-up" condition.
3. Virginia Manufactory of Arms Model 1795/1808 Percussion Musket (altered) - .69 caliber - circa 1797-1808 - Converted from flintlock.
4. C.S.A. Fayetteville Armory Percussion Rifle-Musket - .58 caliber - circa 1862-1865 - Utilized parts captured at Harpers Ferry.
5. C.S.A. Richmond Arsenal Percussion Rifle-Musket - .58 caliber - circa 1861 - A close copy of the U.S. Springfield.
6. Charleville Percussion Conversion Musket - .70 caliber - circa 1850 - Serviceable arms of any type or age, such as this percussion conversion of an older musket, were vitally needed by the Confederacy.
7. S.C. Robinson Sharps-Type Breechloading Percussion Carbine - .52 caliber - circa 1862-1865 - Confederate copy of the Union Sharps carbine, made in Richmond, VA, without the Lawrence pellet priming system for simplicity of manufacture.
8. Sharps New Model 1859 Percussion Carbine - .52 caliber - circa 1859-1866 - The buttstock of this carbine is carved "Rappahannock Station Nov. 7 1863" and was captured from Confederate cavalry forces by Union Gen. John Buford's troopers.

IMPORTED ARMS

Imported Arms

It soon became apparent from the opening battles that the conflict would be lengthy. Both the North and the South realized that more guns would be needed quickly, and looked to Europe for additional arms.

On the Union side, General John C. Fremont, Colonel George Schuyler, and Marcellus Hartley (from the private military outfitting firm of Schuyler, Hartley & Graham) worked tirelessly to obtain new arms. Their efforts served not only to equip Union troops, but also to deprive the Confederates of the opportunity to buy these arms.

The Confederates relied primarily on the efforts of Major Caleb Huse, Major Edward C. Anderson, Commander James D. Bullock, and Captain James H. North. Courtney & Tennant of Charleston, South Carolina, S. Isaacs, Campbell & Company of London, and Nelson Clements of Texas also served as arms procurement agents for the South.

The guns obtained from the foreign markets consisted of a variety of small arms whose quality varied from useless to excellent. Many of the firearms were converted smoothbores that were outdated. Calibers ranged from .54 to .71 caliber. Most of the imported arms came from England, Austria, Prussia, Saxony, Bavaria, France, and Belgium.

1. Barnett English Model 1853 Enfield Percussion Rifle-Musket - .577 caliber - circa 1862 - Type smuggled through the Union blockade in great numbers to arm the South.
2. Suhl German Model 1839 Muzzleloading Percussion Musket - .71 caliber - circa 1839.
3. Charles Ingram English Volunteer Pattern Percussion Rifle - .45 Whitworth - circa 1860 - British Rifle Volunteer units were established to repel a potential French invasion in 1858, but their surplus arms were offered on the world market as the Confederacy began to equip its forces.
4. Lorenz Austrian Model 1855 Percussion Rifle - .54 caliber - circa 1862.
5. Adams Patent Small Arms Company English Army Percussion Revolver - .44 caliber - circa 1857-1861 - Double-action revolvers were more popular in England than in the U.S. This design was made in England by London Armoury Co. and in America by the Massachusetts Arms Co.
6. David Herman English Double-Action Percussion Revolver - .40 caliber - circa 1860 - One of many copies of the Adams revolver.
7. Tranter/Adams English Patent Percussion Revolver - .458 caliber - circa 1855-1860.
8. Austrian Percussion Pistol - .70 caliber - circa 1860-1862.
9. English Double-Action Bar-Hammer Percussion Revolver - .44 caliber - circa 1845 - This gun was seized by the U.S. Navy from a Confederate blockade runner.
10. Caron French Single-Action Pinfire Revolver - 12mm pinfire - circa 1860-1870 - One of the first metallic cartridge designs, Casimir LeFaucheux's pinfire revolvers were among the many foreign arms imported by both Union and Confederate arms buyers.

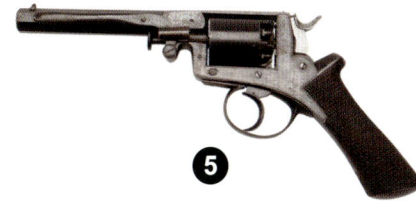

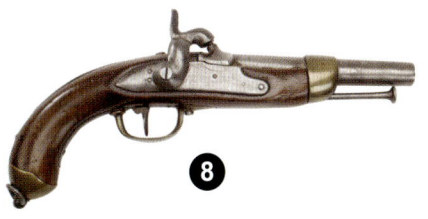
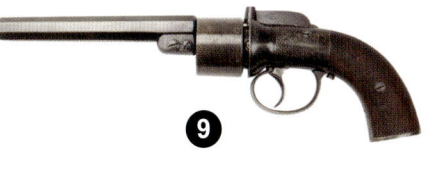
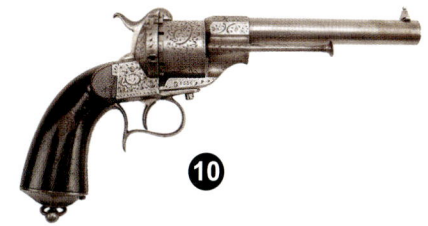

THE AMERICAN WEST

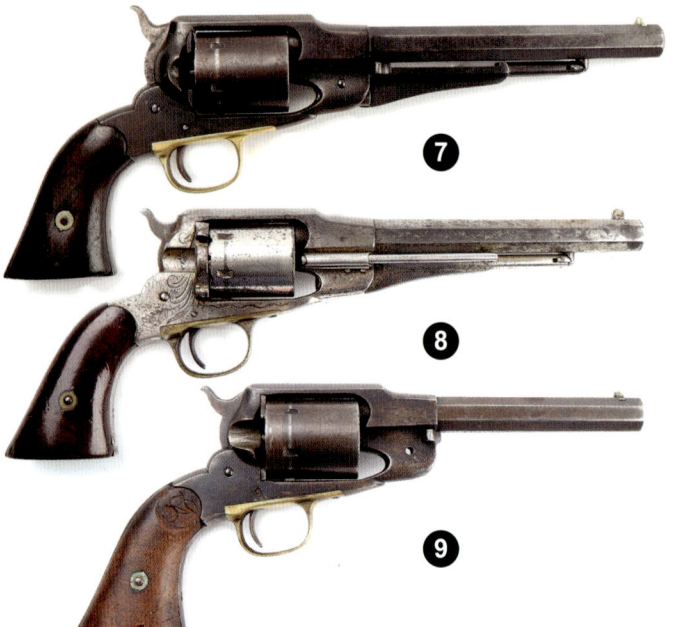
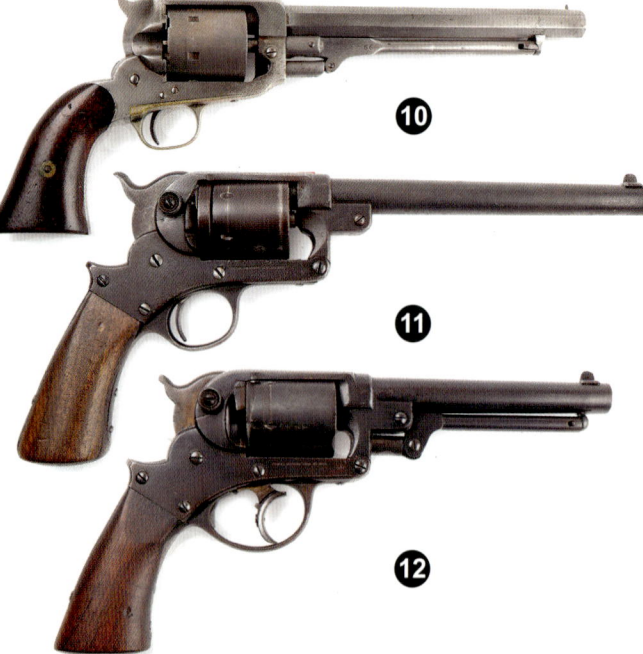

Cartridge Conversions

After the Civil War the advantages of metallic cartridges over the percussion system were clearly apparent. Just as flintlocks had previously been converted to percussion arms, cap and ball revolvers were converted to fire metallic cartridges. This was done both by manufacturers to use up existing percussion revolver parts, and by individual gunsmiths and blacksmiths to modernized older revolvers. The practice was common throughout the 1870s.

1. Thuer Colt factory conversion of 1860 Army Model - .44 Thuer - circa 1868-71.
2. Richards Colt factory conversion of 1860 Army Model - .44 Colt - circa 1873-78 - U.S. military issue.
3. Richards Mason Colt factory conversion of 1861 Navy Model - .38 rimfire - circa 1870s.
4. Colt Pocket Model factory conversion - .38 rimfire -
5. Colt Pocket Navy Model factory conversion - .38 centerfire - "Mont Peg" carved on grips.
6. Colt Model 1861 Navy gunsmith conversion - .38 rimfire.
7. Remington New Model Army factory conversion - originally .46 rimfire, now .45 CF - The first cartridge revolver adopted by U.S. military.
8. Remington New Model Navy factory conversion - .38 rimfire - factory engraved.
9. Remington Old Model Army conversion - .44 centerfire
10. Whitney conversion for U.S. Navy, .38 rimfire.
11. Starr Single Action Army conversion - .45 centerfire.
12. Starr Double Action Army conversion, .45 centerfire.

SIXGUNS

Sixguns

Following the Civil War, veterans and other Americans moved west to start a new life. Firearms were important tools for many, used for sustenance hunting, predator and pest control on ranches and farms, personal defense in unsettled areas, and recreation. The West of this era holds a special spot in America's collective imagination, and certainly the icon of this era is the sixgun.

While cartridge arms were rapidly replacing percussion guns in manufacturer product lines, the older guns were still widely used.

1. Bat Masterson's Colt Single Action Army.
2. Black Jack Ketchum's engraved Colt Single Action Army.
3. John Wesley Hardin's engraved Colt Model 1877 Double Action.
4. U.S. Deputy Marshal Bass Reeves' Colt Single Action Army, courtesy U.S. Marshals Museum.
5. Pat Garrett's engraved presentation Colt Model 1877 Double Action.
6. Jesse James attributed Smith & Wesson Schofield.

THE AMERICAN WEST

The Single Action Army

The Colt Single Action Army Model of 1873 is the gun most widely associated with the American West. Also known as the Colt SAA, Model P, Peacemaker, and Frontier Six Shooter (in .44-40 caliber), this revolver was a vast improvement over the old percussion models.

It used a solid frame with a top strap and screwed-in barrel, similar to the Remington percussion revolvers. One cartridge at a time was loaded through a loading gate on the frame at the rear of the cylinder, and empties were punched out individually using a manual ejector rod mounted on the side of the barrel.

The Colt Single Action Army revolver was offered in 36 calibers during its first 50 years of production, with the most common being .45 Colt, .44-40, .38-40, and .32-20. The last three chamberings were developed for Winchester lever-action rifles. Carrying a handgun in the same caliber as one's rifle minimized the types of ammunition that had to be carried. Standard barrel lengths were 7.5-inch, 5.5-inch, and 4.75-inch. The U.S. Ordnance Department began field-testing the revolver in November 1872. These tests resulted in the government awarding Colt an initial contract in 1873 for 8,000 revolvers in .45 caliber for use by the U.S. Cavalry.

Many famous, as well as infamous, persons are associated with this revolver: Buffalo Bill Cody, Wyatt Earp, Billy the Kid, Calamity Jane, and Gen. George Armstrong Custer. An unknown wit made the remark: *"God created man, but Samuel Colt made them equal!"*

1. Colt Model 1871-1872 Open-Top Revolver - .44 Henry rimfire - circa 1871-73 - The first Colt large revolver designed specifically for metallic cartridges retained the open-top design of its percussion predecessors and cartridge conversions.
2. Colt SAA U.S. Military "Cavalry" Model - .45 Colt - circa 1873-92 - Standard U.S. military sidearm with original 7.5" barrel, called "Cavalry Model" by collectors.
3. Colt SAA U.S. Military "Artillery" Model - .45 Colt - circa 1895-1902 - Some U.S. SAA's were refurbished with shortened 5.5" barrels, called "Artillery Models."
4. Colt Bisley Flat-top Target Model - .32-20 - circa 1894-1912 - The Bisley Model featured a longer more vertical grip. Colt offered their "Flat-top Target" version with adjustable rear sight in both standard SAA and Bisley configurations.
5. Colt Frontier Six Shooter - .44-40 - circa 1889-1919 - In .44 WCF, the SAA was marked "Frontier Six Shooter." 4 3/4" barrel.
6. Colt "Sheriff's Model" SAA - .38-40 - Customers could special order SAA's with shorter than standard barrels, with 3" and 4" being most popular. These "Sheriff's Models" were made without ejector rod and ejector rod housing

SIXGUNS

Largely thanks to Hollywood, the Colt Single Action Army is the best known sixgun of the era. However other revolvers were popular as well. Colt's Double Action models included Mod. 1877s and 1878s; similar to the SAA except for the double-action trigger mechanism. The Remington line of revolvers were similar in style to the Colt, although an argument could be made that Colt adopted the Remington percussion revolver pattern with the topstrap.

1. Colt Model 1878 Double Action Revolvers - circa 1878-1909 - Same standard barrel lengths and major calibers as Single Action Army, some short barrel versions made without ejector housings. Factory Engraved.

2. Colt Model 1877 Double Action Revolvers - in .38 Colt called the Lightning Model, in .41 Colt the Thunderer. Made in a variety of barrel lengths with and without ejectors. Factory engraved.

3. Engraved revolvers from the Remington Factory Collection include (top to bottom) Model 1875, Model 1890, and New Model Pocket Conversion revolver.

THE AMERICAN WEST

Smith & Wesson Model 3 Revolvers

Although most think of the Colt as the typical large cartridge revolver of the post-Civil War 19th century, S&W made more than Colt during that period. Whereas the Colt was more rugged, the S&W had a more advanced top break automatic ejecting design that made it much quicker to load. They were popular in the West; sold for military use to the U.S., Russia, Japan, and Turkey; and offered superior accuracy for target shooters. The various models are collectively known as the "Model 3," a designation for the frame size.

1. S&W Second Model American - .44 American - circa 1870-1874 - New York style engraved.
2. S&W 3rd Model Russian Revolver - .44 Russian - circa 1871-1878 - Large orders of the Model 3 by the Russian military included changes such as the triggerguard spur and extreme knuckle on the backstrap. Period scroll engraved.
3. S&W First Model Schofield - .45 Schofield - circa 1876-1877 - Most were made for the U.S. Army. Wells Fargo purchased some as surplus and shortened the barrels, such as this one, serial number 1.
4. S&W New Model Number Three - circa 1873-1910 - Most production was .44 Russian, but this is serial number 1 of a Model chambered for .38-40 (.38 WCF). Only 74 were produced in this series 1900-1907.
5. S&W Double Actions - *Upper:* Frontier Model in .44-40; *lower:* .44 Double Action 1st Model in .44 Russian - circa 1881-1913 - both with L. D. Nimschke attributed engraving.

SIXGUNS

Merwin Hulbert & Co. Revolvers - Large-frame Merwin revolvers competed with S&W, Colt, and Remington. Production has been estimated low, but based on surviving examples may have actually approached or exceeded that of Remington. They were exceptionally well-made at the Hopkins and Allen plant, to tolerances that are difficult to match today. They featured a unique twist-open design in which barrel and cylinder are rotated 90 degrees clockwise and pulled forward from the frame. This design allows selective extraction of fired cases only. Merwin factory engraving was a distinctive punch-dot style. The style was copied by Spanish and Belgian manufacturers.

Early large-frame Merwins had an open top and scoop flutes, as pictured above, replaced in later production by a topstrap attached to the rear of the barrel and standard cylinder flutes as shown at left. The square butt was the Frontier Model *(above)* and the birdshead, or "skullcrusher" butt was the Pocket Army Model *(left)*. The quick take-down made it easy to change barrels with no tools, and the Pocket Army Model was marketed as a two barrel set, with both short and long options *(left)*. A folding hammer spur was available on double-action models. Large frame models were offered in .44 Russian, .44 Merwin, and .44 WCF (.44-40) calibers. Merwin style revolvers were made from 1876 to 1916.

In addition to .44 cal. large frame, Merwins were offered in medium frame in .32 or .38 S&W and small frame in 32 S&W, with mechanical operation identical to the larger models. A .22 rimfire Baby Merwin was also offered *(not pictured)* which was a close copy of the S&W Model One tip-up.

THE AMERICAN WEST

The Large Handguns of the Old West

The solid-frame single-action design of the Colt and Remington and the top-break design of Smith & Wesson were not the only sixguns in the West. Unusual revolvers from the U.S. and abroad found a market west of the Mississippi.

1. Remington Model 1867 Rolling Block Single-Shot Pistol - .50 centerfire - circa 1867 - This type of pistol was purchased by the U.S. Army and the U.S. Navy after the Civil War.
2. Galand Revolver - .38 Galand - circa 1868-1870 - Unusual European design. Pivoting the trigger guard down and forward pushes barrel and cylinder forward for unloading.
3. Galand-Somerville Revolver - .450 Eley - circa 1868-1870 - Made in England.
4. Enfield Model 1884 Revolver - .476 Enfield - circa 1884 - A heavy hinged-frame revolver, the cumbersome Enfield Mk II revolver relied on an awkward forward-sliding movement for cylinder extraction. Despite these faults, it was selected by the Royal Canadian Mounted Police for issue.
5. VK Belgian Single-Action Revolver - .44 S&W - circa 1880-1890 - The Smith & Wesson top-break design was widely copied in Belgium, Spain, and elsewhere, making it the predominant large-frame revolver design of the late 19th century.
6. Belgian Revolver - .45 caliber - circa 1880-1890 - Loosely based on the S&W .44 Double Action.
7. P. Webley & Son British Metropolitan Police Revolver - .450 Eley - circa 1890-1900 - Webley in England turned out large numbers of rugged top-break and solid-frame double-action revolvers.
8. Hopkins & Allen XL No. 8 Single Action Revolver - .44 centerfire - circa late 1870s to early 1880s - One of the best made H&A revolvers, only a few hundred were produced.

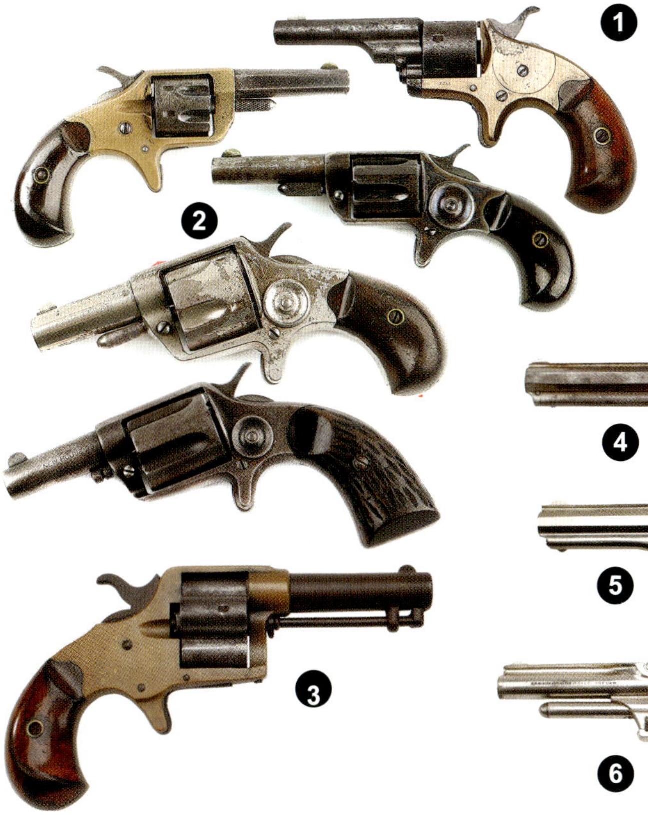

POCKET PISTOLS

Pocket Pistols

Despite Hollywood and TV westerns, the most popular revolver of this era was not the full-size, big-bore "hogleg" six shooter, but rather more compact medium- and small-frame guns. Most popular calibers were .22 and .32 rimfire, and .32 and .38 centerfire. They cost less and were much handier to carry. Many towns prohibited open carry of handguns, and the smaller models could be easily concealed. They are, in fact, sometimes called "pocket pistols."

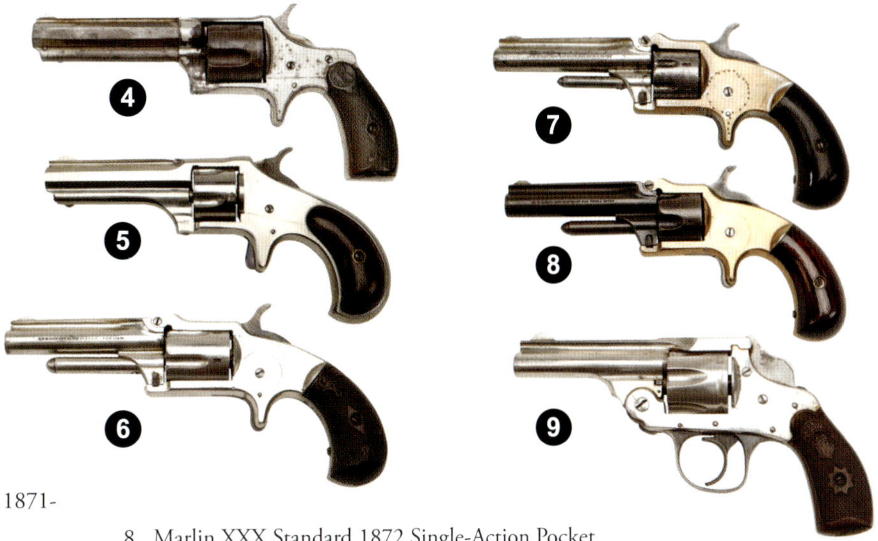

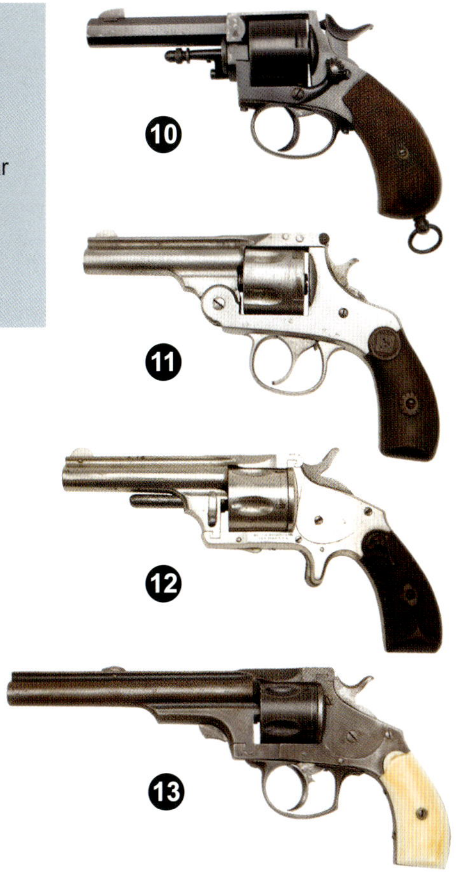

1. Colt Open-Top Pocket Model - .22 rimfire - circa 1871-1877.
2. Colt New Line Revolvers - shown here (top to bottom) in .22, .32, .41, and .38 chamberings - circa 1873-1884.
3. Colt House Model Revolver - .41 rimfire - circa 1871-1876 - The 4-shot model is called the "Cloverleaf due to the 4 lobe cross-section of its cylinder.
4. Remington-Smoot New Model No. 1 Single-Action Revolver - .30 rimfire short - circa 1875-1877 - Around 64,000 Remington spur-trigger small-frame revolvers were produced from 1875 to 1888.
5. Remington-Smoot New Model No. 3 Single-Action Revolver - .38 rimfire - circa 1878-1888.
6. Marlin No. 32 Standard 1875 Single-Action Pocket Revolver - .32 rimfire - circa 1875-1887.
7. Marlin XX Standard 1873 Pocket Revolver - .22 rimfire - circa 1873-1887 - Approximately 10,000 made.
8. Marlin XXX Standard 1872 Single-Action Pocket Revolver - .30 rimfire - circa 1872-1887.
9. Forehand & Wadsworth Model 1890 Hammerless Top-Break Double-Action Pocket Revolver - .38 S&W - circa 1890.
10. Spanish Revolver - 9mm - circa 1885-1900 - Copy of a British Webley with manual safety.
11. Harrington & Richardson Double-Action Pocket Revolver - .32 S&W - circa 1880-1883.
12. Merwin Hulbert & Co. Single-Action Pocket Revolver - .38 S&W - circa 1876-1883.
13. H. Remy Spanish Copy of Merwin Hulbert Double-Action - .38 S&W - circa 1880-1890 - The Merwin pattern was copied in Spain and elsewhere.

Forehand & Wadsworth Swamp Angel - .41 rimfire - circa 1870s.

THE AMERICAN WEST

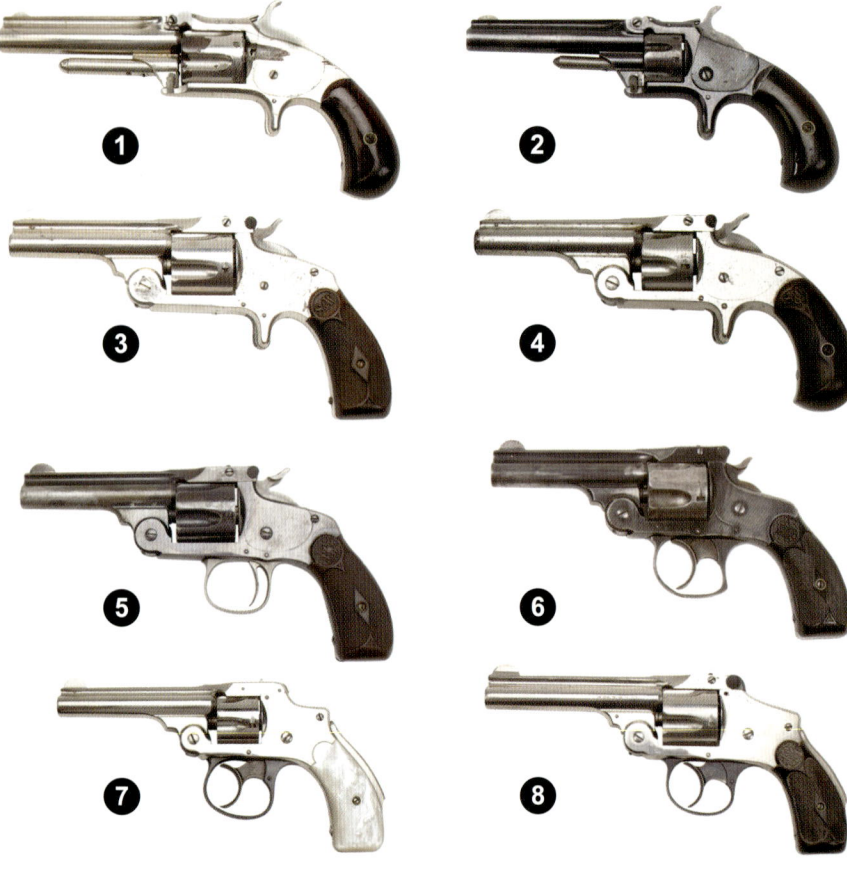

1. Smith & Wesson Model 1 1/2 Second Issue Single-Action Revolver - .32 rimfire - circa 1868-1875 - This model was introduced after S&W was already making a small .22 caliber Model One and a larger six-shot .32 Model Two. Accordingly, this in-between size five-shot .32 wound up with the ungainly moniker, "Model One and a Half."

2. Smith & Wesson Model One, Third Issue, Single-Action Revolver - .22 short - circa 1868-1881 - Third Issue of the Model One is identified by birdshead butt, fluted cylinder, and round ribbed barrel.

3. Smith & Wesson 38 Single-Action Second Model Revolver - .38 S&W - circa 1877-1891 - Around 160,000 .38 SAs were made; the majority were this Second Model configuration.

4. Smith & Wesson .32 Single Action Revolver - .32 S&W - circa 1878-1892 - Nearly 100,000 were made.

5. Smith & Wesson .38 Single-Action Third Model Revolver - .38 S&W - circa 1891-1911.

6. Gen. Leonard Wood's Smith & Wesson .38 Double Action Revolver - .38 S&W - circa 1880-1911 - Wood was Roosevelt's commander in the Rough Riders and he went on to lead the U.S. Army in the Philippines.

7. Smith & Wesson .32 Safety Hammerless First Model Revolver - .32 S&W - circa 1888-1902 - Production of the .32 Safety Hammerless continued until 1937 through two more model variations; nearly 250,000 were made. The Safety Hammerless were also called the "New Departure, and nicknamed the "Lemonsqueezer" due to their grip safety.

8. Smith & Wesson .38 Safety Hammerless Fifth Model Revolver - .38 S&W - Production of five models from 1887 through 1940, with over 250,000 made.

S&W .38 Safety Hammerless attributed to Theodore Roosevelt

S&W Small-Frame Revolvers

Smith & Wesson small-frame revolvers can be grouped into four types. The earliest "tip-ups" (1857-1881) were spur-trigger revolvers in .22 or .32 rimfire with barrels that tipped up allowing the cylinder to be removed for loading or unloading.

The single-action small frames (1878-1892) mostly had spur-triggers as well. These were top-break revolvers, where the barrel and cylinder tipped down, and cartridge cases were automatically ejected.

The double-action small frames (1880-1919) were also top breaks but with traditional triggerguards.

The Safety Hammerless models (1887-1940) were double-action top breaks as well, but with hammers fully enclosed by the frame so they could be fired double-action only, and a grip safety on the backstrap.

All the top-break variations were offered in .32 S&W and .38 S&W only.

Mark Twain on the S&W Model One

While on a train trip Mark Twain wrote, *"I was armed to the teeth with a pitiful little Smith & Wessons seven-shooter, which carried a ball like a homeopathic pill, and it took the whole seven to make a dose for an adult. But I thought it was grand. It appeared to me to be a dangerous weapon. It had only one fault - you could not hit anything with it. One of our conductors practiced a while on a cow with it, and as long as she stood still and behaved herself she was safe; but as soon as she went to moving about, and he got to shooting at other things, she came to grief."*

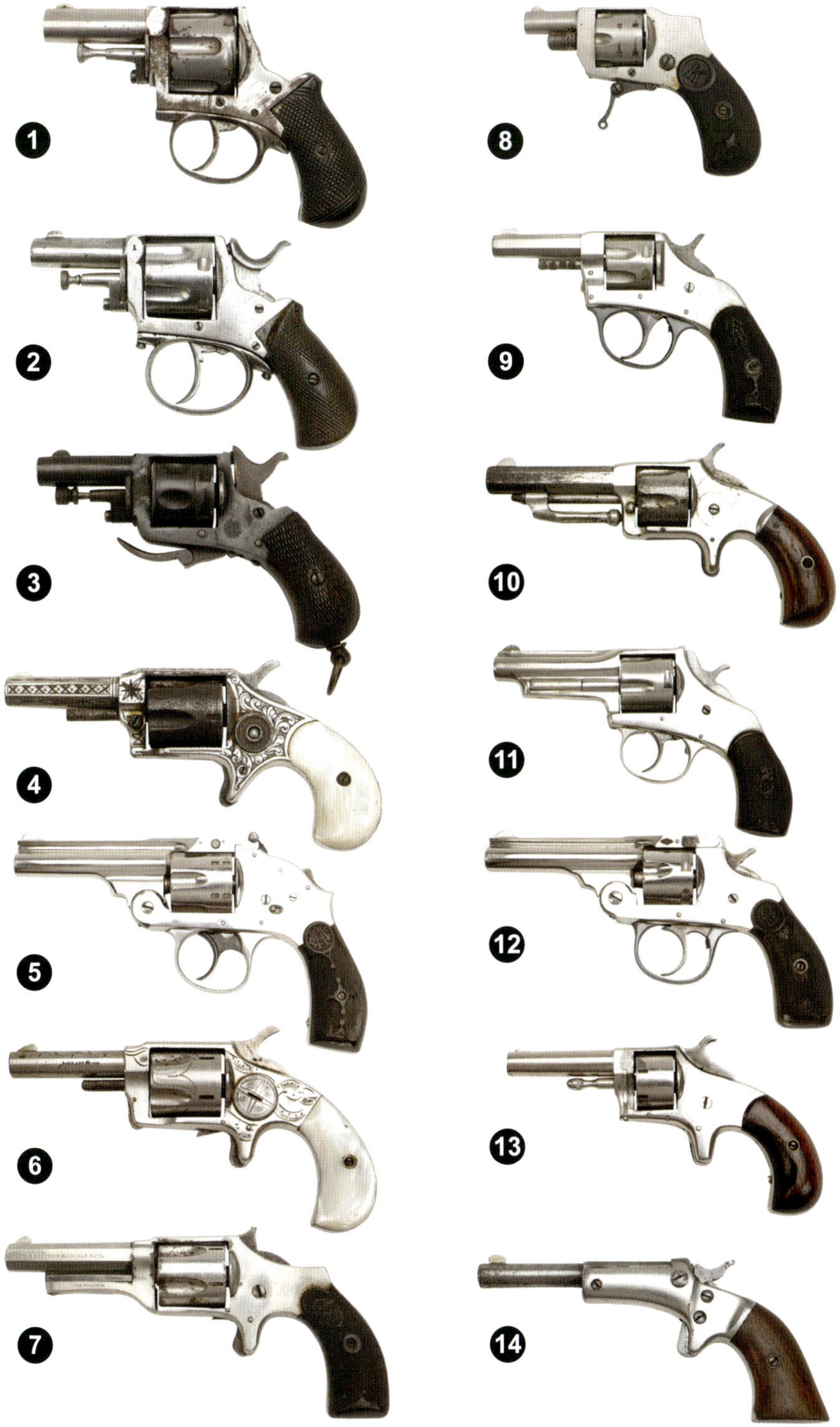

POCKET PISTOLS

1. Belgian British Bulldog Revolver - .38 S&W - circa 1872-1890 - Lt. Col. George Armstrong Custer may have carried a pair of Webley Bulldog revolvers similar to this one with him on his ill-fated Black Hills Expedition in 1876.
2. Belgian Bulldog Revolver - .32 cartridge - circa 1872-1890.
3. German Velo-Dog Revolver - 5mm Velo-Dog - circa 1880-1900 - Velo-dog is a term used for a type of small inexpensive European revolver with folding trigger, usually hammerless, and often chambered for the 5mm Velo-dog centerfire cartridge. Velo is from velocipede, an early term for bicycles. The guns were marketed as ideal for a cyclist's defense against stray canines offended by the new-fangled bicycle.
4. Red Jacket No. 3 Spur-Trigger Revolver - .30 rimfire - circa 1890-1900.
5. American Arms New Safety Hammerless Revolver - circa 1890-1900.
6. Prescott Pistol Co. Crescent Revolver - .30 rimfire - circa 1873-1875.
7. C.S. Shattuck Single-Action Revolver - circa 1880-1900.
8. Henry M. Kolb Baby Hammerless Revolver - .22 rimfire - circa 1900.
9. Harrington & Richardson Young America Revolver - .22 rimfire - circa 1884-1941.
10. Wesson & Harrington No. 3 Rod Ejection Single-Action Revolver - circa 1874-1879.
11. Iver Johnson Model 1879 Revolver - circa 1878-1882 - The Iver Johnson firm also produced bicycles.
12. Iver Johnson Safety Hammer Revolver - circa 1908 - An Iver Johnson revolver of the same model and caliber was used by Leon Czolgosz to assassinate President William McKinley in 1901.
13. U.S. Blue Jacket No. 1 Single-Action Revolver - circa 1890-1900.
14. Stevens No. 41 Tip-Up Single-Shot Pocket Pistol - circa 1864-1916.

Brooklyn Arms Company Slocum Revolver - .32 rimfire - circa 1864 - To circumvent the S&W Rollin White patent, the Slocum used sliding chambers to load the cylinder.

THE AMERICAN WEST

Derringers

Compact single-shot or multi-barrel pistols designed for concealment and personal defensive use at close range picked up the designation "derringer" from the tiny percussion pistols made by Henry Deringer of Philadelphia. These served as hideout guns in gentlemen's vest pockets, ladies' muffs, or up gamblers' sleeves.

1. Remington .41 rimfire derringers - *top to bottom* - Double Derringer, circa 1866-1935, factory engraved. Vest Pocket Pistol, circa 1865-88, factory engraved. Remington-Elliott Derringer, circa 1897-1888.
2. Single shot derringers - *top to bottom* - Frank Wesson Model 1859 Pistol - .30 rimfire - circa 1859. Allen & Wheelock Center Hammer Pistol, .32 rimfire - circa. early 1860s. Brown Southerner - .41 rimfire - circa 1869.
3. Colt First and Second Model derringers. These .41 rimfire pistols were made from 1870-1890.
4. Largest and smallest cartridge derringers of the era - *top* - Connecticut Arms Hammond Bulldog - .44 rimfire - circa 1866-1880. Heavy at 24 oz. *Bottom* - Hopkins & Allen Vest Pocket Derringer - .22 rimfire - 1911-1915

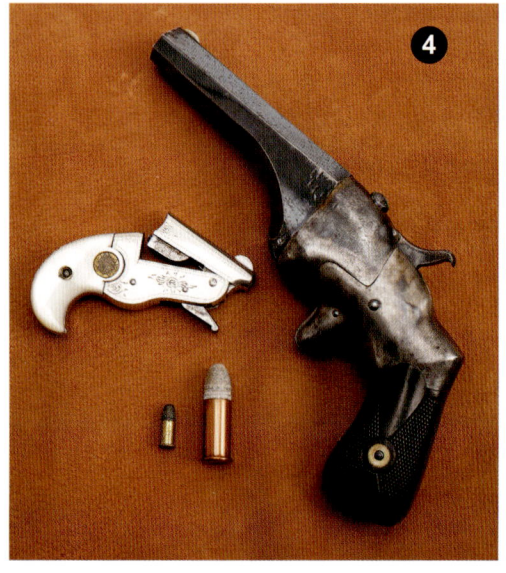

DERRINGERS & CURIOSA

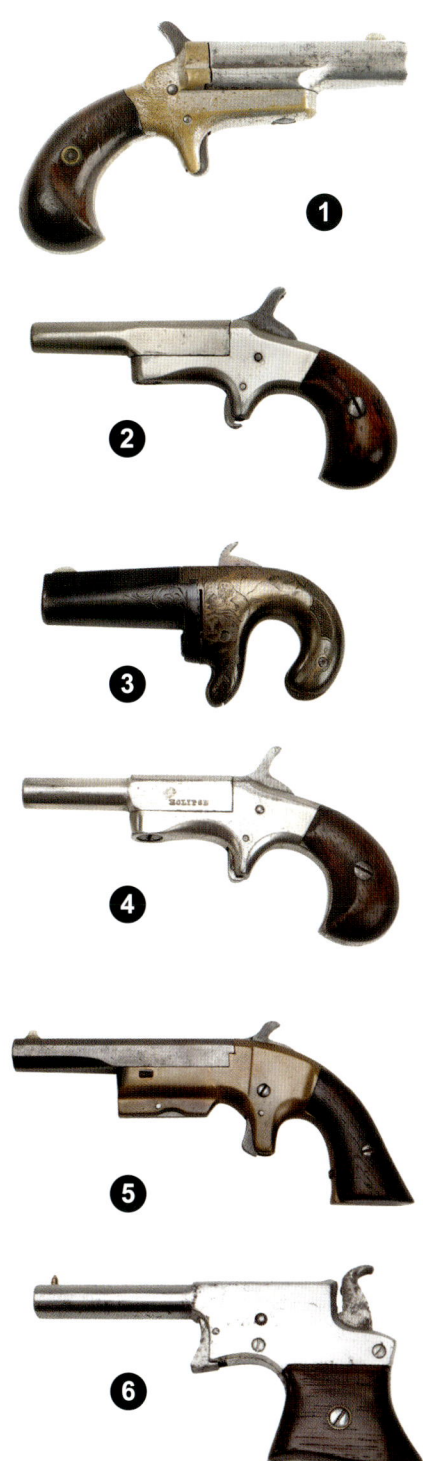

1. Colt 3rd Model Derringer - .41 rimfire - circa 1870-1912.
2. E. Allen & Co. Vest Pocket Derringer - .22 rimfire - circa 1869-1871.
3. Moore's Patent Firearms Co. No. 1 Derringer - .41 rimfire - circa 1860-1865.
4. Eclipse Single-Shot Pistol - .22 rimfire - circa 1870-1887.
5. L. B. Taylor & Co. Single-Shot Pocket Pistol - .32 rimfire - circa 1868-1870.
6. Remington Vest Pocket Pistol - .22 rimfire - circa 1865-1888.
7. Remington Double Derringers - .41 rimfire - circa 1866-1935 - with wrist holster. The archetypical derringer, 150,000 were made. The cartridge only delivered 500 fps muzzle velocity.
8. Frank Wesson Superposed with sliding bayonet - .41 rimfire - circa 1868-1880.
9. American Arms Derringer .22/32 rimfire - circa 1866-1875 - Barrels swivel for 2nd shot.
10. Marston Three Barrel Derringer - .32 rimfire - circa 1865-1872 - Barrel to be fired is selected with switch on right side of frame..

THE AMERICAN WEST

1. Charles Lancaster Four-Barrel Pistol - .455 centerfire - circa 1880.
2. Sharps & Hankins Model 3B pistol - .32 rimfire - circa 1959-1874.
3. Sharps Breechloading Four-Shot Pepperbox Pistol - .22 rimfire - circa 1859-1874. Four stationary barrels with a rotating firing pin on the hammer.
4. Remington-Elliot Derringer - .22 rimfire - circa 1863-1870s.
5. Remington-Elliot Derringer - .32 rimfire - circa 1863-1875. Four fixed barrels with a rotating firing pin.
6. Continental Arms Co. Pepperbox - .22 rimfire - circa late 1860s.

Remington-Rider Magazine Pistol - .32 extra short rimfire - circa 1871-1888. Five shot tubular magazine underneath the barrel.

Collette System Gravity Feed Repeater - 11mm - as displayed at 1855 Paris Exhibition. Open sided tubular magazine above the barrel. Muzzle is raised to feed the next self-contained rocket ball type round. Considered a low powered parlor pistol for indoor practice and recreational shooting.

System Noel Pill-lock Twelve-Shot Pill Lock Turret Pistol. - 7.5mm - circa 1870.

Frankenau's Patent Purse Gun - 5.5mm pinfire - circa 1880.

DERRINGERS & CURIOSA

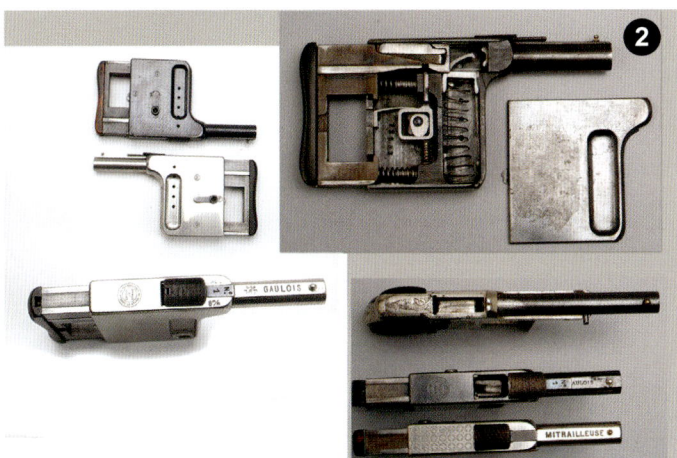

Curiosa

The last half of the 19th century saw production of a number of unusual designs, including hideout or disguised firearms.

1. Early pocket-concealable handguns came in many forms. The simplest that could be fitted into one's palm utilized a squeezing action to discharge and advance to the next cartridge.
2. The French Gaulois, possibly taking its name from the cigarette, was offered in a rectangular format, with its 8mm cartridges held inside a spring-loaded magazine. The Mitrailleuse was similar. Carrying containers resembled cigarette cases so as to not attract attention. Circa 1890s.
3. Minneapolis Firearms Co. Palm Pistol - .32 short centerfire - circa 1891-1892 - The seven chambered rotary disc magazine required disassembly for loading/unloading. The slightly larger Chicago Firearms Protector palm pistol offered eight rounds in a similar "hand"-gun.
4. Retailed by firms across Europe, the French 7.6mm "Apache" designed by Louis Dolne, offered a triple threat: revolver, brass knuckles, and dagger all in one. Its name came from association with 1890s French underworld gangs.
5. Different types of Apache pinfire revolvers with knucks and daggers deployed and ready for use.

THE AMERICAN WEST

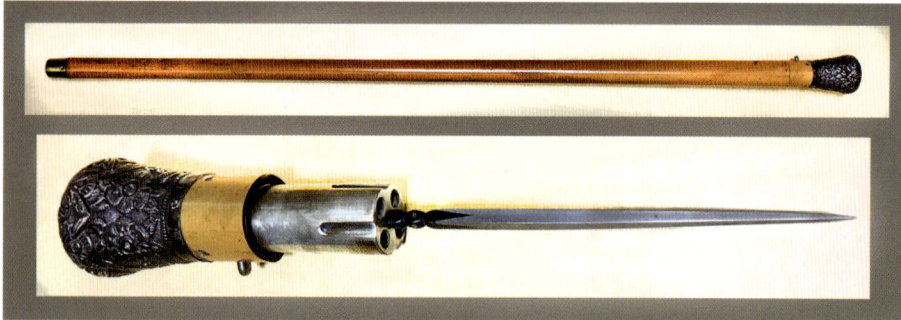

Above: Four-shot pepperbox cane pistol, with dagger.

Below: Numerous types of folding knife pistols were made in the late 19th and early 20th centuries in both percussion and cartridge configurations. The Unwin and Rodgers on left had slots in the handle that held a ramrod and a bullet mold.

1. C.S. Shattuck Arms Unique Palm Pistol - .22 rimfire - circa 1907-1915. Four shots, held in palm and squeezed to fire.
2. Montlahuc & de Bastid Palm Pistol - .22 rimfire - circa 1890.
3. Tribuzio Ring Trigger Pistol - 8mm - circa 1890. When loaded and ready, this pistol is the size and shape of a cigarette pack or deck of cards. As each shot is fired, the barrel cluster rises to bring the next round in line with the firing pin.
4. James Reid "My Friend" Knuckle Duster Revolver - .22 rimfire - circa 1865-1877 - The grip doubles as impromptu brass knuckles, made in .22, .32, and .41 rimfire chamberings. Most had no barrel and fired directly from the front of the cylinder chambers.
5. James Reid New Model Knuckle-Duster - .32 rimfire - circa 1883. This slightly later version is in the form of a revolver rather than a pepperbox.

At left: **Knife pistols.** Blades attached to a percussion pistol provided a viable weapon after the single shot was fired without having to go through a time-consuming reloading process. Folding bayonets, often spring-loaded for deployment, were not uncommon on European pinfire revolvers in the 2nd half of the 19th century.

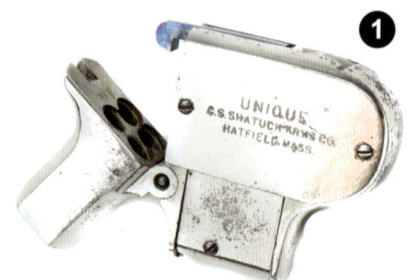

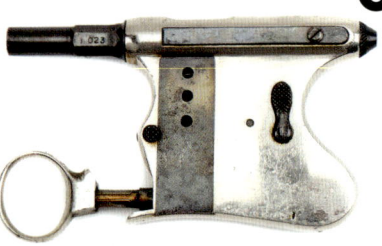

DERRINGERS & CURIOSA

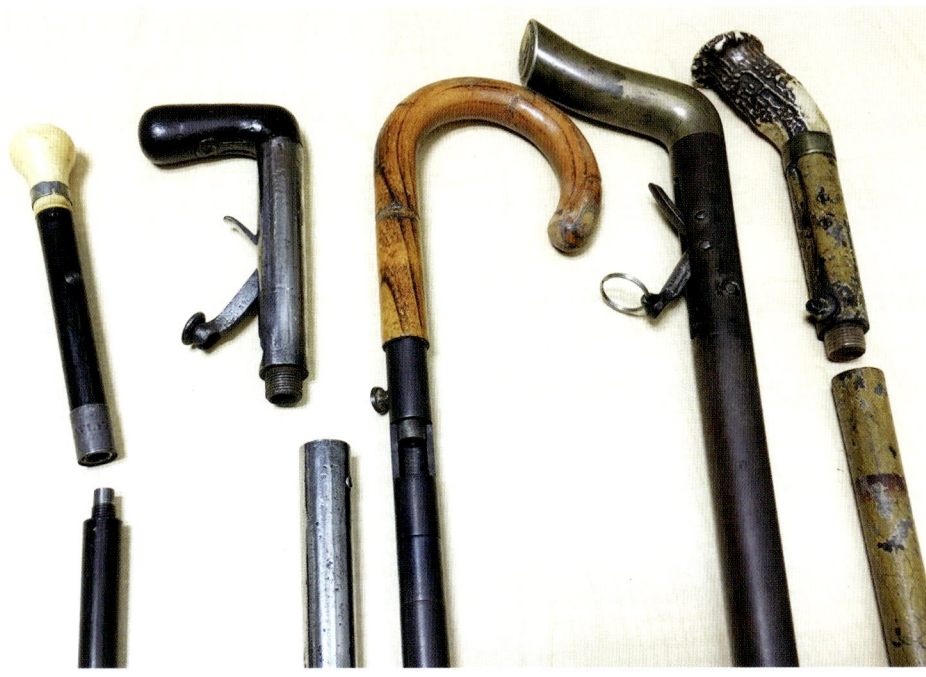

Cane guns

During the Victorian Era, a cane was a common fashion accessory for the well-dressed gentleman. Perhaps not surprisingly, cane guns came into favor as a discreet means of self-defense while out and about. Custom made cane guns are still available today. They are treated as Class III NFA firearms and must be registered with the BATFE.

Probably the best known cane guns were those produced by E. Remington & Sons. These were offered with plain, dogshead, or duckshead *(as at right)* handles. in percussion, .22 rimfire, or .32 rimfire chamberings, produced 1858-1888.

The three pictures at left show views of five different cane guns, disassembled, assembled, and from the muzzle. The 2nd and 4th show the cocked percussion mechanism

At bottom is a take-down large caliber cane air gun. It is cased with a hand pump and handle that are used to charge the air reservoir.

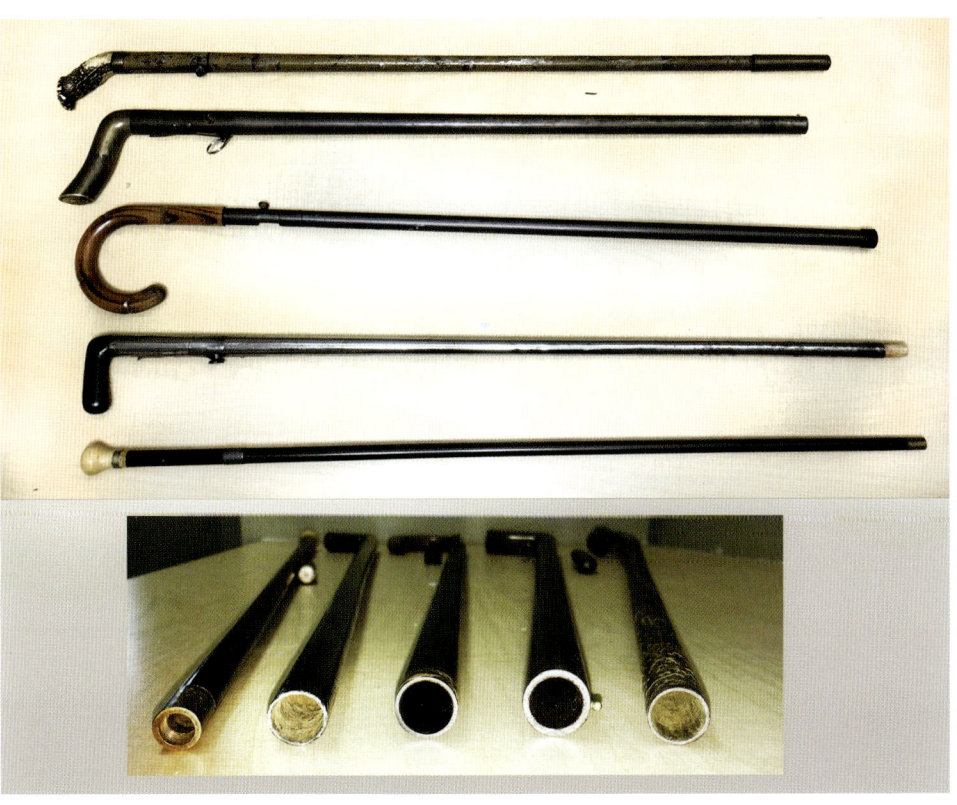

THE AMERICAN WEST

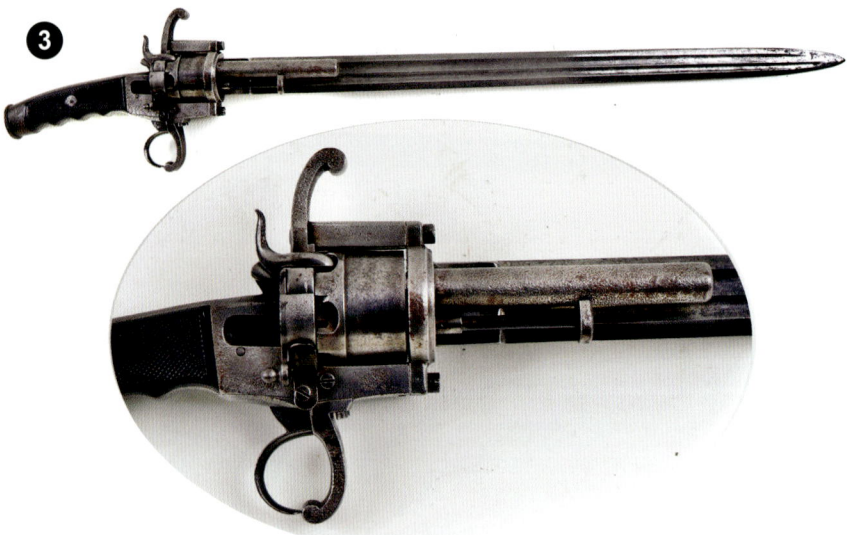

1. Day's Patent Truncheon Pistol - circa 1830s - Combines the constable's (usually) less-than-lethal baton with a percussion blunderbuss. As with many percussion cane guns, cocking the button hammer releases the trigger to lower into place.
2. Blade-barrel Pinfire Revolver - Most knife revolvers have a separate blade attached to the firearm. On this folding trigger pinfire, the blade is a forged extension integral with the barrel.
3. Pinfire Sword Pistol.
4. Single shot Percussion Whip Pistol. The whip is attached to a barrel plug which is removed for firing. Inset shows the plug removed and the button hammer cocked with drop down trigger deployed, ready to shoot.
5. Quirt Pistol. As with the whip pistol, plug is removed from the barrel for firing.
6. Little All Right Revolver - .22 Short - patented 1876 - The trigger folds up from top of barrel. It's fired from inside the shooter's closed fist, risking injury from cylinder gap splatter.
7. Novo folding revolver - 6.35mm - circa 1890s - The grip folds to wrap around the frame and cylinder for compact carry, with a folding trigger.

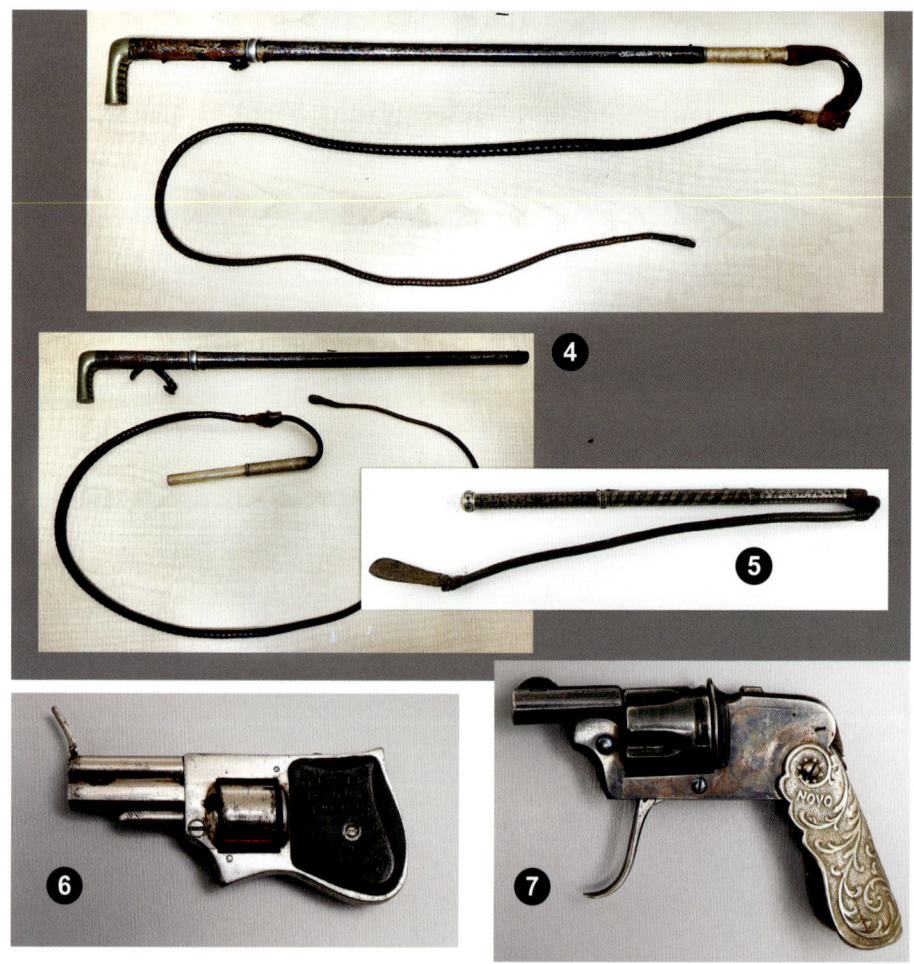

DERRINGERS & CURIOSA

Trap and alarm guns

Animal trap guns, alarm guns, spring guns, and booby trap guns have in common the disconcerting (and today highly illegal) characteristic of firing on their own when their trigger is tripped without a shooter's presence to confirm the legitimacy of the target. They were used for killing pest animals, harvesting furs, or sounding an intrusion alarm (or shooting an intruder!) The potential for tragic unintended consequences is obvious.

1. North & Couch animal trap gun - .31 caliber - circa 1890s - Six-shot percussion pepperbox fires all barrels when a baited string attached to the muzzle is pulled. Reportedly used in Australia for kangaroo control.
2. Reiff & McDowell - .22 blank rimfire alarm gun - circa 1900.
3. S. Coon Door Jamb Alarm Pistol - .28 cal. percussion - circa 1860s.
4. F. Reuthe Double-barrel Percussion Trap Gun - .44 percussion - circa 1860s. Bait is attached to the hooks. When the bait is pulled, both barrels fire.
5. Brass Cannon-Barrel Alarm Gun - 12 gauge pinfire blank - circa 1880s.
6. Never-Fail gopher trap gun - circa 1922 - Set at the entrance to a burrow, when the brass plate is pushed a .38 S&W blank is fired into the varmint's belly.
7. Taylor Fur Getter .22 rimfire - circa 1920s - The stake can be pressed into the ground. When the baited hook is pulled, the round is fired into the furbearer.

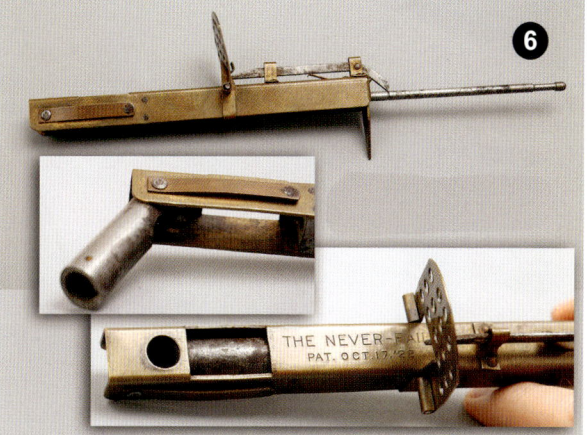

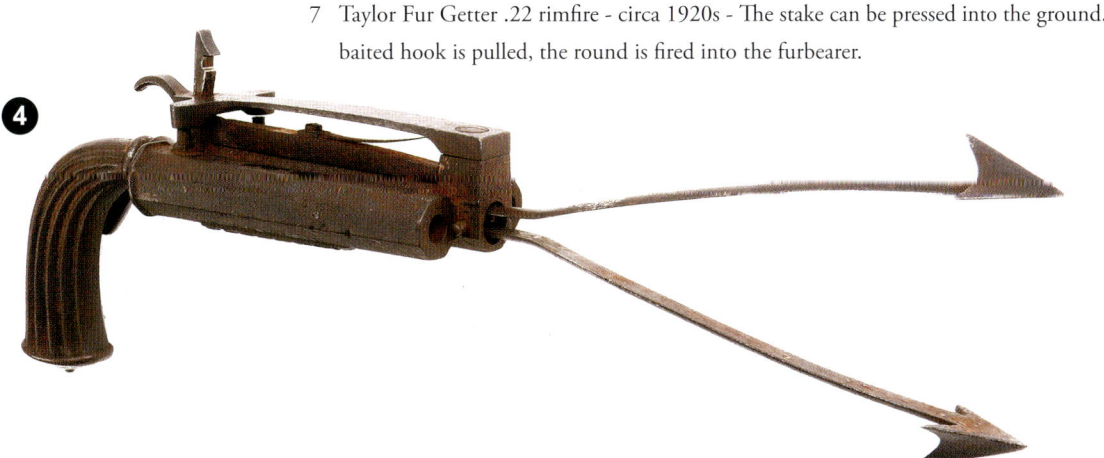

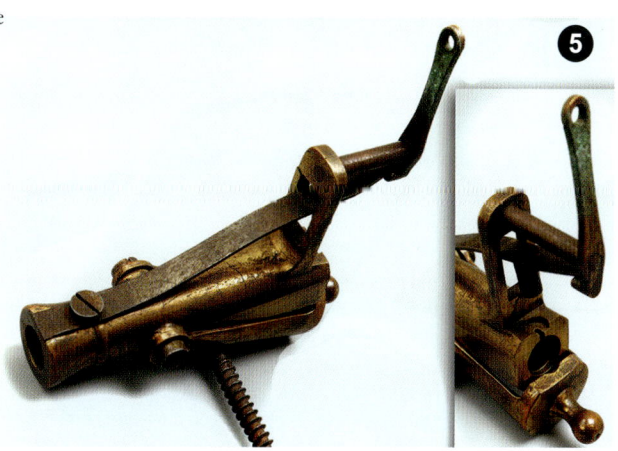

THE AMERICAN WEST

The Lever-Action Rifle

Just as the Colt Single Action Army is considered the handgun of the Old West, the Winchester lever-action rifle is the iconic Old West long gun. Early predecessors included the Hunt, Jennings, and Volcanic rifles.

The 15-shot Henry was the first truly successful lever-action repeating rifle. It was patented by B. Tyler Henry in 1860, and earned its laurels on the battlefields of the Civil War. It was known to Confederates as **"that Yankee rifle you load on Sunday and shoot all week."**

Oliver F. Winchester purchased Henry's company and the patent rights for this unique firearm. In May 1866, he changed the name of the firm from the New Haven Arms Company to the Winchester Repeating Arms Company, thus beginning a long history of legendary firearms.

The Model 1866 Winchester boasted a number of important improvements, principally in the method of loading and ejecting cartridges and in the adoption of a side-frame loading gate. Attempts to market the gun to the federal government failed, but sales to foreign countries flourished.

Improved models based on this design were developed and offered for sale in 1873, 1876, 1886, 1892, 1894, and 1895. These various models gave the public a wide variety of choices, and Winchester lever-action rifles became legendary throughout the United States and the world. The Model 1873 was immortalized in the Hollywood film *Winchester '73* starring James Stewart. The most popular has been the Model 1894, considered America's deer rifle and an iconic presence both in saddle scabbards and pickup truck gun racks well through the mid-20th century, with a total of over six million produced.

1. Jennings by Robbins & Lawrence Rifle - .54 rocket ball - circa 1848-1853 - The Jennings is considered the great-grandfather of the Winchester. Firearms design titans Tyler Henry, Horace Smith, and Daniel Wesson participated in its development. Although a repeater was made, this example is a single-shot and has been "back converted" to percussion. This was to make it usable when the supply of rapidly discontinued proprietary "rocket ball" ammunition dried up.

2. New Haven Arms Company Volcanic Rifle - .41 rocket ball - circa 1857 - Smith & Wesson introduced this lever-action magazine rifle, which was nicknamed "The Volcanic." It was then made by Volcanic Repeating Arms and then by New Haven Arms Company. The rocket-ball ammo had the gunpowder and primer loaded in the base of the hollow bullet.

3. Henry Lever-Action Rifle by New Haven Arms Co. - .44 Henry RF - circa 1860-1866 - Approx. 14,000 were made. It is easily identified by its brass frame and lack of wooden forend. The tubular magazine under the barrel is loaded from the front. The Henry lacks the loading gate of later Winchester lever-actions.

4. Winchester Model 1866 Third Model Lever-Action Carbine - .44 rimfire - circa 1866-1898 - The first true Winchester, known on the Western frontier as the "Yellowboy" for its brass receiver. The first lever-action with a loading gate in the frame; over 170,000 were made.

LEVER-ACTIONS

1. Winchester Model 1866 Lever-Action Rifle - .44 Henry RF - circa 1866-1898.
2. Winchester Model 1873 Lever-Action Rifle - .38-40 - circa 1873-1919.
3. Winchester Model 1876 Lever-Action Rifle - .45-60 - circa 1876-1897.
4. Winchester Model 1886 Lever-Action Rifle, Deluxe Grade - .45-90 - circa 1886-1935 - Special octagonal barrel, and factory single-set trigger.
5. Winchester Model 1892 Rifle - .32-20 - circa 1892-1941.
6. Winchester Model 1894 Rifle - .30-30 - circa 1894-Present.
7. Winchester Model 1895 Lever-Action Rifle - .30-40 Krag - circa 1896-1931.

Winchester Lever-actions
The major models, top to bottom:
MODEL 1866 - 170,000 made 1866-1898. .44 rimfire. Brass frame with loading gate. Yellowboy.
MODEL 1873 - 720,000 made 1873-1919. Relatively low power cartridges, .44-40 (44 WCF), .38-40 (38 WCF), .32-20 (32 WCF). Colt and others made revolvers for the same cartridges. Medium frame with irregularly shaped flat sideplate. The gun that won the West.
MODEL 1876 - 64,000 made 1876-1897. Heavy black powder rifle cartridges 40-60, 45-60, 45-75, and 50-95. Large frame with irregularly shaped flat sideplate.
MODEL 1886 - 160,000 made 1886-1935. Various rifle cartridges from 33 WCF through 50-110 Express. Improved large frame; solid frame (no sideplate) oval loading gate.
MODEL 1892 - Over one million made from 1892 to 1941. Same 44, 38, and 32 WCF calibers as Model 1873, plus .25-20. Light handy solid-frame gun in pistol calibers, identified by distinctive half-oval loading gate with straight front edge. A staple of early Hollywood westerns, even when an anachronism.
MODEL 1894 - Over six million made from 1894 to 2006. The first design made for smokeless powder, in a variety of calibers with the classic being .30-30. Medium solid frame, oval loading port.
MODEL 1895 - 425,000 made 1896-1931. Previous models all had tube magazines. The distinctive box mag of the 1895 allowed it to be chambered for high-powered rifle cartridges with pointed spitzer bullet, in the .30-06 class up to .405 Winchester.

THE AMERICAN WEST

LEVER-ACTIONS

1. Winchester Model 1866 Third Model Musket - .44 Henry RF - circa 1866-1898.
2. Winchester Model 1873 Carbine - .44-40 - circa 1873-1919.
3. Winchester Model 1873 Rifle - .32-20 - circa 1873-1919 - Deluxe pistol grip stock, made in 1884, British proofs.
4. Winchester Model 1873 Rifle - circa 1873-1919.
5. Winchester Model 1876 Rifle - .40-60 - circa 1876-1897.
6. Winchester Model 1886 Rifle - .38-56 - circa 1886-1935 - Nonstandard short barrel and "button" half mag.
7. Winchester Model 1886 Light Weight Rifle - .33 - circa 1886-1935 - The Light Weight Model features a fast taper 22-inch barrel and half mag.
8. Winchester Model 1886 Deluxe Rifle - .50-110 Express - circa 1886-1935 - High-grade wood, checkering, Three folding leaf express rear sight. Most powerful chambering for an 1886.
9. Winchester Model 1886 Rifle - .45-90 - circa 1886-1935 - Western hunters called this model, in .45-90, the "Grizzly bear rifle."
10. Winchester Model 1892 Rifle - .44-40 - circa 1892-1941.
11. Winchester Model 1894 Carbine - .38-55 - circa 1892-1941.
12. Winchester Model 1894 Rifle - .25-35 - circa 1894-Present.
13. Winchester Model 1895 NRA Musket - .30-40 - circa 1903-1906 - Rare variation made for NRA military rifle competition matches
14. Winchester Model 1895 Carbine - .30-06 - circa 1896-1931.
15. Townsend Whelen's Winchester Model 1895 Rifle - .40-72 Winchester - circa 1902 - Noted arms writer and shooter Colonel Townsend Whelen carried this lever-action rifle on hunting trips to British Columbia and South Africa.

Winchester Model 1892 Lever-Action Rifle - .25-20 - circa 1892-1941 - Takedown model.

Most Winchester lever-action rifles were offered in three configurations - carbine, rifle, and musket. Typical standard barrel lengths might be 20" (carbine), 24" (rifle), and 27" (musket). Custom features such as non-standard sights or deluxe wood were generally available on special order. Some could be had as takedown models for ease of storage or transport.

A Chancy Shot by Harry C. Edwards.

THE AMERICAN WEST

Marlin Lever-Action Rifles

The Marlin Firearms Company was founded by former Colt employee John Mahlon Marlin in 1863. The company's first products were handguns and single-shot rifles. In 1881, the company began manufacturing lever-action repeating rifles. Its product line grew to become Winchester's primary competition in that field.

1. Marlin Model 1881 Lever-Action Rifle, Second Style - .45-70 - circa 1881-1892 - 20,000 made. Competitive with the Winchester Model 1876.
2. Marlin Model 1892 Lever-Action Rifle - .32 centerfire/rimfire - circa 1895-1916 - 45,000 made. Wide-firing pin allows the use of either rimfire or centerfire cartridges.
3. Marlin Model 1893 Lever-Action Rifle - .30-30 - circa 1893-1935 - Around one million made, in calibers ranging from .25-36 to .38-55. This was the first Marlin lever-action rifle model to utilize smokeless powder cartridges.
4. Marlin Model 1894 Lever-Action Rifle - .32-20 - circa 1894-1935 - 250,000 made, in the same "pistol class" cartridges as the Winchester 1892.
5. Marlin Model 1897 Lever-Action Rifle - .22 long rifle - circa 1897-1917 - 125,000 made, all in takedown configuration.

One Down - Robert Wesley Amick

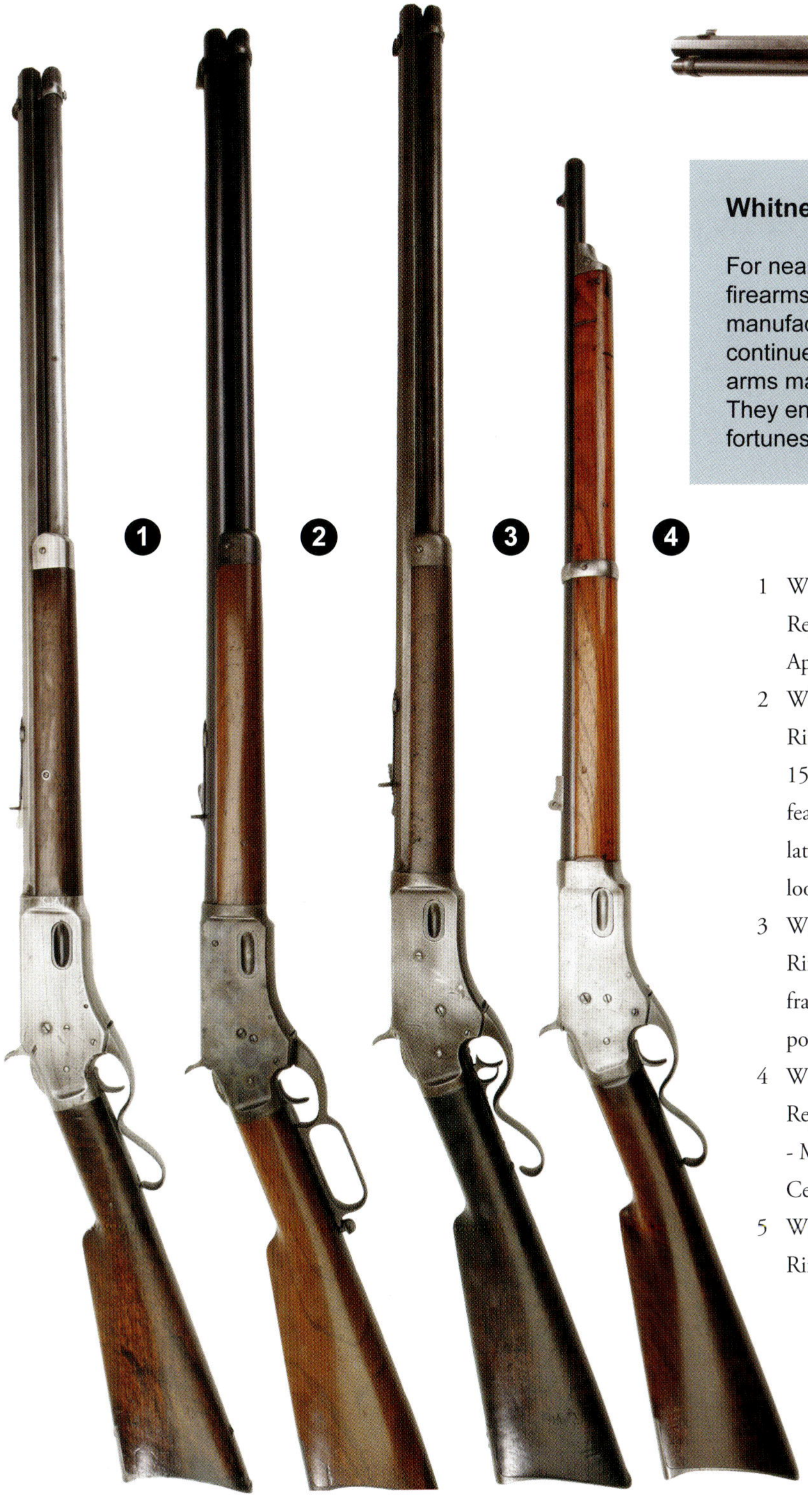

LEVER-ACTIONS

Whitney Repeating Rifles

For nearly a century, Whitney was a major force in American firearms manufacturing. Cotton gin inventor Eli Whitney began manufacturing firearms for the U.S. military in 1798, and continued in that role through the Civil War, in addition to civilian arms manufacture. By that time Eli Whitney, Jr., headed the firm. They entered the lever-action repeater field in 1878, but the firm's fortunes were fading. They were acquired by Winchester in 1888.

1. Whitney-Burgess-Morse Lever-Action Repeating Rifle - .45-70 - circa 1878-1882 - Approximately 3,000 made.
2. Whitney-Kennedy Lever-Action Repeating Rifle - .40-60 - circa 1879-1886 - Approx. 15,000 made. Most Whitney repeaters featured their distinctive S lever, but some later examples were made with the traditional loop, such as this.
3. Whitney-Kennedy Lever-Action Sporting Rifle - .44-40 - circa 1879-1886 - A smaller frame variation, chambered for the less powerful .44, .38, and .32 WCF rounds.
4. Whitney-Burgess-Kennedy Lever-Action Repeating Musket - .45-70 - circa 1878-1882 - Most Whitney repeating muskets went to Central or South America.
5. Whitney Kennedy Lever Action Sporting Rifle - .38-40 - circa 1879-1886.

Swift Approach - Frank Tenney Johnson

THE AMERICAN WEST

OTHER REPEATERS

1. Colt Lightning Slide-Action Rifle, Large Frame - .38-55 - circa 1887-1894 - The large size handled rounds up to .50-110 Express.
2. Colt Lightning Slide-Action Rifle, Medium Frame - .32-20 - circa 1884-1902 - Medium frames handled the "pistol class" cartridges, .44, .38, and .32 WCF.
3. Colt Lightning Slide-Action Rifle, Small Frame - .22 long rifle - circa 1887-1904.
4. Colt-Burgess Lever-action Rifle - .44-40 - circa 1883-1885.
5. Evans Lever-Action Repeating Carbine - .44 Evans - circa 1873-1879 - The Evans repeaters featured a unique helical magazine in the buttstock that could hold 28 to 34 cartridges,
6. H. Pieper Mexican Military Revolving Carbine - 7mm Pieper - circa 1893 - Nine shot.

OTHER REPEATING RIFLES

Colt & Winchester — There's a story that when Colt introduced a lever-action rifle, representatives of Winchester visited the Colt plant with examples of a Winchester revolving handgun design. Deciding that discretion was the better part of valor, Colt abandoned the lever-action rifle market.

High-capacity firearms — 19th century lever-action rifles chambered in cartridges such as the .44-40 commonly held 15 or rounds or more. The Evans held as many as 38, which is more than today's popular AR pattern sporting rifles that typically use 10-, 20-, or 30-round magazines.

Revolving rifles, redux — The self-contained metallic cartridge greatly reduced the risk of chain fires that made percussion models unsafe. However, the tendency to pepper the support hand with burning powder and lead fragments from the cylinder gap led to a less-than-enthusiastic reception for most cartridge revolving rifles.

Smith & Wesson Revolving Rifle - .320 Rev. Rif. - 1879-1887. A long barrel version of the S&W New Model Number Three with a detachable shoulder stock, only 977 were made.

SINGLE SHOTS

Engraved/inlaid Remington Rolling Block shotgun - 16 gauge - circa 1875-1890 - Although most rolling blocks were rifles, shotguns were also produced.

Remington Rolling Block

The sturdy and reliable Remington rolling block was the most popular single-shot action of its time. Thousands of carbines, rifles and pistols were ordered by the US Army and Navy after the Civil War. It was also used as a military arm by over 40 other countries. It was well suited as a civilian hunting rifle, made in multiple frame sizes and calibers from small game .22s through large bore buffalo rifles. Although introduced in the 1860s, the action was strong enough to handle smokeless powder loads and it was produced into the 20th century. It remained popular for decades more as a target, hunting, and recreational shooting rifle.

Prototype Remington Split Breech Rifle, Type I - .40 rimfire - circa 1863 - The prototype for Remington's first cartridge long gun.

Foreign Brass Frame Rolling Block Copy .45 centerfire - circa 1870-1900 - The Remington Rolling Block was the most popular single-shot cartridge rifle design from the 1860s to the early 20th century. It was widely copied.

Detachable Stock Remington Rolling Block Pistol - .22 rimfire - circa 1873-1875 - Remington's pistol carbine utilized a rolling block pistol and a detachable skeleton wire stock.

Remington Rolling Block Cadet Rifle w/ Bayonet - .22 rimfire - circa 1913-1923 - Training rifle produced for military schools.

THE AMERICAN WEST

Belgian 4-bore Rolling Block Rifle - circa late 1860s - The rolling block design was copied by other makers in Europe. This massive single-shot weighs 22 pounds and fires a lead bullet greater than one inch in diameter, suitable for the largest African game animals. This example is crudely stamped "H.M. Stanley" and is attributed to African explorer Henry Morton Stanley who is best known for his expedition to find Dr. Livingston. "Four bore" is the same as 4 gauge. The gauge system is based on the number of lead balls the diameter of the bore that it would take to weigh a pound. Twelve lead balls the diameter of a 12 gauge shotgun bore would weight a pound. Correspondingly, four "4-bore" lead balls would weigh a pound - a quarter pound each.

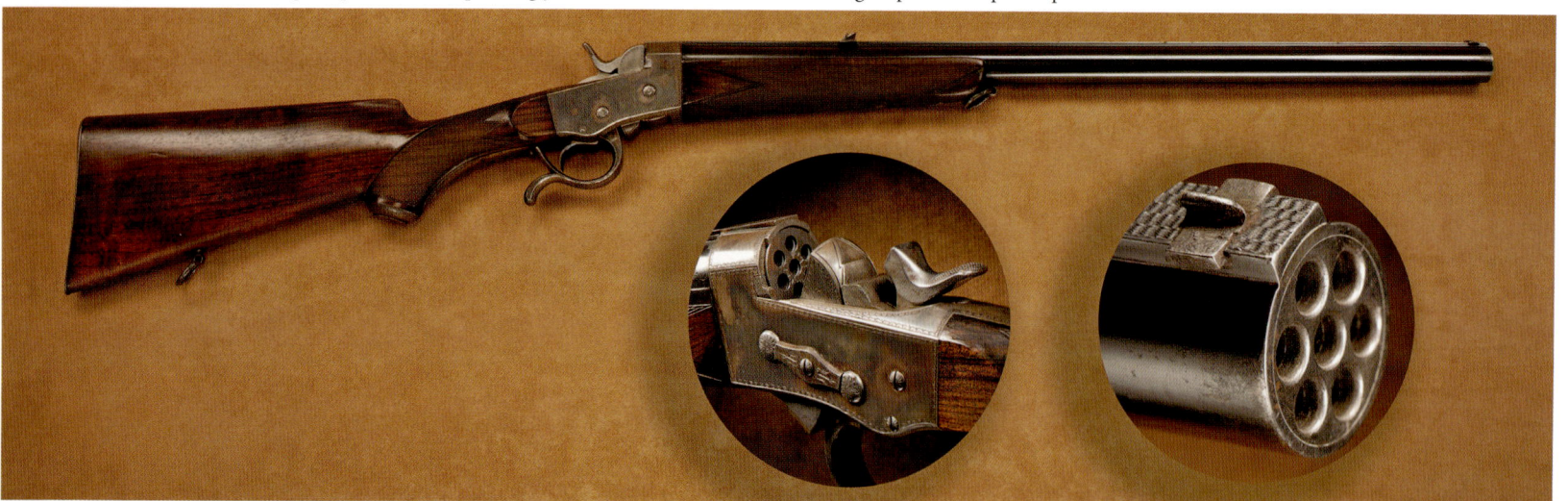

Pieper Rolling Block Multi-Bore rifle - .22 rimfire - circa 1880. This unusual Belgian-made "goose gun" fires all seven cartridges with a single pull of the trigger..

SINGLE-SHOTS

Freund Sharps Rifles

From their Wyoming Armory in Cheyenne, the Freund brothers, Frank and George, created the finest in frontier sporting arms. Modifying falling-block Sharps rifles with custom breechblocks, lockplates and sights, Freund & Bro. built arms uniquely suited to the demands of the mountains and plains, shooting conditions far removed from the East. Their finest grade offered was the "Boss Gun," an embellished single-shot well-suited for buffalo.

Freund & Brother "Boss Gun" Sharps Sporting rifle - 40-90 - circa 1877.

Freund & Brother Sharps Sporting rifle - 40-70 - circa 1877.

Sharps "Big Fifty" in buffalo hunter diorama at NRA National Sporting Arms Museum at Bass Pro Shops.

Buffalo Hunting on the Plains

From Canada to Mexico and from the Mississippi to the Rocky Mountains, an incredible herd of 50 to 100 million American bison, popularly called buffalo, roamed the West. For the Plains Indian, this animal was the staff of life, providing meat for food, fur for warmth, and bones for tools. For the commercial hunter who was primarily interested in obtaining hides and meat to sell, the buffalo was regarded only as a source of wealth. Thousands of hunters traveled west to make their fortune by killing buffalo. The loud noise of a rifle being fired could scare a buffalo herd into a stampede and reduce the number of animals taken by a hunter. For this reason, most hunters armed themselves with rifles capable of scoring a kill at tremendous distances so that the sound of the gunshots would not panic the herd. Many hunters used Civil War surplus arms that had been fitted with new barrels and converted to fire centerfire cartridges. Manufacturers such as Ballard, Marlin, Sharps, Remington, and Winchester soon began to produce and promote rifles that were specifically designed for hunting buffalo.

By 1883, the unchecked harvesting of the buffalo herds left the American Bison in danger of becoming extinct. Due to the enactment of strong and effective conservation measures, however, some limited numbers of buffalo now exist in our national parks.

THE AMERICAN WEST

Remington Hepburn Single-Shot rifles - .44 CF - circa 1880-1907 - Top is a Creedmoor competition rifle. The lower scoped rifle was used by Lewis Hepburn to check ammunition accuracy for Remington.

Ballard No. 5 Pacific Falling Block Single-Shot Rifle - .45-70 - circa 1876-1891

Sharps "Big Fifty" Model 1874 Single-Shot Falling Block Rifle - .50-90 - circa 1871-1881 - Called the "Big Fifty" for its heavy .50 caliber projectile, backed by a powerful 90-grain powder charge. Shipped to Fort Griffin, Texas, for buffalo hunters.

Marlin Ballard Hunter's Rifle - .44 caliber - circa 1875-76 - Features a reversible firing pin that can be changed for centerfire or rimfire cartridges.

Sharps Model 1874 "Old Reliable" Single-Shot Falling Block Rifle - .45 caliber - circa 1871-1881.

Whitney Phoenix Single-Shot Breechloading Rifle - .40-70 - circa 1867-1881 - Hinged breechblock lifts up to load.

SCATTERGUNS

Lancaster Four Barrel Shotgun - 28 gauge - circa 1887.

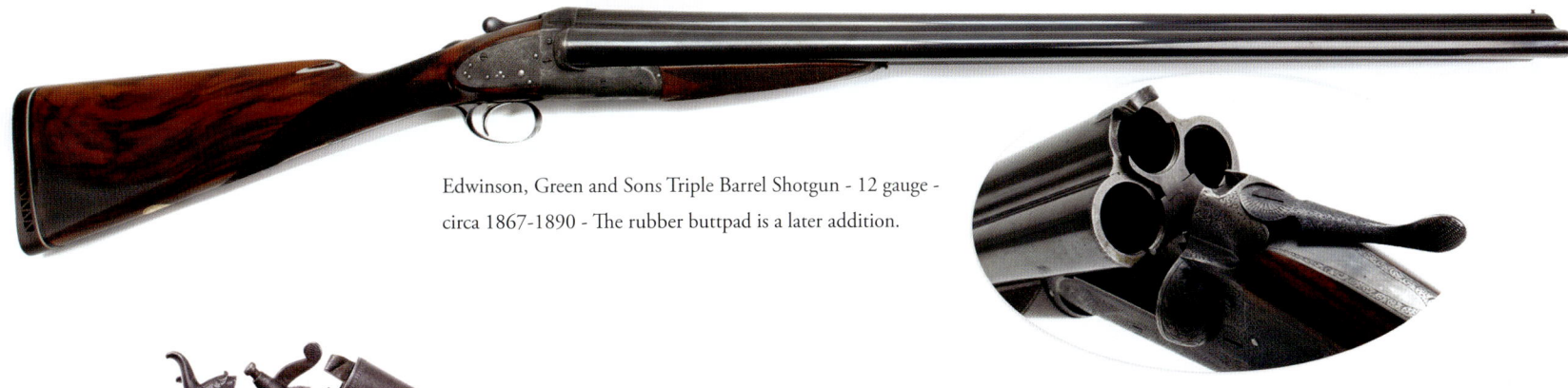

Edwinson, Green and Sons Triple Barrel Shotgun - 12 gauge - circa 1867-1890 - The rubber buttpad is a later addition.

Brugsmueller Drilling - 16x16 gauge & 9mm - circa 1876-1900 - Combining two shotgun barrels with one rifle barrel, drillings were sometimes used for mixed-bag hunting in Europe.

Double-barrels and beyond

Perhaps the most ubiquitous firearms in the Old West, and in post Civil War rural America in general, were double-barrel shotguns, hammer or hammerless, percussion or shotshell. They were a common tool for ranchers and farmers, plus a formidable weapon for lawmen and outlaws, or to defend the homestead. In the late 19th century, repeating shotguns began to gain favor.

Guns combining smoothbore and rifled barrels, or rare shotguns with more than two barrels, were more often found in Europe and England than in the U.S.

THE AMERICAN WEST

1. James Purdey & Sons Side-by-Side Hammer Shotgun - 20 gauge - circa 1877.
2. E. Remington & Sons Side-by-Side Hammer Shotgun - 12 gauge - circa 1882-1889.
3. Roos and Sohn Percussion Side-by-Side Shotgun - 20 gauge - circa 1855.
4. Parker Brothers Lifter Action Side-by-Side Shotgun - 10 gauge - circa 1882.
5. Manton & Co. Double Rifle - .500 Express - circa 1885-1890 - Joseph Manton & Co. were gun makers to the English royal family since 1781.
6. W. W. Greener Double Rifle - circa 1877 - W.W. Greener began in 1829 and in addition to fine arms also produced many scholarly written works on shooting in the 19th century.
7. L. C. Smith Drilling - 12 gauge/.44 caliber - circa 1880-1884 - L.C. Smith began business in 1878 and is considered one of America's finest sporting arms.

James Purdey & Sons Ltd. British Best Grade Side-by-Side Shotgun - 12 gauge - circa 1888 - Best Grade meant that there was no finer gun produced by the firm. Boss & Co. and Purdey only sell "Best Grade" guns.

SCATTERGUNS

1. Roper Repeating Shotgun - 16 gauge - circa 1867 - One of the earliest repeating shotguns, using a revolver-like mechanism. First shotgun to use detachable choke.

2. Model 1887 Lever-Action Shotgun - 10 gauge - circa 1887-1901 - Six-shot capacity, 65,000 made.

3. Winchester Model 1897 Pump Action Shotgun - 12 gauge - 1897-1957 - Successor to the Model 1893.

4. Marlin Model 19 Slide-Action Shotgun - circa 1907 - Winchester and Marlin both made exposed hammer pump shotguns. Some of these early Marlin exposed hammer pump shotguns are unsafe to shoot with modern shotshells.

5. Colt Model 1883 Shotgun - 12 gauge - circa 1884 - 7,300 of these high-grade shotguns made.

6. Burgess Slide-Action Folding Gun - 12 gauge - circa 1892-1899 - Unusual folding design. The company was purchased by Winchester in 1899.

7. Sawed-Off Double-Barrel Shotgun (deactivated) - 12 gauge - circa 1936 - Short-barrel shotguns held some popularity for close-range defense. Today, possession of shotguns with barrels shorter than 18 inches is highly regulated.

THE AMERICAN WEST

Native American Arms

When Europeans arrived in the Western hemisphere, Native American armament for hunting, warfare, and defense consisted of bows and arrows, spears, and stone axes and knives

From about 1630 to 1830, flintlock long guns were widely sold to Native American tribes, often by fur companies such as the Hudson Bay Company. Most were British smoothbores and were known as Northwest Trade Guns or Indian Trade Muskets.

Native Americans continued to acquire firearms by trade or capture. Their guns often show hard use, rawhide reenforcements of stock, and sometimes distinctive decoration including brass tacks. Metal buttplates are often removed to fashion hide scrapers or other tools. Native American guns are sometimes faked and sold to gullible collectors or Old West enthusiasts. Authentic examples are scarce.

Barnett Northwest Trade Gun - 20 gauge smoothbore - circa 1800 - The brass dragon/serpent sideplate was a feature that native Americans came to associate with this type of gun. They offered more in exchange for examples with the sideplate. This example bears the tombstone/fox symbol associated with the Hudson Bay Trading Company.

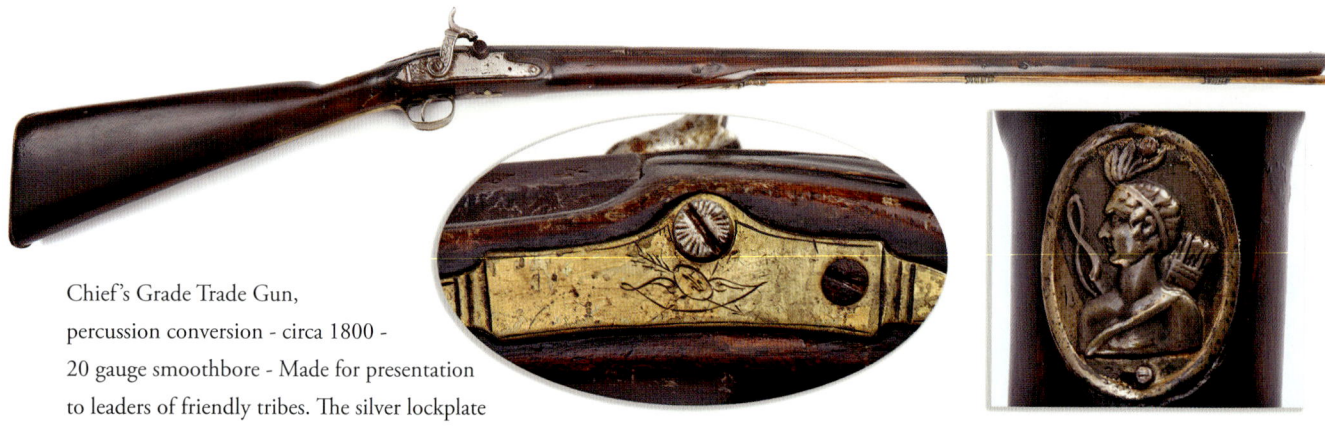

Chief's Grade Trade Gun, percussion conversion - circa 1800 - 20 gauge smoothbore - Made for presentation to leaders of friendly tribes. The silver lockplate and oval at the wrist on this smoothbore were extra bits of bling. These were made with a flat brass sideplate embellished with an engraved bow/quiver that was also represented on the oval. Similar to an officer's fowler of the period, but of cheaper British manufacture.

Sharps Model 1859 Single-Shot Percussion Carbine - .52 caliber - circa 1859-1866 - Captured and later decorated with bone and shell inlays.

Cut-down Springfield M1861 Musket - .62 caliber - circa 1861-1862 - Shortened firearms such as this are sometimes called "blanket guns" because they could be concealed under a blanket worn as a cloak.

NATIVE AMERICAN ARMS

Diorama - NRA National Sporting Arms Museum at Bass Pro Shop

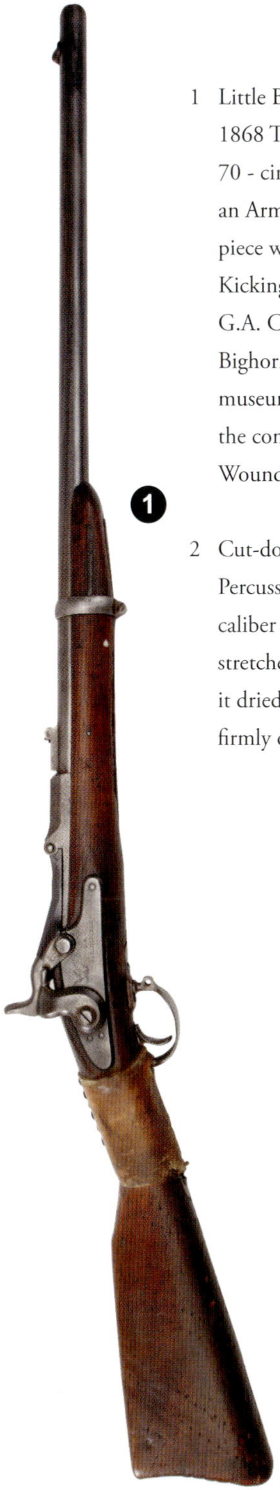

1. Little Bighorn U.S. Springfield Model 1868 Trapdoor Rifle (altered) - .50-70 - circa 1868-1876 - Originally an Army-issued rifle, this cut-down piece was once owned by Lakota chief Kicking Bear, who fought against Gen. G.A. Custer at the Battle of the Little Bighorn in 1876. It was donated to the museum collection by a descendant of the commander of the Indian Scouts at Wounded Knee.

2. Cut-down U.S. Springfield M1816 Percussion Conversion Musket - .69 caliber - circa 1870 - Wet rawhide was stretched over the cracked stock and, as it dried, the shrinking of the rawhide firmly drew the parts together.

THE AMERICAN WEST

1. U.S. Springfield Joslyn Breechloading Rifle - .56-50 rimfire - circa 1865 - First cartridge breechloaders made at Springfield Armory.
2. Parkers Snow Co. Rifle-Musket, Miller Model 1861 .58 Caliber Conversion - .58 rimfire - circa 1863-1864 - One of 2,000 converted to breechloaders in Meridan, CT, after the Civil War in 1865-1867.
3. English Enfield Snider Rotating Block Conversion Rifle - .577 caliber (conversion) - circa 1866-1870 - The Snider side-swing breechblock conversion was used in the British Empire. It was invented by American Jacob Snider.
4. English Barnett Model 1853 Rifle (altered) - .58 Berdan - circa 1866-1870 - This rifle was used by Colt to develop a prototype tested in 1866 at the U.S. Army Board Trials.
5. U.S. Springfield Model 1875 Lee Vertical-Action Rifle - .45-70 - circa 1875 - 150 made for testing and evaluation. Martini dropping-block action; serial number 2.
6. Joslyn-Tomes Model 1870 Straight-Pull Single-Shot Rifle - .58 Martin (conversion) - circa 1872-1873 - Tested by the Army, but rejected.
7. Providence Tool Co. Peabody Lever-Action Single-Shot Carbine - .50 centerfire - circa 1866-1871.

The Army on the Frontier

Prior to the Civil War, U.S. Army garrisons had been established throughout the American West to protect our frontier. Beyond these military posts lay the great American desert and numerous tribes of Native Americans.

U.S. Cavalry troopers stationed throughout the West often found themselves fighting at a disadvantage because the firearms supplied by the government tended to lag behind the most current advances in technology. Troopers engaged in such battles as The Little Bighorn (June 1876) were armed with single-shot breechloaders while their victorious adversaries were armed with the more advanced repeating rifles of the day.

Eventually, as witnessed before during the War Between the States, overwhelming numbers and resources prevailed during the series of battles between the U.S. Cavalry and various Indian tribes that took place over a period of 40 years, culminating with the death of nearly 300 Sioux at the Battle of Wounded Knee on December 29, 1890.

THE ARMY ON THE FRONTIER

1. U.S. Springfield Model 1868 Single-Shot Breechloading Rifle - .50 centerfire - circa 1869-1872.
2. U.S. Springfield Allin Conversion Model 1866 Single-Shot Breechloading Rifle - .50 centerfire - circa 1866 - The Allin trapdoor system was initially used to convert muzzleloaders to cartridge breechloaders.
3. U.S. Springfield Model 1884 Trapdoor Carbine - .45-70 - These Trapdoor arms were to serve throughout the Indian Wars. The initial metallic cartridges issued demonstrated extraction issues, but these .45-70 arms remained in government arsenal through the end of the century.
4. U.S. Springfield Model 1878 Trapdoor Rifle - .45-70.
5. Gen. Wingate's U.S. Springfield Model 1875 Trapdoor Officer's Rifle, Second Type - .45-70 - circa 1877-1881 - Originally owned by NRA founder and president George Wingate. The Officers Model was a unique product of a national armory, in that it was made for private sale to officers for their personal sporting use rather than military issue. It used the action and caliber of the standard military arm, but added deluxe features such as decorative engraving, checkering, target sights, and a detachable pistol grip. Fewer than 500 were made.

The Springfield Trapdoor

At the close of the Civil War, the federal government had an enormous inventory of surplus arms and equipment, including numerous muzzleloading rifled muskets. Rather than destroy these arms, the Chief of Ordnance decided to convert them from their muzzleloading configuration to a breechloading system. E.S. Allin, the Master Armorer at the Springfield Armory, developed a system that converted the old muskets into breechloaders.

The breech of the barrel was cut away and a breech block installed that flipped up and forward to load like a trap door. It was so successful that beginning in 1868, new military arms were manufactured using this system. The cartridge was standardized as the .45-70 in 1873, and trapdoors were manufactured by Springfield Armory well into the 1890s.

At the time the Trapdoor was adopted, there were successful repeaters available, such as the Henry, Winchester 1866, and Spencer.

Military thought of the era was that troopers would waste ammunition if armed with repeating arms. Also, when Trapdoors were first issued, the repeating arms chambered less powerful cartridges with shorter ranges. However, single-shot military arms were still manufactured and issued as full power repeaters were perfected and widely available on the commercial market.

THE AMERICAN WEST

Wm. F. "Buffalo Bill" Cody's show coat and shaving kit. Colt London Navy s/n 1 attributed to Cody and Capt. Jack Crawford "The Poet Scout." "Buffalo Bills Wild West Show" inscribed Colt Lightning Rifle, engraved Colt 1878 DA inscribed "Jack Crawford," and a pair of Colt M1873's inscribed "Pawnee Bill," (Maj. Gordon Lillie). All performed with Buffalo Bill's Wild West and other similar shows.

Above - Annie Oakley's Stevens pistol and Remington Beals rifle, with two cards used by her as targets in her performances.

Below - Frank "Deadshot Doc" Carver's Buffalo Bill Wild West Show trunk and the Winchester 1873 .22 rifle he used in an 1885 six day shoot, hitting 60,000 out of 64,000 thrown targets.

ROMANCE OF THE WEST

Romance of the West - The Wild West Show

After the Civil War, the West was romanticized by dime novels by writers like Ned Buntline and stage shows featuring frontier luminaries such as Buffalo Bill Cody, Wild Bill Hickock, and Texas Jack Omohundro.

Within a few years, traveling open-air Wild West Shows provided live entertainment to millions across this nation as well as Europe. They might feature romanticized reenactments, trick and rodeo riding, wild animals, roping, and exhibition shooting. From 1883 to 1913, Buffalo Bill's Wild West shows were the first and best known. The show had a number of iterations and spin-offs. Over the years, Cody productions featured performers included Annie Oakley, Frank Butler, Gordon "Pawnee Bill" Lillie, and Jack Crawford "The Poet Scout,"

One of the last was the Oklahoma-based Miller Brothers 101 Ranch Wild West Show. They performed from 1907 to 1927. America's fascination with the romance of the west continued in Hollywood movies and TV westerns.

Hambrusch shotgun inscribed "To Annie Oakley 'Little Missy' from Col. Wm. F. Cody London 1890." This shotgun may have been a gift to replace one that was destroyed when Annie used loads with gunpowder provided to her by Cody after she ran out.

Annie Oakley

Born in Darke County, Ohio, in 1860, Phoebe Anne Mosey later adopted the stage name Annie Oakley. As a child she learned to hunt rabbit and quail, which she sold to supplement the family income. She developed a remarkable skill as a marksman, and in five short years, paid off the mortgage on the family farm with earnings from game that she shot and shipped to market.

Her local fame inspired a shooting contest near Cincinnati against noted exhibition shooter Frank E. Butler. She defeated him by a single point, soon fell in love with him, and eventually married him. Butler became Annie's manager and booked her on various show and circus tours. In 1885, she joined Buffalo Bill's Wild West show in Louisville, Kentucky.

Annie became America's first international female super-star. She could hit a dime tossed in the air, shoot a cigarette placed in her husband's lips, and slice in half a playing card that was held edge-on to her at a distance of 30 paces. Perhaps the most famous woman marksman in history, she was further immortalized in the 1946 Broadway musical *Annie, Get Your Gun*.

101 Ranch Wild West Show artifacts - Winchester 1873 rifle inscribed "Bill Pickett / 101 Ranch / World's Champion Bull-Dogger;" a pair of engraved Colt Bisleys inscribed "Lucille Mulhall 101," the first female rodeo champion (carved grips may be later additions); a S&W .44 DA inscribed "Neal Hart / 101;" a "101 Ranch" marked Colt SAA, and C.C. Lee's 101 Ranch travel case and Stevens single-shot rifle.

Below: Bill Pickett, Lucille Mulhall, and Zack Miller of 101 Ranch fame.

THE AMERICAN WEST

The Legend Continues - Fascination with the American West extended long past the frontier era.

1. Western artist Charles Russell (1864-1926) helped shape the image of the West with over 2,000 paintings, sketches, and bronzes. The Merwin Hulbert and holster were presented to Russell by Montana pioneer Granville Stuart.
2. Tom Mix (1880-1940) was a star in over 280 silent movies that helped establish the Western as a Hollywood genre. A pair of his Colt Single Action Army revolvers are shown with his holster rig.

The tradition of live Old West performers and reenactors continued throughout most of the 20th century.

3. Chief Ed Eagle (1902-1984) performed at rodeos and fairs an exhibition shooter with both firearms and bow. Shown here are his Colt 1851 Navy revolver, Colt Lightning rifle, show moccasins, and stone pipe.
4. Marshal Ralph Hooker (1906-2001) was a trick roper, exhibition shooter, professional reenactor, and lawman. This is his Colt Single Action Army with holster. His autobiography was appropriately titled "Born Out of Season."

ROMANCE OF THE WEST & GOLDEN AGE OF ENGRAVING

Engraving

The popularity and quality of American firearms engraving reached a high-water mark in the mid- through late 19th century. German engravers brought their artistry to America and trained successive generations in the demanding craft of sculpting the flat and curved surfaces of iron and steel with hand tools to create works of art.

Engraved arms were signs of prestige and made an impressive presentation piece or gift. In addition to being a firearms design genius, Colt was also a master of marketing and promotion, and had a practice of presenting exquisitely engraved and cased arms to individuals who might exert beneficial influence on behalf of the company's products.

Engraved firearms by independent engravers were commissioned by individuals, distributors, and manufacturers. Manufacturers also hired in-house engravers. A master engraver would often work with apprentices, and multiple artisans might work on the same piece.

Perhaps the two best-known engravers of the era were L.D. Nimschke and Gustave Young. They and other engravers of the era tended to favor ornate floral vine or scroll motifs. Young's style is considered typical of Colt through about 1869, at which time he moved to Springfield and began to do a large number of guns for S&W. The large relief scroll pattern most associated with American arms of the post-Civil War era came to be called Nimschke-style or New York-style engraving, due to the many engravers working in that city. Young's typical tight scroll style was continued by his sons as factory engravers for Smith & Wesson.

THE AMERICAN WEST

Colt Single Action Army - .44 Russian - circa 1903 - Engraved and gold inlaid by Cuno Helfricht.

S&W New Model Number 3 - .44 Russian - circa 1878-1898 - Engraved by Gustave or Oscar Young.

Pidault et Cadier Perrin Pinfire Revolver - 12mm - cica 1860s.

Cased pair of Colt 1878 DA Revolvers - .45 Colt - ca. 1880s - Engraved by Cuno Helfricht for Sam Colt's son Caldwell Colt.

GOLDEN AGE OF ENGRAVING

Rare quadruple cased set of Colt percussion revolvers, two each 1851 Navy Models and 1849 Pocket models, one set engraved and the other decorated with gold damascene.

Period engraved Winchester Model 1866 and 1873 lever-action rifles. Donated by Tom Selleck.

THE AMERICAN WEST

Harrington & Richardson exhibit for the 1876 Philadelphia Centennial Exposition features their spur-trigger .22, .32, and .38 rimfire revolvers with special order decoration including engraving and pearl or ivory carved grips. The four wheels of revolvers were rotated by an electric motor, for display, a novelty at the time.

Engraved Colt Presentation Third Model Dragoon Revolvers - .44 caliber - circa 1851-1861 - Inscribed on backstraps "Prize Shot of Company C, Mounted Riflemen U.S.A." and "George Hess." Likely engraved by Gustave Young.

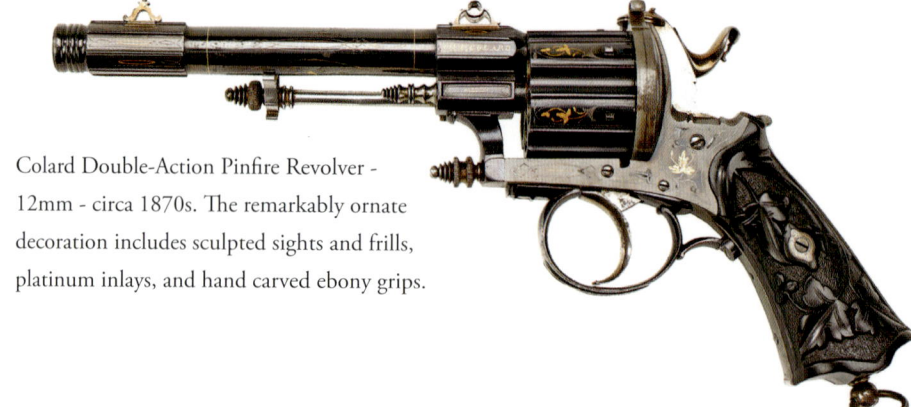

Colard Double-Action Pinfire Revolver - 12mm - circa 1870s. The remarkably ornate decoration includes sculpted sights and frills, platinum inlays, and hand carved ebony grips.

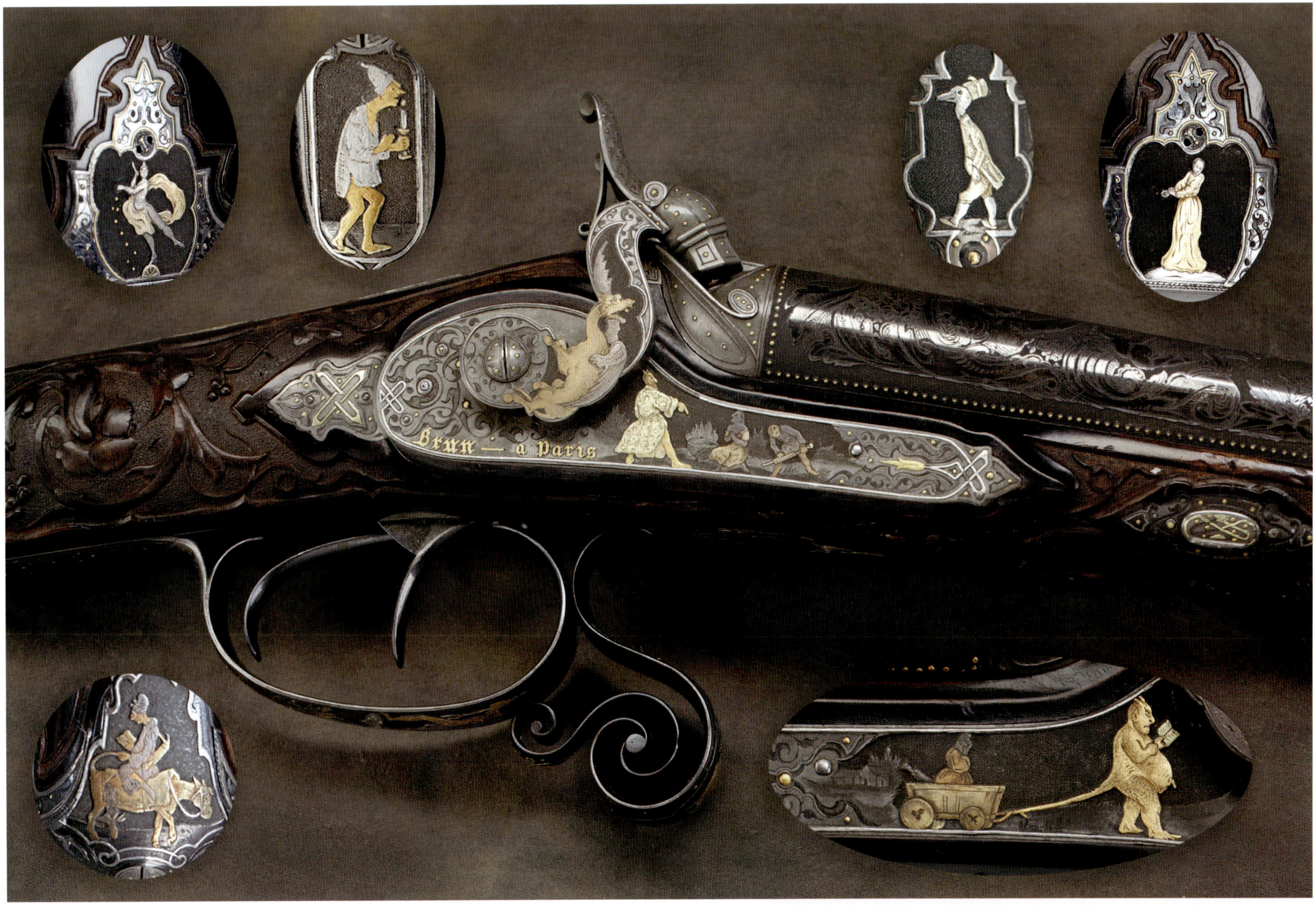

GOLDEN AGE OF ENGRAVING

J.C.A. Brun Percussion Shotgun - 16 gauge - circa 1849 - Nicknamed "The Devil's Shotgun" for the 20 multi-colored gold inlays of demons, imps, and fantasmagoric creatures, this remarkable French piece won a medal at the 1849 Paris Exposition. Exquisitely cased, the ornate accessories include a curved horn powder flask and a ramrod made of baleen.

NEW TECHNOLOGY II

NEW TECHNOLOGY II

The decades before and after the turn of the 19th to 20th centuries saw further leaps in firearms technology.

Propellant and projectile - Again, advances in ammunition led to breakthroughs in firearms design. The introduction of smokeless powder led to higher pressure, higher velocity loads resulting in greater power with a smaller diameter bullet. The new clean burning powder made new types of actions possible. Pointed copper-jacketed spitzer bullets began replacing round-nose lead projectiles. These more aerodynamically efficient rounds meant flatter trajectories and greater range.

Bolt-actions - Bolt-action repeating rifles began gaining favor over lever-actions. The tubular magazines of most lever guns would not safely accommodate spitzer bullets, limiting their range and effectiveness.

Semi-automatic firearms - Clean burning powder allowed firearms designers to find ways to use the energy of the shot to automatically eject the empty case and load a fresh round into the chamber ready to be fired without manual manipulation by the shooter.

U.S. military rounds, also popular in sporting rifles, shown actual size.
.45-70 - introduced 1873 - black powder, round nose lead bullet.
.30-06 - introduced 1906 - smokeless powder, spitzer bullet.

Borchardt C-93 Semi-Automatic Pistol - 7.65x25 - circa 1893-1902 - The Borchardt was the first modestly successful semi-auto pistol. This one is cased with a detachable shoulder stock, holster, and accessories. Three years later, the Mauser 1896 Broomhandle semi-auto would become a major worldwide success. The Luger borrowed and improved the Borchardt toggle-link action.

The Mexican-designed Mondragon was the first successfull semi-automatic rifle, introduced in 1885. See the WWI chapter for more information on combat use. By 1910, both Winchester and Remington were producing multiple models of semi-auto centerfire rifles with detachable box magazines for the hunting and law enforcement markets.

POWDER & PROJECTILE, BOLT-ACTIONS, & SEMI-AUTOS

Bolt-Action: The Rifles of the Brothers Mauser

In the world of firearms, few people have left a greater mark than brothers Wilhelm and Paul Mauser. The genius of the Mausers' first bolt-action design was such that many subsequent Mauser designs were merely adaptations of the original brought about by advances in technology.

The Mauser brothers originally encountered difficulty in attracting the attention of their own government to the possibilities of a bolt-action rifle and sought financial backing in the United States. At one point the Remington Arms Company was approached and seemed interested. But the Ilion, New York, gunmaker backed out of a pending contract just as the German government showed renewed interest.

Eventually the Mausers' designs became the most produced and copied of all firearms innovations. Most sporting and military bolt-action rifles (and some shotguns) can trace their development to the efforts of the brothers Mauser.

The four rifles on this page are all prototypes by the Mauser brothers as they perfected the bolt-action rifle. When the French Chassepot needle-fire rifle debuted in the Franco-Prussian War, developments in metallic cartridges were already conspiring to make this arm obsolete. Among the individuals that observed the rifle's flaws were Remington's European sales representative, Samuel Norris, and Wilhelm and Paul Mauser. Norris knew that metallic cartridges were the future for military arms and worked with the Mausers to create a conversion of the French Chassepot rifle that would take metallic cartridges. In 1869, the conversion received a U.S. patent and prototypes were made by the Mauser brothers for use in convincing European military leaders to adopt a new bolt-action rifle system. A number of intermediate prototypes, based on reworked Chassepot rifles, reflected changes in extractors, spring location and self-cocking capabilities. The end result, the Mauser M1871 rifle, utilized an 11mm centerfire cartridge and features a reliable bolt design that cocked on closing. This bolt-action design was the foundation for other designs such as the Mauser Model 1898, which in turn came to influence many other rifle designs including the American Springfield Model 1903 rifle.

Mauser prototype: Chassepot French Model 1866 Bolt-Action Rifle with Norris-Mauser Patent Self-Cocking Bolt - 11mm - circa 1869-1870 - Thought by historians to be the first Mauser ever made, predating any patent models.

Mauser prototype: Norris-Mauser Belgian Model 1867/69 Bolt-Action Rifle - 11mm - circa 1869-1870.

Mauser prototype: Chassepot French Model 1873 Bolt-Action Rifle with Kynoch Metallic Centerfire Cartridge Conversion - 11mm - circa 1875-1879.

Mauser prototype: Chassepot French Model 1866 Bolt-Action Rifle with Mauser Experimental Bolt and Hook Cocking Piece - 11mm - circa 1869-1870.

NEW TECHNOLOGY II

The bolt-action was adopted by European armies before the U.S. The American military experimented with bolt-actions, but stayed with single-shot trapdoors until the 1890s. Likewise, the American sporting market continued to be dominated by single-shots and lever-action repeaters into the early 20th century.

1. Mauser Belgian Interim Model 1869/70 Bolt-Action Rifle; Model #1 - 11mm - circa 1869-1870.
2. Mauser Belgian Interim Model 1869/70 Bolt-Action Rifle, Model #2 - 11mm - circa 1869-1870.
3. Dreyse German M1860 Needle-Fire Rifle - .50 Needlefire - circa 1865 - Used by the Prussian army during the Franco-Prussian War of 1871, the needle gun was rapidly replaced by the Mauser 1871.
4. Mauser German Modified Gewehr 71 Bolt-Action Rifle - 11mm - circa 1867 - This bolt-action rifle would replace the needle gun as Germany's main service rifle following the Franco-Prussian War of 1871.
5. Societe Industrial Swiss Model 1871 Vetterli Bolt-Action Rifle - 10.35 Vetterli - circa 1871-1887.
6. Brescia Italian Model 1871 Vetterli Bolt-Action Carbine - 10.35 Vetterli - circa 1871-1887.
7. Brescia Italian Model 1871/87 Vetterli-Vitali Bolt-Action Rifle - 10.35 Vetterli - circa 1871-1887 - Single shot bolt-actions were redesigned for fixed box magazines.
8. Dutch Beaumont-Vitali Bolt-Action Rifle - 10.35 Vetterli - circa 1870-1887.
9. Waffenfabrik Bern Swiss Model 1881 Bolt-Action Rifle - 10.35 Vetterli - circa 1881-1883.

EVOLUTION OF THE EARLY BOLT-ACTION

1. U.S. Springfield Model 1871 Ward-Burton Single-Shot Bolt-Action Rifle - .50 centerfire - circa 1871 - Slightly more than 1,000 Ward-Burton rifles were tested in trials, but this early bolt-action was the first bolt-action centerfire rifle brought into American military service. Following a tradition begun after the American Revolution, the front sight of the rifle doubled as a lug point for a socket bayonet.
2. Winchester-Hotchkiss Model 1879 First Model Bolt-Action Carbine - .45-70 - circa 1880-1881 - This rifle represents Winchester's first significant military contract with the U.S. government.
3. Winchester-Hotchkiss Second Model Bolt-Action Musket - .45-70 - circa 1880-1881.
4. Winchester-Hotchkiss Second Model Bolt-Action Carbine - .45-70 - circa 1880-1881.
5. U.S. Winchester-Hotchkiss Model 1883 Third Model Bolt-Action Musket - .45-70 - circa 1883-1899.
6. Remington-Keene Magazine Bolt-Action Rifle - .40-60 - circa 1880-1883 - 500 of these rifles marked "USID" were used by Indian Police on reservations.
7. U.S. Remington-Lee Model 1882 Magazine Bolt-Action Rifle - .45-70 - circa 1882-1886. One of the first bolt-actions with a detachable box magazine.
8. Remington-Lee Model 1882/1885 Magazine Bolt-Action Rifle - .45-70 - circa 1886-1888.
9. Winchester Civilian Model 3rd Hotchkiss Musket - .45-70 - circa 1879-1889.

NEW TECHNOLOGY II

The Genius of John M. Browning

The son of a gunsmith, John Moses Browning was born in Ogden, Utah, on January 21, 1855. From his earliest youth, Browning displayed a remarkable talent for invention. By age 13 he had made his first gun - of scrap iron - in his father's gunshop. By age 24 he had been granted his first patent - for a breechloading single-shot rifle. Browning's first firearm patent was bought by the Winchester Repeating Arms Company and marketed as the Model 1885 (the renowned High Wall and Low Wall rifles). Browning's inventive genius produced 128 patents for breechloading rifles, magazine rifles, auto-loading guns, repeating shotguns, gas-operated firearms, semi-automatic firearms, and machine guns. His designs were manufactured by Winchester, Remington, Colt, Stevens, and the Fabrique Nationale d'Armes de Guerre in Herstal, Belgium. Several of his designs were adopted by the U.S. Army, notably the Model 1911 pistol, the Model 1917 Browning water-cooled machine gun, and the Model 1918 Browning automatic rifle. Perhaps the greatest inventor in small arms history, John M. Browning died of a heart attack on November 26, 1926.

1. Colt Model 1905 .45 Semi-Automatic Pistol - .45 rimless smokeless - circa 1905-1911
2. U.S. Colt Model 1911 Semi-Automatic Pistol - .45 ACP - circa 1917.
3. Colt Model 1902 Sporting Semi-Automatic Pistol - .38 Rimless Smokeless - circa 1903.
4. Colt Model 1902 Military Semi-Automatic Pistol - .38 Rimless Smokeless - circa 1916.
5. Colt Model 1903 Pocket Semi-Automatic Pistol - .38 Rimless Smokeless - circa 1927.
6. Colt Model 1903 Hammerless Type III Pocket Semi-Automatic Pistol - .32 ACP - circa 1927.
7. Fabrique Nationale/Browning Model 1910 FN Semi-Automatic Pistol - .32 ACP - circa 1930-1935.
8. Fabrique Nationale/Browning P-35 Hi-Power Semi-Automatic Pistol - 9mm Parabellum - circa 1973 - Considered the last handgun design to be created by John Browning prior to his death in 1926. It was completed by Dieudonné Saive of Fabrique Nationale. The P-35 pistol has been issued to the military of over 50 countries. A single-action semi-automatic pistol with a double-stack magazine holding 13 9mm cartridges, the P-35 or Hi-Power pistol provided significant handgun firepower for the period it was developed.

JOHN MOSES BROWNING

1. Browning Model 1878 Standard Single-Shot Rifle - .45-70 - circa 1878-1882 - An early example of John Browning's single-shot rifle design as built in his Ogden, UT, gunshop, Browning sold the manufacturing rights for this design to Winchester in 1883.
2. Winchester Model 1907 Semi-Automatic Rifle - .351 Winchester - circa 1908.
3. Winchester Winder Single-Shot Musket - .22 short - circa 1918-1919 - Lt. Col. C.B. Winder adapted the Browning single-shot design to crate a gun with military rifle lines with a target arm that could be used for both training and competition.
4. Browning Grade 1 Semi-Automatic Takedown Rifle - .22 rimfire - circa 1976.
5. Remington Model 11 Autoloader Shotgun - 12 gauge - circa 1915.
6. Winchester Model 1911 SL Autoloader Shotgun - 12 gauge - circa 1912.
7. Remington Model 17 Slide-Action Shotgun - 20 gauge - circa 1917-1933.

Browning Long Gun Designs

In addition to the guns on this page, Browning designed Winchester lever-action Models 1886, 1892, 1894, and 1895. Many of his designs are still in production today.

A BRIGHT NEW CENTURY

THEODORE ROOSEVELT

1. Theodore Roosevelt's Fabrique Nationale Model 1900 Semi-Automatic Pistol - .32 ACP - circa 1900 - Full-coverage engraving with gold line inlays, it was presented to Pres. Theodore Roosevelt. This pistol was given to the museum by Roosevelt's grandson, Corneilus V.S. Roosevelt.

2. Theodore Roosevelt's Smith & Wesson New Model No. 3 Single-Action Revolver - .38 Long Colt - circa 1898 - Shipped by S&W to Roosevelt prior to his forming the Rough Riders in the spring of 1898. Custom sighted and engraved, and specially chambered for the U.S. Service cartridge, it is believed Roosevelt intended to take this revolver to Cuba in the Spanish-American War.

3. Theodore Roosevelt's Fred R. Adolph Hammerless Double Rifle - .450 Cordite - circa 1909-1911 - Made for Roosevelt following his African Safari of 1909-1910, this gun was displayed in the window of Abercrombie & Fitch in New York City for many years before Roosevelt gave it to an associate.

4. Gen. Roosevelt's Winchester Model 1895 Lever-Action Rifle - .405 Winchester - circa 1923 - Owned by one of Roosevelt's sons, Theodore, Jr., and used on his hunting trips. He rose to the rank of brigadier general and was awarded the Congressional Medal of Honor in WWII.

Theodore Roosevelt

Theodore Roosevelt is an icon of his era. He was a prolific writer, historian, politician, military hero, and loving father and husband. He is also the only person to receive both the Congressional Medal of Honor and the Nobel Peace Prize. Born in 1858, he labored under the ravages of asthma as a child. His father stressed the need for a vigorous personal regimen to combat the asthma, and Theodore (he was never called Teddy by his family) began to thrive in the outdoors.

He earned his spurs as a cowboy during a two-year stint as a rancher in the Badlands of South Dakota, and also became an excellent hunter. Well aware of the fact that he was not a great marksman, he humorously remarked that he **"didn't shoot well, but did shoot often."**

His firearms collection was perhaps the largest ever assembled by any president of the United States. He was known for insisting upon exacting standards for his guns, and favored Winchesters and Colts. He also treasured a pinfire shotgun that was a gift from his father.

An ardent lover of nature and a staunch conservationist, Teddy Roosevelt was responsible for the establishment of the National Forest Service, the conservation and rebuilding of the buffalo herds, the National Conservation and Waterways Commission, the National Monument system within the National Park Service, and the first 51 bird sanctuaries in the United States.

Roosevelt expressed the balance between conservation and sport, saying, **"thus the encouragement of a proper hunting spirit, a proper love of sport, instead of being incompatible with a love of nature and wild things, offers the best guarantee for the preservation of wild things ...."**

Following his years as president, Roosevelt embarked in 1909 upon a year-long African safari. Carrying a sporterized Model 1903 Springfield, a Holland and Holland double rifle, a Fox 12-gauge shotgun, and three Winchester Model 1895s, his adventure acquired 4,897 mammals and more than 4,000 birds, 2,000 reptiles, and 500 fish, all of which were carefully preserved and shipped to the Smithsonian Institution for study and display.

Teddy's Bear

Roosevelt's love for hunting the grizzly bear inspired numerous journalists to compare his squinting eyes and toothy smile to that of a grizzly. The grizzly bear soon became a political symbol for his presidency.

When Roosevelt refused to shoot a motherless bear cub during a hunting expedition, the story of his compassion quickly spread across the country. An enterprising toy merchant labeled all of his stuffed toy bears "Teddy's Bear," and the teddy bear soon became a national sensation that endures to this day as a favorite toy and stuffed companion.

Theodore Roosevelt and the NRA

Theodore Roosevelt was an active proponent of military rifle practice and an ardent supporter of legislation that established the National Rifle and Pistol Matches in 1903. Roosevelt signed Public Law 149 on March 3, 1905, authorizing the sale of surplus military rifles, ammunition, and equipment to National Rifle Association affiliated clubs. Competitions were held for affiliated shooters to qualify as National Marksman who would be listed by the War Department as members of the National Marksmen's Reserve (called the "Third Line of Defense" for the Army).

On February 16, 1907, the following correspondence was sent to the NRA by President Theodore Roosevelt:

"I am so heartily interested in the success of the National Rifle Association of America and its work done in cooperation with the National Board for the Promotion of Rifle Practice that I take pleasure in sending you herewith my check for $25 for life membership therein."

A BRIGHT NEW CENTURY

An Age of Elegance

Theodore Roosevelt inspired many persons to take up "the strenuous life," a lifestyle that encouraged hard, outdoor work and various types of outdoor recreation that included hunting, hiking, fishing, rowing, and rifle practice. Legions of persons followed his example and began enjoying the numerous positive aspects of hunting. Hunting trips and expeditions, including African safaris, became a popular form of recreation for millions of Americans.

From 1880 to 1930, a period that became known as the Age of Elegance, the world's finest gunmakers produced some of the most exquisite firearms ever created.

Purdey Side-by-Side Shotgun - 12 gauge - circa 1902 - A gift from King Edward VII to the Shah of Persia. Engraved by Messer. Barre.

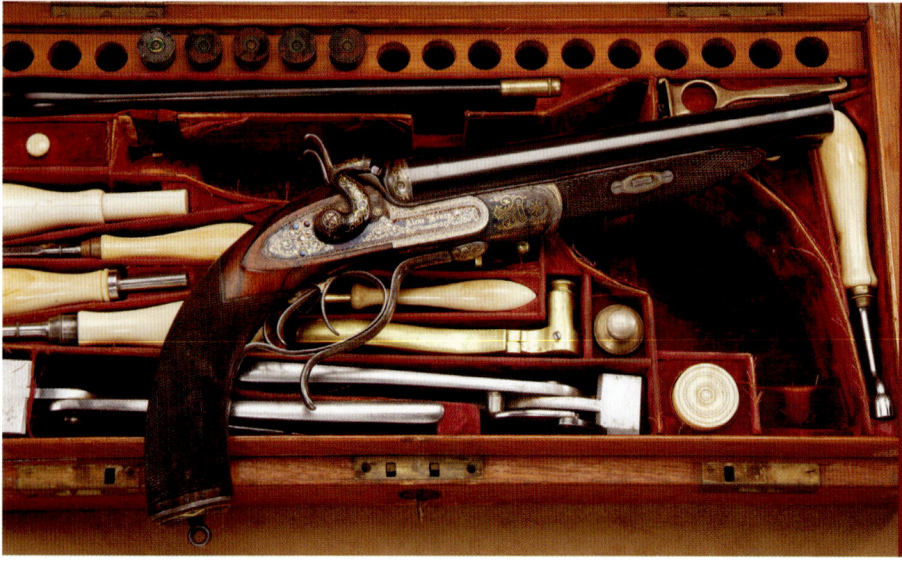

Alexander Henry Howdah Pistol - .577 Snyder - circa 1870 - Heavy caliber double-barreled pistol used as a backup gun when hunting tigers from elephant-back in India

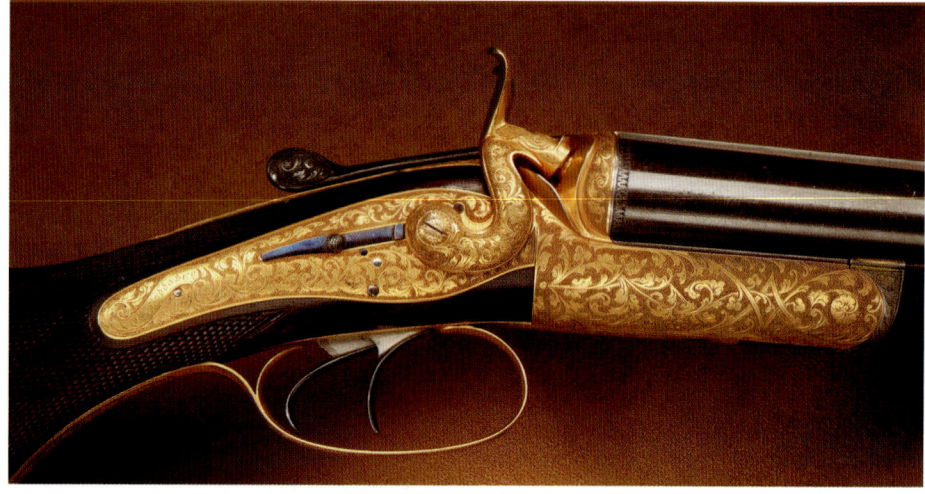

Rodda Double Rifle - 15 bore - circa 1900-1940 - Exhibition grade with gold damascene.

Holland & Holland Maharaja Grade Double Rifle - .500/.465 Nitro Express - circa 1924 - Rare cloisonne enamel gold sideplates.

AN AGE OF ELEGANCE

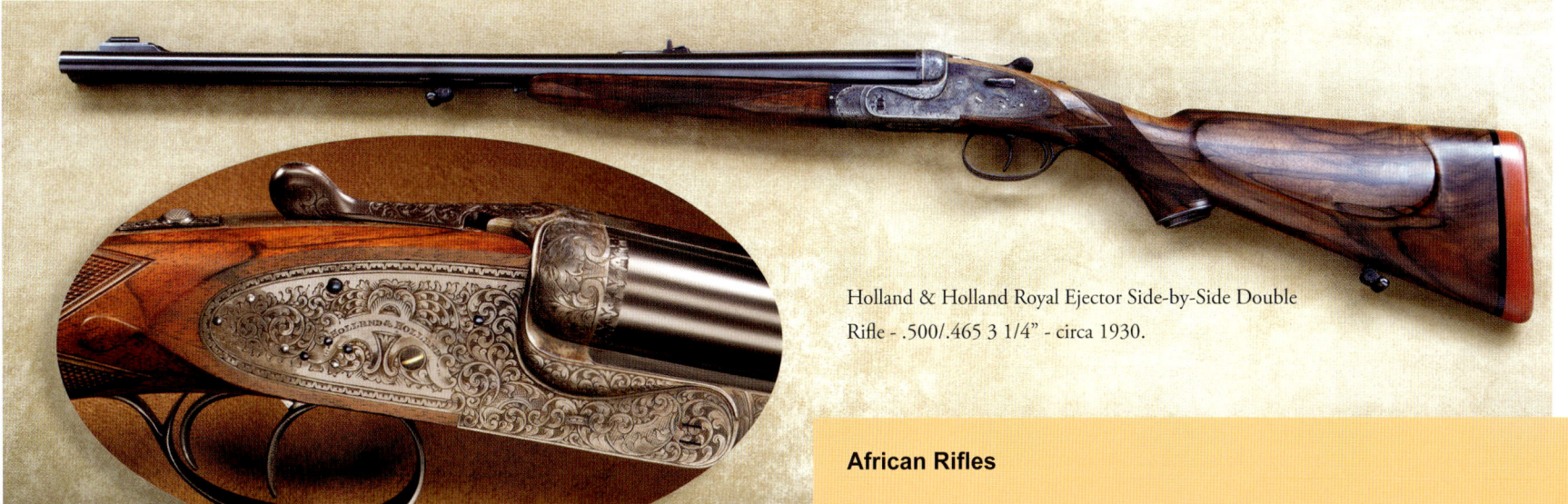

Holland & Holland Royal Ejector Side-by-Side Double Rifle - .500/.465 3 1/4" - circa 1930.

African Rifles

The decades immediately preceding and following the turn of the 20th century saw an era of British, European, and American hunting and exploration in Africa. The term "elephant gun" indicated a rifle suitable for harvesting of, or defense against, large dangerous animals such as the "big five" - lion, buffalo, elephant, rhino, and leopard. The classic gun for this application was a double-barrel rifle, accommodating a quick and sure second shot, firing a large caliber bullet in the half-inch diameter range over a large charge of powder.

W.J. Jeffery & Co. Double Rifle - .600 Nitro Express - circa 1903-1920. Hammerless falling block design patented in 1872.

A BRIGHT NEW CENTURY

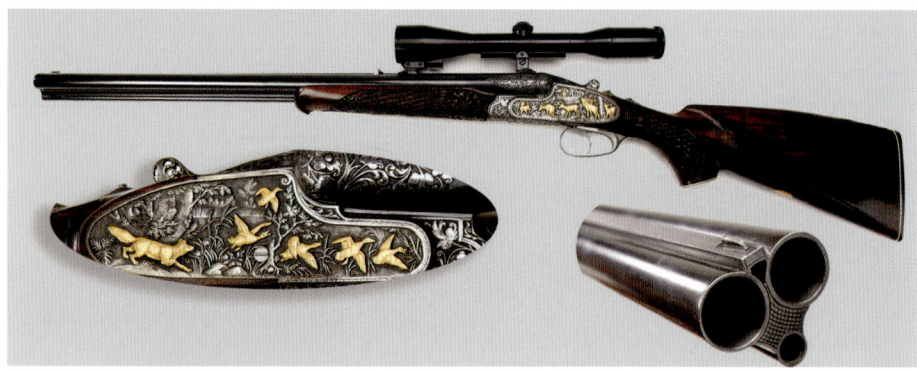

Suhler Jagd-und Sportwaffen GmbH Drilling - 12 gauge x 12 gauge / 7.65x65R - circa early 20th century - Exhibition grade.

Cased pair of Woodward James Over/Under Shotguns - 12 gauge - circa 1913.

William Evans Cast Stock Shotgun - 12 gauge - circa 1931. View from above. Top Quality with an extreme cast stock to allow a right handed shooter to aim with his left eye.

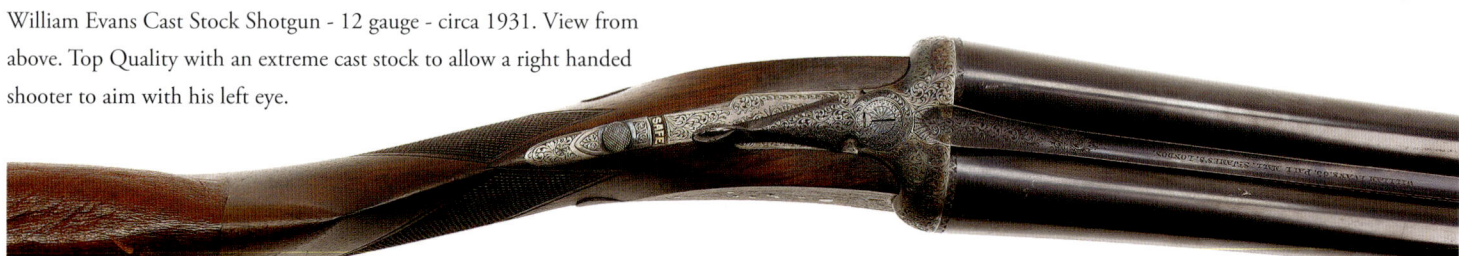

Bottom - Triple cased set of Stephen Grant shotguns - 12 gauge - circa 1902.

AN AGE OF ELEGANCE

President Grover Cleveland's Colt Model 1883 Hammerless Side-by-Side Damascus Shotgun - 8 gauge - circa 1895 - The only 8 gauge shotgun ever to be manufactured by the Colt factory, this side-by-side was presented to U.S. President Grover Cleveland and engraved with his name on the trigger guard. Cleveland was the only U.S. President to serve two non-consecutive terms (1885-1889 and 1893-1897).

The Golden Guns of the Yacht *United States*

The yacht *United States* was owned by Col. Edward H.R. Green, whose mother Hetty Green was dubbed the "Witch of Wall Street" and was considered the richest woman in America at the time. Green's vessel was the most luxurious American vessel afloat, being twice the length of the presidential yacht and having a stateroom for every state in the Union. As a sea-going arsenal, Green commissioned six Winchester rifles (an 1895 in .30-06, two 1894s in .30-30, and three .22 rimfire Lightnings, all with birdseye maple stocks), along with four Colt semi-automatic .22 pistols. Each gun was gold-plated and engraved "Yacht United States."

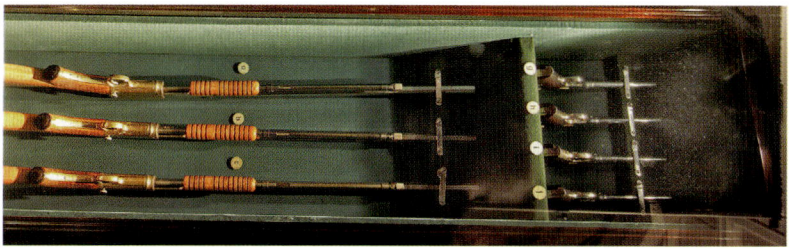

A BRIGHT NEW CENTURY

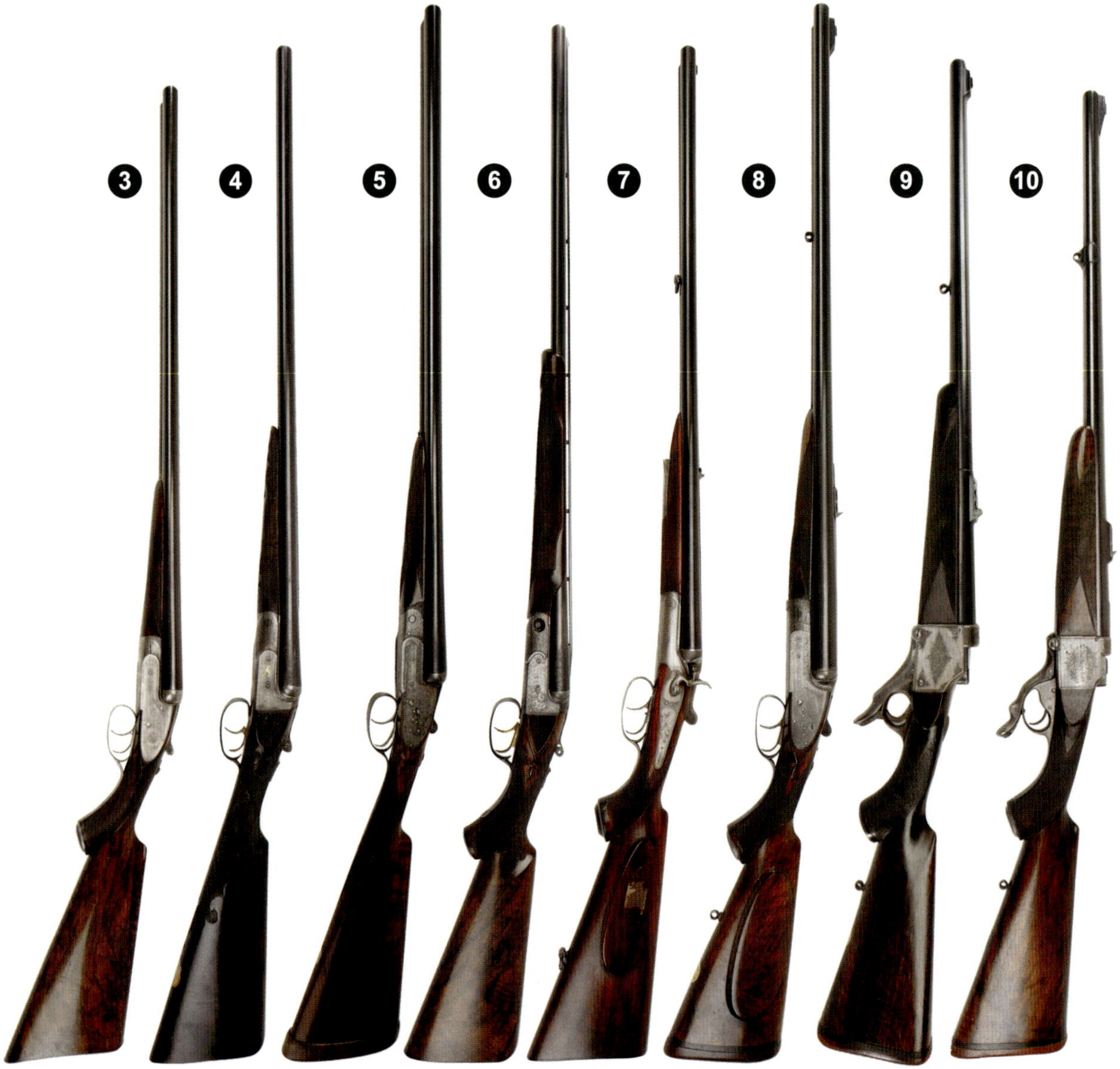

1. Mauser Model 1896 Broomhandle Semi-Automatic Pistol with matching serial number shoulder stock - 7.63 Mauser - circa 1897-1901 - The wooden buttstock was hollow and the pistol itself could be stored inside and the stock used as a holster.
2. DWM Model 1902 Luger Semi-Automatic Carbine with matching serial-numbered shoulder stock. - .30 Luger - circa 1902-1905 - Shoulder-stocked pistol carbines like this Model 1902 commercial example were favored by Kaiser Wilhelm I, who had a withered arm and had difficulty holding a full-sized rifle in firing position.
3. James Purdey & Sons Side-by-Side Shotgun - 12 gauge - circa 1892 - Since 1814, still one of the world's premiere arms makers.
4. Parker AAHE-Grade Side-by-Side Shotgun - 12 gauge - circa 1901 - Parker Brothers of Connecticut is considered one of the finest of American sporting arms manufacturers.
5. Cogswell & Harrison British Side-by-Side Shotgun - 12 gauge - circa 1937 - Cogswell & Harrison was originally established in 1770.
6. Parker A-1 Special Side-by-Side Shotgun - 20 gauge - circa 1920.
7. Austrian Cape Gun - 16 gauge/6.5mm rimmed - circa 1890-1900.
8. Stephen Grant & Sons Double Rifle - .500/.450-3 1/4 inch - circa 1901-1905 - Stephen Grant worked for Charles Lancaster and Boss & Co. before opening his own firm in 1867.
9. Webley & Scott Single-Shot Falling-Block Rifle - .450 caliber - circa 1920 - Webley & Scott began in 1790 and made fine arms in the U.K. for nearly 200 years.
10. Rigby Farquharson Single-Shot Lever-Action Rifle - .470 Nitro Express - circa 1898-1900 - Hammerless falling-block design patented in 1872, in a caliber suited for heavy African game.

AN AGE OF ELEGANCE

The Parker Invincibles

The Parker Company's Invincible line of shotguns were envisioned as the ultimate flagship smoothbore of the day and were priced accordingly at $1,500 each, twice the price of a fine English Purdey shotgun or a Parker A-1 special-order gun. With the onset of the Great Depression, even the most affluent captains of industry could not afford this high pricing and, as a result, only three Parker Invincible shotguns were ever manufactured and sold, all between 1924 and 1929. Two 12-gauge Invincibles and one 16-gauge Invincible are the only three examples ever produced, notable for their gold triggers, full-coverage engraving with gold inlays, and their finely figured wood stocks. They are believed to be the most valuable set of American-made shotguns ever produced.

A BRIGHT NEW CENTURY

1. Paul Jung Drilling - circa 1890 - Drilling combination guns are popular in European countries where owning more than one firearm can be problematic. A drilling is a three-barrel gun, most often two shotgun barrels and a rifle barrel.
2. G. Knaak German Vierling Combination Gun - 12 gauge/.22 rimfire/.25-35 Win. - circa 1900. A *vierling* is a four-barrel gun.
3. W. W. Greener Ltd. British Peabody-Martini Single-Shot Rifle - .45 caliber - circa 1910 - This Peabody-Martini action was popular with competition shooters at the turn of the 19th century.
4. Lefever G Grade Side-by-Side Shotgun - 12 gauge - circa 1894.
5. Parker Brothers BH Grade Side-by-Side Shotgun - 12 gauge - circa 1898.
6. Kleszczewski Excelsior Drilling - circa 1900 -
7. Wilhelm Collath German Over/Under Combination Gun - 12 gauge/9.3 x 65mmR - circa 1900.
8. Westley Richards Super Magnum Paradox Side-by-Side Shotgun - 12 gauge - circa 1890-1900.
9. Ithaca Engraved Hammerless Shotgun attributed to D.B. Wesson - 20 gauge - circa 1909.

AN AGE OF ELEGANCE

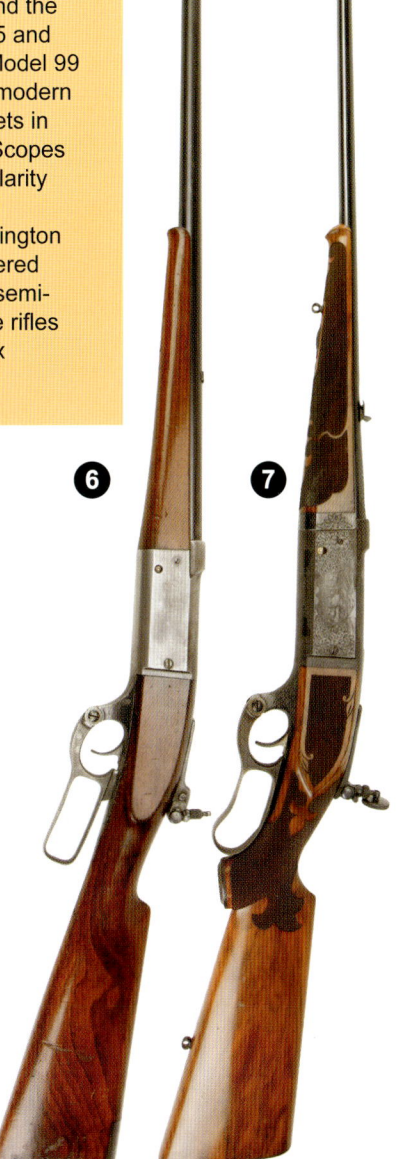

1. Charles Daly Side-by-Side Shotgun - 10 gauge - circa 1895.
2. Franz Jager Herold Three-Barrel Shotgun - 16 gauge - circa 1910-1920 - Built with three smoothbore barrels, this Franz Jager triple shotgun was created for an individual seeking the capability to utilize three different shot types while hunting.
3. Remington Model 10 Slide-Action Shotgun - 12 gauge - circa 1915-1925.
4. Ross Rifle Co. Canadian Deer-Stalking-Pattern Bolt-Action Sporting Rifle - .280 Ross - circa 1901.
5. Mauser German Type B Bolt-Action Rifle with telescopic sight - 8x57mm Mauser - circa 1920-1925 - Commercial scoped sporter.
6. Savage Model 1895 Lever-Action Carbine - .303 British - circa 1898 - Cartridge counter magazine with cocked indicator. Rotary magazine allowed use of pointed spitzer bullets, which are unsafe in tube magazine lever-actions.
7. Savage Model 99 Lever-Action Rifle - circa 1920.
8. Remington Model 81 Woodmaster Semi-Automatic Rifle - .35 Remington - circa 1938-1940.

Repeater Preferences

In the early 20th century, pump shotguns began to gain ground on the traditional double-barreled guns, and bolt-action rifles took some of the lever-action market. With box magazines, the Winchester 1895 and the Savage Model 1895 and its successor, the Model 99 allowed the use of modern pointed spitzer bullets in lever-action rifles. Scopes began to gain popularity

By 1910, both Remington and Winchester offered multiple models of semi-automatic centerfire rifles with detachable box magazines.

A BRIGHT NEW CENTURY

A Splendid Little War

On February 15, 1898, the American battleship U.S.S. *Maine* exploded in Havana harbor. The United States, believing that Spain was responsible for the loss of the ship and over 200 men, declared war on Spain. The Secretary of State called the conflict "a splendid little war." Victory for the United States came within nine months as America's army troops in Cuba and naval forces in the Philippines dismantled the last vestiges of the once-powerful Spanish Empire.

The Spanish Mauser rifles and the American Krag rifles that were used in the Spanish-American War were evenly matched in effectiveness. Eventually, the Model 1903 Springfield, a licensed copy of the Spanish Mauser, replaced the Krag as the primary service rifle for American troops.

1. U.S. Springfield Model 1896 Krag-Jorgensen Bolt-Action - .30-40 Krag - circa 1896-1898 - The Krag was the U.S. issue long gun during the Spanish American War.
2. Winchester-Lee Straight-Pull U.S. Navy Rifle - 6mm Lee Navy - circa 1895-1902 - The first U.S. Navy-adopted military bolt-action rifle that used both smokeless ammunition and jacketed bullets, the straight-pull Winchester Lee had limited issue. U.S. Marine detachments stationed in China during the Boxer rebellion were among the limited units to see combat service with this rifle. Stripper clips became widely used to load bolt-action and semi-auto firearms with fixed box magazines.
3. U.S. Springfield Model 1884 Trapdoor Rifle - .45-70 - circa 1885-1890 - Although issued to some American troops, these obsolete black powder rifles were no match against the smokeless mausers of the Spanish in Cuba.
4. U.S. Springfield Model 1896 Krag-Jorgensen Bolt-Action Rifle - .30-40 Krag - circa 1896 - Named for Norwegian inventors Ole Hermann Johannes Krag and Erik Jorgensen, the Krag-Jorgensen rifle was the first U.S. Army rifle that used smokeless powder ammunition with jacketed projectiles. In 1898 it was replaced by the similar Model 1898, which itself was replaced five years later by the U.S. Springfield Model 1903.
5. Mauser Spanish Contract M1893 rifle - 7mm - circa 1893-1898.

A SPLENDID LITTLE WAR

Roosevelt's Rough Riders

Theodore Roosevelt resigned his office as Assistant Secretary of the Navy in 1898 in order to organize a cavalry regiment to fight in the Spanish-American War in Cuba. The regiment was commanded by Colonel Leonard Wood, a Medal of Honor recipient under whom Roosevelt served as a lieutenant colonel.

The response to recruiting advertisements was overwhelming, attracting cowboys, rangers, Indians, and even gentlemen riders from the Harvard, Yale, and Princeton polo clubs!

On the morning of July 1, 1898, near Santiago, Cuba, Roosevelt's Rough Riders, as his regiment was popularly known in the press, attacked the Spanish forces along San Juan ridge and adjoining Kettle Hill. In the mid-afternoon, the Rough Riders overran the Spanish positions and made their heroic way into the history books. Roosevelt's popularity soared upon his return to the United States, resulting in his election as vice president.

Colt Gatling Gun - .30-40 Krag - This tripod mounted Gatling is one of four used by the Rough Riders. Gatling guns were manufactured 1862 to 1911. This early rapid-fire crew-served weapon consists of a cluster of barrels, rotated around an axis by a hand crack. Each barrel fires as it comes in line with the firing pin, and is reloaded by a vertical stick magazine.

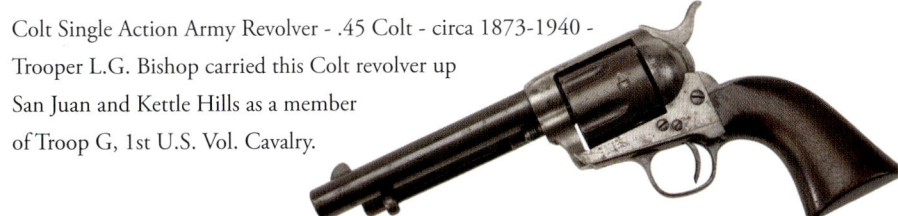

Colt Single Action Army Revolver - .45 Colt - circa 1873-1940 - Trooper L.G. Bishop carried this Colt revolver up San Juan and Kettle Hills as a member of Troop G, 1st U.S. Vol. Cavalry.

Colt Model 1905 Machine Gun, aka "Potato Digger" - 7mm - One of two Colt machine gun presented to the 1st US Volunteer Cavalry by two sisters of a Rough Rider and a wealthy gentleman. These were the first full-auto firearms used in combat by the U.S. Army. On loan from the Theodore Roosevelt Birthplace National Historic site, where it was recently discovered in the basement.

THE WORLD AT WAR

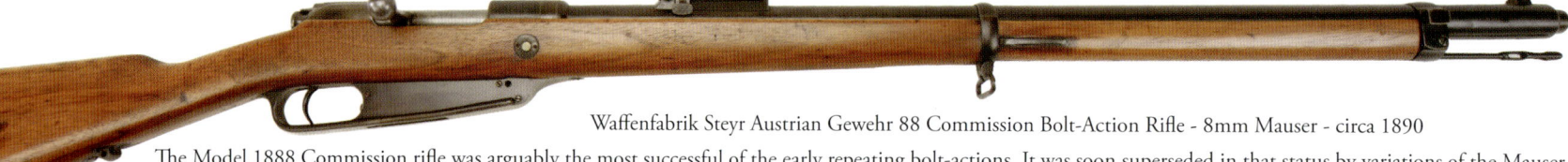

Waffenfabrik Steyr Austrian Gewehr 88 Commission Bolt-Action Rifle - 8mm Mauser - circa 1890

The Model 1888 Commission rifle was arguably the most successful of the early repeating bolt-actions. It was soon superseded in that status by variations of the Mauser 1898 pattern. In the arms race between France and Germany in the 1880s, the Commission 88 became the first German military rifle to employ smokeless ammunition. It was also the only German military bolt-action rifle design not actually manufactured by Mauser but by other contractors, in part to settle a patent infringement claim by Steyr Mannlicher.

1. Mauser German Model 1871 Bolt-Action Carbine - 11mm.
2. Waffenfabrik Steyr Austrian Model 1874 Gras Bolt-Action Rifle - 11mm Gras - circa 1874-1877.
3. Chatelerault French Model 1874 Gras Bolt-Action Carbine - 11mm Gras - circa 1880.
4. French Chassepot Model 1866 rifle - 11mm - circa 1873 - The standard service rifle of the French Army during the Franco-Prussian War of 1871, this rifle, far superior to the Prussian needle gun, proved that superior firepower cannot make up for bad leadership in combat.
5. Tula Arsenal Russian Model 1879 Berdan II Bolt-Action Rifle - 11mm - circa 1879-1881 - Designed by U.S. Civil War General Hiram Berdan, founder of the USSS (United States Sharp Shooters). This model was adopted by the Russian military.
6. U.S. Springfield Model 1882 Chaffee-Reese Bolt-Action Magazine Rifle - .45-70 - circa 1884.
7. Amberg Arsenal German Model 71/84 Bolt-Action Rifle - 11mm Mauser - circa 1884.
8. St. Denis French Daudeteau/Dovitiis Conversion Single-Shot Bolt-Action Carbine - 6.5mm Daudeteau - circa 1877.
9. Carl Gustafs Stads Gevarsfaktori Swedish Model 1894 Mauser Bolt-Action Carbine - 6.5mm Swedish - circa 1904.
10. Danish Model 1889 Krag-Jorgensen Carbine - 8mm - circa 1890 - The design of the Krag-Jorgensen with its side mounted box magazine was borrowed for the first smokeless powder repeating rifle adopted as the primary arm for the U.S. Army.

TURN OF THE 20TH CENTURY MILITARY RIFLES

1. Carl Gustafs Stads Gevarsfaktori Swedish Model 1896 Mauser Bolt-Action Rifle - 6.5x55mm - circa 1911.

2. Ludwig Loewe Waffenfabrik German Model 1895 Chilean Contract Bolt-Action Rifle - 7mm Mauser - circa 1897-1900.

3. Waffenfabrik Steyr Norwegian Contract Model 1894 Krag-Jorgensen Bolt-Action Rifle - 6.5x55mm - circa 1897 - This design was the basis for the adoption of the Krag Jorgensen by the U.S. military.

4. Ludwig Loewe & Co. German Argentine Contract Model 1891 Bolt-Action Carbine - 7.65mm Mauser - circa 1891-1907.

5. Gevaerfabriken Kjobenhaven Danish Model 1899 Krag-Jorgensen Bolt-Action Rifle - .30-40 Krag - circa 1892.

6. Ludwig Loewe Waffenfabrik Model 1895 Spanish Contract Mauser Bolt-Action Rifle - 7mm Mauser - circa 1893-1898.

7. Mauser Model 1896 Spanish Contract Bolt-Action Rifle - 7mm Mauser - circa 1896-1900.

8. Tokyo Arsenal Siamese Contract Mauser Model 1903/Type 45 Bolt-Action Rifle - 8mm - circa 1903-1908.

9. Fabrica Nacional de Arms Mexican Model 1910 Mauser Bolt-Action Rifle - 7mm.

THE WORLD AT WAR

1. U.S. Springfield Model 1898 Gallery Practice Bolt-Action Rifle - .22 rimfire - circa 1906 - This example is a .22 caliber training rifle variant.

2. Danzig Arsenal German Gewehr 98 Bolt-Action Rifle - 8mm Mauser - circa 1916 - The Gewehr 98 or 98 Mauser, as it is known, became the finest bolt-action rifle ever produced. It was, in minor variants, the standard service rifle of Germany from 1898 to 1945.

3. Mauser German Karabiner 98A Bolt-Action Rifle - 8mm Mauser - circa 1918-1920 - This '98 Mauser carbine was popular in the trenches of World War I due to its short and maneuverable length.

4. Blake Bolt-Action Repeating Rifle - .30-40 Krag - circa 1892-1910.

5. Fabrique Nationale Belgian Mauser Model 1916 Bolt-Action Carbine - 7.65mm Mauser - circa 1916-1918.

REMINGTON MILITARY PROTOTYPES

Top to bottom:

Remington Elliott Rifle - .45 centerfire - One of 15 rifles submitted from various manufacturers for 1872 U.S. military trials.

Prototype Remington Keene Rifle - .45 centerfire - circa 1880 - A later version was submitted for 1882 Army trials and purchased by the Navy and U.S. Office of Indian Affairs.

Remington Cook Rifle, - .40 centerfire - Made for U.S. Navy trials in 1894.

Remington Lee rifle, 6mm. Non-standard chambering made for 1872 U.S. military trials.

U.S. MILITARY PISTOL TRIALS

1. Colt Single Action Army Revolver - .45 Colt - circa 1873-1940 - This near-relic example was captured from Mindanao Moro guerillas by a lieutenant of the Phillipine Scouts in 1912.
2. Colt Model 1892 New Army Revolver - .38 Colt. In 1892 the U.S. military decided to modernize its standard issue sidearm with .38 caliber double-action swing-out cylinder revolvers, replacing the larger .45 Colt single-action. However, during the Philippine Insurrection, the .38 U.S. service cartridge was found to have inadequate stopping power against suicide attacks by Moro *juramentados*. The big .45 was called back into service while the Army sought a better replacement. Theodore Roosevelt used U.S. Colt Model 1892 serial number 16334 in the fight up Kettle and San Juan Hills, July 1, 1898. His revolver was recovered from the sunken battleship USS *Maine*.
3. Colt U.S. Model 1902 Army Revolver - .45 Colt - circa 1902-1904 - To fill the stopgap need for a handgun with .45 stopping power, the 1878 DA Colt is modified with an enlarged triggerguard, allegedly to allow small-statured Filipino combatants to use two fingers on the trigger.

U.S. Military Pistol Trials

With the failure of .38 caliber revolvers in the Philippines and the adoption of semi-auto military pistols in Europe, the U.S. was looking for a new handgun. In 1901 they purchased 100 each of Luger and Colt pistols for field trials.

In 1904 the Army commissioned the Thompson-LaGarde tests to determine optimum caliber for a military sidearm. Testing included killing livestock and firing rounds into human cadavers. The report recommended .45 caliber.

In 1907, nine different .45 caliber handguns were submitted for testing. Of these, the Colt, Savage, and Luger were deemed superior. Luger declined to participate in further trials, but Savage and Colt produced examples for field trials and continued to improve their designs. At a 6,000 round head-to-head shoot-out in March 1911, the Savage experienced a variety of failures while the Colt performed flawlessly. The Model 1911 Colt was adopted.

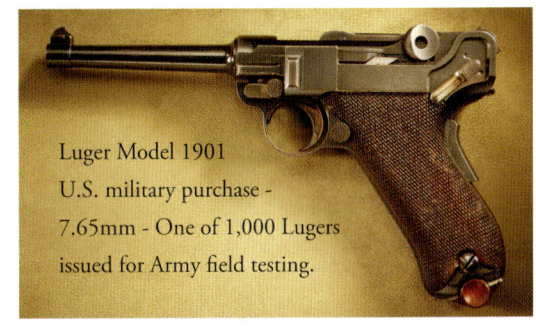

Luger Model 1901 U.S. military purchase - 7.65mm - One of 1,000 Lugers issued for Army field testing.

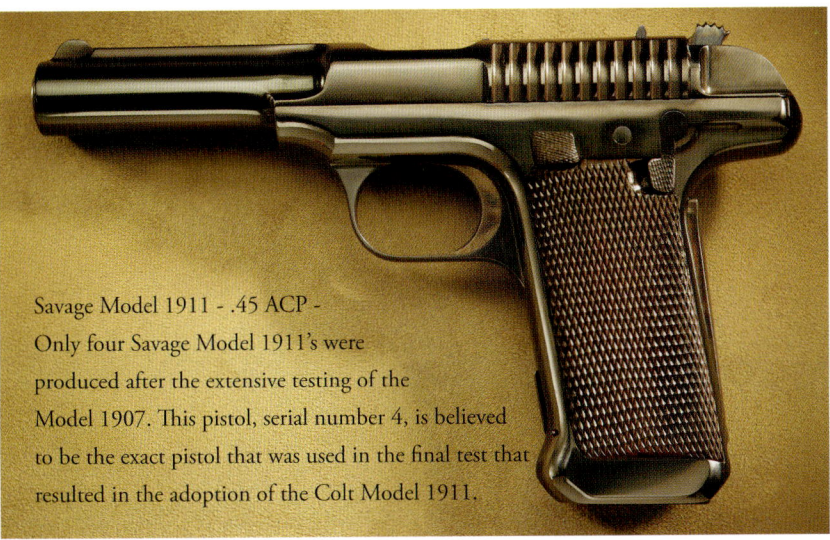

Savage Model 1911 - .45 ACP - Only four Savage Model 1911's were produced after the extensive testing of the Model 1907. This pistol, serial number 4, is believed to be the exact pistol that was used in the final test that resulted in the adoption of the Colt Model 1911.

Colt Model 1907 - .45 ACP. - This is one of 200 Model 1907s that were manufactured exclusively for the trials. They were issued to cavalry units in Minnesota and the Philippines. Changes made from the commercial Model 1905 included the introduction of a grip safety.

THE WORLD AT WAR

A Second Bite at the Apple

During WWI, the U.S. Navy and Marines conducted another round of tests for a service handgun, despite the fact that the Colt 1911 had been adopted only a few years prior. The guns tested were the Colt 1911, the Remington Model 53, and the Grant Hammond, all chambering the .45 ACP cartridge. Side-by-side shooting tests were held in 1918, including sand and mud tests.

The Grant Hammond was found to be extremely accurate. However it was mechanically complicated, experienced more failures, and automatically ejected its magazine when the last round was fired, which was considered a liability in a military pistol.

The Remington was an upsized version of the .380 ACP Remington Model 51. It was found to be accurate and reliable with good handling characteristics.

Considered the best of the three, the Navy made an order to replace all handguns then in service with the Navy and Marines, including the new 1911. However, Remington came in with a price that was considered higher than acceptable. Revised pricing was requested. However, by the time it was submitted, WWI was winding down, and Remington was busy producing 1911s, and the project was abandoned.

Only two examples of the Remington M53 are known to survive. The one shown here is on loan to the NRA National Sporting Arms Museum from the Remington Factory Collection.

U.S. Colt Model 1911 Semi-Automatic Pistol .45 ACP - circa 1912-1925.

Above: Grant Hammond Serial Number 1 - .45 ACP. Only 13 were ever made.

At right: Remington Model 53 - .45 ACP.

THE GREAT WAR

The Great War

The Great War, now commonly referred to as World War I, began after the assassination of Archduke Franz Ferdinand of Austria in June 1914. By mid-August 1914 most of the major European powers were at war. The United States entered on the side of the British and French in April 1917. World War I signaled the end of the age in which conflicts were settled with some semblance of chivalry. It was a war of rapidly changing technology, fought using tactics of the Napoleonic era. Companies, even battalions of soldiers, were thrown against squads of men, each squad manning a single machine gun capable of firing 800 rounds a minute. One General responded to the rapid destruction of his entire Division by telling his men to **"dig, dig, dig, until you are safe."** By Christmas 1914 a trench system wound its way from the Belgian coast on the North Sea to the Swiss border some 1500 kilometers away! For four years, until November 1918, the trenches remained in place, virtually unchanged. The word stalemate entered the dictionary to describe a useless situation with no foreseeable conclusion. The result was 8.5 million dead and 21 million maimed and disabled, plus 12.5 million civilian casualties.

The bolt-action rifle was standard armament among the 30 nations involved in this global conflict, with some members of the Allies - countries at war with Germany - paying licensing fees for their rifles to the German firm of Waffenfabrik Mauser. The dominating firearm of the war was the machine gun. Once thought wasteful and expensive, its use ensured that neither side could advance on the other without incurring horrifying losses. The war was brought to an end on November 11, 1918, by the combination of overwhelming Allied offensive action and the spread of revolution throughout Germany that forced the Kaiser's abdication and the replacement of the monarchy with a civilian government willing to surrender.

Colt Model 1914 Machine Gun (deactivated) - Manufactured by Marlin - .30-06 - circa 1914-1916 - Sometimes called the potato digger after the reciprocating action of its low-mounted operating rod, this Browning-designed machine gun served in primarily training roles during World War I.

U.S. Springfield Model 1903 Bolt-Action Rifle - .30-06 - circa 1903-1930 - The Springfield '03 was the American standard service rifle from 1903 to 1936. It first saw service in the Philippines in 1903. Issued in WWI and WWII, it was still in service as a sniper rifle in Korea and Vietnam.

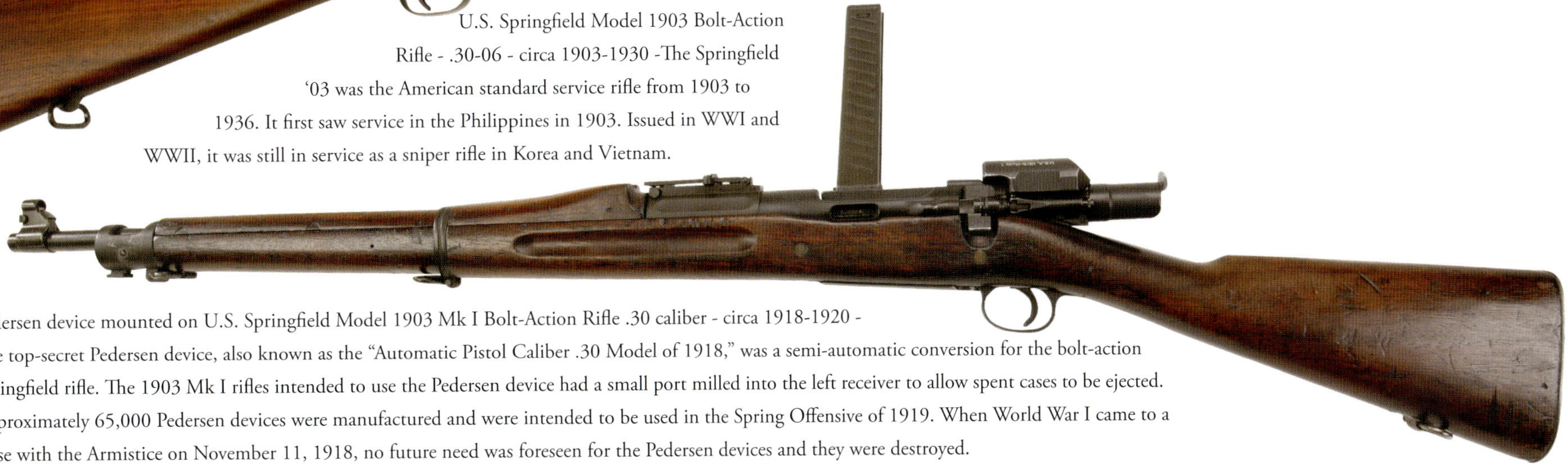

Pedersen device mounted on U.S. Springfield Model 1903 Mk I Bolt-Action Rifle .30 caliber - circa 1918-1920 - The top-secret Pedersen device, also known as the "Automatic Pistol Caliber .30 Model of 1918," was a semi-automatic conversion for the bolt-action Springfield rifle. The 1903 Mk I rifles intended to use the Pedersen device had a small port milled into the left receiver to allow spent cases to be ejected. Approximately 65,000 Pedersen devices were manufactured and were intended to be used in the Spring Offensive of 1919. When World War I came to a close with the Armistice on November 11, 1918, no future need was foreseen for the Pedersen devices and they were destroyed.

THE WORLD AT WAR

1. U.S. Remington Model 1917 Bolt-Action Rifle - .30-06 - circa 1917-1919 - Over two million M1917s were manufactured by Eddystone, Remington, and Winchester.
2. U.S. Winchester Prototype Model 1917 Bolt-Action Magazine Rifle - .30-06 - circa 1917 - This unmarked tool room example of a Winchester Model 1917 bolt-action rifle was part of a collection assembled by a former production line superintendent at Winchester.
3. U.S. Winchester Model 1897 Slide-Action Trench Shotgun - 12 gauge - circa 1918 - Winchester's military slide-action shotgun was fitted with a barrel handguard and bayonet lug. It was adopted for the close quarters combat of trench warfare.
4. U.S. Springfield Model 1903 Bolt-Action Rifle (relic condition) - .30-06 - circa 1903-1907 - Buried in a French field, this relic M1903 rifle was recovered in 1963.
5. U.S. Springfield Model 1903 Gallery Practice Bolt-Action Rifle - .22 rimfire - circa 1915 - A rare variant of the 1903 Springfield, this .22 was made for training purposes.

THE GREAT WAR

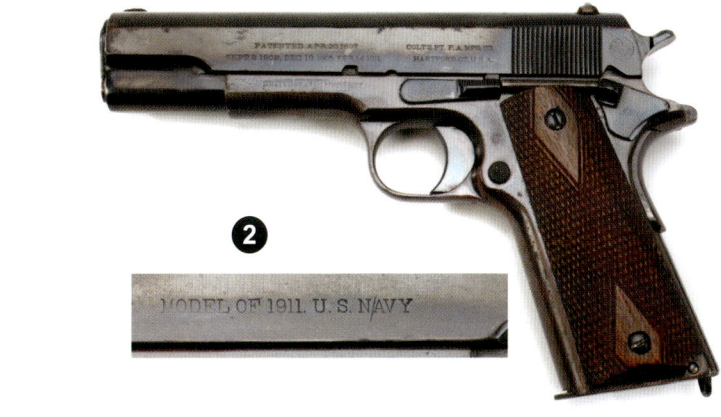
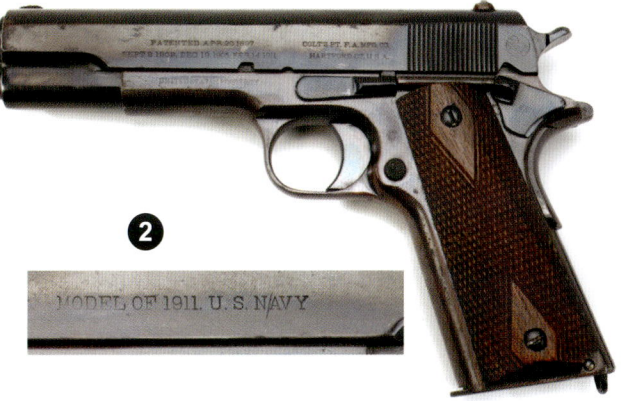

1. **U.S. Colt Model 1911 Semi-Automatic Pistol** - .45 ACP - circa 1912-1925 - Lanyard loops were added to pistols and magazines prior to WWI for retention purposes. This pistol was carried by an American officer during the 1919 Siberian Expedition in Russia.

2. **U.S. Navy Colt Model 1911 Semi-Automatic Pistol** - .45 ACP - circa 1912-1925 - Over 31,000 M1911 pistols were produced for U.S. Navy contracts and marked on the slide.

3. **U.S. North American Arms Model 1911 Semi-Automatic Pistol** - .45 ACP - circa 1918 - To provide additional supplies of the Model 1911 semi-automatic pistol, U.S. government contracts were issued to many potential suppliers, including the North American Arms Company of Quebec, Canada. Just over 100 pistols were completed before the end of World War I, but none of these were found to conform to U.S. Ordnance specifications for serial number and model marking.

4. **U.S. Remington-UMC Model 1911 Pistol** - .45 ACP - circa 1918-1919 - Less than 22,000 M1911 pistols were made by Remington-UMC.

5. **U.S. Springfield Model 1911 .22 Caliber Prototype Semi-Automatic Pistol** - .22 long rifle - circa 1914 - Springfield Armory began a .22 rimfire training pistol based on the M1911 platform that was shelved by World War. I. Roughly 25 of these semi-automatic .22 pistols were constructed.

THE WORLD AT WAR

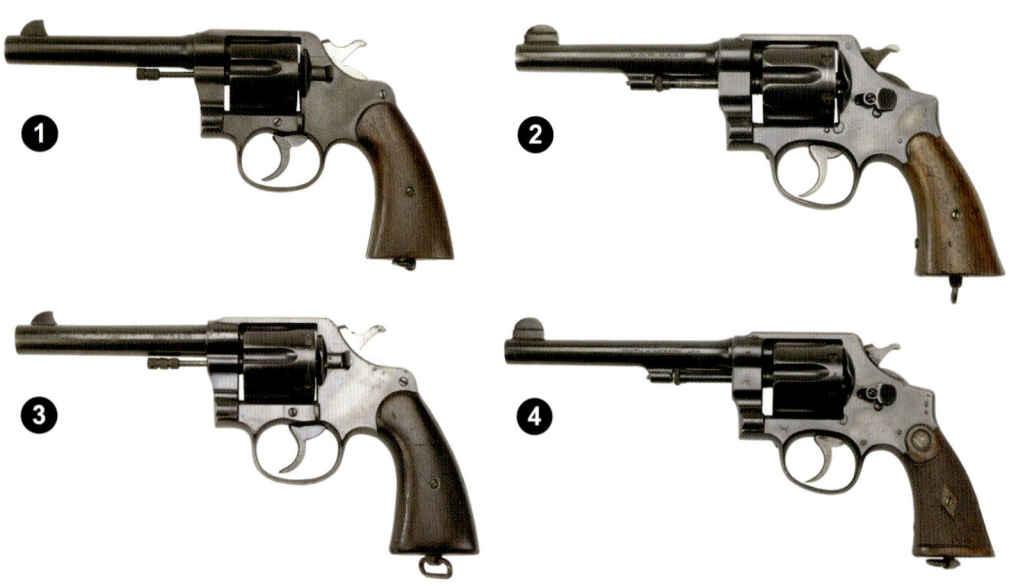

1. U.S. Colt Model 1917 Revolver - .45 ACP - circa 1917 Over 151,000 double-action Colt M1917 revolvers were produced.
2. U.S. Smith & Wesson Model 1917 Revolver - .45 ACP - circa 1917-1919 - Over 209,000 S&W M1917 revolvers were produced.
3. U.S. Colt Model 1909 U.S. Army Revolver - .45 Colt - circa 1909 - Colt's M1909 was a military version of the commercial New Service model revolver.
4. U.S. Smith & Wesson 2nd Model Hand Ejector Revolver - .455 Mk II - circa 1902-1903 - S&W produced almost 70,000 revolvers in .455 caliber for British/Canadian military orders.

U.S. Remington Mk III Flare Pistol - 10 gauge - circa 1917-1918 - The brass frame of the Mk III was intended to resist corrosion from firing flares.

U.S. Springfield Model 1903 Bolt-Action Sniper Rifle - .30-06 - circa 1907-1919 - The U.S. Warner-Swazey-scoped sniper was the first .30-06 bolt-action sniper rifle. Note extended "Air Service" 20-round magazine.

British Farquhar-Hill Model 1909 Experimental Semi-Automatic Rifle - .303 British - circa 1909 - The long recoil-operated Farquhar-Hill was intended as a squad automatic rifle and was tested by British Ordnance's Small Arms Committee in 1908. A 20-round drum magazine was intended as the standard configuration although other magazine capacities were also tested. This example is one of the rarer semi-automatic-only versions.

THE GREAT WAR

WWI Allies

A variety of bolt-action arms were used by the Allied nations to equip their infantry units. Some countries found that demand for rifles could not keep pace with production so other models for which tooling and machinery already existed were put into service production. Canadian soldiers, for example, were armed with either homegrown Ross rifles the Models 1905 or 1910, the British Enfield SMLE #1 Mk III, or American-made Pattern 14 Enfields!

1. British Enfield No. 3 Mk I Bolt-Action Rifle - .303 British - circa 1914.

2. Canadian Ross Rifle Co. Model 1910 Straight-Pull Rifle - .280 Ross - circa 1910 - Found to have a potentially dangerous bolt design, Ross rifles were sidelined from active service.

3. Canadian Ross Rifle Co. Model 1905 Straight-Pull Rifle - .303 British - circa 1906 - The straight-pull line of Ross rifles had a reputation for being unsafe firearms due to a complicated bolt that could be incorrectly reassembled and would fail to lock the action correctly during firing. During the interwar period and during World War II, the Ross rifles still in inventory were utilized for non-firing training duties.

4. British SMLE Mk III Bolt-Action Rifle - .303 British - circa 1942-1943 - The fast-firing SMLE could empty its ten-shot magazine in less than 20 seconds with an adept shooter.

5. British BSA Sparkbrook Model 1893 Mk II Magazine Lee-Metford Bolt-Action Rifle - .303 British - circa 1893 - In WWI, British forces employed earlier Lee-Enfield models that were updated for issue.

6. Remington Mosin Nagant Model 1891 Bolt-Action Rifle - 7.62mm x 54 Russian - circa 1917 - This Mosin Nagant rifle was tested by NRA during the WWI period.

7. Russian Mosin Nagant Model 1891 Bolt-Action Rifle - 7.62mm x 54 Russian - circa 1911 - Russia's standard service rifle in World War I held five cartridges.

THE WORLD AT WAR

1. French Tulle Model 1886/93 Lebel Bolt-Action Rifle - 8mm Lebel - circa 1900-1918 - The French Lebel was one of the first rifles to employ both jacketed bullets and smokeless powder.

2. French Berthier Model 1916/27 Bolt-Action Carbine - 8mm Lebel - circa 1892-1920 - Shorter carbines were used for cavalry and artillery units.

3. French St. Etienne French Model 1917 Semi-Automatic Rifle - 8mm Lebel - circa 1917-1925 - French semi-auto rifle designs did not come into use until late in WWI.

4. Belgian Hopkins & Allen Contract Mauser Model 1889 Bolt-Action Rifle - 7.65mm Mauser - circa 1889-1915 - H&A's contract with Belgian authorities resulted in 180,000 M1889 rifles for WWI.

5. French Lebel Model 1907-15 Bolt-Action Rifle (sectionalized) - 8mm Lebel - circa 1907 - This cutaway of a military firearm illustrates many of its otherwise hidden internal mechanisms.

6. French Berthier Model 1907/15 Bolt-Action Rifle - 8mm Lebel - circa 1917.

7. Russian Contract Winchester Model 1895 Lever-Action Rifle - 7.62x54 Russian - circa 1915 - 1916 - Winchester made M1895 rifles for Russia that used military stripper clips.

THE GREAT WAR

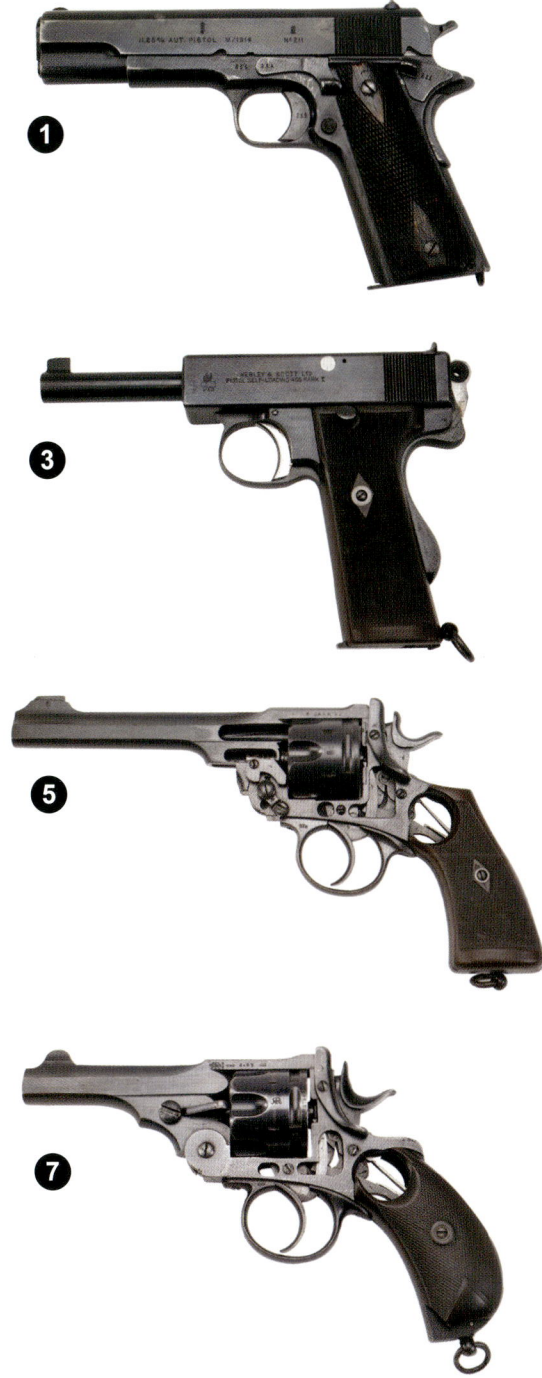

Revolvers

Revolvers were produced in great quantities and became indispensable on nightly trench raids. From 1915 to 1917, Britain purchased quantities of Colt Model 1911 pistols and both Colt and Smith & Wesson revolvers in .455 caliber to keep up with demand.

1. Norwegian Model 1914 Pistol - .45 ACP - circa 1914 - The Model 1911 semi-automatic pistol design proved popular in other nations. Almost 33,000 copies of the M1911 design were built in Norway. This is the last one made.

2. British P. Webley & Sons Pryse Revolver - .455 Webley - circa mid-1870s.

3. British Webley & Scott Model 1912 Mk I Semi-Automatic Pistol - .455 W&S Self-Loader - circa 1909-1938 - Semi-auto Webley pistols were issued to Horse Artillery units.

4. British Webley Mk IV Revolver - .455 Webley - circa 1899-1914 - Webley's Mk IV .455 revolver was the last British military blackpowder-proofed model.

5. British Webley Mk VI Revolver (sectionalized) - .455 Webley - circa 1915-1919 - Sectionalized handguns are created by military armorers as a means of instruction in operating mechanisms. Strategically cut windows in the side of frames, cylinders, and barrels reveal how springs are mounted and the correct alignment or working relationship of parts. Sectionalized or cutaway pieces are often created from condemned pistols no longer suitable for shooting.

6. Webley Mk V Revolver - .455 Webley - circa 1914-1915 - Most MARK V Webleys were shipped to former colonies such as Australia or New Zealand.

7. British Webley Mk I Revolver (sectionalized) - .455 Webley - circa 1894-1897.

8. Belgian Montenegrin Single-Action Revolver - 11.75mm Gasser - circa 1914-1918 - A Montenegrin Air Corps individual reportedly received this revolver in 1914.

9. British Webley No. 1 Mk 1 Flare Pistol - 26mm - circa 1917-1918 - A strong break-open design, Webley's flare pistols were made of brass to resist corrosion.

THE WORLD AT WAR

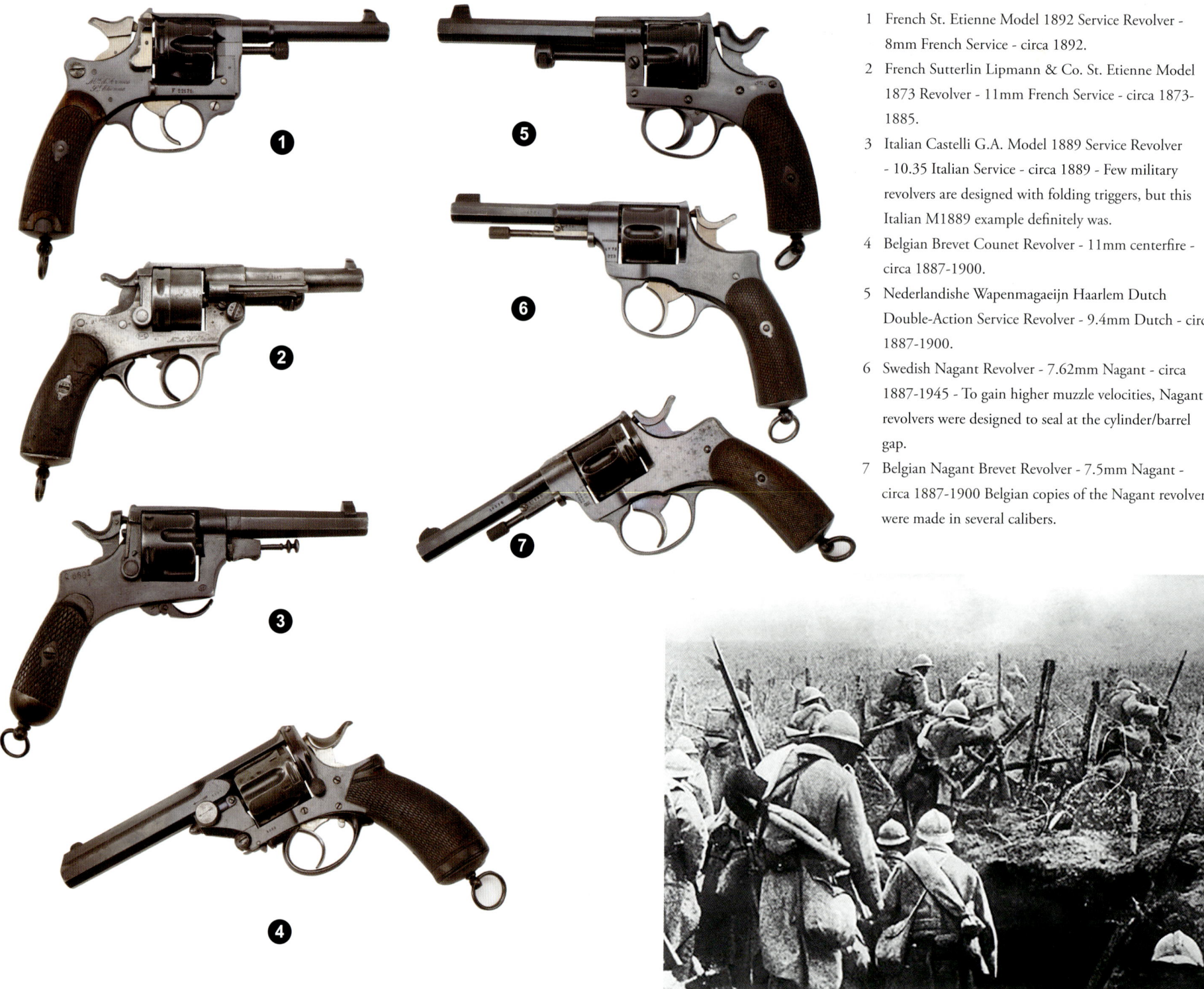

1. French St. Etienne Model 1892 Service Revolver - 8mm French Service - circa 1892.
2. French Sutterlin Lipmann & Co. St. Etienne Model 1873 Revolver - 11mm French Service - circa 1873-1885.
3. Italian Castelli G.A. Model 1889 Service Revolver - 10.35 Italian Service - circa 1889 - Few military revolvers are designed with folding triggers, but this Italian M1889 example definitely was.
4. Belgian Brevet Counet Revolver - 11mm centerfire - circa 1887-1900.
5. Nederlandishe Wapenmagaeijn Haarlem Dutch Double-Action Service Revolver - 9.4mm Dutch - circa 1887-1900.
6. Swedish Nagant Revolver - 7.62mm Nagant - circa 1887-1945 - To gain higher muzzle velocities, Nagant revolvers were designed to seal at the cylinder/barrel gap.
7. Belgian Nagant Brevet Revolver - 7.5mm Nagant - circa 1887-1900 Belgian copies of the Nagant revolver were made in several calibers.

THE GREAT WAR

German Waffenwerke Oberspree Kornbusch Gew98 Bolt-Action Rifle - 8mm Mauser - circa 1917 - The Gew98 featured a Lange-pattern rear sight with a curved range elevator.

German Mauser Model 1888 Commission Bolt-Action Rifle - 8mm Mauser - circa 1894 - The Commission 88 rifle featured a barrel jacket and a Mannlicher-style box magazine.

German J.P. Sauer & Sohn Gew98 Sniper Rifle - 8mm - circa 1916-1917 - A limited number of German Gew98 bolt-action rifles were converted to utilize a monocular sight that superimposed a pyramidal aiming point in the field of view. This sniper system was intended for quick target acquisition under low light conditions as this optic proved faster to use than traditional iron sights, but magnification also had to be low to maximize field of view.

German Deutsche Waffen und Munitionsfabriken Model 1917 Artillery Luger Semi-Automatic Pistol with holster, shoulder stock, cleaning rod, and loading tool - 9mm - circa 1917 - Red-painted "9" grip markings refer to the caliber of the pistol to distinguish it from other 7.63mm caliber guns.

German Erfurt Luger LP-08 Artillery Semi-Automatic Pistol - 9mm - circa 1915 - The Luger pistol was manufactured in different barrel-length configurations; the longer Lange Pistole 08 was intended for artillery and ancillary specialty units. A special elevation-adjustable rear sight was mounted at the rear of the barrel and could be adjusted to 800 meters.

THE WORLD AT WAR

Central Powers' Rifles

The bolt-action design of the Mauser brothers and the straight-pull bolt of the Austrian Mannlicher system accounted for the majority of arms carried by the Central Powers. Most arms accepted a 7.92mm cartridge, the "8mm," as the Mauser cartridge is also known.

1. Austrian Waffenfabrik Steyr Model 1895 Bolt-Action Carbine - 8x57mm - circa 1895-1940 - Used in both WWI and WWII.

2. Austro-Hungarian Model 1867 Werndl Rifle - 11mm Werndl - circa 1870-1879.

3. German Erfurt Arsenal Model 1891 Commission Bolt-Action Carbine - 8mm Mauser - circa 1896 - Recalled Erfurt carbines were upgraded to take new 8mm service ammunition for WWI.

4. German Erfurt Arsenal German Karabiner 98a Bolt-Action Carbine - 8mm Mauser - circa 1918 - Original issue configuration complete with breech and muzzle covers.

5. Swiss S.I.G. Mondragon Semi-Automatic Rifle - 7.5mm Mondragon - circa 1914-1916 - The Mexican-designed Mondragon was one of the first semi-automatic rifles. Prior to the usage of machine guns in aerial combat, it was employed by German aviators, offsetting the pistols and rifles brought aloft by their French and British counterparts for aerial combat. The ability to mount a 100-round drum magazine later offered enhanced firepower capability for the Mondragon's selective-fire light machine gun version.

6. German Mauser Gew 98 Bolt-Action Sniper Rifle - 8mm Mauser - circa 1916 - Sniper rifles had both optical and iron sight capability.

THE GREAT WAR

Tank Warfare

Chemical weapons, machine guns, and tanks were first widely used in WWI. France and Britain produced a total of more than 6,500 tanks. Germany only produced 20. Instead, Germany developed a heavy anti-tank rifle resembling an enlarged Mauser that fired a cartridge roughly equivalent to the later .50 BMG that would easily penetrate the thin metal armor of early tanks. The German approach proved effective. For example, only 28% of the allied tanks deployed in the battle of Amiens survived four days of combat.

At left: German Mauser Waffen Munitionsfabrik Single-Shot Bolt-Action Anti-Tank Rifle - 13mm - circa 1917 - Heavy with bipod and ammunition, the Mauser anti-tank rifle was the first anti-tank rifle. This massive gun fired a high-velocity tungsten-core 13.2mm projectile, which proved effective against the early Allied tanks.

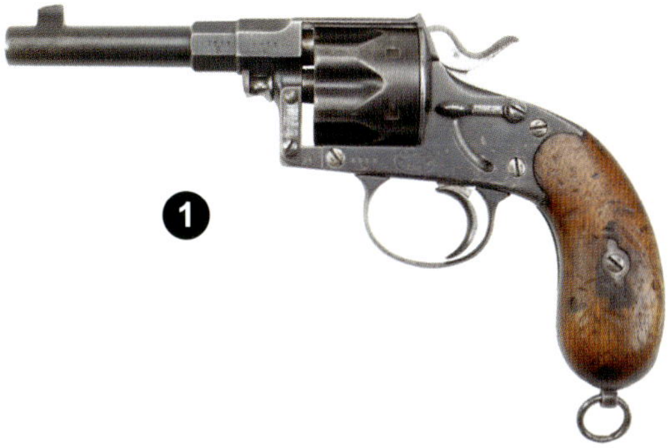

1. German CS CGH Suhl Single-Action Model 1883 Commission Reichsrevolver - 10.6mm German Service - circa 1890.
2. German Gebruder Mauser und Cie Model 1879 Double-Action Reichsrevolver - 10.6mm German Service - circa 1890-1895 - Mauser produced both revolvers and rifles for German military contracts.
3. German Dreyse Model 1879 Commission Single-Action Reichsrevolver - 10.6mm German Service - circa 1880-1914 - Reichsrevolvers were issued in both single-action and double-action versions, with the cylinder chambers individually numbered. This example bears unit issue markings from two artillery units.
4. German Mauser Model 1896 Broomhandle Semi-Automatic Pistol - .30 Mauser - circa 1920 - Post WWI, many Mauser pistols received shortened barrels to comply with Versailles Treaty requirements.

THE WORLD AT WAR

1. German Mauser Model 1896 Broomhandle Export Semi-Automatic Pistol - 9mm Mauser - circa 1914-1918 - The 10-shot Mauser M1896 was widely exported both before and after WWI.
2. German Deutsche Waffen und Munitionsfabriken Model 1914 Artillery Luger Semi-Automatic Pistol with snail drum magazine - 9mm - circa 1917 - Luger pistol carbines offered better range capability than standard sidearms.
3. German Bergmann Model 1896 Semi-Automatic Pistol - 5mm Bergmann - circa 1896-1910 - Bergmann's compact pistol design utilized a recoil spring within its bolt.
4. German Mauser Model 1896 Broomhandle Semi-Automatic Pistol - 7.63 Mauser - circa 1912-1916 - Mauser's M1896 had an integral magazine that could be quickly reloaded with a 10-shot stripper clip.
5. Belgian Charles Clement Model 1910 Semi-Automatic Pistol - 7.65mm - circa 1910-1914 - Private-purchase pistols were popular officer choices for personal protection.
6. Austrian Steyr Daimler Puch A.G. Model 1907 Roth Steyr Semi-Automatic Pistol - 8mm Roth-Steyr - circa 1909-1920 - Steyr's striker-fired design was later applied to the modern Glock pistol.
7. Austrian Steyr Daimler Puch A.G. Model 1911 Steyr-Hahn Semi-Automatic Pistol - 9mm Steyr - circa 1912-1916 - Steyr's M1911 design had an integral magazine using stripper clips.
8. Argentine Mannlicher Model 1905 Semi-Automatic Pistol - 7.63 Mannlicher - circa 1909-1929 - Mannlicher's M1905 pistol had limited European military acceptance.
9. Austrian Werder Single-Shot Pistol - 11mm Werder - circa 1869-1880 - Single-shot Werders were issued to horse-drawn artillery units.

THE GREAT WAR

1. Austrian Waffenfabrik Steyr Steyr-Mannlicher Model 1890 Bolt-Action Rifle - 8mm x 50R - circa 1890-1893.
2. Austrian Steyr Oester Waffenfabrik Ges. Model 1909 Semi-Automatic Pistol - 7.65mm - circa 1909-1939 - Lower barrel axis for lighter apparent recoil.
3. German Jager Waffenfabrik Semi-Automatic Pistol - 7.65mm - circa 1913-1915 - Jager's stamped construction pistol failed German military review in WWI.
4. German Schwarzlose Gmbh Model 1908 Semi-Automatic Pistol - 7.65mm - circa 1908-1911 - Austrian Andreas Schwarzlose designed this pistol to function in a unique blow-forward recoil system. The barrel of this pistol moves forward on firing, exposing the expended cartridge casing, which is knocked away by a mechanical ejector. An unusual feature of this pistol is the grip safety that can be locked into the fire position by depressing a frame-mounted button.
5. Belgian Anciens Etablissements Pieper Model 1908 Bergmann-Bayard Semi-Automatic Pistol - 9mm Bergmann-Bayard - circa 1908-1918 - Bergmann-Bayard's M1908 Spanish military pistols were made in Belgium.
6. German Langenhan FL Selbstlader Semi-Automatic Pistol - 7.65mm - circa 1914-1916 - A worn Langenhan's breechblock could blow into the shooter's face.
7. German Mauser Model 1896 Broomhandle Semi-Automatic Pistol - 9mm Mauser - circa 1916-1918 - 9mm Mauser M1896 pistols bore special grips marked with a red "9" to show they used a different ammunition.
8. Swiss Waffenfabrik Bern Model 1906 Luger Semi-Automatic Pistol - 7.65 Parabellum - circa 1906-1919 - Swiss Lugers continued in secondary military service into the 1950s.
9. German Deutsche Waffen & Munitions Fabriken P.04 Naval Luger Semi-Automatic Pistol - 9mm Parabellum - circa 1916 - Adopted after a series of trials culminating in 1904 by the Kaiserliche Marine, the Luger P.04 was intend to replace revolvers in the hands of landing parties. This example bears issue markings from the dockyards of Wilhemshaven. Larger German capital ships, such as battleships, received up to 100 pistols.
10. German Mauser Model 1896 Broomhandle Semi-Automatic Pistol with shoulder stock - 7.63 Mauser - circa 1914-1916.

THE WORLD AT WAR

Inter-War Arms Development

WWI saw the introduction of submachine guns. These are shoulder-fired arms chambered for pistol-power cartridges capable of full auto fire — that is, they will fire continuously so long as the trigger is held back and there is ammunition in the magazine. The American Thompson was introduced too late for extensive usage. There was also limited use of self-loading or semi-automatic rifles. These fire one round per pull of the trigger and were generally chambered for full-power rifle cartridges of the class used in bolt-action rifles of the era. Both trends continued between the wars.

U.S. M1A1 Thompson - .45 ACP - WWII - Brought back from WWII by Lt. Dwight Edwin Markley. His B-17, Sweet Chariot, was part of the 8th Air Force, participating in several missions over Europe, even surviving a mid-air collision with another bomber.

INTER-WAR ARMS DEVELOPMENT

Top - 1928 Navy-issue Thompson submachine gun with 50 round drum, .45 ACP. Later overstamped for the Maryland State Police.

Bottom - Early Model 1921 Thompson, .45 ACP, with 100 round drum, also shown open *(inset)*.

Thompson

John T. Thompson was born in Kentucky in 1860 and graduated from the U.S. Military Academy at West Point in 1882. He joined the U.S. Army Ordnance Department and retired as a Brigadier General in 1914. He patented numerous devices for automatic small arms. His greatest invention, however, was the Thompson submachine gun. Chambered for the .45 ACP cartridge, this air-cooled selective-fire firearm used a delayed blowback action, creating an extremely reliable firearm. The submachine gun, manufactured on contract by Colt and the Auto Ordnance Company, was capable of firing from a two-column box magazine, holding 20 rounds or drum magazines with either 50- or 100-round capacity.

Thompson's gun was first used in combat by the U.S. Marine Corps in Nicaragua in 1925. Widely purchased by police departments and the U.S. military, the Thompson submachine gun was widely used by both U.S. and allied troops during World War II. The use of this firearm in the hands of legendary lawmen and infamous gangsters alike in the early part of the 20th Century earned it the moniker "the gun that made the '20s roar!"

U.S. Auto Ordnance Model 1928 Thompson Submachine Gun (deactivated) - .45 ACP - circa 1940 - Discovered on the Anzio beachhead, this M1928 SMG was reportedly used to eliminate 19 Germans by a British soldier.

THE WORLD AT WAR

Oversized Instructional Cutaway M1 Garand Training Model - circa 1950 - Shown with standard M1 Garand for scale. Constructed of painted wood, this large-scale model of an M1 Garand rifle is cutaway on one side to demonstrate the operating mechanism. Equipped with inert cartridges, the model could be shown in front of an audience as part of a small arms training familiarization.

The Garand

John C. Garand was born in Canada on New Year's Day 1888. Moving to Connecticut at an early age, he developed an interest in firearms while helping his brother operate a shooting gallery. He obtained a position at the Springfield Armory and in 1919 began his work on developing a semi-automatic operating system for a rifle action. His design, popularly known as the Garand Semi-Automatic Rifle, was ready for testing by 1930. Officially adopted by the U.S. Army in 1936, as the U.S. Rifle, Caliber .30, M1, the Garand is a gas-operated rifle with an 8-round en bloc clip inserted from the top. Ejecting each spent cartridge, the gun automatically loaded a new one with each trigger pull. General George S. Patton, Jr., dubbed the M1 "**the finest battle implement ever devised**."

The United States was the only nation in World War II to equip its infantry with a semi-automatic rifle as a standard service arm. As such, arms historians have credited the M1 Garand with an important role in the Allies' victory in World War II. Over four million M1 Garand rifles were manufactured during World War II. More were built during the Korean War and M1 Rifle serial numbers reach into the six million range.

Detail of Garand en bloc loading system.

U.S. Springfield T3E2 Semi-Automatic Rifle - .276 Pedersen caliber - circa 1931 - Forerunner of the M1 Garand, 20 of these rifles were tested in 1931. Although this general design was chosen, the caliber was changed to .30-06 for military service.

Vickers Armstrong Ltd. Vickers-Pedersen Semi-Automatic Rifle - .276 Pedersen - circa 1926-1928
The Pedersen was the primary competitor of the Garand for adoption as the U.S. military semi-auto service rifle. It relied on a upward-acting toggle-joint action similar in operation to the Luger pistol, but improved with delayed blowback operation. To work within the special parameters of this design, Vickers-Pedersen rifles were intended to be used with wax-coated ammunition.

INTER-WAR ARMS DEVELOPMENT

U.S. Harrington & Richardson M1 Semi-Automatic Rifle (sectionalized) - .30-06 - circa 1953 - This cutaway Garand was part of an electronic demonstration exhibit used by the U.S. Army.

U.S. Springfield M1 Garand Semi-Automatic Rifle with Grenade Sight, M7A3 Grenade Launcher - .30-06 - circa 1945 - Firing rifle grenades from an M1 Garand required a special blank cartridge.

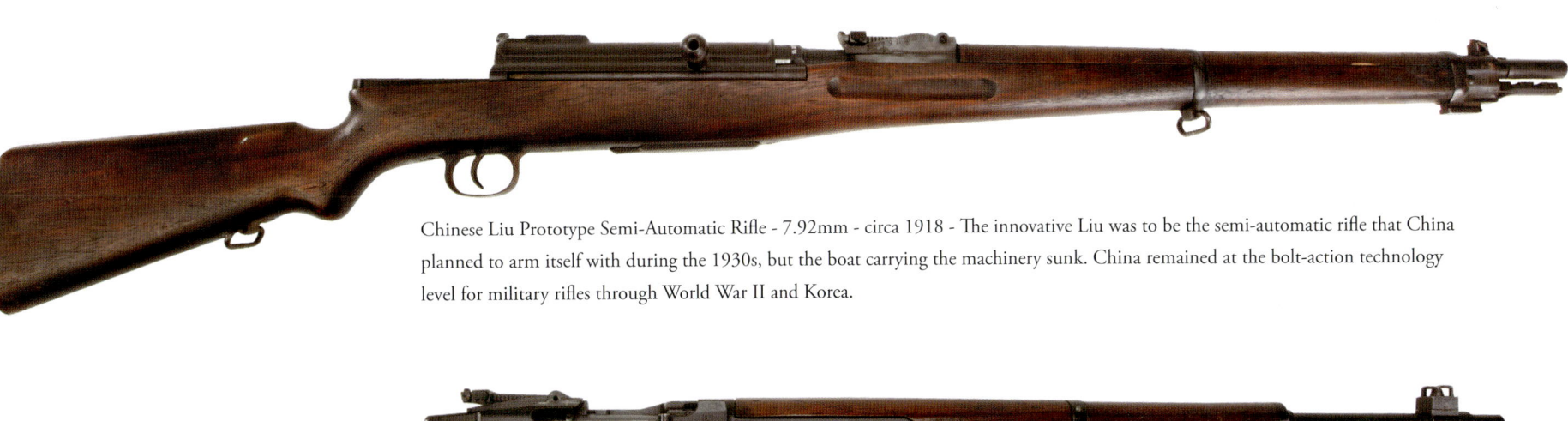

Chinese Liu Prototype Semi-Automatic Rifle - 7.92mm - circa 1918 - The innovative Liu was to be the semi-automatic rifle that China planned to arm itself with during the 1930s, but the boat carrying the machinery sunk. China remained at the bolt-action technology level for military rifles through World War II and Korea.

Japanese Type 5 Semi-Automatic Rifle - 7.7mm - circa 1945 - Japanese semi-automatic rifle development during World War II resulted in the Type 5, a direct copy of the American Garand rifle in 7.7mm. A few unissued examples were located in a Japanese naval arsenal at the end of the war.

THE WORLD AT WAR

1. U.S. General Motors - Inland Manufacturing Division M1A1 Semi-Automatic Carbine - .30 Carbine - circa 1943.

2. U.S. Remington Model 1903A1 Bolt-Action Rifle - .30-06 - circa 1942 - Rock Island Arsenal machinery was adapted by Remington to produce M1903A1 rifles in WWII.

3. U.S. Smith-Corona Model 1903A3 Bolt-Action Rifle - .30-06 - circa 1944 - Smith-Corona, a former typewriter company, tooled up to make M1903A3 rifles in WWII.

4. U.S. Johnson Automatics Model 1941 Semi-Automatic Rifle - .30-06 - circa 1941 - The Johnson's 10-round magazine could be quickly loaded with stripper clips.

5. U.S. Winchester Model of 1918 Browning Automatic Rifle (BAR) - .30-06 - circa 1944 - The Browning Automatic Rifle was developed to replace unreliable French light machine guns, and although it entered service late in World War I, this firearm was a mainstay of American forces through WWII and Korea. A gas-operated, selective-fire arm intended for squad-level automatic fire, the BAR suffered only from the limited firepower capacity of its 20-round box magazine.

The World at War: World War II

The global conflict, fought between 1939 and 1945, is considered the largest and most destructive war in history. Truly a world war, campaigns were fought in Europe, Asia, Africa, North America (Alaska), and the islands in the Pacific. Total casualties numbered 60-80 million, including the largest number of civilians ever to die as a result of one war. The submachine gun, light machine gun, and semi-automatic sidearms were used in great numbers, further changing the shape and scope of infantry tactics as platoon and squad strength unit actions defined typical combat experiences.

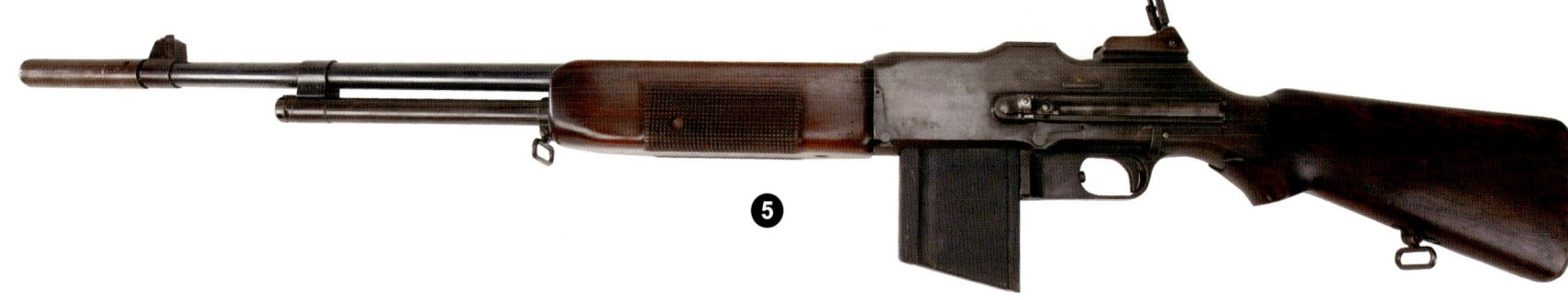

WORLD WAR II

1. Winchester Model 69 Bolt-Action Rifle with Sectionalized Maxim Suppressor - .22 long rifle - circa 1935-1941 - Reportedly sent to England for training in covert use of suppressed arms.
2. U.S. Stevens Model 620 Slide-Action Shotgun - 12 gauge - circa 1944-1945 - Many WWII-era commercial shotguns, such as this Stevens 620, were adapted for military service with the addition of metal handguards and bayonet lugs. These shotguns were used for secondary military roles, freeing up rifles that could be sent to the front lines.
3. U.S. Winchester Model 12 Slide-Action Riot Shotgun - 12 gauge - circa 1943 - Winchester slide-action shotguns were modified to take a rifle bayonet with a ventilated barrel handguard.
4. U.S. Remington Model 11 Shotgun - 12 gauge - circa 1944 - Semi-auto shotguns were used by Army Air Corps trainees in aerial target shooting simulations.
5. U.S. Victory Training Rifle - circa 1941 - Wooden training rifles were utilized in both WWI and WWII eras to allow more drilling and arms handling instruction for soldiers without the need for ammunition.

WWII: U.S.

Products of "The Great Arsenal of Democracy," arms and equipment made in the United States, were directly responsible for the victory of democratic ideals over those of dictators and fascists. The entire country was placed on a war economy in 1942 and all manufacturing and even agricultural resources were turned to the war effort. With men serving on the battlefront, women workers replaced them at their posts in the armories and firearms manufacturing plants throughout the country, becoming competent and skilled contributors to the war effort. Millions of rifles, pistols, tanks, and planes were produced in the greatest manufacturing effort in history. Major gun manufacturers suspended their sporting lines and produced arms for the infantry and Marines. Colt and Winchester produced a dizzying array of arms with Remington and Smith & Wesson supplying a great deal of needed firepower. Companies that in peacetime produced items such as jukeboxes, sewing machines and typewriters produced rifles and pistols. In just the field of small arms, the list of manufacturers is impressive:

Company - Peacetime Goods - War Production

Guide Lamp Division General Motors - Automotive Components - OSS Liberator Pistol
National Postal Meter - Metering Machines - M1 Carbines
Remington Rand - Typewriters - M1911A1 Pistols
IBM - Business Machines - M1 Carbines
Smith-Corona - Typewriters - M1903A3 Rifles
Quality Hardware - Sheet Metal Fabricating Machines - M1 Carbines
Union Switch & Signal - Railroad Equipment - M1911A1 Pistols
Rock-Ola Manufacturing - Jukeboxes - M1 Carbines
Singer Manufacturing - Sewing Machines - M1911A1 Pistols
Inland Division General Motors - Automobile Steering Wheels - M1 Carbines
Standard Products Co. - Automobile Windows - M1 Carbines

THE WORLD AT WAR

U.S. Underwood-Elliot-Fisher Semi-Automatic M1 Carbine - .30 Carbine - circa 1944 - Designed to serve as a longer-ranged replacement for handguns and for military personnel who did not require the full-sized M1 Garand, the M1 carbine was a lightweight semi-automatic rifle that was widely issued in both European and Pacific campaigns. Over six-and-a-half million M1 carbines were produced during the WWII years. Underwood-Elliot-Fisher made 19 components for the 62-part M1 carbine that were used by 10 different contractors to assemble guns.

U.S. Remington Model 1903A4 Bolt-Action Rifle with Telescopic Sight - .30-06 - circa 1944 - A quick adaptation for the venerable Springfield M1903 pattern rifle to convert it for sniping service was done by the addition of a modified Weaver 330 telescopic sight. While expedient, the low magnification and low moisture resistance of the optic challenged long-range shooters of the M1903A4 rifle. Its telescopic mount base prevented reloading via stripper clips.

Winchester Accuracy Test Fixture - .50 Browning - circa 1942 - Wartime production requirements resulted in faster manufacturing. To test sample lots many companies relied on test fixtures that could be used to chronograph ammunition for velocity and pressure, ensuring that only quality materials were forwarded to the armed forces.

Smith & Wesson Model 1940 Semi-Automatic Light Rifle - 9mm Parabellum - circa 1940-1941 - A flawed design, these were never issued and almost all of the S&W Light Rifles were destroyed after WWII.

WORLD WAR II

WWII: Allies

In the first years of World War II (Sept. 1939 to June 1941), the British Empire and Commonwealth stood alone, allied against the German-Italian tide. The Soviet Union joined the Allies after Germany invaded Russia in June 1941. The United States maintained a formal stance of neutrality until the Japanese sneak attack at Pearl Harbor on December 7, 1941, brought the nation into the war as an Allied Power. Prior to that time the American public had been generally sympathetic toward the plight of the British. Legislation was passed in Congress allowing for the transfer of arms, ammunition, and vitally needed equipment such as planes, ships, and vehicles to England under the provisions of the Lend-Lease Act. Because British society lacked a heritage of personal firearms ownership, American citizens were encouraged to ship their personal firearms to England in an effort to save a British home. Over 7,000 arms were sent and issued to Home Guard units for local defense.

The Sixguns of World War II

Although the 1911A1 pistol was the standard American issue sidearm of WWII, the demand was such that large numbers of revolvers were produced as well. During WWI, S&W and Colt each adapted their large-frame revolvers to fire the standard-issue rimless .45 ACP cartridges by using sheet metal "moon clips" that held six rounds in position to be fired. These were both named the Model 1917 and continued in use during WWII.

The production of the Smith & Wesson factory during WWII went to the war effort, primarily making military versions of their popular six-shot .38 Special Military & Police revolvers. These came to be known as Victory Models, and a V prefix was added to the serial number. The Colt counterpart was the Commando Model. S&W also made the Military & Police in .38 S&W for the British Commonwealth nations, including Britain, Canada, Australia, and New Zealand, with the model designation .38-200 British Service Revolver.

1. Smith & Wesson 38-100 British Service Revolver - .38 S&W - circa 1941 - Identical to the S&W U.S. Victory Model, except for the chambering. Over 500,000 were produced during the war years; replaced grips.
2. U.S. Colt Commando Revolver - .38 Special - circa 1942-1945 - After WWII, many Victory Models were transferred to law enforcement agencies.
3. U.S. Smith & Wesson Model 1917 Revolver - .45 ACP - circa 1935 - Ensign John Wesson (grandson of the S&W founder) received this M1917 when he graduated from the U.S. Naval Academy.
4. Smith & Wesson 38-100 British Service Revolver - .38 S&W - circa 1944 - Note the late war "Black Magic" phosphate-type finish compared to the earlier commercial finishes. After the war, many Victory and 38-100 revolvers were issued to European police forces, and marked accordingly, such as this one.
5. U.S. Smith & Wesson Model 1917 Revolver - .22 rimfire (converted) - circa 1943 - This M1917 was used by Norwegian resistance fighters in WWII.
6. U.S. Union Switch & Signal Model 1911A1 Semi-Automatic Pistol - .45 ACP - circa 1943 - Second smallest producer of the M1911A1 pistol in WWII.
7. U.S. Colt Model 1911A1 Semi-Automatic Pistol - .45 ACP - circa 1943 - Finishes on the M1911A1 went from bluing to parkerizing as the war went on.

THE WORLD AT WAR

1. British Enfield No. 5 Mk I Bolt-Action Jungle Carbine with No. 5 Mk I Bayonet - .303 British - circa 1945.

2. Savage No. 4 Mk I Bolt-Action Rifle w/ No. 7 Folding Bayonet - .303 British - circa 1941 - Tool room prototype built prior to U.S. entry into WWII at Savage.

3. British Enfield SMLE Mk III Bolt-Action Rifle - .303 British - circa 1917 - Older WWI British rifles were recycled for WWII use.

4. French MAS Model 1936 Bolt-Action Rifle - 7.5mm M29 - circa 1937-1940 - The French MAS rifle had a weaker action than the Mauser.

5. French St. Etienne Model 1886/93 (R-35) Bolt-Action Carbine - 8mm Lebel - circa 1939 - Rebuilt with spare parts, older French rifles went into WWII service.

6. French Lebel Model 1907/15 Bolt-Action Rifle - 7.5mm - circa 1917 - Altered for more powerful cartridges, older French rifles were pressed into service.

7. Canadian Ross Model 1905 Straight-Pull Bolt-Action Rifle - .303 British - circa 1914 - Many Canadian Ross rifles were used only as training arms.

WORLD WAR II

1. Finnish Mosin Nagant Model 27 Bolt-Action Rifle - 7.62mm x 54R - circa 1933 - Captured Russian rifles served Finnish forces in WWII.

2. Russian Mosin Nagant Model 1944 Bolt-Action Carbine - 7.62mm x 54R - circa 1944-1945 - Late-war M/N carbines were fitted with a folding bayonet.

3. Russian Tokarev Model 1938 SVT Semi-Automatic Rifle - 7.62mm x 54R - circa 1940 - Early semi-auto Soviet rifles had operating issues in cold weather.

4. Russian Mosin Nagant Model 1891 Bolt-Action Rifle - 7.62mm x 54R - circa 1897-1905 - Russian-rebuilt rifles for WWII included pre-1900 contract arms.

5. Russian SVT-40 Semi-Automatic Sniper Rifle - 7.62mm x 54R - circa 1941 - This later gas-operated arm supplemented traditional bolt-actions in the Russian infantry. About 51,710 SVT snipers were built out of the total of 1.6 million rifles manufactured by 1945.

THE WORLD AT WAR

1. Mexican Fabrica de Armas Obregon Semi-Automatic Pistol - .45 caliber - circa 1930-1936 - Built in Mexico City, the semi-automatic Obregon pistol combines elements of the Steyr-Hahn barrel system with the Colt-Browning M1911 design. Most of the 1,000 pistols made were sold through the Mexican commercial market.
2. Swedish Husqvarna Model 1903 Semi-Automatic Pistol - .380 ACP - circa 1903-1940 - Re-chambered for U.S. post-war importation.
3. British Enfield No. 1 Mk VI Revolver - .455 Webley - circa 1923 - A between-the-wars Webley pattern .455 revolver.
4. British Ballester-Molina British Contract Pistol - .45 ACP - circa 1940 - British military contracts for WWII sidearms included more than 10,000 Argentine Ballester-Molina-built copies of Colt's M1911 semi-automatic design. Similar to the Colt M1911A1, Ballester-Molina pistols had no grip safety feature.
5. British Enfield No. 2 Mk I Revolver - .38 S&W (.38-200 British) - circa 1932 - Bobbed hammers were done for better maneuvering in tight quarters.
6. Fabrique Nationale/Inglis P-35 Hi-Power Semi-Automatic Pistol - 9mm Parabellum - circa 1944-1945 - Chinese contract copies of the P35 pistol were made by flame pantograph.
7. French St. Etienne French Nagant Model 1892 Double-Action Ordnance Revolver - 8mm - circa 1904 - Older obsolete French revolvers continued in WWII service.
8. Russian Nagant Model 1895 Double-Action Service Revolver - 7.62mm Nagant - circa 1931 - Well after military semi-auto pistols were in production, Russia continued to make military revolvers.
9. Russian Tokarev Model 1933 Semi-Automatic Pistol - 7.62 Tokarev - circa 1943 - Copying certain Colt-Browning handgun features, the Tokarev T33 semi-automatic pistol incorporates a modified hammer/sear assembly that can be removed as a unit.
10. Philippine Resistance Revolver - .38 cartridge - circa 1942 - Crudely constructed, this handmade handgun was built by members of the Philippine resistance using only a file and drill. Reportedly, it claimed the lives of six enemy soldiers and was fired several hundred times without failure.

WORLD WAR II

British B.S.A./Holland & Holland No. 4 Mk I (T) Bolt-Action Sniper Rifle - .303 British - circa 1944-1945 - Selected No. 4 rifles in World War II, chosen for accuracy, were forwarded to Holland & Holland for further accurizing and telescopic sight fitting. The completed sniper rifles were placed in transit crates, paired with scout regiment telescopes.

Japanese Nagoya Army Arsenal Type 97 Arisaka Bolt-Action Sniper Rifle with telescopic sight - 6.5mm - circa 1942 - Japanese sniper rifles were standard production guns fitted with optics.

Japanese Type 99 Bolt-Action Sniper Rifle with Scope - 7.7mm - circa 1943 - Unlike European tradition, Japanese sniper rifle optics were aligned on each rifle to a specific point of aim at a set distance. There were no external adjustments on Japanese sniper optics and as the rifle's point of impact changed due to changes in humidity, their users learned to compensate.

Swiss Schmidt-Rubin Swiss K-31/43 Straight-Pull Sniper Rifle - 7.5mm - circa 1943 - Nearly 2,000 of these Swiss K-31/43 straight-pull sniper rifles were manufactured with an integral 2.8X telescopic sight mounted on a swing-out base that allowed the iron sights to also be utilized.

THE WORLD AT WAR

Above: John Hession U.S. Springfield Model 1903 Bolt-Action Rifle - .30-06 - circa 1907 - Maj. John Hession was one of the best long range target shooters of his era. The plaque on the butt lists the many competitions he won and records he set. In the early dark days of World War II, it looked as if only the British Isles stood against the crushing might of Hitler's war machine. The English, with little tradition of civilian arms ownership, turned to America for the guns to defend their homeland. Individual Americans responded, sending their privately owned firearms across the Atlantic for the defense of England, including Hession, who sent his prize target rifle. He added a second plaque to the stock stating, "For obvious reasons, the return of this rifle after Germany is defeated would be deeply appreciated."

At right: Merkel shotgun, 12 gauge, circa 1937. presented by Generalissimo Franco of Spain to Hermann Goering, German WWI ace who was head of the WWII Luftwaffe, and Hitler's designated successor. It was captured at the end of WWII and presented to General of the Army Dwight D. Eisenhower, who in turn presented it to WWI General of the Armies, John J. "Blackjack" Pershing.

WORLD WAR II

Joe Foss's Colt 1911 Pistol - .45 ACP circa 1918, refurbished 1942. This pistol was issued in 1942 at Guadalcanal to Marine aviator and WWII ace Joe Foss, who received the Medal of Honor in 1943. Between Oct. 1942 and Jan. 1943, "Foss's Flying Circus" squadron shot down 72 enemy aircraft, 26 of those by Foss himself, including five Japanese Zeroes in a single day. He went on to become the Governor of South Dakota, the first Commissioner of the NFL, and the President of the NRA.

Admiral Lee's Colt M1911Pistol - .45 ACP - circa 1915. Service sidearm of Admiral Willis Augustus "Ching" Lee (1888 - 1945). Lee won five Olympic gold medals, one silver and one bronze in the 1920 Olympics. During WWII he was awarded the Navy Cross for his actions during the naval battle of Guadalcanal. He was the first American commander to use radar to engage in night naval combat, and the only American commander to engage the Japanese Navy in a one-on-one battleship-to-battleship fight, which he won.

THE WORLD AT WAR

U.S. General Motors Guide Lamp Division FP-45 Liberator Single-Shot Pistol - .45 ACP - circa 1943 Classified as a flare projector to keep its wartime development a secret, General Motors produced each Liberator pistol for less than $2.40, including 10 rounds of .45 ammunition and a pictorial guide sheet on its usage. Approximately one million Liberators were manufactured to be dropped to resistance forces behind enemy lines. However they were never widely issued and most were scrapped after WWII ended.

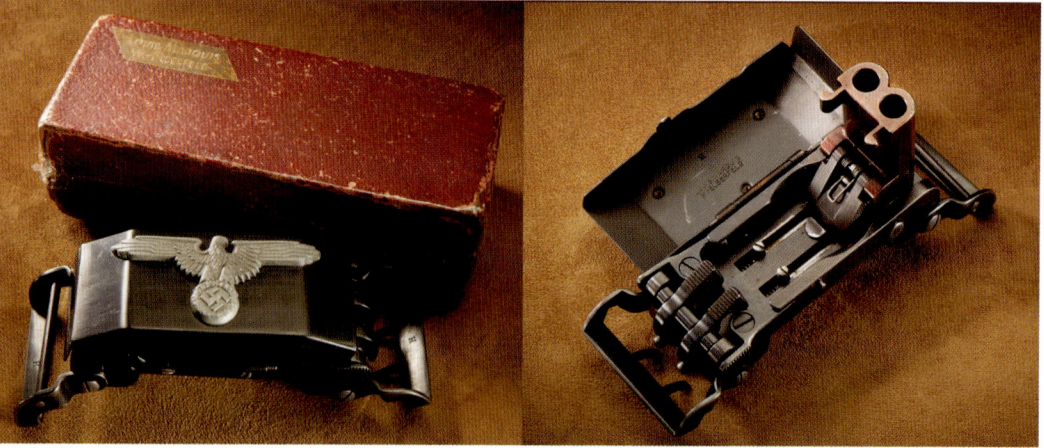

German J. P. Sauer & Sohn M30 Luftwaffe survival drilling - 9.3x74mmR, 12 gauge Considered one of the first pilot "survival" guns, this was made for German Luftwaffe pilots and was standard equipment to some German aircraft in the early years of the WWII. Two shotgun barrels mounted over a rifle barrel were intended to allow a downed pilot to forage for food.

German SS-Waffenakademie Koppelschloßpistole (belt buckle pistol) - .32 ACP - circa 1940 - Designed and manufactured by Louis Marquis, this is one of the great weapons rarities of World War II. This covert "belt buckle" pistol has a dropping front plate that exposes two twin pistol barrels ready to be fired. It is complete with original issue cardboard box.

U.S. Sedgely Glove Pistol - 38 caliber - This single-shot pistol is mounted to a glove, with a trigger mechanism extending past the muzzle. Between 50 and 200 were made for the U.S. Navy during WWII. Intended usage is unclear, although it may have been a covert assassination tool for the O.S.S. The official name was Hand Firing Mechanism Mk II.

WORLD WAR II

WWII: Axis

Germany, Italy, and Japan, known as the Axis powers, were the aggressor nations in the global struggle known as World War II. Their primary infantry armament did not differ much from that used in World War I. For these nations, the standard infantry rifle was still a bolt-action, although squads and platoon-size units were supplemented with submachine guns and light machine guns on an unprecedented scale, making them very effective.

1. German Mauser (byf) K98k Sniper Rifle - 8mm Mauser - circa 1941-1945.
2. German Mauser G41 (m) rifle - 8mm - circa 1942 Issued only in limited numbers in Italy. The Mauser-made G41(m) semi-automatic rifle had the capability to use a rearward bolt handle to continue to function the action if the gas-operated semi-automatic mechanism failed.
3. DWM (Deutsche Waffen und Munitions Fabriken) P.08 Luger Semi-Automatic Pistol - 9mm - circa 1918 British-captured handguns such as this one required proofing in the U.K. before re-issue.
4. Japanese Type 1 Folding Stock Paratrooper rifle - 6.5mm Japanese - circa 1941 - To provide a compact unit while parachuting, Japanese armorers adapted a hinged, folding stock for the Type 1 Paratrooper rifle, constructed from an otherwise standard Arisaka bolt-action rifle.
5. German Walther Gewehr 43 Semi-Automatic Rifle with Telescopic Sight - 8mm Mauser - circa 1943-1944 - Utilizing roughly cast parts, along with forged and stamped components, Germany's Gewehr 43 provided an expedient semi-automatic service rifle that blended a gas system similar to the Russian Tokarev with a bolt mechanism derived from the earlier G41 rifles made by Walther.

THE WORLD AT WAR

1. German J. G. Anschütz Wehrsportkarabiner Bolt-Action Carbine - .22 rimfire - circa 1937-1938 - Anschütz's training rifles were part of the Third Reich mobilization for military service; school-age programs featured small arms familiarization with rimfire counterparts resembling the larger 98k rifles.

2. Italian Scotti Model X Semi-Automatic Rifle - 6.5 Italian - circa 1933 - Only 250 of these semi-auto rifles were tested by the Italian military.

3. Czech Waffenfabrik Brunn AG DOT Karabiner 98k Bolt-Action Rifle with Grenade Launcher - 8mm Mauser - circa 1943-1944 - This Czech K98k has a grenade launcher attachment and side-mounted sights.

4. German Mauser-Werke K98k/ZF-41 Bolt-Action Sniper Rifle - 8mm - circa 1941-1944 - WWII German army marksmen employed rifles fitted with the low-power ZF-41 optic.

5. German Walther Volksturm Gewehr VG1 Rifle - 8mm Mauser - circa 1945 - Built by Walther as a last-ditch firearm, the VG1 bolt-action was a crudely constructed blend of components from other German military guns that could no longer be produced at the time. VG1s were distinguished by rejected magazines, barrels, and other parts from Gewehr 43 rifles as well as crudely band-sawed wood stocks.

6. Hungarian Metallwaren Budapest Model 98/40 Bolt-Action Rifle - 8mm Mauser - circa 1943 - Hungarian contract M98/40 rifles had expedient two-piece stocks.

7. Czech Waffenfabrik Brunn AG Mauser Model 33/40 Bolt-Action Carbine - 8mm Mauser - circa 1941-1943 - WWII German mountain troops employed the light M33/40 carbine.

WORLD WAR II

1. German Walther Model 41W Semi-Automatic Rifle - 8mm Mauser - circa 1942 - Walther built semi-auto rifles in early WWII to provide firepower for German infantry.

2. Swedish Carl Gustafs Stads Gevarsfaktori Model 96 Sniper Bolt-Action Rifle with Telescopic Sight - 6.5mm - circa 1917 - Germany seized occupied armaments and reissued these to their own forces.

3. German Walther K43 Semi-Automatic Rifle - 8mm Mauser - circa 1945 - K43 rifles were crudely assembled.

4. German Berliner-Luebecker Maschinenfabrik Gewehr 41 Semi-Automatic Rifle - 8mm - circa 1942-1943 - The G41 was intended to replace the aging bolt-action rifles that Germany had used in World War I and also to counter Russian semi-auto arms such as the Tokarev rifle. The intricate machining required for manufacture led to production delays, resulting in the design being replaced by the Gewehr 43 rifle.

5. Polish F. B. Radom WZ-29 Bolt-Action Short Rifle - 8mm Mauser - circa 1939.

6. Polish Radom Wz 29 Bolt-Action Rifle - 8mm Mauser - circa 1931.

THE WORLD AT WAR

1. Italian Mannlicher Carcano Model 41 Bolt-Action Rifle - 6.5mm Italian - circa 1942.

2. Brescia Italian Mannlicher Carcano Model 91/24 Bolt-Action Rifle - 6.5mm Italian - circa 1942.

3. Italian R. E. Terni Mannlicher Carcano Model 38 Bolt-Action Rifle with Model 1938 Folding Bayonet - 7.35mm Italian - circa 1939 - This Italian Carcano carbine variant incorporated a permanently affixed folding bayonet. While chambered for the 7.35mm cartridge, many arms were rechambered for the earlier 6.5mm to mitigate ammunition distribution issues later in the war.

4. Italian Brescia Mannlicher Carcano Model 1938 Bolt-Action Rifle - 7.35mm Italian - circa 1938-1942.

5. Italian Terni Arsenal Mannlicher-Carcano Model 91/29 Bolt-Action Carbine with Tromboni Launchi Bombe Grenade Launcher - 6.5 Italian - circa 1930 - Fitted with a side-mounted grenade launcher that required removing the rifle's bolt to fire grenades, the Italian Tromboni Launchi Carabini was reported to generate substantial recoil on firing.

6. Italian Gardone Fascist Youth Bolt-Action Carbine - 6.5mm Italian - circa 1942-1943 - Fascist youth groups received small-scale arms to match the size of their members.

7. Italian Gardone Model 1891 Mannlicher Carcano Bolt-Action Rifle - 6.5mm Italian - circa 1924.

WORLD WAR II

1. Japanese Tokyo Juki Kogyo Type 99 Arisaka Bolt-Action Rifle - 7.7mm - circa 1942-1943.
2. Japanese Type 38 Arisaka Bolt-Action Rifle - 6.5mm - circa 1939.
3. Japanese Type I Bolt-Action Rifle - 6.5mm - circa 1938-1939 - Italian contractors produced Carcano-based Type I rifles for Japanese military contracts.
4. Japanese Type 44 Bolt-Action Carbine - 6.5mm - circa 1912-1942.
5. Japanese Toyo Kogyo Type 99 Arisaka Bolt-Action Rifle with Nagoya Arsenal Type 30 Bayonet - 7.7mm - circa 1941 - This Type 99 was captured on Guadalcanal.
6. Japanese Type 20 Murata Bolt-Action Carbine - 8mm - circa 1880-1898 - The Type 20 was the first Japanese-designed magazine bolt-action repeater.

THE WORLD AT WAR

1. Japanese Koishikawa Arsenal Type 30 Arisaka Bolt-Action Rifle - 6.5mm - circa 1897-1905.
2. Japanese Kokura Army Arsenal Type 99 Arisaka Bolt-Action Carbine - 6.5mm - circa 1943-1944 - Two-piece stocks were required because the Japanese mainland did not support large trees.
3. Japanese Koishikawa Arsenal Type 35 Arisaka Bolt-Action Rifle - 6.5mm - circa 1944-1945.
4. Japanese Kokura Army Arsenal Type 38 Arisaka Bolt-Action Rifle - 6.5mm - circa 1905-1938.
5. Japanese Nagoya Army Arsenal Type 2 Arisaka Bolt-Action Rifle - 7.7mm - circa 1940. This takedown model disassembles in the middle for carry by paratroopers.
6. Japanese Kokura Army Arsenal Type 99 Arisaka Bolt-Action Rifle - 7.7mm - circa 1942. Folding monopod provides a stable rest for more accurate prone shooting

WORLD WAR II

1. Japanese Ceskoslovenska Zbrojovka Brno Contract VZ-24 Bolt-Action Rifle - 8mm Mauser - circa 1937 - Czech VZ-24 rifles were ordered for Japanese Special Naval Landing Forces.
2. Japanese Tokyo Arsenal Arisaka Bolt-Action Pressure Test Gun - 6.5mm - circa 1940 - Pressure test guns allowed quality checks on wartime ammunition.
3. Chinese Chiang Kai-Shek Short Model Mauser-Pattern Bolt-Action Rifle - 8mm Mauser - circa 1936-1949 - Also known as the Type 24, this rifle was based on the German K98 and was used by China against Japan.
4. Japanese Model 1922 Light Machine Gun Trainer - circa 1930 - Japanese military training for the invasion of China used an unusual machine gun trainer that required no ammunition. A hose brought carbide gas to a sparking element inside the receiver that detonated the gas as it was cranked. The sound of the detonations emulated actual firing for familiarization purposes.
5. Japanese Nagoya Army Arsenal Type 99 last-ditch Arisaka Bolt-Action Rifle - 7.7mm - circa 1944-1945 - Throughout World War II, Japan suffered from lack of resources. In the final months of the conflict, marginal-quality bolt-action rifles, missing non-essential features, were the best that could be manufactured. Even these last ditch rifles were made with chrome-lined bores to protect against corrosive effects of wartime ammunition.

THE WORLD AT WAR

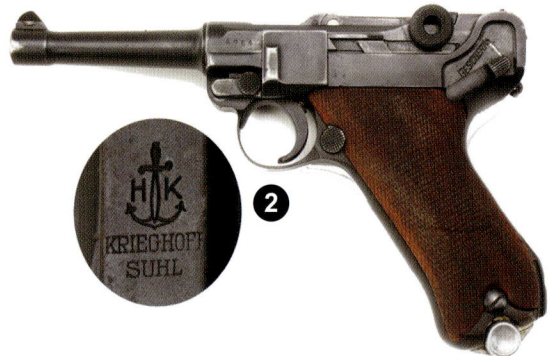
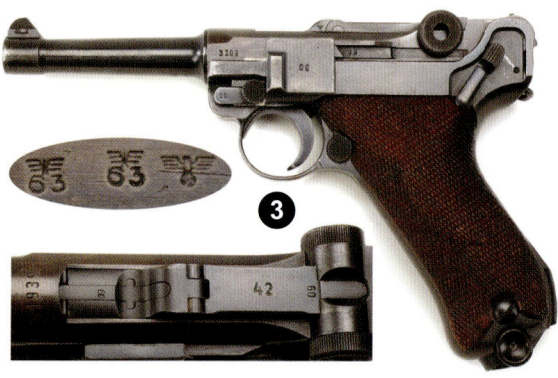

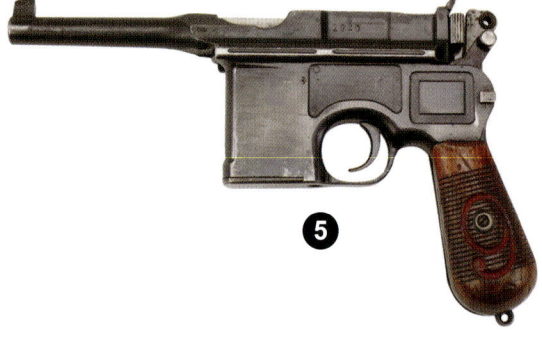

1. German Mauser P.08 Luger Black Widow Semi-Automatic Pistol - 9mm - circa 1941 These Luger variants were called "Black Widows" by collectors because of the gun's black plastic grips.

2. German Kreighoff P.08 Luger Semi-Automatic Pistol - 9mm Parabellum - circa 1936-1937 - Kreighoff received a contract for 10,000 pistols for the German Luftwaffe in 1935.

3. German Mauser/Deutsche Waffen und Munitions Fabriken P.08 Luger Semi-Automatic Pistol - 9mm Parabellum - circa 1939.

4. German Mauser P.38 Semi-Automatic Pistol - 9mm Parabellum - circa 1942 - To increase military handgun manufacturing in World War II, Germany sought a design that could be mass produced faster than their existing Luger pistol. Walther's double-action HP design, a 9mm semi-automatic that could be made cheaper than the Luger, was adopted as the P.38 and subsequently contracted for production by Mauser and Spreewerke.

5. German Mauser Model 1896 Broomhandle Military Semi-Automatic Pistol - 9mm Parabellum - circa 1913-1914 - Versailles Treaty requirements resulted in shorter-barreled German military handguns.

6. German Fabrique Nationale/Browning P-35 Hi-Power Semi-Automatic Pistol - 9mm Parabellum - circa 1942-1944 - FN's P-35 provided 13 shots from its double-stack magazine.

7. German Spreewerke GmbH Metallwarenfabrik P.38 Semi-Automatic Pistol - 9mm Parabellum - circa 1943-1944 - Speerwerke produced the lowest-quality P.38 pistols during WWII.

WORLD WAR II

1. German J. P. Sauer & Sohn Model 38H Double-Action Semi-Automatic Pistol - 7.65mm - circa 1938-1945 - During World War II, German government requirements resulted in most of the production run of the Sauer 38 pistol being taken. This pistol was one of the first modern pistols with a de-cocking capability.

2. Czech CZ Model 1924 Semi-Automatic Pistol - 9mm Kurz - circa 1924-1938.

3. German Deutsche Werke A.G. Ortgies Semi-Automatic Pistol - 7.65mm - circa 1920-1928 - Ortgies pistols had a grip safety whose spring also served as the driving force for the striker.

4. German Sauer Model 1930 Berhorden Semi-Automatic Pistol - .32 ACP - circa 1930-1937 - Fitted with chamber indicator, trigger also had a security lock to prevent firing.

5. German Walther PPK Semi-Automatic Pistol - 7.65mm - circa 1942 - This pistol is one of two confiscated from Nazi saboteur teams landed by submarine in 1942. Two four-man teams were set ashore on Long Island and in Florida with explosives.

6. Hungarian Fegyvergyar Model 37 Semi-Automatic Pistol - 7.65mm - circa 1941 - Part of 50,000-gun order in 1941 for Luftwaffe.

7. German Walther Model PP Semi-Automatic Pistol - 7.65mm - circa 1942.

8. German Mauser Model 1934 Semi-Automatic Pistol - 7.65mm - circa 1942 - This pistol is the second seized from Nazi saboteur teams landed in 1942 on Long Island and Florida.

9. German Mauser HSc Pistol - .32 ACP - circa 1945 - War trophy brought home by Frank Drummond, 75th Infantry.

THE WORLD AT WAR

1. Polish Radom P-35 VIS Semi-Automatic Pistol - 9mm Parabellum - circa 1943-1944 - Late war pistols lacked takedown latches.
2. Italian Beretta Model 1934 Semi-Automatic Pistol - 9mm Kurz (short) - circa 1942.
3. Italian Glisenti Model 1910 Semi-Automatic Pistol - 9mm Glisenti - circa 1910-1920 - Glisenti pistols were intended to fire a lower-power 9mm cartridge.
4. German Mauser Model 712 Schnellfeuer Machine Pistol with Detachable Shoulder Stock - 7.63 Mauser - circa 1932-1936 - Machine pistols based on the Mauser M1896 design offered selective fire as an option. However, in the abbreviated package of a handgun, the high firing rate did not translate to more hits on target.

WORLD WAR II

1. Spanish Unceta y Compania S.A. Astra Model 900 Semi-Automatic Pistol - .30 Mauser - circa 1928-1936 - Astra 900 pistols were used by Spanish Civil Police and National Guard units during WWII.
2. Handmade Japanese copy of Mauser Model 1896 Broomhandle Semi-Automatic Pistol - 8mm Nambu circa 1944 - This handmade pistol was captured by PFC Edward A. Baldin, USMC, during the invasion of Peleliu.
3. Japanese Nagoya Army Arsenal Type 14 Nambu Semi-Automatic Pistol - 8mm Nambu - circa 1944 - Fitted with both rotating safety and magazine safety.
4. Japanese Tokyo Artillery Arsenal Type 26 Revolver - 9mm - circa 1893-1925 - The 9mm Nambu round used in the Type 26 revolver is used by no other handgun in the world.
5. Japanese Baby Nambu Semi-Automatic Pistol - 7mm Mauser - circa 1909-1929 - Presentation arms were given to graduates of Japanese military schools.
6. Edgar Rice Burroughs' Japanese Nagoya Army Arsenal Type 94 Semi-Automatic Pistol - 8mm Nambu - circa 1944 - Burroughs, creator of Tarzan, received this pistol while a Pacific war correspondent.
7. Japanese Tokyo Artillery Arsenal Model 1902 Papa Nambu Semi-Automatic Pistol - 8mm Nambu - circa 1909-1926 - The Papa Nambu pistol incorporated a grip safety and could mount a shoulder stock.
8. Japanese Type 14 Nambu pistol - 8mm Nambu - circa 1937 - Pre-war Nambu pistols had rounded, small trigger guards.
9. Japanese Type 90 3-Barrel Flare Pistol - 28mm - circa 1943 - Japanese naval units with poorly functioning radio systems communicated though aerial flares and these triple-barrel flare pistols allowed the ability to launch multiple colored signals.
10. German Walther SLE Stainless Steel Flare Pistol - 26mm - circa 1941 - Intended for submarine service, a very limited number of flare pistols were constructed of stainless alloys to resist corrosion.
11. German Flare Pistol - 26mm - circa 1943-1944 - Stampings were used to build German machine pistols, carbines, as well as flare pistols.

THE WORLD AT WAR

British BSA (Birmingham Small Arms) Sten Mark II Submachine Gun (deactivated/dummy receiver) - 9mm Parabellum - circa 1943 - Inexpensively produced in small workshops where individual stamped and welded components could be forwarded for assembly, Britain's Sten gun incorporated fewer than 50 parts and took less than five man-hours of labor to produce each example.

U.S. Harrington & Richardson Reising Model 50 Submachine Gun - .45 ACP - circa 1944-1945 - Firing from a closed bolt, the Reising M50 submachine gun created by Harrington & Richardson was ordered for service with U.S. Navy, Marine Corps. and Coast Guard units. Problems with reliability foreshortened the service life of this delayed blowback, which was considered more accurate than the Thompson submachine gun.

German MG42 Machine Gun - circa 1943 - 8mm Mauser - The MG42 high rate of fire of 1200 rounds per minute was double or better that of other machine guns of the era such as the U.S. Browning or the British Vickers. The rapid fire earned the MG42 the nickname "Hitler's buzzsaw."

WORLD WAR II

1. Chinese Mukden Arsenal Manchurian Mauser 98 Bolt-Action Rifle - 8mm - circa 1933-1939 - Built in Mukden Arsenal for the army of Manchukuo during 1933-1939, this bolt-action rifle design incorporates both Arisaka and Mauser elements. The two-piece stock and ovoid bolt handle knob are typical of Arisaka arms, and the barrel bands are thinner than German Mauser counterparts.

2. Austrian Steyr Daimler Puch Mauser Model 98k Bolt-Action Carbine - 8mm Mauser - circa 1944 - This '98 Mauser was the standard service rifle of Germany during World War II.

3. Mexican Fabrica Nacional de Arms Mauser Model 1936 Bolt-Action Rifle - 7mm Mauser - circa 1936-1947.

4. Venezuelan Fabrique Nationale Contract Model 1924/30 Bolt-Action Rifle - 7mm Mauser circa 1930-1950.

5. Belgian Fabrique Nationale Model 1924/30 Bolt-Action Rifle - 7mm - circa 1930-1947.

6. Czech Ceskoslovenska Zbrojovka Brno Model 98/29 Persian Contract Bolt-Action Rifle - 8mm Mauser - circa 1930-1938.

7. Ceskoslovenska Zbrojovka Brno Czech Copy of Kar 98K Bolt-Action Rifle - 7mm Mauser - circa 1942-1945.

8. Danish Madsen G1A Bolt-Action Rifle - .30-06 - circa 1958 - The Madsen G1A rifle was the last of a long line of military issue bolt-actions. Produced in Denmark for a Colombian military order in 1958, this .30-06 rifle had modern features including an integral muzzle brake and a high comb stock with rubber buttpad.

MODERN WARFARE

BATTLE RIFLES

Following the success of the M1 Garand in WWII, many countries adopted "battle rifles" - box-magazine-fed semi-auto rifles chambered for full-power rifle cartridges such as .30-06 or 8mm Mauser. The FN49 was used by Argentina, Belgium, the Belgian Congo, Brazil, Colombia, Egypt, Indonesia, Luxembourg, and Venezuela.

1. Egyptian Fabrique Nationale Model FN-49 Semi-Automatic Rifle - 8mm Mauser - circa 1952-1958 - FN-49 rifles were used in the Suez Conflict and in the Korean War. Other countries adopted the FN49 in .30-06, 7.62x51 NATO, 7mm Mauser, and 7.65 Argentine. Variations were produced 1948 to 1961.

2. Savage SMLE No. 4 Mk I/3 Bolt-Action Rifle with Bayonet - .303 British - circa 1948 - Savage made No. 4 rifles for British/Canadian contracts as well as U.S. training purposes.

3. Indian Ishapore Arsenal SMLE No. 1 Mk III Bolt-Action Rifle (altered) - .303 British - circa 1954 - Modified for grenade launching had wire-wrapped forestocks.

4. Czech VZ-52 Semi-Automatic Carbine - 7.62mm x 45 - circa 1953-1954 - VZ-52 carbines utilized a different 7.62mm cartridge than SKS carbines.

5. U.S. Springfield Armory M1D Sniper Semi-Automatic Rifle - .30-06 - circa 1942 - Late in WWII, M1D snipers were fielded with offset M84 scopes.

6. U.S. Colt Model 1918A2 Browning Automatic Rifle (BAR) - .30-06 - circa 1942-1945.

7. Inglis Mk I Semi-Automatic Pistol - 9mm Parabellum - circa 1945 - Canadian copies of FN P-35 pistols continued in service with British Commonwealth nations.

POST-WAR DEVELOPMENT - AK47 & M16

Assault Rifles - The AK47 and the M16

WWII proved the advantages of full-auto shoulder arms. However full-power rifle cartridges were difficult to control in full-auto, and submachine guns chambering pistol-level cartridges did not have the range for distant encounters. Late in the war Germany developed a select-fire shoulder arm chambered for an intermediate power cartridge. Hitler named it the "Sturmgewehr" - literally "storm rifle," with the meaning of storm being to assault. The model was designated the StG44.

After the war, Mikhail Kalashnikov's team of Russian designers developed a similar concept in 1947 - the *avtomat kalashnikova* or AK47, chambered for a 7.62x39mm cartridge. Used throughout the Soviet Bloc, it has become the most produced military rifle in history.

In the early 1960s, the U.S. began developing their own version of the assault rifle concept, ultimately adopting Eugene Stoner's Armalite design as the M16 in 1964.

It also was a select-fire gun with detachable magazine, but chambered for the 5.56 NATO round, nearly identical to the .223 Remington cartridge.

Refinements and improvements of the AK47 and M16 concepts are the most widely used military arms today. A true "assault rifle" uses an intermediate cartridge and has full-auto fire capability.

MODERN WARFARE

Modern Warfare: Korea

The United States entered this conflict - often called a police action - on behalf of the United Nations in June 1950. The war pitted the Democratic People's Republic of Korea (North Korea) - who were backed by the Communist Chinese and the Soviet Union - against the Republic of Korea (South Korea) - backed by the United States and the United Nations. The M1 Rifle remained the standard service rifle of the United States and many of our United Nation allies. Some countries still clung to the effective and powerful, but slow, bolt-action rifle. Australian infantry continued to use the same rifle that they had used on the shores of Gallipoli some 40 years before.

U.S. General Motors Inland Division M2 Selective Fire Carbine with flash hider - .30 Carbine - circa 1945 - With six million M1 carbines in service, conversion to selective-fire began as an armorer conversion package offered in late 1944. The Korean conflict saw many semi-auto M1 carbines upgraded to M2 (selective-fire) capability.

U.S. Ithaca Model 1911A1 Semi-Automatic Pistol - .45 ACP - circa 1943-1945.

U.S. General Motors Guide Lamp Division M3 Submachine Gun - .45 ACP - circa 1943-1945 - Approximately 680,000 M3 Grease Guns were manufactured by General Motor's Guide Lamp Division and by the Ithaca Gun Company during WWII and Korea. This inexpensive .45 caliber submachine remained in U.S. military inventory through the Gulf Wars for tanker crews.

Brophy's .50 BMG Korea Sniper Rifle - .50 Browning - circa 1950 - Converted from a Russian PTRD anti-tank rifle by major William Brophy during the Korean War, this single-shot rifle was fitted with a barrel from a U.S. M2 .50 BMG and a Unertl telescopic sight. Brophy's experiment foreshadowed adoption of .50 caliber sniper rifles in the early 21st century.

KOREA

U.S. Springfield Model T44 E4 Selective Fire Rifle (deactivated) - .30 T65 - circa 1957 - Forerunner of the M14, T44 prototypes based on a modified Garand receiver in 7.62mm competed successfully against the FN FAL (T48) rifle, with the design being adopted for military service in 1957.

Armalite AR-10 Semi-Automatic Rifle (deactivated) - 7.62mm - circa 1956-1957 - Fewer than 10,000 Armalite AR-10 rifles were originally produced as this selective-fire rifle design by Eugene Stoner failed in U.S. military and Nicaraguan army testing. Small quantities of the rifles were sold to military forces in Portugal and the Sudan.

Colt AR-15 Automatic Rifle (deactivated) - 5.56mm NATO (.223) - circa 1964 - Adapted by the U.S. Air Force in selective-fire configuration, Armalite's AR-15 later became the M16A1 for Army issue.

Shangshei Arsenal Mauser Model 1896 Broomhandle Semi-Automatic Pistol - .45 ACP - circa 1930-1935 - Chinese M1896 pistol copies were made in .45 ACP.

U.S. Remington Rand M1911A1 Semi-Automatic Pistol - .45 ACP - circa 1944 - 1911-pattern pistols were widely distributed in Vietnam, as they had been in previous conflicts.

MODERN WARFARE

Vietnam

Perhaps the most controversial conflict in modern times, the Vietnam War began with North Vietnamese communist-led terrorist attacks against the government of the Republic of Viet Nam (South Viet Nam) in the late 1950's. Fought as a jungle guerrilla war, American forces began to be involved in the conflict in 1959 and remained until the fall of Saigon in 1975 suffering 58,000 men and women killed in action. As a guerrilla conflict, the war was fought with a variety of arms. U.S. soldiers captured enemy rifles of the type used during the War Between the States 100 years earlier! In the end the North Vietnamese won the conflict not with a combination of ancient surplus arms or conventional communist bloc equipment, but with superior propaganda, extraordinary patience, diplomatic skill, and a crushing military defeat delivered to South Vietnamese forces.

1. Czech VZ54 Sniper Bolt-Action Rifle - 7.62x54R - circa 1954 - SHE-marked for the Czech arsenal, this model was built for only three years.
2. Hungarian Mosin Nagant Model 1891/30 Bolt-Action Rifle with telescopic sight - 7.62x54R - circa 1970 - This Hungarian MN rifle was captured from a Vietcong sniper in 1970.
3. Chinese SKS Type 56 Semi-Automatic Carbine - 7.62x39mm - circa 1980 - Chinese copies of the SKS carbine had wide distribution in Vietnam.
4. Viet Cong Bolt-Action Carbine - 7.62x39mm - circa 1964-1970 - A crude bolt-action fitted to a scavenged US M1 carbine stock, this single-shot rifle is chambered for the same 7.62x39mm cartridge used in SKS and AK-47 arms.
5. Viet Cong Slam-Fire Blow-Back Rifle - 7.62x39mm - circa 1964-1970 - A spring-loaded bolt is drawn back to load or fire this gun.
6. Viet Cong Muzzleloading Thumb-Trigger Rifle - 11/16 caliber - circa 1964-1970 - Crudely built from pipe, this single-shot gun has a sheet metal trigger.

VIETNAM

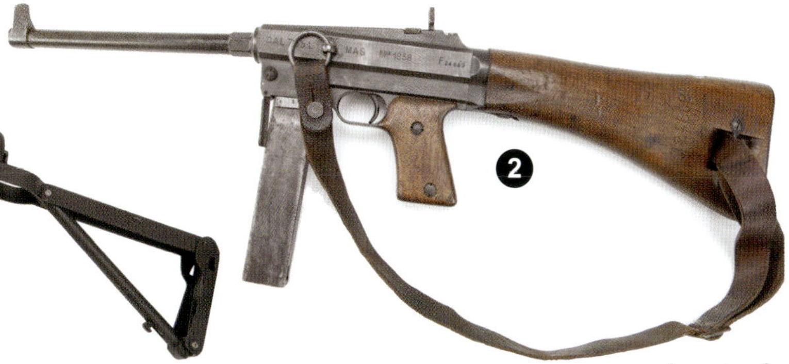

1. Sterling (Parker Arms import) Semi-Automatic Carbine - 9mm - circa 1990 - Sterling SMGs utilized a pair of rollers as followers to enhance magazine feeding.
2. French MAS Model 1938 Submachine Gun - 7.65mm MAS - circa 1954-1956 - French MAS SMGs employed a folding trigger as a safety mechanism.
3. Polytech/KFS AK-47S Legend Folding-Stock Rifle - 7.62x39mm - circa 1984 - Modern commercial copies of the AK-47 rifle are manufactured in semi-automatic configuration for sale in markets including the United States by the same manufacturers that produced selective-fire editions for the world's military forces. This Polytech folding-stock rifle utilizes components that also appear in the Chinese Type 56 rifle. Visual appearance is similar to AK-47s used in Vietnam.
4. Chinese Mosin Nagant Type 53 Bolt-Action Rifle - 7.62mm x 54R - circa 1954-1960 - Chinese copies of Soviet arms included M/N carbines.
5. Chinese Chiang Kai-Shek Short Model Bolt-Action Rifle - 7.92mm - circa 1936-1949.
6. U.S. Remington Model 1903A4 Bolt-Action Rifle with M82 Telescopic Sight - .30-06 - circa 1945 - M1903A4 snipers utilized low-power scopes adapted from commercial sporting optics.
7. French MAS1949 Semi-Automatic Rifle - 7.5mm M29 - circa 1955 - Semi-auto MAS rifles retain the capability to launch grenades using a tilting bolt system.
8. French St. Etienne MAS 1936 Bolt-Action Training Rifle - .22 rimfire - circa 1947-1950 - Former training rifles were pressed into service by Vietcong insurgents.
9. Viet Cong Semi-Automatic Pistol - .45 ACP - circa 1965-1968 - Handmade using only sections of railroad track and a file and drill, this .45 caliber semi-automatic pistol is a crude copy of the Model 1911 design, but does fire and extract reliably.
10. Handmade Vietnamese 1911 Pattern Pistol - .45 ACP - circa 1965-1968 - Crudely built from steel rail, Viet Cong gunsmiths improvised this copy of a 1911 pistol.

MODERN WARFARE

General Officer Pistols

American General Officers, by virtue of their rank, have the privilege to carry sidearms, in part as a symbol of rank and command, as the handgun replaced the sword. During WWII, Colt semi-automatic pistols, the M1903 in .32 ACP, and the M1908 in .380 ACP were the most common models of pocket pistols issued. Some GOs elected to carry the standard M1911 pistol, captured enemy pistols, or privately purchased handguns. On retiring from active service, only General Officers have the unique opportunity to retain their issued pistol.

1. U.S. Colt Model 1903 Semi-Automatic General Officer Pistol - .32 ACP - circa 1943 - This Colt Model 1903 semi-automatic pistol was presented to Major General Richard Anthony Bresnahan. Bresnhan received his first set of general's stars in January of 1972.
2. U.S. Colt Model 1903 Semi-Automatic General Officer Pistol - .32 ACP - circa 1943 - In July of 1959, General Bruce Palmer, Jr., received this Colt Model 1903 semi-auto pistol in token of his new rank.
3. U.S. Colt Model 1908 Semi-Automatic General Officer Pistol - .380 ACP - circa 1943 - One of the few General Officer pistols to actually see combat, this Colt Model 1908 handgun was with Lieutenant General Ridgely Gaither during Operation Varsity. Gaither jumped with the 17th Airborne to attack German positions held near the Rhine. Using this .380 pistol and his GI issue .45 pistol, Gaither and his men were able to suppress an enemy 20mm gun emplacement.
4. U.S. Colt Model 1903 Semi-Automatic General Officer Pistol - .32 ACP - circa 1943 - Elaborately engraved and fitted with carved wooden grip panels, this Colt Model 1903 pistol was presented to General Frank Thomas Mildren in 1960, then re-presented after his subordinates in Germany borrowed the pistol in 1968 to have it specially embellished to mark Mildren's advancement to lieutenant general.
5. U.S. Colt Model 1903 Semi-Automatic General Officer Pistol - .32 ACP - circa 1943 - General Hugh Pate Harris received this Colt Model 1903 .32 caliber pistol in December 1953, when he served as Deputy Chief of Staff for the 8th Army and was in charge of all military operations in Korea.
6. U.S. Colt Model 1908 Semi-Automatic General Officer Pistol - .380 ACP - circa 1943 - Recommended personally for promotion by General George S. Patton, General Issac Davis White received his first general's stars in May 1944, along with this Model 1908 Colt pistol.
7. U.S. Colt Model 1903 Semi-Automatic General Officer Pistol - .32 ACP - circa 1944 - Lt. General Richard Meyer received this Colt General Officer pistol.

GENERAL OFFICER PISTOLS

Medal of Honor Recipient Brig. Gen. Marion P. Maus' Savage Model 1907 Pistol - .32 ACP - circa 1911 - Maus was awarded the medal when as leader of Apache Scouts in 1887, his patrol was ambushed by Geronimo's forces. Maus single-handedly killed the attackers while rescuing a wounded trooper. Geronimo wrote "Maus was the bravest man I have ever seen."

Smith & Wesson Model 39 U.S. Air Force General Officer Semi-Automatic Pistol - 9mm Parabellum - circa 1969 - The U.S. Air Force was one branch of the armed services that broke with tradition in ordering General Officer pistols. A Smith & Wesson Model 39 9mm pistol was presented to General Bryce Poe in 1969. The grips were later modified by USAF armorers to reflect Poe's rank at retirement.

Colt Model 1903 Semi-Automatic Pistol - .32 ACP - circa 1921 - General Douglas MacArthur received this pistol during his term as superintendent of West Point.

Beretta M9 Presentation General Officer Pistol - 9mm - circa 1993 - Former USMC Commandant P.X. Kelley received this presentation Beretta pistol.

MODERN WARFARE

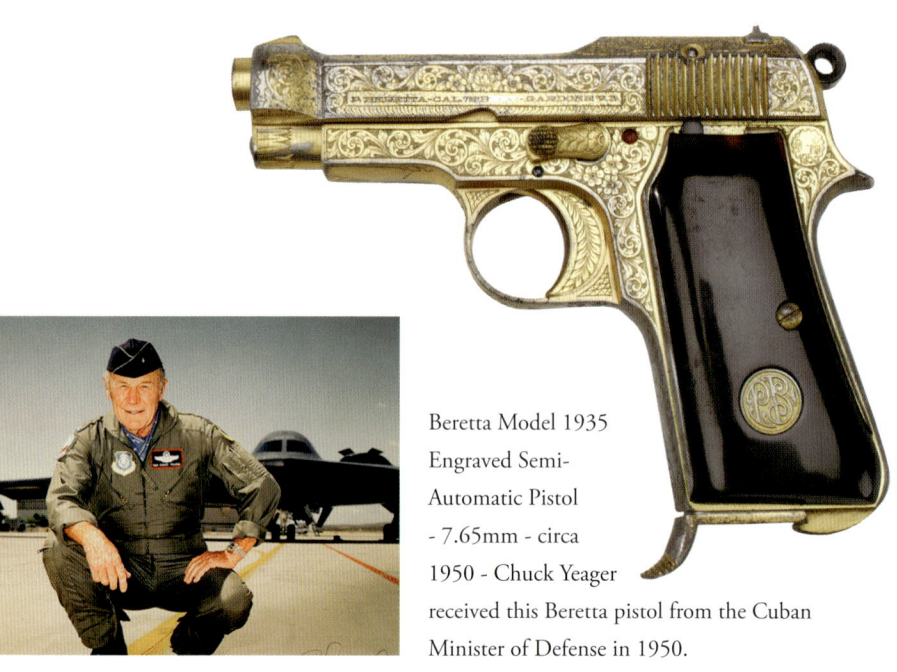

Beretta Model 1935 Engraved Semi-Automatic Pistol - 7.65mm - circa 1950 - Chuck Yeager received this Beretta pistol from the Cuban Minister of Defense in 1950.

U.S. Colt M15 Semi-Automatic General Officer Pistol - .45 ACP - circa 1973 - After originally receiving a .32 caliber Colt Model 1903 pistol, Maj. Gen. John Carpenter Raaen exchanged that handgun in 1973 for a Rock Island Arsenal-built .45 caliber General Officer pistol, SN GO2. Raaen was the commanding general of Rock Island Arsenal at that time.

U.S. Colt Model 1911A1 Semi-Automatic Pistol - .45 ACP - circa 1943 - General Eisenhower gave this pistol to an aide involved in the 1942 North Africa invasion.

Chinese M20 Tokarev Pistol - 7.62 Tokarev - circa 1969 - Captured in Vietnam, this Tokarev was presented to Major General Donn Royce Pepke.

MILITARY ARMS TODAY

Desert Storm and the Global War On Terrorism

Beginning on January 17, 1991, in an unprecedented six-week campaign, United States and Allied forces numbering 450,000 commanded by U.S. Army General Norman Schwarzkopf won a sweeping victory against an Iraqi army of nearly 1,000,000 troops. A brilliant two-pronged ground force attack routed the entire Iraqi Army in 100 hours. An estimated 100,000 Iraqi troops were killed and 65,000 captured. The allies suffered only 234 dead, 479 wounded, and 57 missing in action. A variety of selective-fire arms, standard among the coalition forces proved to be more than a match for the communist bloc arms of the Iraqi soldier.

Beretta XM9 Semi-Automatic Pistol - 9mm Parabellum - circa 1979 - Tests of this XM9 model and other 9mm pistols led to the adoption of the similar M9 Beretta as the US issue sidearm in 1986 replacing the 1911. In 2017 the M9 was replaced by the SIG M17, a military version of the SIG P320.

Lewis Machine & Tool Defender 2000 semi-automatic rifle with Trijicon ACOG scope and Surefire flashlight, 5.56x45mm, circa 2005 - This semi-auto is in the same configuration as the current U.S. issue M4 select-fire military rifle, as adopted in 1994, although the flashlight attachment varies depending on need. At this writing the U.S. is considering adopting a 6.8mm cartridge as its new standard issue ammunition.

Cugir Arsenal SAR-2 semi-automatic rifle with Russian Kobra red dot sight, 5.45x39mm, circa 2005 - This semi-auto is in the same configuration as the current Russian select-fire military AK74. In 1974, the Soviet Union adopted the Kalashnikov design in this smaller caliber.

Russian SVD Dragunov Sniper Semi-Automatic Rifle - 7.62 x54 Russian - circa 1975 - Designed by Eugenie Dragunov, a former Russian Olympic competitive shooter, the SVD Dragunov semi-automatic rifle was incorporated as a squad sniper arm in 1963. Its optic can be set to detect active infrared night vision sources on the battlefield and includes an illuminated reticle.

MODERN WARFARE

1. MAS French FAMAS Bullpup Semi-Automatic Carbine - 5.56mm - circa 1989 - Compact and light, the French FAMAS bullpup rifle has its magazine behind the trigger.
2. Fabrique Nationale FAL Semi-Automatic Rifle - 7.62mm NATO - circa 1985 - Rejected by the U.S. military, the FN FAL was adopted by other NATO nations.
3. Harrington & Richardson T48 Selective Fire Rifle (deactivated) - .30 T65 - circa 1950-1952 - Three firms were contacted to provide FAL pattern rifles for U.S. military testing; this Harrington & Richardson T48 is one of the arms tested for the Light Self-Loading Rifle trials to find the replacement for the M1 Garand rifle.
4. DPMS M160 Selective-Fire Rifle - 5.56mm - circa 2003 - Commercial production M16A2 with three-shot burst capability.
5. Israeli Military Industries Galil Sniper Semi-Automatic Rifle - 5.56mm - circa 1993 - Galil design blends American cartridge with Russian action for desert reliability.
6. Heckler & Koch Mark 23 Offensive Handgun System with Suppressor and Laser Aiming Module - .45 ACP - circa 2000 - H&K's special ops mission pistol was designed to take a suppressor and laser/IR aiming system.
7. SIG Sauer M11 Semi-Automatic Pistol - 9mm Parabellum - circa 2009 - Made for the NCIS in Europe. It was a contract overrun sold commercially.

MILITARY ARMS TODAY

U.S. Remington M24 Sniper Bolt-Action Rifle - 7.62mm NATO circa 1989-1990 - Since 1988, the M24 has been standard issue for U.S. Air Force and Army snipers.

Prototype Remington XM24 Sniper Bolt-Action Rifle - .300 Winchester Magnum - circa 1987 - Original prototype rifle made for the M24 sniper project.

U.S. Barrett M82A1 Semi-Automatic Sniper Rifle (deactivated) - .50 Browning - circa 1990 - The first U.S. military orders for the Barrett M82A1 semi-automatic rifle came in 1990 with the first Desert Storm campaign. Initially, 125 rifles were ordered for the U.S. Marine Corps. This example is one of that initial lot. The Barrett "Light .50" is a massive semi-automatic rifle, weighing over 30 lbs. and chambering a round previously used only in heavy machine guns.

MODERN WARFARE

MILITARY SNIPER RIFLES

U.S. MILITARY SNIPER RIFLES

Top - U.S. Winchester Model 70 Bolt-Action Sniper Rifle with Lyman 20X Target Scope - .30-06 - circa 1942 - WWII era sniper rifles were called back into service for Vietnam.

Middle - U.S. Remington USMC M40 Bolt-Action Scout/Sniper Rifle with Redfield 3 x 9 Variable Range Sight - .308 Winchester - circa 1968 - U.S. Marine Corps requirements for a heavy-barrel sniper rifle were fulfilled by Remington Arms of Ilion, NY. The initial 995 rifles ordered were to be equipped with an auto-ranging reticle optic provided by Redfield.

Bottom - U.S. Remington USMC M40A1 Bolt-Action Scout/Sniper Rifle w/ 10X Scope - 7.62mm NATO - circa 1968 - Originally a Vietnam-era Remington M40 rifle, during upgrades by U.S. Marine Corps armorers this rifle was refitted with a synthetic McMillan stock and re-barrelled with a heavier-contour 7.62mm barrel. The optic on this rifle was manufactured by U.S. Optics, a California firm contracted to replace the original Unertl 10X scopes on the M40A1 rifles.

TO SERVE AND PROTECT

POLICE FIREARMS

Law Enforcement Revolvers

In the 19th century, police sidearms were rarely standardized. During his service as New York City Police Commissioner 35 year old Theodore Roosevelt chose the .32 caliber Colt New Police to be the issue handgun of the NYPD. For most of the 20th century double action revolvers by Smith & Wesson or Colt were the most common police sidearms. In the 1970s through 1990s classic blue steel, fixed sight, 38 Special revolvers began to be replaced by stainless steel, adjustable sights, and .357 Magnum.

Clockwise from top left: Colt Python, .357 Magnum, circa 1963. New York City Transit Police. Smith & Wesson Model 60 stainless steel Chiefs Special, .38 Special, circa. 1970. Backup gun, Lt. Thomas Sefton, San Diego PD. S&W Model 681, .357 Magnum, circa 1982. Trooper Robert T. Starr, Troop C Norwich Barracks, Chenango County, NY. Ruger Model SP101, .38 Special, circa 1990. State Police of New York.

Bill Jordan's Colt Border Patrol Revolver - .38 Special - circa 1952 - This Model was designed by famed lawmen Harlon Carter and Bill Jordan. This early production prototype, one of only 400 made in .38 Special, was Jordan's personal sidearm, with his name inscribed on the frame.

Texas Ranger Lt. Richard Sweeney's Smith & Wesson Model 19 - .357 Magnum - circa 1988 - In the 1970s through 1990s many police agencies replaced wood grips with rubber Pachmayrs.

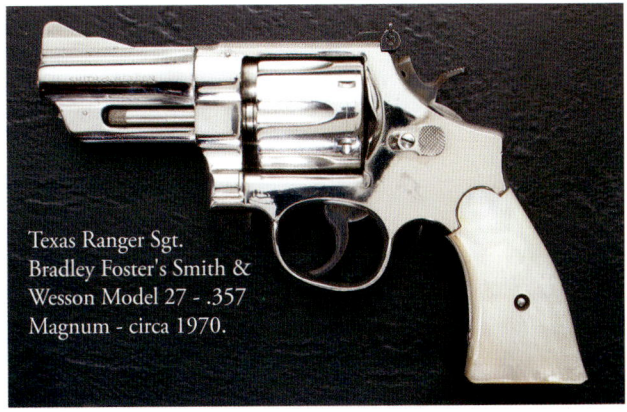

Texas Ranger Sgt. Bradley Foster's Smith & Wesson Model 27 - .357 Magnum - circa 1970.

TO SERVE AND PROTECT

Police Forces

The establishment of police forces can trace its roots to England and to the Magna Carta, agreed to by King John in 1215. This document established the offices of sheriff and constable and provided guidelines for their authority and actions. Local and state militia forces provided protection for cities and townships in the early 19th century, but the political office of sheriff remained the mainstay of the police force. By the early 19th century, larger cities such as Boston and Philadelphia had organized volunteer police forces known as Watch and Ward. By 1850, many cities had police commissioners and forces of officers under them.

Police forces were gradually absorbed into civil service systems. August Vollmer, the police chief of Berkeley, California, in 1910 is generally considered the father of the modern police department. During his term, he introduced motorized patrols and college education for members of the force.

NRA Police Shooting Competition

1 Smith & Wesson Model 10 Military & Police Revolver with Billy Club Extension - .38 Special - circa 1952-1953 - The famous S&W M&P revolver became the standard police officer's sidearm from 1910 to the 1980s. This one is fitted with a rare 1920s era billy club attachment, which is hollow so the gun can be fired with the club attached, a concept which would give modern police administrators continuum-of-force nightmares.

2 Smith & Wesson Model 14-3 Revolver - .38 Special - circa 1974. Beauty is as beauty does. This Wesley Barksdale-modified revolver was used by Alabama State Trooper Sergeant James Collins in recording the first 1500 score in 1978 police revolver competition.

3 Championship Springfield Armory 1911-A1 Semi-Automatic Pistol - .45 ACP - circa 1993 - Customized by Alan Tanaka and used by Dwight Van Horn to win the Harry Reeves Trophy in police competition.

4 Remington Factory Experimental Law Enforcement Long Arms. *Upper* - Model 870 shotgun with double handgrips - 12 gauge - circa 1980. *Lower* - Model 7600 folding stock pump action rifle - 6mm - circa 1977.

5 Smith & Wesson Model 64-3 Revolver (altered) - .38 Special - circa 1988 - This modified Smith & Wesson revolver was used by Lt. Philip Hemphill of the Mississippi Highway Patrol in winning five National Police Shooting Championships.

6 DEA Agent Frank White's Colt Combat Commander Semi-Automatic Pistol - .45 ACP - circa 1971 - This customized Colt pistol was used by Drug Enforcement Administration Agent Frank E. White, including a number of cases involving drug interdiction in Florida. The TV series *Miami Vice* is reported to be modeled in part on events from his career.

POLICE FIREARMS

④

⑤

⑥

TO SERVE AND PROTECT

1. Colt Police Positive Special - .32-20 - circa 1924.
2. Colt Marshal - .38 Special - circa 1955.
3. Smith & Wesson M&P Semi-Automatic Pistol - 9mm - circa 2006 - Law enforcement agencies transitioned from revolvers to semi-automatics in the mid-1980s. S&W introduced this semi-auto version to follow up on their classic M&P revolver.
4. Glock Model 17 Semi-Automatic Pistol - 9mm Parabellum - circa 1990 - Its polymer "plastic" frame and absence of a traditional active safey were controversial when the Glock was first introduced. However, it gained rapid acceptance and became the issue sidearm of many law enforcement agencies. This example is from the Metropolitan Washington, D.C., Police Department.
5. Beretta Model 92 SB Texas Ranger-Issue Semi-Automatic Pistol - 9mm - circa 1980-1985.
6. Dwight Van Horn's Presentation Colt Gold Cup Pistol - .45 ACP - circa 1993 - Dwight Van Horn received this engraved and cased pistol as the winner of the Harry Reeves Trophy, awarded to the champion of the NRA Police Semi-Automatic Service Pistol Match at the NRA National Police Shooting Championships.
7. Smith & Wesson Chemical Co. Model 277 Tear Gas Pistol - 37mm - circa 1980 - The S&W revolver N-frame formed the platform for this single-shot police arm for teargas and non-lethal rounds.
8. Smith & Wesson 1st Model Ladysmith Revolver - .22 rimfire - circa 1905 - The tiny seven-shot Ladysmith was significantly smaller than any traditional double-action revolver made today. This one was carried as a back-up gun by a law enforcement officer in Freedom, NH. Replaced oversize grips.

At left - Smith & Wesson Chiefs Special Revolver - .38 Special - circa 1956 - Carried by Sheriff "Bus" Harmon of Walker County, Georgia.

IN THE LINE OF DUTY

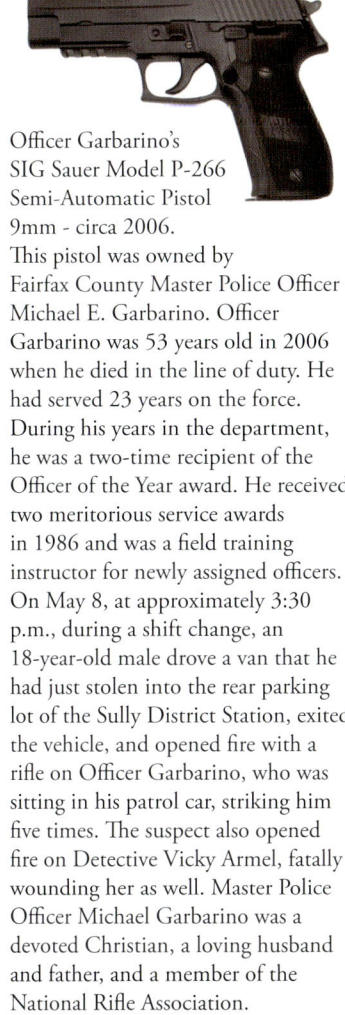

Officer Garbarino's SIG Sauer Model P-266 Semi-Automatic Pistol 9mm - circa 2006. This pistol was owned by Fairfax County Master Police Officer Michael E. Garbarino. Officer Garbarino was 53 years old in 2006 when he died in the line of duty. He had served 23 years on the force. During his years in the department, he was a two-time recipient of the Officer of the Year award. He received two meritorious service awards in 1986 and was a field training instructor for newly assigned officers. On May 8, at approximately 3:30 p.m., during a shift change, an 18-year-old male drove a van that he had just stolen into the rear parking lot of the Sully District Station, exited the vehicle, and opened fire with a rifle on Officer Garbarino, who was sitting in his patrol car, striking him five times. The suspect also opened fire on Detective Vicky Armel, fatally wounding her as well. Master Police Officer Michael Garbarino was a devoted Christian, a loving husband and father, and a member of the National Rifle Association.

September 11, 2001 - Officer Walter Weaver *(above right)* was an NRA member and as part of New York City's Emergency Services Truck Number 3. He was one of the first to arrive at the World Trade Center. His stainless steel Smith & Wesson back-up revolver was with Weaver as the 30-year-old officer struggled to rescue those trapped in an elevator in the South Tower when the tower fell. Found later in the rubble, this sidearm was donated to the NRA National Firearms Museum by his family. Working nearby was his friend, Sgt. John D'Allara *(above left)*, an 18-year department veteran of Squad 2 of the Emergency Services Unit. With D'Allara was his Smith & Wesson service pistol, a Model 5946 9mm handgun. As the World Trade Center fell, D'Allara was one of the 71 law enforcement officers, and 343 members of the New York City Fire Department, as well over 2,800 civilians that perished that day. His pistol, recovered from the rubble next to D'Allara's body, is on loan to the NRA National Firearms Museum from his family.

TO SERVE AND PROTECT

1. High Standard Model 10B Semi-Automatic Tactical Shotgun - 12 gauge - circa 1968 - A compact semi-automatic shotgun, the High Standard Model 10 incorporated a high intensity flashlight whose bulb had a habit of breaking under shotgun slug recoil.

2. Heckler & Koch MP5A3 Submachine Gun - 9mm - circa 1980-1985 - The roller-locked blowback operation of the Heckler & Koch MP5 submachine gun allows it to function efficiently with a closed bolt. Widely issued by both law enforcement and military units, this H&K SMG design is among the world's most recognizable firearms.

3. Remington 31R Slide-Action Riot Shotgun - 12 gauge - circa 1938-1940.

4. Remington Model 81 Police Semi-Automatic Rifle - .35 Remington - circa 1940 - Along with the Remington Model 31 shotgun, the Model 81 rifle was the favorite of law enforcement in the field and among prison guards during the mid-20th century.

5. SIG 550-2SP CounterSniper Semi-Automatic Rifle - 5.56mm NATO (.223) - circa 2005 - A current favorite of law enforcement SWAT teams.

6. Handmade Pistol - .22 rimfire - circa 1989 - This crude .22 zipgun was reportedly handmade in a prison from parts found in the machine shop.

THE LONG ARMS OF THE LAW

NRA National Police Shooting Championship

1. Colt M1921 Thompson Submachine Gun - .45 ACP - circa 1921-1923 - This Colt-made Tommy gun is in near mint and unfired condition.
2. Remington 11-87 Police Semi-Automatic Shotgun - 12 gauge magnum - circa 2004.
3. Winchester Model 1897 Slide-Action Shotgun - 12 gauge - circa 1942 - This cut-stock shotgun was used as an entry weapon by a Florida police department. Winchester's slide-action Model 1897 has been popular with law enforcement since its introduction. Offered in both takedown and solid-frame versions, the 1897 has also been manufactured in riot and trench configurations for the U.S. military.
4. Winchester Model 1907 Police Semi-Automatic Rifle - .351 Winchester - circa 1955 - Nearly 59,000 Model 1907 Winchester semi-auto rifles were manufactured from 1907 to 1957. The .351 Winchester cartridge used in these rifles was popular with law enforcement; extended magazines were made that offered increased capacity.
5. Colt AR15A3 Tactical Semi-Automatic Carbine - .223 Remington - circa 1994 - Law enforcement carbine with collapsible stock, removable carrying handle, and flash hider.

TO SERVE AND PROTECT

TEXAS RANGERS

Guns of Texas Ranger Captain Jay Banks:
Top: Remington Model 870 Shotgun - 12 gauge - circa 1975 - Inscribed "NEVER DRAWN IN ANGER NOR DROPPED THRU FEAR." Presented in 1979.
Bottom: Pair of Colt Government Model Pistols - .45 ACP - circa 1944 and 1950 - Mexican silver grips.

The Texas Rangers

Originally organized in the 1820s as a local militia force to protect settlers from attacks, the Texas Rangers became a full-time, paid corps in 1835. They served the U.S. Army as cavalry and scouts during the Mexican War of 1847 and many individual Rangers served in various Confederate cavalry units during the War Between the States. The Rangers were reconstituted in 1874 as a statewide law enforcement agency. Active today, the Texas Rangers were placed under the authority of the Texas Department of Public Safety in 1935.

COMPETITION

EARLY TARGET GUNS

1. S. S. Baird Underhammer Percussion Muzzleloading Target Rifle - .44 caliber - circa 1860 - Underhammer target rifles provided a cleaner line of sight on barrel top as well as faster ignition.

2. Massachusetts Arms Co. Maynard Falling-Block Rifle - .41 caliber - circa 1875 - Maynard rifles could be had with interchangeable barrels in different calibers.

3. Mexican Percussion Target Rifle - .41 caliber - circa 1845 - Percussion target rifles like this Mexican example were used in many countries; competitive shooters followed a variety of activities using targets ranging from paper to longer-range painted metal discs or squares that resounded on impact.

4. Ford Brothers Percussion Target Rifle - .36 caliber - circa 1835-1855 - In the time when turkey shoots offered community entertainment, many gunsmiths produced heavy-barreled rifles to compete in informal competition.

5. Winchester/Schoyen Model 1885 Falling Block Single-Shot Target Rifle - .32-40 - circa 1885 - Fitted with a George Schoyen heavy target barrel. In competition, often a single cartridge case was reused, again and again, with cast/paper-patched projectile being muzzleloaded down the barrel to rest just outside the chamber.

6. H. Sauer German Percussion Target Rifle - .45 caliber - circa 1870-1890 - European target shooters preferred back-action locks that could be cocked with a forward push from the firing position.

The Era of the Scheutzenfest

Competitive shooting has been a favorite sport among Americans since before the American Revolution. One of the oldest forms of organized shooting in the United States was introduced about 1850 in the Midwest by Swiss and German immigrants, and was known as the Scheutzen match or scheutzenfest. The first competitive shooting club, called a scheutzenbund, was organized in 1865. These competitions were quite stylized in form, and shooters used customized small-caliber rifles equipped with pronged buttplates, hand rests, elaborate sights, and heavy barrels. Shooting took place from a standing position at targets placed at a distance of 150-200 yards. The scheutzenfest was more than just a rifle competition. It was an important social event. By 1890, nearly all large American communities with a German heritage had large scheutzenbunds.

COMPETITION

1. German Zimmershutzen Rifle - 4mm rimfire - circa 1900-1920 - Utilized in Europe for indoor competition, the zimmerschuetzen incorporated a port near the muzzle that loaded into the back of a short rifled section of the barrel.
2. Stevens-Pope Single-Shot Schuetzen Rifle - .22 rimfire - circa 1920-1930 - Under the supervision of noted barrel-maker Harry Pope, this Stevens single-shot was fitted with a target barrel.
3. J. Blattman Peabody-Martini Free Rifle - .22 rimfire - circa 1920-1930 - Made for international free rifle competition.
4. Winchester Model 1885 Falling Block Single-Shot Rifle - .32-40 - circa 1885-1920 - Fitted with Harry Pope false muzzle barrel.
5. Marlin-Ballard Lever-Action Schuetzen Rifle - .38-55 - circa 1875-1891 - Re-rifled by Harry Pope and rechambered by Zetler Brothers for sale by dealer Axel Petersen.
6. Stevens-Pope Single-Shot Schuetzen Rifle - circa 1885-1895 - H. M. Pope was renowned as a gunsmith whose attention to detail in rifling barrels was legendary. Pope was hired in 1901 by the Stevens Rifle Company to produce a line of single-shot target rifles and continued to do so until 1905.

EARLY TARGET GUNS

1. Stevens Ideal No. 49 Walnut Hill Single-Shot Rifle - .22 rimfire - circa 1895-1930 - Walnut Hill was the Massachusetts Rifle Association range in Woburn, MA, founded in 1876.
2. Winchester Model 1885 Falling-Block Single-Shot Schuetzen Rifle - .38-55 - circa 1893 - Made for left-handed shooter.
3. Remington-Hepburn No. 3 Mid-Range Creedmoor Rifle - .40-65 - circa 1880 - A shorter vernier tang sight denoted the Mid-Range model.
4. Massachusetts Arms Maynard Model 1873 Single-Shot Rifle - .35 centerfire - circa 1875 - Thick-headed cartridges were used in the Maynard target guns.
5. Redfield Prototype Single-Shot Rifle - .25-20 - circa 1950 - Redfield, a company better known for aperture sights and optics, built a prototype rifle to show what a modern single-shot rifle could represent. Based on the falling-block Ballard action, this rifle never went into full production and only a handful of prototypes exist.
6. Sharps-Borchardt Model 1878 Mid-Range Single-Shot Rifle - .40-90 Sharps - circa 1878-1881 - The hammerless Sharps-Borchardt rifle was manufactured only from 1878 to 1881, at the close of the Sharps Rifle Company's existence, and fewer than 9,000 were ever made.

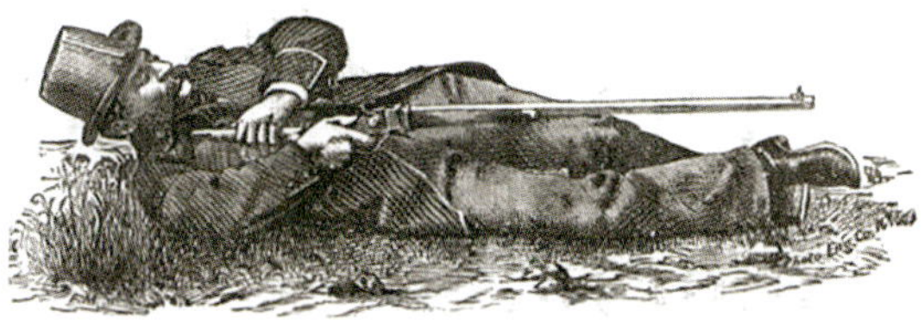

COMPETITION

1. Remington Creedmoor Long-Range Rifle - .45-70 Sharps - circa 1880-1907 - Creedmoor, the first NRA range on Long Island, was a facility with specific rifle rules. Rifles like this Remington could be used in competition only with single triggers and had to conform to strict weight limits. Adjustable pistol grip patented by H.H. Handy.

2. Sharps Model 1877 Creedmoor Falling-Block Single-Shot Target Rifle - .45-100 Sharps - circa 1877-1878 - About 100 M1877 rifles were made with Rigby barrels.

3. Frank Wesson No. 2 Mid-Range Underlever Falling-Block Single-Shot Rifle - .44 caliber - circa 1870 - Rifle has rear stock tang mounts to allow reclining shooting position.

4. Marlin-Ballard No. 4 A-1 Mid-Range Single-Shot Target Rifle - .40-65 - circa 1878-1880 - Fitted with best-grade vernier sights by Marlin.

5. Winchester Model 1885 High Wall Falling-Block Single-Shot Rifle - .30-06 - circa 1885-1920 - One of 40 rifles built for U.S. International Match shooting and believed used at Camp Perry in 1913.

The Mists of Creedmoor

In 1872, the Range Committee of the National Rifle Association negotiated with the State of New York to establish a target range for the training of the National Guard and other personnel. The establishment of a range was the principal goal of the NRA at that time. A 70-acre parcel known as Creed's Farm on Long Island was purchased from the Central and Northside Railroad for the new range. Colonel Henry G. Shaw, editor of the *New York Sun*, viewed the property on one misty morning and remarked it was just like the moors of southern England. Perhaps we should call it Creed's Moor, rather than Creed's Farm. The name Creedmoor, now synonymous with firearms and target shooting, was agreed upon as the new name for NRA's target range. The first shots on the new range were fired on April 25, 1873, by George Wingate. The dedication match was held on June 21, 1873, with two individual matches followed by a regimental team competition. Prizes included a purse and a gold-mounted Winchester Model 1866 Rifle. The establishment of the Creedmoor range attracted hundreds of new members to the NRA, as well as inquiries from all over America regarding match competitions. Although urban growth eventually forced the closing of the range at Creedmoor, the name came to imply the highest standard of quality. Arms manufacturers such as Remington, Sharps, and Marlin used the name Creedmoor in their advertising for their top-of-the-line target rifles.

A New Range at Sea Girt

When the Creedmoor range closed, nearly every state in the Union had developed its own rifle teams and private clubs. Many of them had their own ranges based upon NRA rules and patterned after Creedmoor. In 1890, the New Jersey State Rifle Association established a new 148-acre range in the resort community of Sea Girt. In 1892, the National Rifle Association transferred its national and international matches to the new range. The success of these competitions brought national attention to Sea Girt, and the National Rifle Association became internationally recognized as a governing organization.

EARLY TARGET GUNS

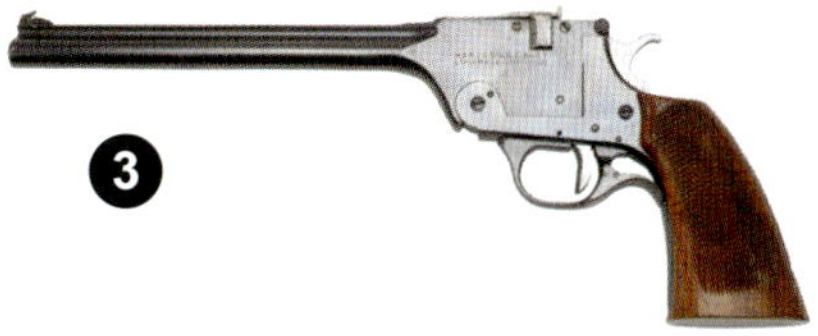

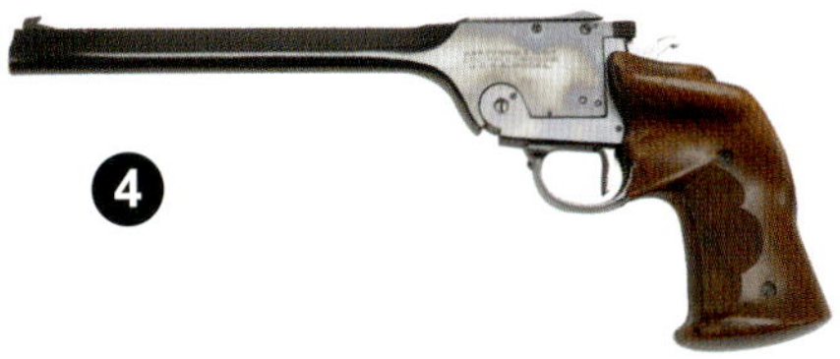

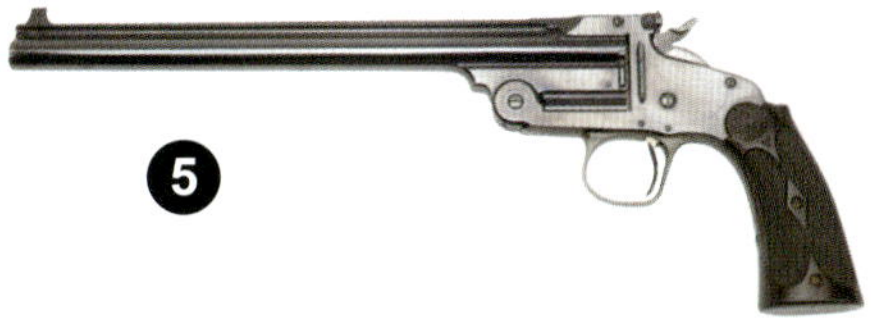

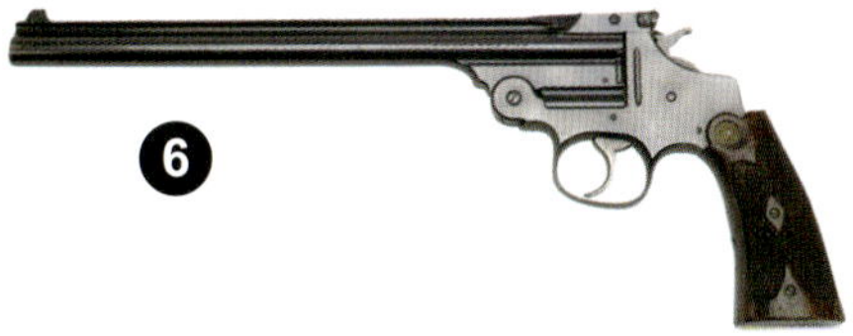

1. Wurfflein Single-Shot Pistol - .44 Russian - circa 1890-1910.
2. Stevens No. 41 Tip-Up Single-Shot Pistol - .32 rimfire - circa 1903-1916.
3. Harrington & Richardson Model USRA Single-Shot Target Pistol - .22 rimfire - circa 1928-1941. Variable front sight could be moved to regulate sight distance.
4. Another H&R USRA Single-Shot Pistol, with custom thumb-rest grip.
5. Smith & Wesson Second Model Single-Shot Pistol - .22 rimfire - circa 1905-1909. About 4,600 were made.
6. Smith & Wesson Third Model Single-Shot Pistol - .22 rimfire - circa 1909-1923. Almost 7,000 made.
7. Smith & Wesson Fourth Model Single-Shot Pistol - .22 long rifle - circa 1925-1936. Also known as the Straight Line.
8. Colt Camp Perry Double-Action Single-Shot Target Pistol - .22 rimfire - circa 1929-1941 - Colt changed the round cylinder on an Officer's Model revolver to a flat single-shot chamber insert for their Camp Perry Model.
9. Smith & Wesson Model 14 K-38 Target Masterpiece Revolver - .38 Special - circa 1955 - Owned by Colonel John Lee, former Director of Civilian Marksmanship.
10. Smith & Wesson Model 41 Semi-Automatic Pistol - .22 rimfire - circa 1947-present.
11. Smith & Wesson Model 52-1 Semi-Automatic Pistol - .38 Special - circa 1963-1970 - Fires rimmed .38 Special ammunition, which is unusual in a semi-auto pistol.
12. Smith & Wesson Model 24 Revolver - .44 Special - circa 1954.
13. Crown City/Kart .22 Conversion Semi-Automatic Pistol - .22 rimfire - circa 1975.
14. High Standard Trophy Semi-Automatic Pistol - .22 rimfire - circa 1957.
15. Colt Model 1911 Semi-Automatic Pistol - .38 Special - circa 1911-1925 - Converted from .38 Super to .38 Special by gunsmith A.E. Berdon.

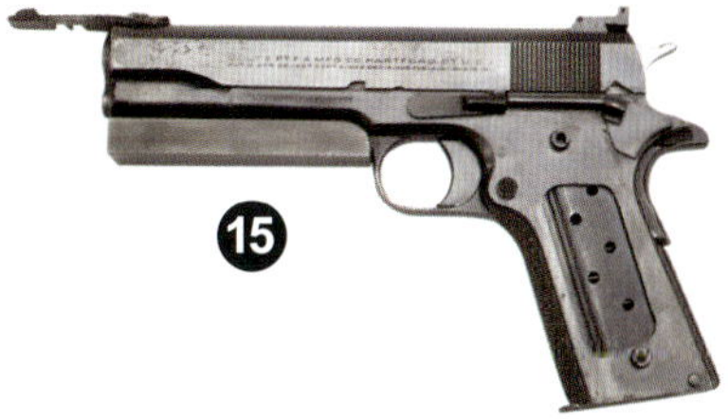

COMPETITION

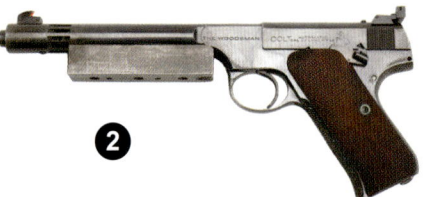

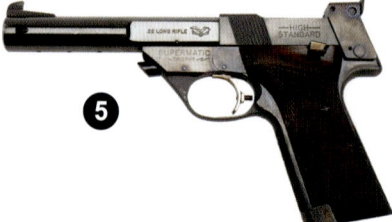

1. Colt Model 1911 Semi-Automatic Pistol - .45 ACP - circa 1911-1925 - Accurized by gunsmith A.E. Berdon for National Match competition.

2. Colt Woodsman Semi-Automatic Pistol - .22 rimfire - circa 1927-1947 - USMC Captain Thurman Barrier won the .22 aggregate championships in 1949 with this pistol. Only one inch of barrel is rifled.

3. U.S. Remington Rand Model 1911A1 Semi-Automatic Pistol - .45 ACP - circa 1943-1945 - Accurized by gunsmith A.E. Berdon for target competition

4. Smith & Wesson Model 46 Semi-Automatic Pistol - .22 rimfire - circa 1957-1966 - Cheaper version of S&W Model 41 pistol.

5. High Standard Military Model 106 Pistol - .22 rimfire - circa 1969 - Presented to Trudy Schlernitzauer as 1969 Camp Perry Woman's Pistol Champion.

6. Essex Arms M1911 Race Gun - .45 ACP - circa 1998 - Modern competition handguns are often crafted by gunsmiths using match-grade barrels and finely adjustable target sights. This example was rescued from a police department evidence locker where it had been scheduled for destruction after having been taken from its owner.

7. Fabrique Nationale GP Competition pistol - 9mm - circa 1998 - FN competition model not marketed in the U.S.

8. Colt Model 1911A1 National Match Semi-Automatic Pistol - .45 ACP - circa 1959-1964.

9. Colt Model 1911 Semi-Automatic Pistol - .45 ACP - circa 1911-1925 - Accurized by gunsmith James Clark for inter-service competition.

Camp Perry

The range at Sea Girt, New Jersey, served the NRA and the National Matches well in its initial years. But after 15 years of heavy use, the range began to suffer from overcrowding and outdated camping facilities.

A new site was located by Ammon B. Critchfield, the Adjutant General of Ohio and an NRA vice president. The property was located on a level plain measuring 1 mile long and 1/2 mile deep. It stretched along the shore of Lake Erie just south of Put-in-Bay and was less than 45 miles east of Toledo.

In 1905, the Ohio state legislature appropriated $25,000 toward the purchase and development of a National Guard rifle range and camp. The Ohio State Rifle Association and the Ohio National Guard Association agreed to purchase 30 additional acres to be the site of a clubhouse. Dedicated in August 1907, this new installation was named Camp Perry in honor of Captain (later Commodore) Oliver Hazard Perry who triumphed over the British during the War of 1812 at the Battle of Lake Erie. The National Matches were held each summer at Camp Perry though 2018.

Camp Atterbury

In 2017, the NRA began the process of moving the NRA National Championships from Camp Perry to Camp Atterbury, an active National Guard base near Indianapolis, Indiana. Beginning that year the National High Power Rifle Championship was held there, with National Smallbore and National Pistol Championships moving there in 2020.

A new NRA Military Heritage Museum is planned for this site.

CAMP PERRY & OTHERS

1. Col. McMillan's Colt M1911A1 National Match Semi-Automatic Pistol - .45 ACP - circa 1959-1964 - Later fitted with ornate Mexican silver & gold grip panels, this National Match pistol was awarded in 1963 to Lt. Colonel William McMillan, a Triple Distinguished competitive shooter.
2. Colt Mark IV Series 70 Gold Cup National Match Semi-Automatic Pistol - .45 ACP - circa 1970-1983 - Originally intended to be a trophy presented at the 1990 National Matches at Camp Perry, OH. Torrential rain showers resulted in the cancellation of the match where this pistol was to be awarded.
3. Colt Government Model Semi-Automatic Pistol - .45 ACP - circa 1911-1925 - Fitted with modern Aimpoint sight.
4. H. Stotzer Single-Shot Target Pistol - .22 rimfire - circa 1937-1940.
5. Hämmerli Model 150 Single-Shot Free Pistol - .22 rimfire - circa 1989.
6. Hämmerli Model 103 Free Pistol - .22 long rifle - circa 1959-1960.
7. Sako Finnmaster Pistol - .22 rimfire - circa 1971.
8. Hämmerli Single Shot Air Pistol - .177 pellet - circa 1961-1970 - Owned by Stan Mate, recipient of UIT Blue Star Award.
9. Hämmerli Model 208 Standard Semi-Automatic Pistol - .22 rimfire - circa 1966-1968.
10. Feinwerkbau Model 65 Air Pistol - .177 pellet - circa 1961-1971 - Owned by Stan Mate, recipient of UTI Blue Star Award.

COMPETITION

1. Walther Free Pistol - .22 rimfire - circa 1977.
2. Walther Model LP 2 Air Pistol - .177 pellet - circa 1967-1972.
3. Beretta Tipo Olimpionico Semi-Automatic Pistol - .22 rimfire - circa 1959-1964 - Handmade prototype.
4. Hämmerli Master Air Pistol - .177 pellet - circa 1964-1977.
5. Walther OSP Semi-Automatic Target Pistol - .22 rimfire - circa 1961-1970.
6. Hämmerli Model 200 Olympia Semi-Automatic Pistol - .22 rimfire - circa 1958-1963.
7. Russian TOZ 8 Bolt-Action Target Rifle - .22 rimfire - circa 1950.
8. Russian MU-55 Target Pistol - .22 long rifle - circa 1975 - Russian single-shot target pistols, like this MU-55 .22 pistol built by Anschütz, Hämmerli, and Walther, compete with other international handguns in free pistol events.

CAMP PERRY & OTHERS

1. U.S. Springfield Model 1903 Bolt-Action Rifle - .30-06 - circa 1920-1930 - Refitted with Remington match barrel for competition.
2. VMT State Metal Works Finnish Lion Bolt-Action Single-Shot Target Rifle - .22 rimfire - circa 1937-1972.
3. Dunlap Custom Bolt-Action Rifle - .308 Winchester - circa 1950-1960.
4. Winchester Model 70 Bolt-Action Rifle - .30-06 - circa 1942 - Named "Old Yeller," the rifle set a 998-45X National Record in 1968.
5. Champlin Firearms Left-Hand Bolt-Action Rifle - .220 Swift - circa 1966 - Left-hand action customized by Roy Ivan Baldwin.
6. Anschütz Model 1813 Bolt-Action Rifle - .22 rimfire - circa 1979-1988.

COMPETITION

1. U.S. Springfield Model 1903 National Match Bolt-Action Rifle - .30-06 - circa 1921-1928 - Rifle was sold through Director of Civilian Marksmanship to former NRA magazine editor.

2. U.S. Springfield M1 Garand National Match Semi-Automatic Rifle - .30-06 - circa 1953-1963 - About 3,600 National Match Garands were made.

3. U.S. Springfield Model 1903 NRA/NBA President's Match Presentation Bolt-Action Rifle - .30-06 - circa 1932 - During the years of the Great Depression, the National Matches were reduced in scale to small regional competitions held at military bases around the country. This Model 1903 bolt-action rifle was awarded to USMC Corporal W.A. Easterling in 1932 at the Quantico matches that year.

4. Waffenfabrik Steyr Austrian Mannlicher Model 1893 Bolt-Action Rifle - 6.5mm - circa 1901 - Shot in 1901 Sea Girt match between Ireland and NJ teams, rifle was presented to NRA in 1976 after Palma Match competition. Note rear sight is mounted for the "Creedmore" shooting position, which is prone, lying on the back.

5. U.S. Springfield Krag Jorgensen Rifle with Pope Barrel - .30-40 Krag - circa 1901 - The rifle was owned by Col. John Caswell, noted sportsman and competitive shooter, who donated in 1923 the Winged Victory statue that is used as the Caswell Trophy.

6. Winchester Model 52 Bolt-Action Rifle - .22 rimfire - circa 1919-1979 - Owned by former NRA President Alonzo Garcelon. Favored in smallbore competition since its inception in 1919, Winchester's Model 52 rifle could be had with standard or heavyweight barrels.

CAMP PERRY & OTHERS

George Farr's Springfield Model 1903 rifle - .30-06 - circa 1921 - It was George Farr's first time at the Camp Perry National Matches. On the last relay of September 9, 1921, the 62-year-old Washington State resident was issued a rifle from an armory rack and made history. Using the iron sights on a Springfield M1903 he had never fired before, along with a crude spotting scope, Farr shot an incredible string of 71 consecutive bull's-eyes at his 1000-yard target, using government issue tin-plated .30-06 ammunition. Only fading twilight prevented further shooting. Farr's world record feat quickly attracted the attention of his fellow shooters on the line, who pooled their dollars to make a presentation of the rifle.

COMPETITION

Modern Target Shooting

Thousands of Americans enjoy the sport of competitive target shooting as their principal hobby. It is enjoyed today in a variety of disciplines such as smallbore and high-power rifle, pistol, air gun, shotgun and black-powder muzzleloading. Modern technology has given the sport a new look as accurate firearms, specifically manufactured for these competitions, have been developed along with highly efficient, scientifically designed cartridges.

Today, thousands of shooting clubs across the nation at the local, state, and national levels provide safe firearms handling, marksmanship, and competition training for interested individuals and teams. Numerous colleges and universities offer scholarships in a variety of shooting disciplines. Outdoor and indoor ranges, dotted across the country, hold monthly and annual competitions among members. On a global scale, national shooting teams and individuals compete in many international competitions held throughout the world.

1. Colt Sporter Target Model AR-15 Semi-Automatic Rifle - .223 Remington - circa 1989-1994 - AR-15 based rifles have become the most popular competition rifles in America.
2. Tubb 2000 Bolt-Action Rifle - 6mm - circa 2007 - Chambered in 6mm XC, this Tubb 2000 rifle offers an extended sight radius which can translate to a significant long-range accuracy advantage for an advanced marksman. Note that this bolt-action adopts modern AR platform features that enhance accuracy, ergonomics, safety, and manufacturing efficiency including a pistol grip stock, modern materials, elevated sights, straight-line configuration, and collapsible/adjustable buttstock.
3. Ljutic Industries Space Gun - 12 gauge - circa 1980 - Ljutic shotguns, offered in several models, provide competitive shotgunners with unmatched handling characteristics. Again, features widely associated with AR type rifles are incorporated in this single-shot shotgun, including pistol grip stock, raised sighting rail, and straight-line design.

MODERN COMPETITIVE SHOOTING

1. Anschütz Model 54 Super Match Bolt-Action Rifle - .22 rimfire - circa 1971.
2. Winchester Model 70 Palma Centennial Bolt-Action Rifle - .308 Winchester - circa 1976 - Unfired rifle from 1976 Palma Centennial Match; one of 80.
3. Anschütz Model 220 Air Gun - .177 pellet - circa 1959-1967.
4. Anschütz Model 380 Air Gun - .177 pellet - circa 1971.
5. Anschütz Model 1811 Bolt-Action Rifle - .22 long rifle - circa 1981.
6. Anschütz Model 1827 Fortner Bolt-Action Biathlon Rifle - .22 long rifle - circa 1990 - The biathlon combines cross-country skiing with rifle target competition.

COMPETITION

The Olympics

The first Olympic Games were held in 776 B.C. in Greece and repeated at four-year intervals until they were discontinued in 392 A.D. In 1896, Baron Pierre de Coubertin revived the Olympic games and organized the first international event in Athens, Greece. There were nine sporting disciplines represented, but as a former French shooting champion, de Coubertin included shooting - three pistol and two rifle events - as one of the nine, on the Olympic program. Only four nations competed for shooting medals in 1896, while some 80 countries met on the firing line in more recent games. The shooting events now attract the third-largest participation of any sport represented in the modern Olympic Games.

The United States has over 45 Olympic shooting medals to its credit. Shooter Carl Osburn has won 11 Olympic medals. In 1976, Margaret Thompson Murdock became the first woman in history to win an Olympic shooting medal (silver). In 1984, separate women's shooting events were instituted. In that year American Pat Spurgin became the first woman in history to capture an Olympic Gold for shooting. In recent decades, Launi Meili (1992), Kim Rhode (1996, 2004, & 2012), Nancy Johnson (2000), Matthew Emmons (2004), Walton Eller (2008), Vincent Hancock (2008 & 2012), Jamie Lynn Gray (2012) and Ginny Thrasher (2016) have continued the tradition of U.S. shooting gold-medal winners.

Morris Fisher's *(right)* Olympic Gold J. Hartman Hämmerli/Martini Free Rifle - .30-06 - circa 1920 - Used by Morris Fisher in 1920 Olympics to win gold in international position shooting.

Pistol Wizard A.P. Lane's *(left)* Olympic Gold Colt Officer's Model Match Revolver - .38 Colt - circa 1912 - A.P. Lane, nicknamed "The Pistol Wizard," used this .38 revolver in Olympic competition in the 1912 and 1920 games, bringing home five Olympic gold medals and a bronze team medal.

OLYMPICS

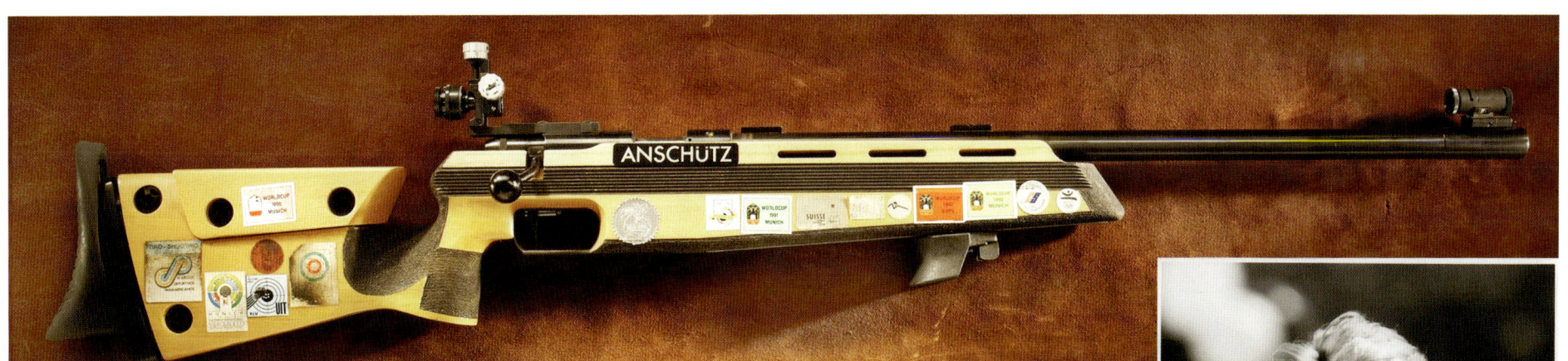

Launi Meili's Olympic Gold Medal Anschütz Model 54 Bolt-Action Rifle - .22 long rifle - circa 1990 - In the 1992 Olympic games in Barcelona, Spain, 29-year-old American smallbore shooter Launi Meili used this Anschütz .22 rifle to win the gold medal in the women's 50-meter, three-position shooting event.

Art Cook's Olympic Gold Remington Model 37 Rangemaster Bolt-Action Rifle - .22 long rifle - circa 1947 - In the 1948 Olympic games in London, American Art Cook took gold in the 50-meter smallbore rifle match, firing a 599 (with 43 Xs) score with the Remington Model 37 rifle, fitted with an adjustable barrel bedding system.

COMPETITION

Bill McMillan's Olympic Gold High-Standard Supermatic Citation Semi-Automatic Pistol - .22 long rifle - circa 1959 - The 1960 Olympic Games in Rome pitted U.S. Marine Corps Capt. Bill McMillan against shooters from Finland and the Soviet Union. Using this High Standard .22 pistol, McMillan won the gold medal for the 25-meter event following a three-way shoot-off after his score of 587 was posted.

Lanny Bassham's Olympic Gold Medal Walther GX-1 Bolt-Action Rifle - .22 rimfire - circa 1974 - After winning Silver in the 1972 Olympics, Bassham developed a stock design that suited him better. He dropped the buttplate, angled the pistol grip so the wrist doesn't bend while shooting, offset the rail for his offhand rest, lowered the barrel below the edges of the stock, raised the sight bases, and angled the forend up. Firearms engineers disagreed with the design, but Walther built this rifle to his specifications. Other shooters jokingly called it "the oar", but in the 1976 Winter Olympics, Bassham tied for first place with Margaret Murdock. Bassham suggested they both be awarded gold medals, but the judges used the established tie-breaking rules to award him gold. At the awards ceremony, Bassham invited Murdock to share the first place pedestal with him, which she did. His 35 international medals rank him 3rd of all time among U.S. shooters, and include four world records.

OLYMPICS

Thurman Randle's Remington Model 37 Rifle - .22LR - circa 1938 - Used in Camp Perry matches. Randle was a world record holder and served as President of NRA.

Winchester Model 52 Bolt-Action Rifle - .22 rimfire - circa 1929 - Named "Old Bacon Getter" by owner Thurman Randle, a former NRA president, this Winchester Model 52 rifle has a crudely painted stainless barrel to minimize glare when shooting in bright sunlight.

Thomas D. Smith's World Record Colt Government Model Semi-Automatic Pistol - .38 Special - circa 1960-1963 - In the 1963 Pan American Games, Lt. Colonel T.D. Smith used this .38 caliber semi-automatic pistol to set a world record in center-fire pistol competition that remains unbroken. He also shot in the 1964 Olympics.

Colt Olympic National Match Semi-Automatic Pistol - .45 ACP - circa 1933 - This Colt National Match .45 semi-automatic pistol belonged to the coach of the 1936 American Olympic team and was used in training exercises prior to competition in Germany.

COMPETITION

Ed McGivern

Born in Omaha, Nebraska, in 1874, Ed McGivern earned a reputation as the fastest gun in the world. One of this country's most celebrated exhibition shooters, he learned the art of fast shooting with astounding accuracy by pursuing a rigorous path of discipline and self-training in his youth. Ed McGivern became a scientific expert with a handgun. Every spare moment was spent developing championship shooting skills along with a variety of scientific timing devices designed to measure intervals of time as short as 1/20th of a second. At the age of 58 he set a world record for accurate rapid fire shooting - five shots, fired in less than 9/20th of a second into a group that could be covered by a half-dollar coin from a distance of 20 feet.

Some of McGivern's records have been equaled, and in some instances, bested by more modern shooters like Jerry Miculek. However, McGivern's more famous exploits took place as he was in his mid to late 50s and arthritis was threatening his shooting career.

Throughout his life, McGivern relied on single-action revolvers for fast-fanning shooting. His Colt Single Action Army revolvers still retain the original tape wrapped around their triggers. Fitted with custom grip panels, sized and checkered to his specifications for double-action speed shooting, he favored S&W revolvers. HIs handguns also had special sights fitted, notably a gold bead on black post front sight that came to be known as the "McGivern sight." McGivern's final years were supported by protégé Walter Groff, who brought McGivern east to live in Philadelphia. In gratitude, McGivern's gun collection was given to Groff, whose widow in turn donated 14 of McGivern's handguns to the National Firearms Museum in 1974.

Below: McGivern's World Record Smith & Wesson 38-44 Police Target Model Revolver - .38 Special (Heavy) - circa 1931 - The revolver used by Ed McGivern to shoot his five shots in 9/20ths of a second, setting a world record, was commemorated by the brass plaque added to the sideplate. Enlarged trigger guard by gunsmith Sukalle. Gold bead front sight.

At right: Ed McGivern's traveling trunk.

Other McGivern guns appear on the facing page.

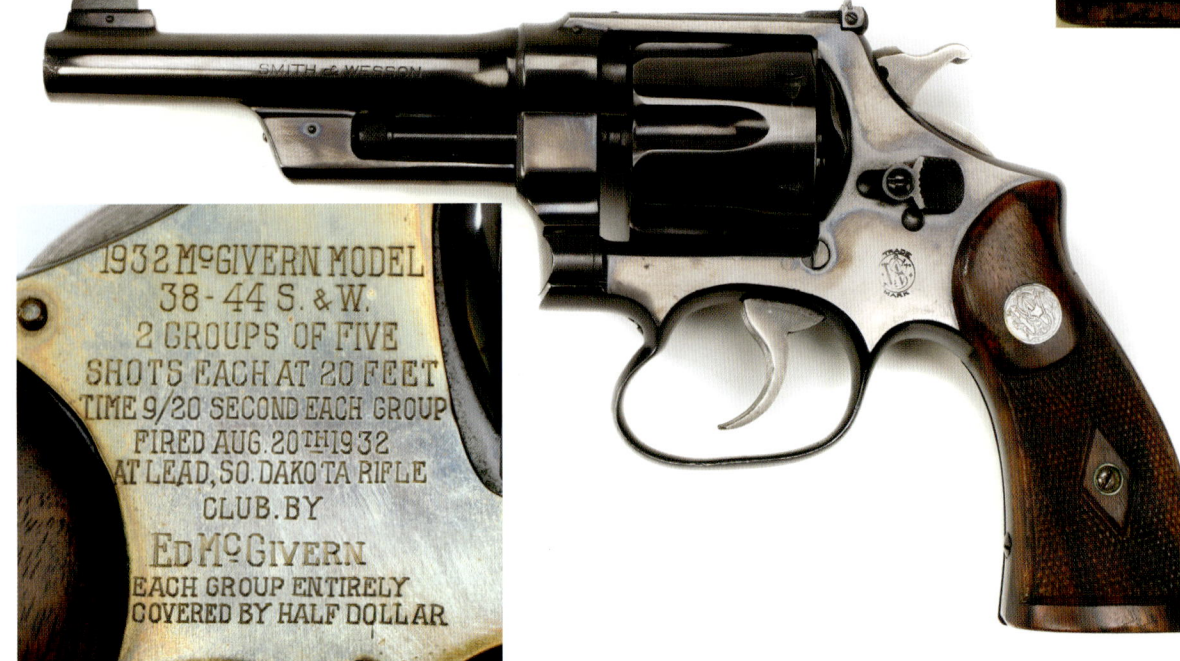

Ed McGivern

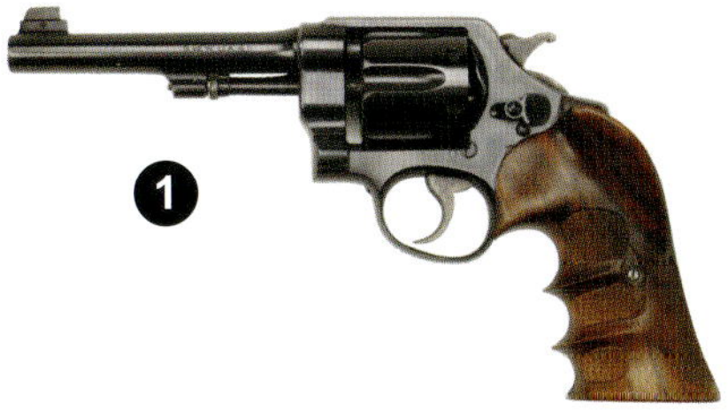

EXHIBITION SHOOTERS, WRITERS & OTHERS

Ed McGivern's revolvers:

1. Smith & Wesson Model 1917 Revolver - .45 ACP - circa 1935 - Gold bead front sight with finger groove grips.
2. Smith & Wesson Model 1917 Revolver - .45 ACP - circa 1935 - Cut down with modified trigger guard and no hammer spur.
3. Smith & Wesson K-38 Revolver - .38 Special - circa 1947 - Stock gun with McGivern carved grips.
4. Colt Model 1873 Single Action Army Revolver - .38 Special - circa 1898 - Adjustable-sighted Single Action Army with checkered grips.
5. Smith & Wesson Military & Police Revolver - .38 Special - circa 1915-1942 - Snub-nosed with gold bead front sight; no hammer spur.
6. Colt Model 1873 Single Action Army Revolver - .38 Special - circa 1933 - Slip hammer target-sighted SAA with checkered grips.
7. Smith & Wesson Military & Police Revolver - .38 Special - circa 1915-1942 - Snub-nosed with target sights with gold bead front sight.
8. Smith & Wesson Military & Police Revolver - .38 Special - circa 1917-1940 - Target sights with gold bead front.
9. Smith & Wesson Hand Ejector First Model .44 Triple-Lock Revolver - .44 Special - circa 1915-1920 - Target sights with smooth grips.
10. Smith & Wesson Military & Police Revolver - .38 Special - circa 1915-1942 - Custom reformed rear trigger guard stop.
11. Smith & Wesson First Model Hand Ejector Revolver - .44 Special - circa 1911 - Custom-carved grips.
12. Colt Model 1873 Single Action Army Revolver - .45 Colt - circa 1893 - McGivern's fanning gun with taped trigger.
13. Smith & Wesson New Model No. 3 Single-Action Revolver - .38-40 - circa 1885-1908 - Engraved "Ed McGivern of Montana 1919."

COMPETITION

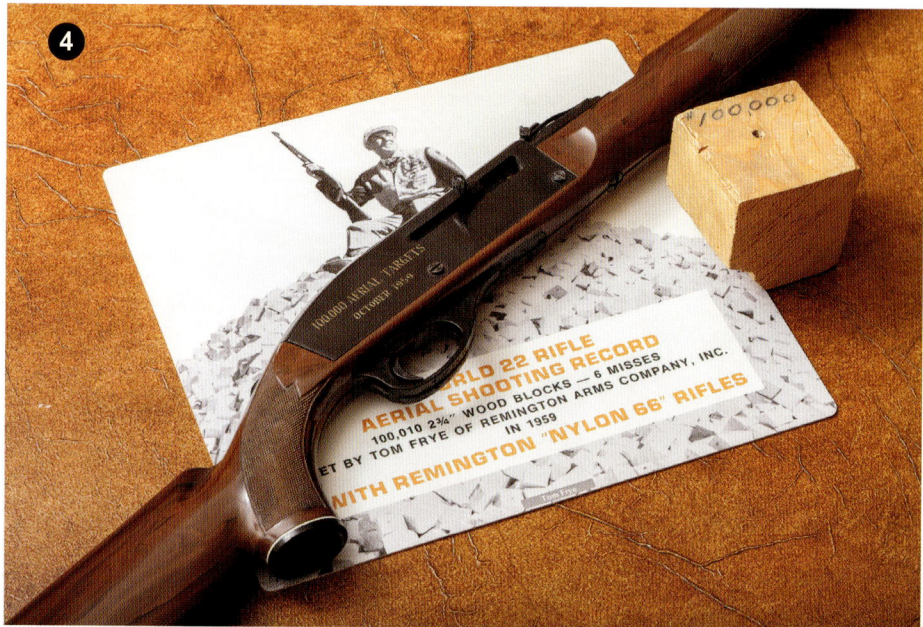

1. Ad Topperwein's Colt Officer's Model Revolver - .38 Special - circa 1904-1908 - Ad and Plinky Topperwein, a husband-and-wife exhibition shooting team for Winchester, were renowned for their skills, which included drawing pictures with bullet holes. In 1906 Plinky (Elizabeth) became the first woman to compete in NRA National Matches. She was the best female shooter of her era.

2. Herb Parsons' Smith & Wesson Outdoorsman Revolver - .22 LR - circa 1931-1940, and his S&W Model 1905 Military & Police 4th Change - .38 Special - circa 1915-1942 - Noted exhibition shooter Herb Parsons was employed by ammunition companies, including Winchester and Remington, to give presentations showing the capabilities of their products in the hands of an expert. *Parsons is pictured kneeling at left.*

3. Arlayne Brown's Colt Officer's Model Target Revolver - .38 Colt - circa 1929 - This custom target revolver was specially ordered from Colt in 1929 by Arlayne Brown, a noted female pistol competitor, for use at the Camp Perry National Matches. She won her first Camp Perry matches at age 13. *Brown is pictured at left.*

4. Tom Frye's Remington Model 66 Rifle - .22 LR - circa 1959 - Exhibition shooter Frye broke Ad Topperwein's aerial shooting record with this rifle hitting 100,004 out of 100,010 hand thrown wooden blocks. The image of him sitting on a mountain of blocks was a Remington advertising staple in the early 1960s.

EXHIBITION SHOOTERS, WRITERS & OTHERS

Elmer Keith's Keith/Falcon Test Enfield Prototype Rifle - .334 Wildcat. Keith is best known for his experiments with high power loads contributing to the development of the .44 Magnum.

Col. Charles Askins' Aguirre Y Aranzibal Over/Under - 10 gauge - circa 1958. Believed to be the first 10 gauge over/under shotgun made.

Elmer Keith's modified Colt Bisley, converted to .357 Magnum with adjustable sights and vent rib added.

Julian Hatcher's 1903 Springfield rifle and Colt Camp Perry single-shot pistols, used in the 1938 National Matches. Hatcher was head of U.S. Army Ordnance during WWII, and technical editor of NRA's American Rifleman magazine.

Skeeter Skelton's Smith & Wesson Model 34-1 Kit Gun - .22 LR. - circa 1971 Border Patrolman Skelton was known for his books and his popular "Hipshots" column in *Shooting Times* magazine.

Townsend Whelen's Springfield Sporter Bolt-Action Rifle - .30-06 - circa 1920 - Incorporating elements of the Mauser 1898 bolt-action design, the 1903 Springfield became a popular sporter.

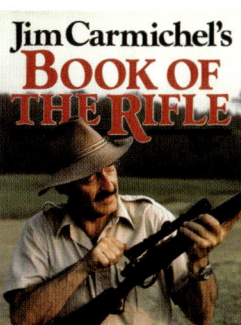

Jim Carmichel's Jarrett/Remington XP-100 Rail Gun - .22 Wildcat - circa 1980. These types of benchrest rifles are made for maximum accuracy, designed to be fired from a solid rest.

Tennessee Ernie Ford's Browning Superposed Shotgun - 12 gauge - circa 1954 - Owned by the popular singer and television host, known for songs such as "Sixteen Tons."

FOR THE FUN OF IT

Johnny Cash's Stevens Single-Shot Rifle - .32 cartridge - circa 1910-1920 - Once owned by the famous singer/songwriter.

1. Remington Model 6 Single-Shot Rifle - .22 rimfire - circa 1901-1933.
2. Stevens Favorite Single-Shot Rifle - .32 rimfire - circa 1893-1939.
3. Harrington & Richardson 1920 Single-Shot Shotgun - .410 gauge - circa 1920 - This was a beginner shotgun for many first-time shooters who wanted a dependable, yet inexpensive shotgun.
4. Flobert Belgian Model 5 Rifle - .22 Flobert rimfire - circa 1890-1900 - Low-powered Flobert rifles and pistols were popular for indoor shooting in a parlor.
5. Quackenbush Convertible Air Rifle - circa 1884-1913 - Could fire .22 rimfire or airgun pellets.
6. Stevens No. 12 Marksman Single-Shot Rifle with Weaver B4 Scope - .22 rimfire - circa 1912-1933.
7. Hopkins & Allen Falling Block Rifle - .32 rimfire - circa 1888-1892.
8. Remington Model No. 4S "Military Model" Rolling Block Sporting Rifle - .22 rimfire - circa 1913-1923 - Remington's Model 4S was originally designed for American Boy Scouts and was stamped with their name But in 1915, the designation was changed to "Military Model" and the majority of the 15,000 rifles produced were so marked until manufacture ceased in 1923.

Plinking

Since the turn of the 20th century, the .22 caliber single-shot rifle has been the most popular first firearm for young boys and girls. Teaching the art and responsibility of safely handling a gun to a child or an adolescent is as old as firearms themselves. The craft and manufacture of specialized firearms for youth is nearly as old. By the late 19th century, well-known arms manufacturing companies regularly engaged in the design and sale of the boys' or ladies' rifles, as they were then termed. Many of America's youth came of age, as had their forefathers, learning to handle a gun safely and effectively. This instruction in safe gun handling, shared between parent and child, has become a traditional American rite of passage from childhood to adult responsibility.

PLINKING

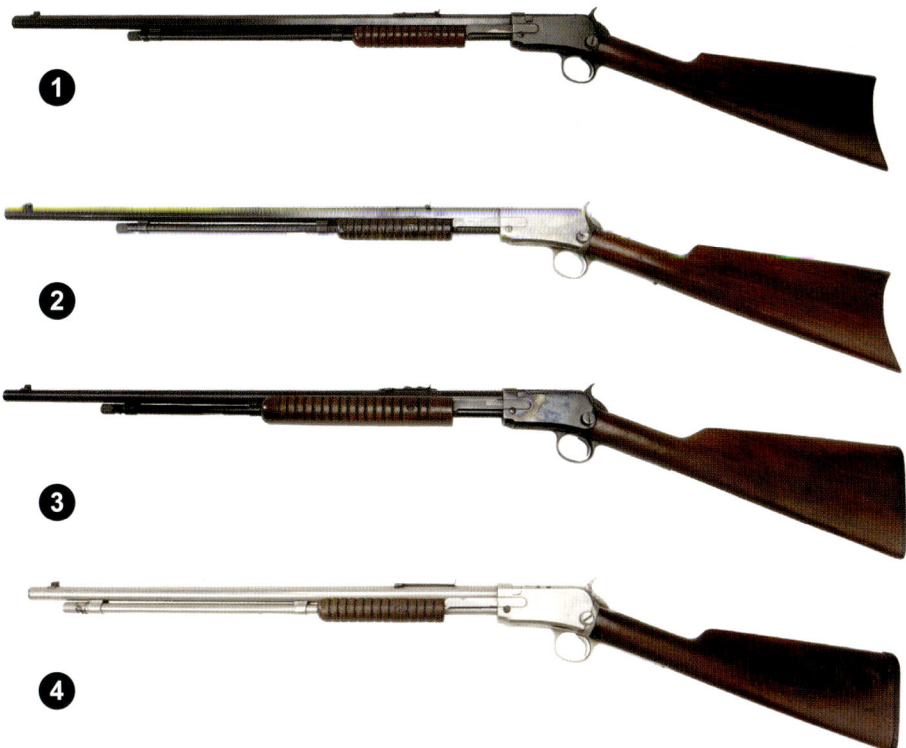

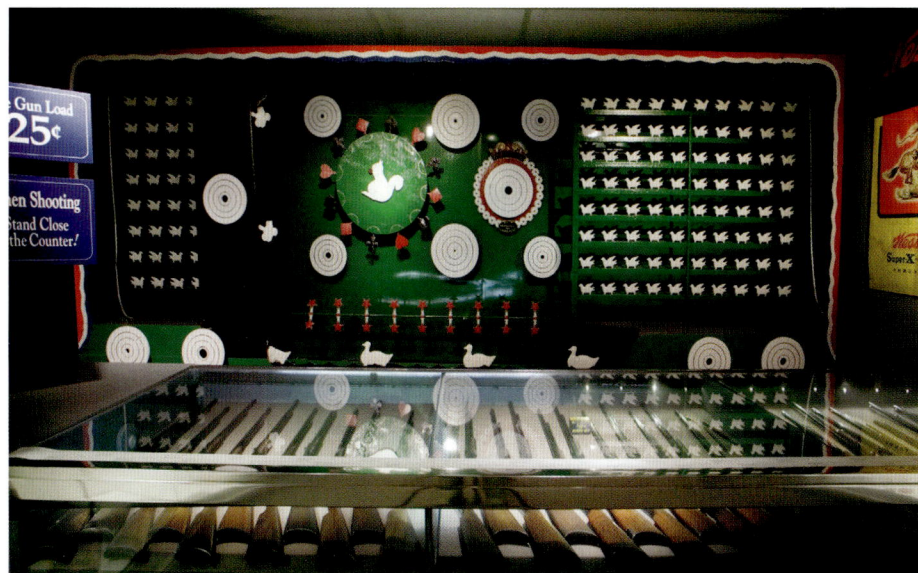

Original Coney Island Shooting Gallery, created in the first decade of the 20th century, on display at the National Firearms Museum.

Shooting Galleries

People have always been fascinated with testing their skill and marksmanship by shooting at a variety of objects. The development of the shooting gallery as a game at fairs, carnivals, and amusement parks is a distinctly American phenomenon. At the height of its popularity, amusement companies designed and produced elaborate galleries, which included still targets, knock downs, bells and chain-driven moving wheels, silhouettes, and bullseye targets. So popular was the pastime that all major firearms manufacturers produced lines of gallery rifles and pistols chambered for .22 rimfire ammunition, and ammunition makers turned out millions of .22 gallery cartridges.

1. Winchester Model 1890 Slide-Action Rifle - .22 rimfire - circa 1913.
2. Winchester Model 1890 Slide-Action Rifle - .22 rimfire - circa 1912.
3. Winchester Model 62A Slide-Action Rifle - .22 rimfire - circa 1936.
4. Winchester Model 1906 Slide-Action Rifle - .22 rimfire - circa 1926 - Almost 850,000 Model 1906 slide-action rifles were manufactured by Winchester from 1906 to 1932. It differed from the earlier Model 1890 in that it was only offered in a round barrel configuration.
5. Winchester Model 1906 Slide-Action Rifle - .22 rimfire - circa 1924 - rear tang sight.
6. Savage Model 29B Slide-Action Rifle - .22 rimfire - circa 1929-1950.
7. Remington Model 25 Slide-Action Rifle - .32-20 - circa 1886-1890.

FOR THE FUN OF IT

1. Hopkins & Allen Junior Rifle - .32 rimfire - circa 1905-1914.
2. Mossberg Model L Single-Shot Rifle - .22 rimfire - circa 1929-1932.
3. Quackenbush Model 1886 Bicycle Pump Rifle - .22 rimfire/pellet - circa 1886-1890 - These youth rifles could be tied to a bicycle for transport. Retractable wire stock.
4. Anschütz Woodchucker Bolt-Action Rifle - .22 rimfire - circa 1960.
5. Winchester Model 36 Single-Shot Shotgun - 9mm rimfire shotshell - circa 1920-1927.
6. Browning BL-22 Rifle - .22 long rifle - circa 1970-2003.
7. Daisy Model 2201 Bolt-Action Single-Shot Rifle - .22 rimfire - circa 1988-1991.
8. Detroit Rifle Co. No. 11 Rifle - .22 rimfire - circa 1899-1905.
9. Armalite AR-7 Explorer Semi-Automatic Rifle - .22 rimfire - circa 1959-1960 - Designed to be broken down, with the collapsed parts stored in the water proof stock. A variation was used as a USAF pilot survival rifle.
10. Winchester Model 59 single-shot bolt-action rifle- .22 rimfire - circa 1930-1931.
11. Winchester Model 290 Deluxe Semi-Automatic Rifle - .22 rimfire - circa 1965-1973.
12. Hamilton No. 27 Single-Shot Rifle - .22 rimfire - circa 1907-1930.
13. Atlas Single-Shot Rifle - .22 rimfire - circa 1886-1890.
14. Hopkins & Allen Junior Repeater Rifle - .22 rimfire - circa 1902-1914.

PLINKING

1. Meriden Arms Co. Single-Shot Rifle - .22 rimfire - circa 1913-1918.
2. Winchester Model 67 Bolt-Action Rifle - .22 rimfire - circa 1934.
3. Stevens No. 65 Little Krag Single-Shot Bolt-Action Rifle - .22 rimfire - circa 1903-1910.
4. Simpson Bolt-Action Rifle - .22 rimfire - circa 1928-1941.
5. Marlin Model 101 Crown Prince Single-Shot Bolt-Action Rifle - .22 rimfire - circa 1959.
6. Thompson Center Classic Semi-Automatic Rifle - .22 rimfire - circa 2000.
7. Remington Nylon 76 Lever-Action Rifle - .22 rimfire - circa 1972-1974 - This nylon stocked rifle reflected the changing times and styles of the 1970s.
8. Savage Stevens Model 87 Semi-Automatic Rifle - .22 rimfire - circa 1938-1945.
9. Remington Model 512 Sportmaster Bolt-Action Rifle - .22 rimfire - circa 1940-1962.
10. Browning T-Bolt T-2 Straight-Pull Bolt-Action Rifle - .22 rimfire - circa 1965-1974 - Browning's T-Bolt .22 rifle offered a fast, straight-pull action that was built to move straight back and then forward without the turn up / pull back / push forward / turn down manipulation required a traditional bolt-action rifle.
11. Noble Model 70 Slide-Action Shotgun - .410 gauge - circa 1953-1971.
12. Winchester Model 190 Semi-Automatic Rifle - .22 rimfire - circa 1967-1980.
13. Marlin Model 20S Slide-Action Rifle - .22 rimfire - circa 1922-1927.

FOR THE FUN OF IT

Air Guns

The firing of a projectile through the use of compressed air, gas, and spring-loaded guns has a long history of development and goes back as far as the 16th century. By the late 19th century, these guns developed into a popular toy for young boys and girls. While some are still used today for serious Olympic target and sporting purposes, the great majority of those manufactured are intended for recreational plinking by the youth of the world. In 1870, Henry M. Quackenbush patented an air gun that accepted both BBs and darts. In 1882, Clarence Hamilton of Plymouth, Michigan, developed an all-metal air gun. The Hamilton air gun was given the now-familiar name Daisy. The very first Daisy is on display at the National Firearms Museum, a gift of the present-day Daisy Manufacturing Company. In a child's world, the name Daisy has become as recognizable and familiar as Colt and Winchester. In 1890, Daisy was selling about 85,000 air guns per year. By 1960, annual production and sales were close to 1.5 million.

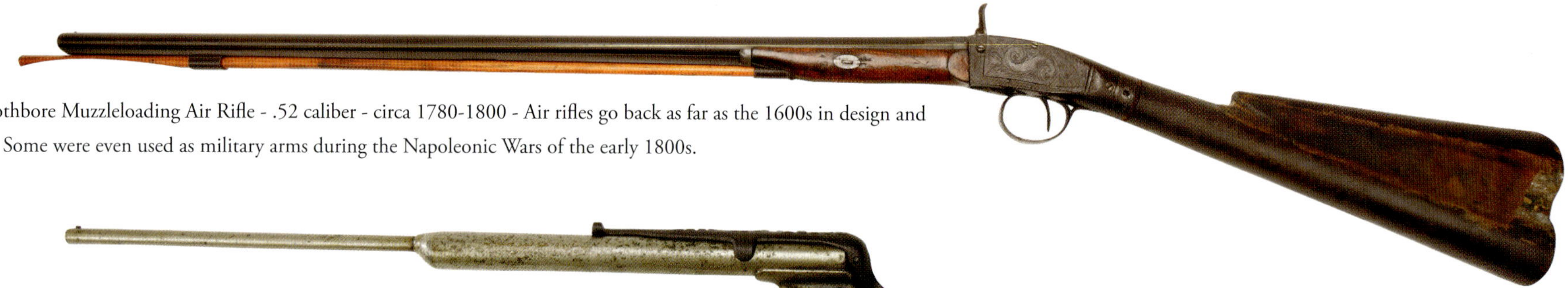

English Smoothbore Muzzleloading Air Rifle - .52 caliber - circa 1780-1800 - Air rifles go back as far as the 1600s in design and manufacture. Some were even used as military arms during the Napoleonic Wars of the early 1800s.

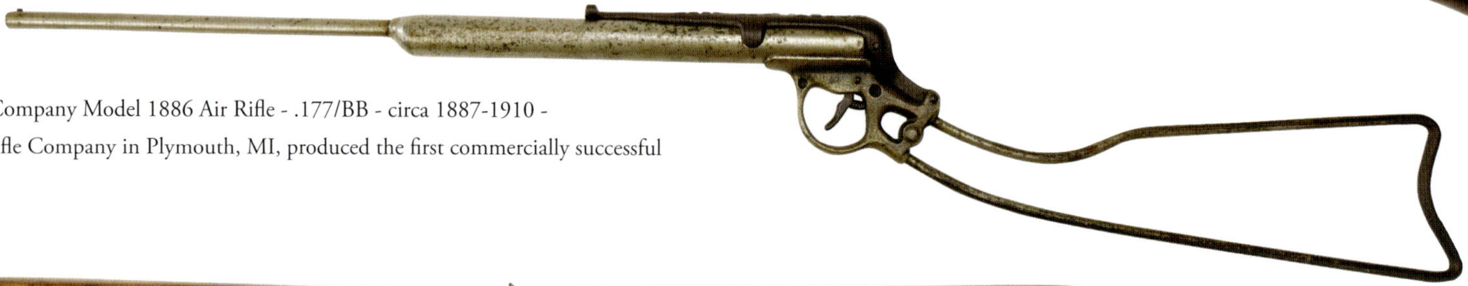

Markham Air Rifle Company Model 1886 Air Rifle - .177/BB - circa 1887-1910 - The Markham Air Rifle Company in Plymouth, MI, produced the first commercially successful BB guns in 1887.

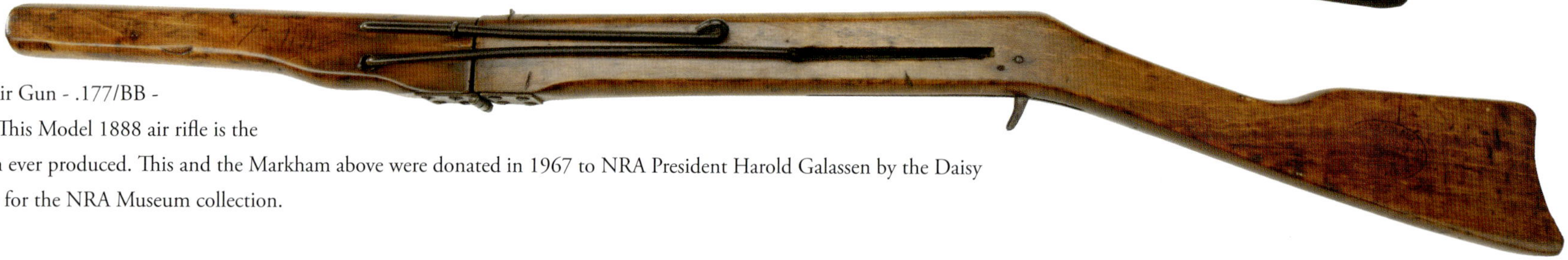

The First Daisy Air Gun - .177/BB - circa 1889-1900 This Model 1888 air rifle is the first Daisy air gun ever produced. This and the Markham above were donated in 1967 to NRA President Harold Galassen by the Daisy company as a gift for the NRA Museum collection.

AIR GUNS

1. Crosman Model 130 Single-Shot Air Pistol (sectionalized) - .22 pellet - circa 1955-1970.
2. Daisy Model 177 Repeating Air Pistol - .177/BB - circa 1959-1978.
3. Daisy NRA Centennial Commemorative Peacemaker Repeating Air Pistol - .177/BB - circa 1971 - Part of an NRA Centennial set with a Winchester-styled Daisy lever-action BB rifle, this single-action revolver-styled BB handgun was sold by the Daisy company in 1971 and 1972.
4. Daisy Model 118 Target Special Air Pistol - .118 pellet - circa 1937-1952.
5. Diana German Model No. 1 Air Pistol - .177/BB - circa 1924-1940.
6. Webley Junior Air Pistol - .177/BB - circa 1929-1938 - The last firearms produced by the venerable Webley firm, founded in 1790, were air guns.
7. Crosman Model 116 Air Pistol (sectionalized) - .177/BB - circa 1951-1954.
8. Crosman Hahn 45 Single-Action Air Pistol - .177/BB - circa 1959-1969.
9. Crosman Single-Action 6 CO2 Pistol - .22 rimfire - circa 1959-1969.
10. Healthways Model 175 Plainsman CO2 Pistol - .177/BB - circa 1969-1980.
11. Hahn Model 45 Single-Action CO2 Pistol - .177/BB - circa 1959-1969.
12. Hy-Score Model 800 Air Pistol - .22 pellet - circa 1948-1970.
13. Daisy Model 188 Air Pistol - .177 pellet/BB - circa 1980.
14. Crosman Marksman BB Pistol - .177/BB - circa 1977.
15. Crosman Model 150 CO2 Pistol (sectionalized) - circa 1956-1967.
16. Webley Tempest Air Pistol - .177 pellet - circa 1979-1981.

FOR THE FUN OF IT

1. Sheridan Blue Streak Single-Shot Air Rifle - 5mm pellet - circa 1952-1963.
2. Crosman M1 Carbine Air Rifle - .177/BB - circa 1968-1976 - This air rifle appealed to the post-war baby boomers who desired a realistic copy of the M1 Carbine.
3. Hy-Score Model 808 Single-Shot Air Rifle - .177 pellet - circa 1970-1980.
4. Crosman Model 700 Pellmaster Air Rifle - .22 pellet - circa 1967-1971.
5. Atlas Single-Shot Air Rifle - .177/BB - circa 1886-1890.
6. Daisy Buck Jones Special BB Gun - .177 pellet - circa 1934-1942 - This slide-action BB gun manufactured by Daisy from 1934 to 1942 featured sundial markings on the stock as well as a small embedded compass.
7. Daisy Model 104 Double-Barrel Air Gun - .177/BB - circa 1938-1940.
8. Crosman V-350 Air Rifle - .177/BB - circa 1961-1969.
9. Daisy Model 25 Slide-Action Air Rifle - .22 pellet - circa 1972.
10. Markham King Model D Air Rifle - .22 pellet - circa 1907-1909.
11. Crosman Experimental Air Rifle - .177/BB - circa 1960-1961.
12. Benjamin Model 362 CO2 Carbine - .22 pellet - circa 1956-1957.
13. Daisy Model 300 CO2 Rifle - BB - circa 1968-1975.

AIR GUNS

1. Daisy Red Ryder No. 111 Model 40 Lever-Action Air Rifle - .177/BB - circa 1947 - The Red Ryder is still in production, a favorite among youngsters.
2. Quackenbush Single-Shot Air Rifle - .21 pellet - circa 1881-1919.
3. Benjamin Model 30/30 Carbine - .177 pellet/BB - circa 1972-1976.
4. Daisy Model 25 Slide-Action Air Rifle - .177 pellet/BB - circa 1972.
5. Daisy Model 99 Lever-Action Air Rifle - .177 pellet/BB - circa 1960-1970.
6. Daisy Model 917 Powerline Air Rifle - .177 pellet/BB - circa 1979-1982.
7. Crosman Powermaster 760 Air Rifle - .177 pellet/BB - circa 1966-1970.
8. Crosman Model 140 Single-Shot Air Rifle - .22 pellet - circa 1956-1962.
9. Daisy Model 1894 Lever-Matic Repeating Air Rifle - .177/BB - circa 1970-1980.
10. Crosman CO2 Rifle - .22 pellet - circa 1946-1950.
11. Sheridan VM-68 Lady Magnum Paintball Gun - .69 caliber - circa 1992 - Anodized in pink, this one-of-a-kind paintball gun was used in competition by a former *American Rifleman* magazine editor, Jessica Sparks, and loaned to the National Firearms Museum collection.
12. German Crank-Action Air Rifle - 7mm - circa 1870.
13. Paul Giffard French Single-Shot CO2 Rifle - 8mm - circa 1880-1890.
14. Mayer & Grammelspacher German Diana Model 27 Air Rifle - .177 pellet - circa 1910-1936.
15. German Lever-Action Single-Shot Air Rifle - 6.5mm - circa 1870.

FOR THE FUN OF IT

Hollywood Guns: Real Guns of Reel Heroes.

We have all sat fixated before televisions watching the heroes save whomever was in need of saving with their six gun or an M1 Garand. Whether it was the dusty streets of Dodge City or the beaches of Normandy, the Duke, Clint and a host of others wielded their firearms with ease and unfailing accuracy against the bad guys. We developed our fascination for the tools of their trade while watching them on the silver screen. The NRA Museums feature the actual guns used to create the iconic scenes we've all come to know and remember by heart. So, go ahead, make my day, enjoy the Hollywood Guns of the NRA Museums.

Smith & Wesson Schofield - Actor Tom Selleck has been a patron of NRA Museums for decades and has generously given many of his film-used firearms to the museum for display in our Hollywood Guns exhibit. This revolver was used in the 2001 film *Crossfire Trail*.

Shiloh Sharps # 3 Rifle - .45-110 - Filmed entirely in Australia, 1990's *Quigley Down Under* was a unique western featuring Tom Selleck's eponymous character Matthew Quigley. The film rekindled interest in Sharp's rifles so much that thirty years after the film's release, factories are still backordered for Quigley rifles. - Gift of Tom Selleck

HOLLYWOOD GUNS

Sig Sauer 1911 - *Criminal Minds* actor Joe Mantegna portrays FBI Special Agent David Rossi. For the 14th and final season of the show, Sig made a special USMC edition of the 1911 for agent Rossi. Joe presented the pistol and his character badge to the National Firearms Museum in 2018. Mantegna regularly films episodes of the Outdoor Channel's "Gun Stories" at the NRA Museums.

Beretta 92 & HK P7 - The 1988 Christmas siege of the Nakatomi Plaza in Downtown LA will be forever remembered every holiday season, following showings of *It's a Wonderful Life* (1946) and *Miracle on 34th St.* (1947) Bruce Willis and Alan Rickman ushered in a new era of Holiday Favorites with *Die Hard* (1988) and created an instant sensation for both of these pistols. This Beretta had previously been used by Mel Gibson in *Lethal Weapon* (1987).

Walther PP - Gold plated, engraved with ivory grips this pistol was created from an original World War II Walther to mimic the PP supposedly owned by Adolph Hitler. It is featured prominently in the 2020 film *Boss Level* starring Mel Gibson. A silencer has been added to enhance its use in the movie's story line.

FOR THE FUN OF IT

Italian reproduction Colt M-1847 Walker. As with many Hollywood guns, once they have finished doing their job on one film, they go back into storage until called upon for another rental. Some guns can appear in as many as a dozen separate feature films and television shows. Such is the case for this Walker Colt reproduction. Initially used in *True Grit* (1969) by Kim Darby and John Wayne, it was subsequently used by Clint Eastwood in *The Outlaw Josey Wales* (1976).

Gatling Gun Model 1883 - .45-70 - This Gatling gun is one of two used in the final scenes of *Gunga Din* (1939). Shown mounted on an original Colt factory barrel dolly, the museum is fortunate to own both of the guns used in this iconic film.

Left: Star Model B Semi Auto 9mm - For decades, before the development of the .44 Win Mag. cartridge, most armorer's in Hollywood had to rely on Colt 1911 look-a-likes to fire blank cartridges. Star Model B's fit the bill nicely with the exception of the exposed extractor on the right side of the gun. Actor William Holden used this Star in the classic western *The Wild Bunch* (1969).

Right: Book of Eli Remington Mod. 870 shotgun and Heckler & Koch HK45 pistol - 12 gauge & .45 ACP. Used by Denzel Washington as Eli in this 2010 film.

HOLLYWOOD GUNS

Smith & Wesson Model 29 - "…the most powerful gun ever made…" and with those lines, San Francisco Police Inspector Harry Callahan as portrayed by Clint Eastwood changed film history and firearms history forever. As Dirty Harry, his .44 Magnum became a worldwide sensation and phenomenon. The demand for Model 29 revolvers has hardly diminished since the film was released in 1971. Thought to be the most famous handgun of all time. - From the collection of John Milius, writer and director on the *Dirty Harry* series of films, to whom it is inscribed from Warner Brothers and Clint Eastwood.

No Country for Old Men Silenced Remington 11-87 shotgun - 12 gauge - A suppressed semi-automatic shotgun is one of the unusual arms used by bad guy killer Anton Chigurh (played by Javier Bardem) in this 2007 film for which he received an Oscar.

M1 Garand - Since the M1 Garand was adopted in 1936, literally thousands of films have been made showing US G.I.'s defeating the evil forces of fascism armed with the Garand. Not since John Wayne led US Marines ashore in *The Sands of Iwo Jima* (1949) has an M1 Garand been wielded with such menacing alacrity than when Clint Eastwood invited his delinquent neighbors to "Get off my lawn" while shouldering the M1. *Gran Torino* (2008) shared this particular Garand with *Lost* (2004).

Moses Brothers Self-Defense Engine Frontier Model B Pistol. This stylized pistol is actually a .38 Taurus revolver fitted inside a futuristic bronze housing. It was the primary sidearm of Captain Malcolm "Mal" Reynolds (Nathan Fillion) aboard the spaceship *Serenity* in the 2005 film of the same name. Previously showcased in a short-lived television series, *Firefly*, Fillion and his small crew practice a frontier moral code in the dark vastness of outer space, wielding many unusual arms based on American Western standards.

MODERN FIREARMS

William B. Ruger

Born in Brooklyn, New York, William B. Ruger developed an early interest in firearms by shooting on his high school rifle team. Studying gun books and patents, he developed a strong interest in firearms design. Just prior to World War II, Ruger took a job at the Springfield Armory, where he designed a machine gun and obtained a patent. In 1948, he and a partner, Alex Sturm, developed a .22 caliber self-loading pistol, and began Sturm, Ruger & Company. The .22 caliber Standard semi-automatic pistol was the first firearm they produced. The success of the design set Ruger to work developing a high-quality revolver. These products were followed by a long line of firearms including the Blackhawk series of single-action revolvers, black-powder revolvers, police revolvers, self-loading carbines, falling block single-shot rifles, bolt-action rifles, semi-automatic rifles and pistols, and Red Label shotguns. Today, Ruger guns are made for every interest from plinking to big game hunting. The genius and marketability of Ruger's designs have made Sturm, Ruger & Company an American success story.

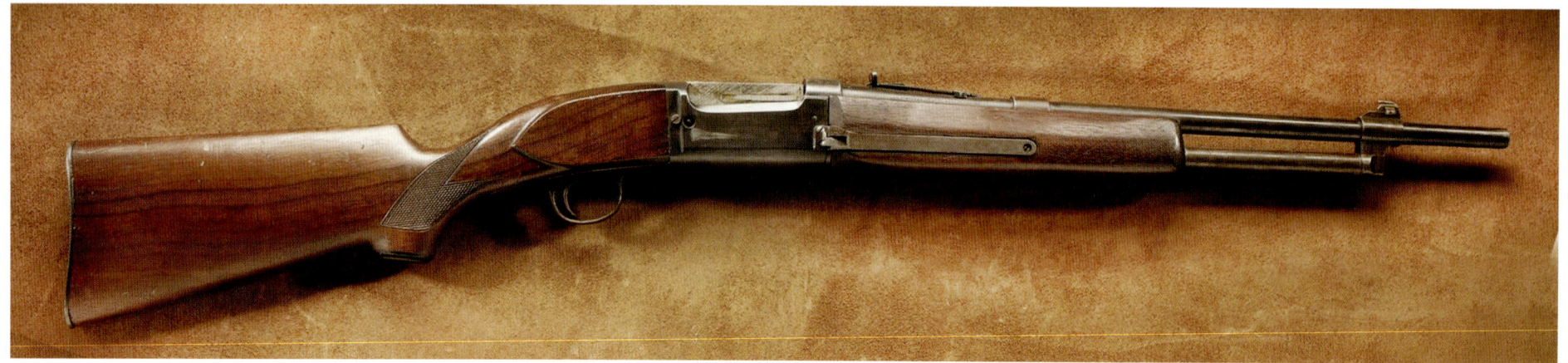

Prototype Ruger/Savage Model 1899 Semi-Automatic Conversion - .250/3000 - circa 1942 - In 1942, young arms designer William Batterman Ruger visited Springfield Armory with a modified Savage Model 99 rifle in hand. Altered from a lever-action to a semi-automatic design, Ruger's new rifle prototype impressed the military, and Ruger was hired to work as a military firearms design specialist.

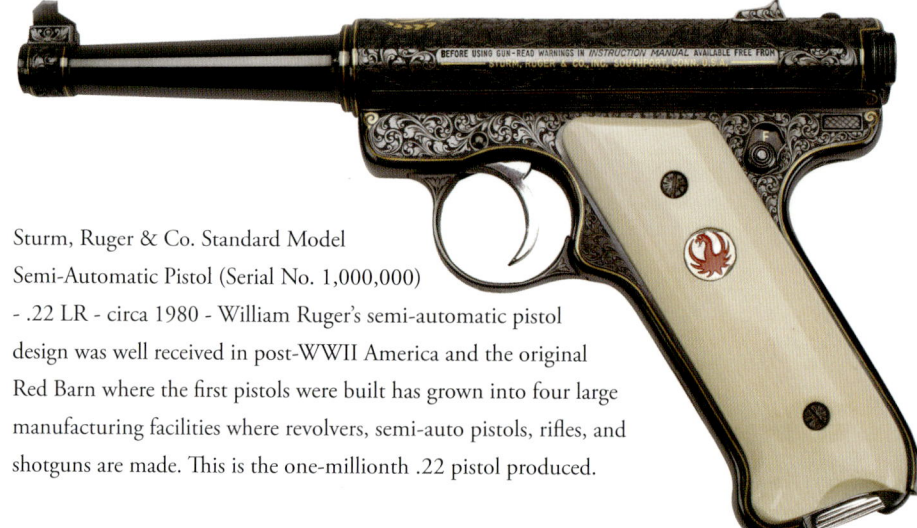

Sturm, Ruger & Co. Standard Model Semi-Automatic Pistol (Serial No. 1,000,000) - .22 LR - circa 1980 - William Ruger's semi-automatic pistol design was well received in post-WWII America and the original Red Barn where the first pistols were built has grown into four large manufacturing facilities where revolvers, semi-auto pistols, rifles, and shotguns are made. This is the one-millionth .22 pistol produced.

William B. Ruger holding the Outstanding American Handgunner Award for 1975

INNOVATIONS & ODDITIES

Winchester Model 70 Bolt-Action Rifle with Radio Stock - .30-06 - circa 1955 - Someone in the marketing department decided that what the American hunter needed was a shiny chrome plated rifle with a built-in transistor radio so he could listen to "Rock Around the Clock" in the deer stand. It was only displayed at one trade show before the concept was abandoned.

Radio Rifles, Automatic Revolvers, and Bolt-Action Double-Barrels.

Not every firearms innovation is as successful as Ruger's Standard Model. Here are some of the "also-rans," some of which led to new developments while others beg the question "What were they thinking?"

At right: In the late 19th and early 20th centuries, firearms innovators were working with new designs that utilized the energy generated by the firing of the cartridge to eject an empty case and load a new round into firing position. Originally called "auto-loaders," today these types of pistols, rifles, and shotguns are referred to as "semi-automatics." The concept was also applied to revolvers, albeit with less success. These two handguns used the energy of the firing cartridge to rotate the cylinder to the next chamber and cock the hammer so the shooter was ready for a successive single action shot.

Upper - Webley-Fosbery Automatic Revolver - .455 centerfire - circa 1901-1924.
Lower - Union Firearms Co. Auto Revolver - .32 centerfire - circa 1903-1913.

Szecsei & Fuchs Double-Barrel Bolt-Action Rifle - .416 Remington Magnum, circa 1998-2002. This unique double-barrel bolt-action rifle loads two cartridges at the same time and is the world's only repeating double rifle design. It has an eight round capacity. Hungarian inventor Joseph Szecsei reportedly has said he developed his innovative design after being charged simultaneously by three elephants in 1989.

MODERN FIREARMS

1. Savage Albree Prototype Model 7 Semi-Automatic Rifle with Scope - .22 rimfire - circa 1939. Experimental slam-fire design.
2. Experimental/Prototype Mauser Semi-Automatic Pistol Carbine - 7.63 Mauser - circa 1900. Combining the semi-automatic action of the Mauser M1896 pistol with a well-balanced carbine profile, this rifle never saw commercial production.
3. Loosemore Prototype Open Bolt Rifle - .22 rimfire - circa 1988-1990. Firing sample made for corporate presentations.
4. Daisy-Heddon V/L Single-Shot Caseless Cartridge Rifle - .22 V/L - circa 1968-1969. Daisy's V/L system combined airgun and caseless ammunition technology. Designed to ignite a propellant charge moulded on the base of the projectile by compression, the Daisy was a hybrid airgun/firearm that met with little market acceptance.
5. Armalite Golden Gun Semi-Automatic Shotgun - circa 1964-1965. The glowing golden anodizing of the aluminum barrel and receiver gave the Golden Gun its name. Armalite produced only 2,000 examples of its AR-17 semi-automatic shotgun, with innovative ultra-lightweight construction and plastic stock ahead of its time, from 1964 to 1965.
6. Winchester Model 52C Bolt-Action Rifle - .22 long rifle - circa 1955. Toolroom prototype.
7. Loosemore Destroyer Semi-Automatic Pistol/Carbine Prototype - .30 Carbine - circa 1988-1990. Handmade pistol blending Thompson and M1 carbine features.
8. Sommer & Ockenfuss GmbH German Marksman Tactical Rifle with Schmidt & Bender 3-12 x 50 Variable Scope - .308 Winchester - circa 2001. An unusually compact countersniper rifle, the Sommer & Ockenfuss utilizes a pump-action mechanism as part of its bullpup configuration.

INNOVATIONS & ODDITIES

Winchester Model 70 Bolt-Action Rifle with Radio Stock - .30-06 - circa 1955 - Someone in the marketing department decided that what the American hunter needed was a shiny chrome plated rifle with a built-in transistor radio so he could listen to "Rock Around the Clock" in the deer stand. It was only displayed at one trade show before the concept was abandoned.

Radio Rifles, Automatic Revolvers, and Bolt-Action Double-Barrels.

Not every firearms innovation is as successful as Ruger's Standard Model. Here are some of the "also-rans," some of which led to new developments while others beg the question "What were they thinking?"

At right: In the late 19th and early 20th centuries, firearms innovators were working with new designs that utilized the energy generated by the firing of the cartridge to eject an empty case and load a new round into firing position. Originally called "auto-loaders," today these types of pistols, rifles, and shotguns are referred to as "semi-automatics." The concept was also applied to revolvers, albeit with less success. These two handguns used the energy of the firing cartridge to rotate the cylinder to the next chamber and cock the hammer so the shooter was ready for a successive single action shot.

Upper - Webley-Fosbery Automatic Revolver - .455 centerfire - circa 1901-1924.
Lower - Union Firearms Co. Auto Revolver - .32 centerfire - circa 1903-1913.

Szecsei & Fuchs Double-Barrel Bolt-Action Rifle - .416 Remington Magnum, circa 1998-2002. This unique double-barrel bolt-action rifle loads two cartridges at the same time and is the world's only repeating double rifle design. It has an eight round capacity. Hungarian inventor Joseph Szecsei reportedly has said he developed his innovative design after being charged simultaneously by three elephants in 1989.

MODERN FIREARMS

1. Standard Arms Model G Semi-Automatic Rifle - .35 Remington - circa 1910-1912. While produced for less than four years (1910-1914), Standard Arms rifles were the first gas-operated longarms produced in America and offered the capability of shifting from slide-action to semi-automatic functioning; nearly 5,000 were made.

2. Heineman Experimental Prototype Semi-Automatic Carbine - 8mm Heineman - circa 1925. Experimental 1920s' semi-auto design with sideways toggle-link action like a Luger pistol.

3. W.H.B. Smith Prototype Lever-Action Rifle - circa 1955. Intended for sale by Marlin as an inexpensive youth rifle.

4. W.H.B. Smith Prototype Semi-Automatic Rifle - .22 rimfire - circa 1955. Demonstrator used in sales presentations.

5. W.H.B. Smith Prototype Single-Shot Shotgun - 12 gauge - circa 1955. Fitted with interchangeable barrel assemblies.

6. Winchester Model 99 Thumb Trigger Rifle - .22 rimfire - circa 1904-1923. An unusual .22 rimfire rifle intended to be fired by pushing the thumb instead of pulling a trigger with a finger, Winchester's Model 99 had excellent sales abroad in Australia and in the first three years of production (1904-1906) much of the production was exported there.

7. Darne Sliding Breech Side-by-Side Shotgun - circa 1920-195, Incorporating an unusual action, the French Darne shotgun was popular in humid tropical environments because its powerful camming action was able to force moisture-swollen paper shotshells into the chambers and reliably extract them after firing.

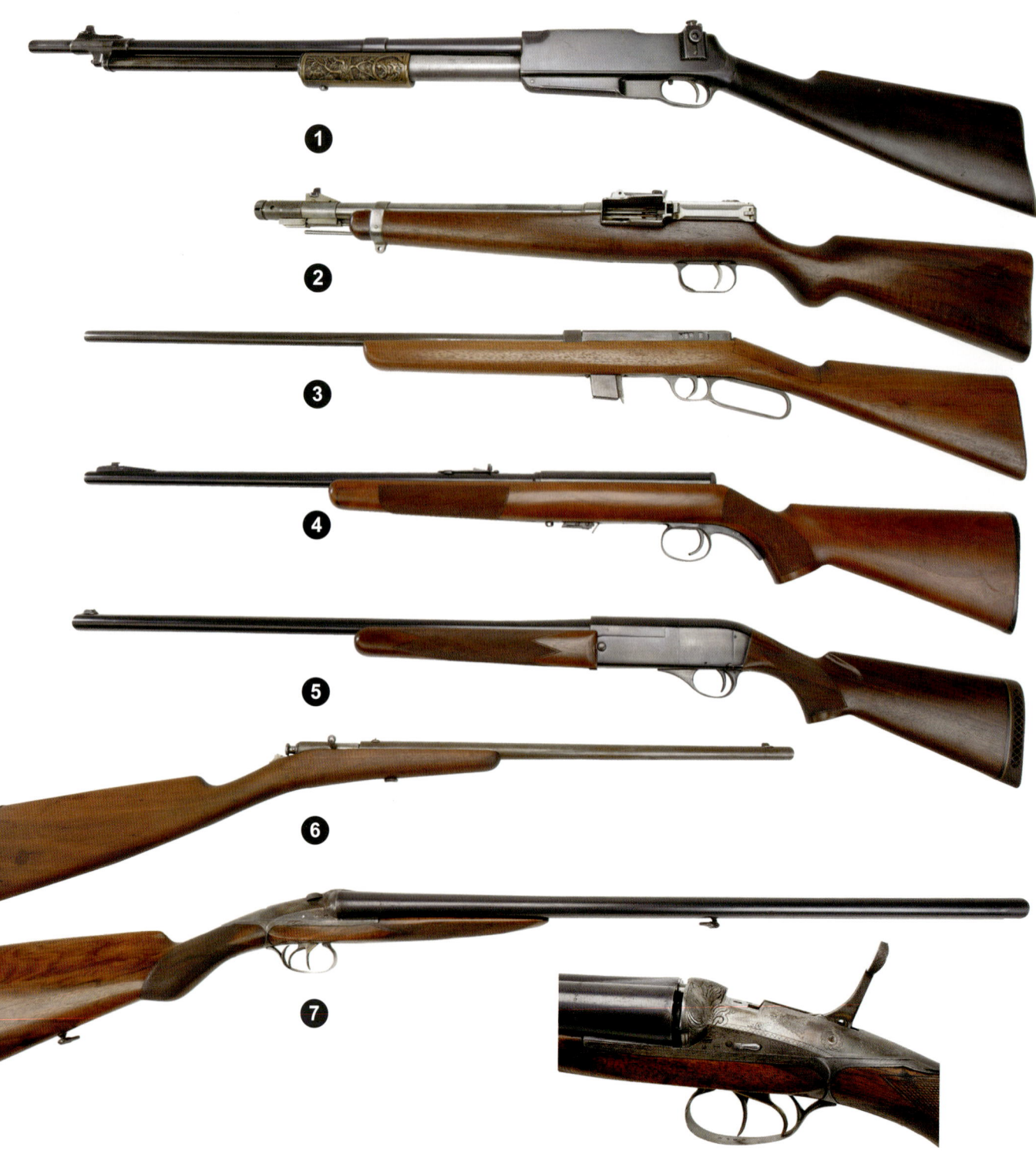

INNOVATIONS & ODDITIES

W.H.B. Smith

In the post-WWII era, W.H.B. Smith was a designer of firearms who incorporated expedient sintered-metal processes originally created by wartime German factories. Smith's prototypes included innovative toggle-link, break-open, and other handgun, rifle, and shotgun actions that were offered to companies including Winchester, Ithaca, and Marlin to serve as the foundation of new product lines. Smith authored the first editions of *Small Arms of the World*. The National Firearms Museum houses many of his design prototypes.

W.H.B. Smith WSP-65 Prototype Single-Shot Pistol - .44 caliber - circa 1955 - Built as a test platform for .44 magnum ammunition then in production for the S&W Model 29 revolver; this pistol never made it past prototype status. It could have preceded the S&W .44 Magnum and the Ruger Blackhawk as the first .44 Magnum and could have introduced the concept of interchangeable barrels later popularized by Thompson/Center.

1. W.H.B. Smith WSP-50 Prototype Single-Shot Pistol - .22 rimfire - circa 1955 - Toggle-activated single-shot.
2. Smith Prototype WSP-90 Pistol - .22 rimfire - circa 1955 - Locked-cam single-shot.
3. W.H.B. Smith Prototype Straight-Pull Semi-Automatic Pistol - .22 rimfire - circa 1955 - Straight-pull semi-automatic.
4. Smith Prototype WSP-70 Single-Shot Pistol - .22 rimfire - circa 1955 - Break-open.
5. W.H.B. Smith Prototype WSP-75 Single-Shot Pistol - .22 rimfire - circa 1955 - Unfinished alloy frame.
6. W.H.B. Smith Prototype WSP-200A Single-Shot Pistol - .38 Special - circa 1955 - Break-open design made on alloy frame to test durability.
7. W.H.B. Smith Prototype WSP-20 Semi-Automatic Pistol - .22 rimfire - circa 1955 Sintered metal technology was used to create the receiver for this pistol.
8. W.H.B. Smith Prototype WSP-10 Single-Shot Pistol - .22 rimfire - circa 1955 - Manual-cocking single-shot.
9. W.H.B. Smith WSP-40 Second Model Prototype Semi-Automatic Pistol - .22 rimfire - circa 1955 - Unfinished toolroom sample.

MODERN FIREARMS

1. Savage Albree Prototype Model 7 Semi-Automatic Rifle with Scope - .22 rimfire - circa 1939. Experimental slam-fire design.
2. Experimental/Prototype Mauser Semi-Automatic Pistol Carbine - 7.63 Mauser - circa 1900. Combining the semi-automatic action of the Mauser M1896 pistol with a well-balanced carbine profile, this rifle never saw commercial production.
3. Loosemore Prototype Open Bolt Rifle - .22 rimfire - circa 1988-1990. Firing sample made for corporate presentations.
4. Daisy-Heddon V/L Single-Shot Caseless Cartridge Rifle - .22 V/L - circa 1968-1969. Daisy's V/L system combined airgun and caseless ammunition technology. Designed to ignite a propellant charge moulded on the base of the projectile by compression, the Daisy was a hybrid airgun/firearm that met with little market acceptance.
5. Armalite Golden Gun Semi-Automatic Shotgun - circa 1964-1965. The glowing golden anodizing of the aluminum barrel and receiver gave the Golden Gun its name. Armalite produced only 2,000 examples of its AR-17 semi-automatic shotgun, with innovative ultra-lightweight construction and plastic stock ahead of its time, from 1964 to 1965.
6. Winchester Model 52C Bolt-Action Rifle - .22 long rifle - circa 1955. Toolroom prototype.
7. Loosemore Destroyer Semi-Automatic Pistol/Carbine Prototype - .30 Carbine - circa 1988-1990. Handmade pistol blending Thompson and M1 carbine features.
8. Sommer & Ockenfuss GmbH German Marksman Tactical Rifle with Schmidt & Bender 3-12 x 50 Variable Scope - .308 Winchester - circa 2001. An unusually compact countersniper rifle, the Sommer & Ockenfuss utilizes a pump-action mechanism as part of its bullpup configuration.

INNOVATIONS & ODDITIES

Weird Ammo for Weird Guns

Dardick - In 1950 the U.S. Military was looking at alternative feeding devices for firearms and found that a triangular cased cartridge used less room in a magazine that a cylindrical one. The military did not use it but David Dardick did. He also decided to use a plastic called Celanese Fortiflex to replace the expensive brass casing. The triangular cartridge had a lead .38 bullet in it. His revolver cylinder had three open pie shaped chambers and an 11- or 15-round magazine to feed it, resulting in a magazine fed revolver. The ammo was nicknamed "trounds" for Triangular Rounds.

Gyro Jet - The 1950's and 60's was the age of rocketry. Everything was going to be rocket powered — cars, planes, trains and even firearms. MBA Inc. started producing rocket firing pistols to the public in 1963 called Gyro Jets. The solid-nose 13mm rocket round has a cylinder of solid rocket fuel in its hollow base, and is ignited by a standard pistol primer. The barrels were smoothbore. Instead of rifing in the barrel, the rocket nozzles on the base of each round were angled to make the rocket spin in flight and stabilize it. The rockets left the muzzle at 350 feet per second and accelerated to 1,250 fps. Since there is no empty case to eject, functioning is simplified. The hammer drives the projectile rearward against a fixed firing pin in the breechface. As the projectile moves forward, it rides over the hammer, forcing it back down into the cocked position, allowing the next round to be raised into position by the spring fed magazine follower.

Dardick Series 1500 Pistol (Double-Action, Magazine-Fed Revolver) - .38 Dardick Tround - circa 1958-1960 - Dardick pistols could be converted to carbine configuration by replacing the pistol barrel with a long barrel and stock assembly.

MB Associates Gyrojet Mk I Model B 007 Semi-Automatic Carbine - 13mm Gyrojet - circa 1966-1967 - Made for a James Bond movie with SN 007.

MB Associates Gyrojet Semi-Automatic Carbine - 13mm Gyrojet - circa 1966-1967 - with scope.

MB Associates Gyrojet Mark I Pistol - 13mm Gyrojet - circa 1966-1967 Also manufactured in 12mm due to concerns that the 13mm chambering might run afoul of regulations restricting caliber of handguns.

Gyrojet rockets *(left)* and Dardick trounds *(right)*. The rockets were made with 2, 3, or 4 angled ports in the base. Shown approximately actual size.

MODERN FIREARMS

Colt Stainless Steel Prototype Semi-Automatic Pistol - 9mm Parabellum - circa 1972 - Less than 50 of the Stainless Steel Pistol (SSP) prototypes were manufactured by Colt after solicitation from the U.S. military to develop a double-action 9mm replacement for the Model 1911A1 pistol.

Colt Prototype Pistols
Top: Colt Experimental Prototype Target Pistol - .22 LR - circa unknown - s/n X24694. The factory describes this as an "exotic advanced experimental and prototype design concept."
Middle: Colt Experimental Match Target Pistol - .22 LR - circa unknown - s/n GX4524. The top rib extends back over the slide, which is machined so that the rear of slide surrounds steel which is integral with the frame.
Bottom: Colt Woodsman Experimental Prototype Pistol - .22 LR - circa pre-1978 - s/n GX-704.

Colt Prototype WSP-60 Semi-Automatic Pistol - .22 rimfire - circa 1955 - Alternative pistol design for Colt Woodsman II.

Miniature Martial Flintlock Pistol - #10 shot - circa 1986 - Once considered a test of a journeyman gunsmith's skills, modern miniature arms are a specialized collector field with fully functional muzzleloading pistols, like this diminutive martial single-shot pistol, offering intriguing shooting opportunities. Shown at approximate actual size, with dime for scale.

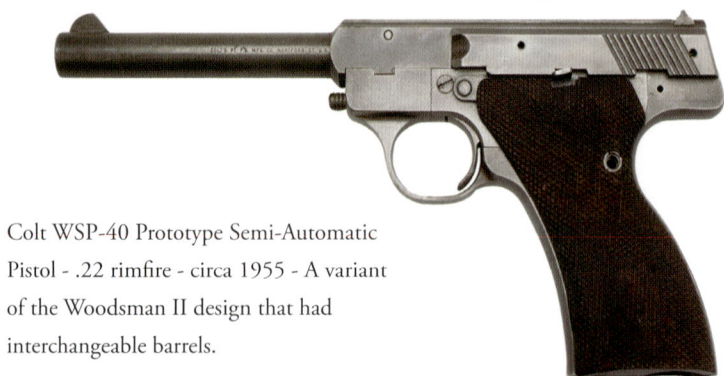

Colt WSP-40 Prototype Semi-Automatic Pistol - .22 rimfire - circa 1955 - A variant of the Woodsman II design that had interchangeable barrels.

INNOVATIONS & ODDITIES

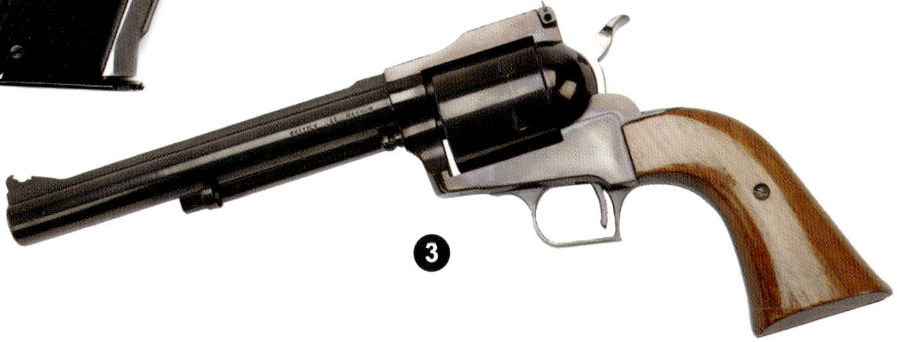

Above: Semmerling LM-4 and LM-3 pistols - .45 ACP - circa 1978-1982 - Less than 600 Semmerling LM-4 ultra compact pistols were built for deep concealment applications. This smaller example *(right)* was designed as a manually operated repeater. The slide required a forward push and a backward pull to eject the spent case and reload from the magazine. A long striker-cocking trigger pull was also part of the safety mechanism for this pistol. The larger Semmerling LM-3 *(right)* was designed as the ultimate in .45 caliber backup handguns and was a double-action-only semi-automatic. This example bears serial number 001.

1. Bridgeport Firearms Co. Prototype P66 Pistol - .22 rimfire - circa 1966 - Semi-auto design made to compete with Colt/Ruger handguns: production ceased after Ruger lawsuit.
2. Dornaus and Dixon Bren Ten Semi-Automatic Pistol - 10mm - circa 1983 - The first tactical semi-automatic pistol chambered for the 10mm cartridge, Dornhaus & Dixon's Bren Ten failed as a commercial success due to a lack of magazines available as the handguns were completed by the manufacturer.
3. Mikkenger Arms Grizzly Single-Action Revolver - .44 Magnum - circa 1976-1977 - Only American single-action revolver design to not utilize frame screws.
4. Danish Rifle Syndicate Schouboe Semi-Automatic Pistol - 11.35mm Schouboe - circa 1907 - Firing a lightweight wooden core bullet, the Schouboe was tested in U.S. Army trials in 1907.

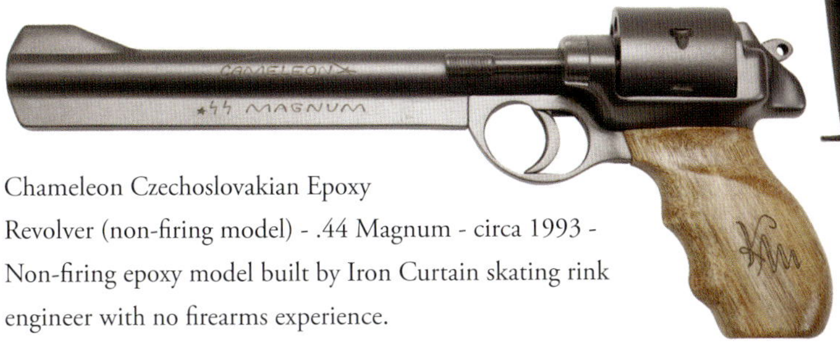

Chameleon Czechoslovakian Epoxy Revolver (non-firing model) - .44 Magnum - circa 1993 - Non-firing epoxy model built by Iron Curtain skating rink engineer with no firearms experience.

MODERN FIREARMS

Smith & Wesson
Model 342 AirLite Ti
Revolver - .38 Special +P

Modern Firearms

Since WWII, more types of firearms are available to the American public than ever before. In rifles, the AR pattern is by far the most popular, with over 16 million AR and AK platform rifles produced or imported between 1990 and 2016, although bolt, lever and single-shots still have adherents. In handguns, semi-autos have become prevalent, with revolvers still popular. The use of new materials such as polymer, stainless steel, titanium, and lightweight alloys serve a market in ultra-light concealed carry handguns. Semi-auto and pump shotguns prevail, with classic doubles still popular for some sporting uses. A wide variety of optical and electronic sights have gained extensive popularity for all types of firearms.

HANDGUNS

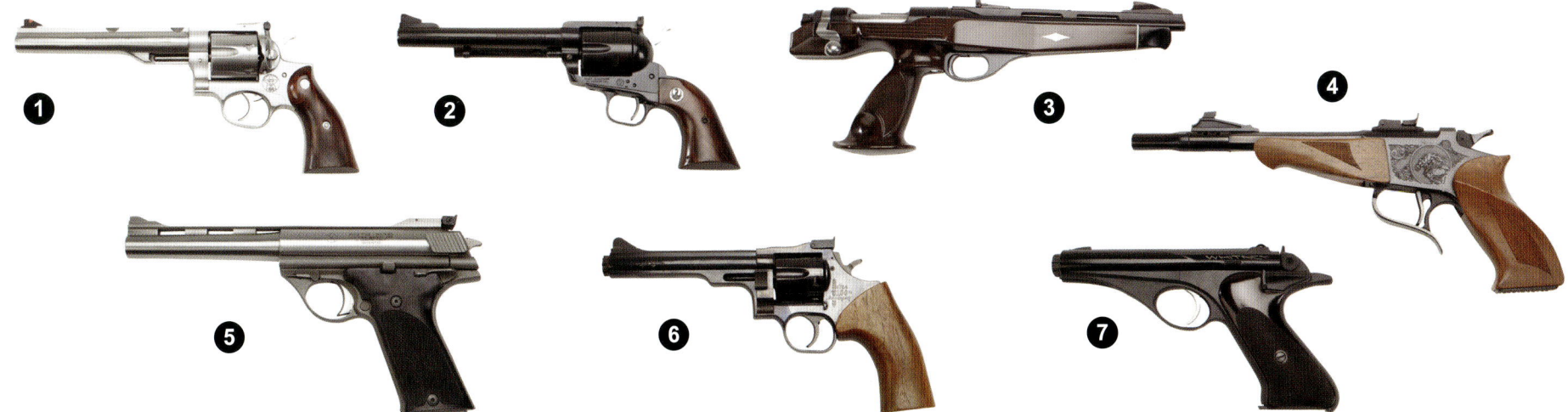

1. Sturm, Ruger & Co. Redhawk Revolver - .44 Magnum - circa 1985.
2. Sturm, Ruger & Co. Old Model Blackhawk Single-Action Revolver - .44 Magnum - circa 1971 - Ruger Blackhawk Models combined the classic Single Action Army lines with modern design including coil springs, adjustable sights, and modern metallurgy. The .44 Magnum Blackhawk was only offered for a brief time before being replaced by the beefier Super Blackhawk.
3. Remington XP-100 Bolt-Action Pistol - .221 Fireball - circa 1963-1967 - One of the early specialty single-shot handgun designs made for high-power hunting and long-range target competition.
4. Thompson/Center Arms Contender Single-Shot Pistol - .45 Colt/.410 shotshell - circa 1967-1969 - Few firearms have the capability to fire as many cartridge types as the Thompson-Center Contender. Interchangeable barrels and selective firing pins allow this single-shot handgun design to fire rimfire or centerfire ammunition without disruption.
5. Arcadia Machine Tool AutoMag Semi-Automatic Pistol - .44 AMT/.357 AMT - circa 1971-1973 - Built as a semi-custom hot rod handgun, the stainless Automag pistol allowed owners to handload ammunition to meet metallic silhouette and hunting requirements. Interchangeable barrel assemblies allowed swapping from .357 to .41 or .44 Automag calibers.
6. Dan Wesson Model 12 Revolver - .357 Magnum- circa 1971 - Wesson revolvers featured interchangeable barrels, allowing users to go from snub nose concealment barrels to longer hunting barrels.
7. Whitney Firearms Corp. Wolverine Semi-Automatic Pistol - .22 rimfire - circa 1955-1962.

Smith & Wesson Sigma SW40F - .40 S&W - circa 1994 - The polymer frame Sigma was introduced to compete with the Glock. Glock sued over patent infringement and the case was settled out of court. Although the Sigma has been overshadowed in the S&W product line by the M&P series the .40 S&W round is popular as a compromise between 9mm and .45ACP. This is the first production Sigma, s/n SGM0001.

Glock Model 17 Semi-Automatic Pistol (sectionalized) - 9mm - circa 1987 - Featuring polymer construction, the Glock 17 is the invention of Austrian Gaston Glock. The Glock has been adopted by many law enforcement agencies to replace their revolvers. In addition to its 17-round magazine capacity, a factor in its selection may have been the pistol's simple operation, which would ease the transition to the new gun. Like the double-action revolver, the Glock has no external safety devices to manipulate and requires only a single pull on the trigger for each shot. Its popularity led to a rush to polymer frame pistols by other manufacturers. Cutaway samples such as this one are used as sales demonstration samples and armorer training.

MODERN FIREARMS

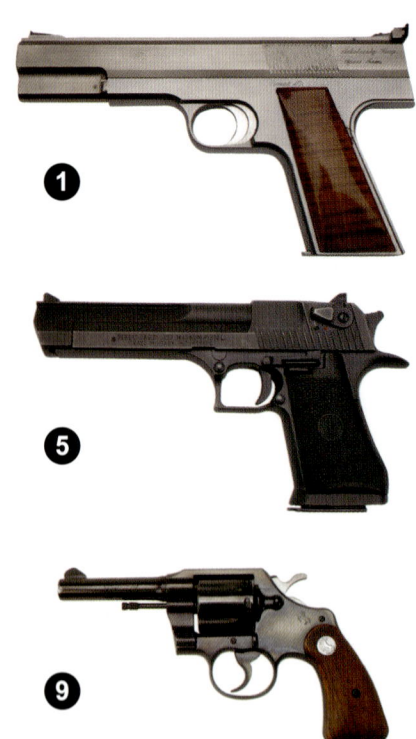
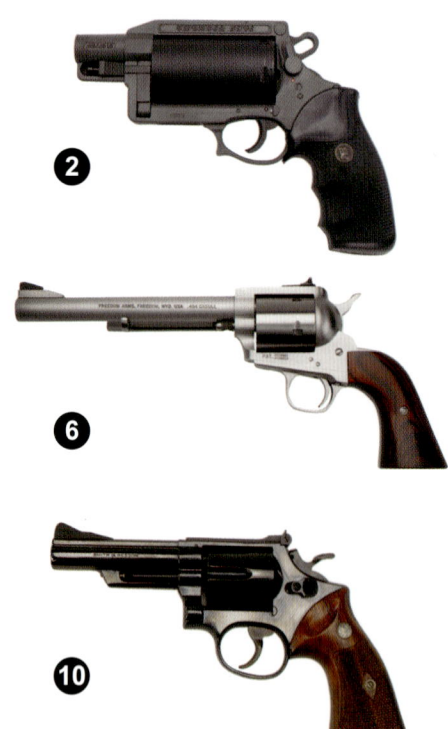
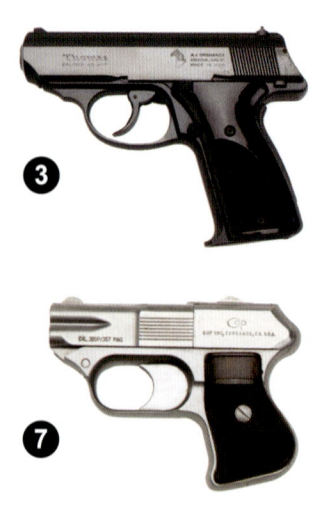
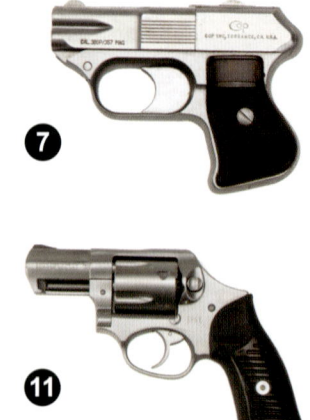

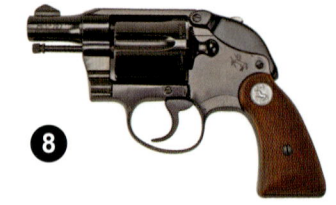

1. Sokolovsky .45 Automaster Semi-Automatic Pistol - .45 ACP - circa 1984-1985 - Handbuilt in Grass Valley, CA, about 20 of the Sokolovsky semi-automatic pistols were manufactured in versions that included a heavier target handgun. No screws were used in the Automaster design. The trigger had safety, magazine release, and firing functions.

2. MIL, Inc., Thunder Five Revolver - .45 Colt / .410 shotshell - circa 1994-1998.

3. Thomas /AJ Ordnance Semi-Automatic Pistol - .45 ACP - circa 1971 - Short-lived design with unique features for the time, including blowback action, double-action only, and stainless steel barrel.

4. Dan Wesson Model 15 Revolver - .357 Magnum - circa 2000 - Interchangeable barrels.

5. Israel Military Industries Desert Eagle Semi-Automatic Pistol - .357 Magnum - circa 2001 - Gas-operated semi-auto for high-power Magnum cartridges traditionally chambered in revolvers.

6. Freedom Arms Model 83 Premier-Grade Single-Action Revolver - .454 Casull - circa 1999 - Briefly eclipsed the .44 Magnum as the most powerful production revolver until the introduction of the .500 Magnum.

7. COP Four-Barrel Derringer - .357 Magnum - circa 1982 - COP is short for "Compact Off-Duty Police." Its small, heavy weight (28 oz.), and limited four-shot capacity restricted its popularity as a back-up.

8. Colt Agent Revolver - .38 Special - circa 1956-1972 - This model featured a shortened grip frame for better concealment.

9. Colt Marshal Model Revolver - .38 Special - circa 1955 - Round-butt variant of Official Police model. Only 2,500 were made.

10. Smith & Wesson Model 19 Combat Magnum Revolver - .357 Magnum - circa 1958 - Classic mid-size K-frame .357 Magnum. Widely popular police sidearm, made from 1955 to 1999.

11. Sturm, Ruger & Co. KSPNY-182 Double-Action-Only Revolver - .38 Special - circa 1990 - It has a factory-bobbed hammer and was made under a special law enforcement contract for State Police of New York.

12. Smith & Wesson Model 645 Double-Action Semi-Automatic Pistol - .45 ACP - circa 1988.

13. Coonan Arms, Inc. .357 Magnum Semi-Automatic Pistol - .357 Magnum - circa 1991 - Carried by a Vermont sheriff in the performance of his law enforcement duties.

HANDGUNS

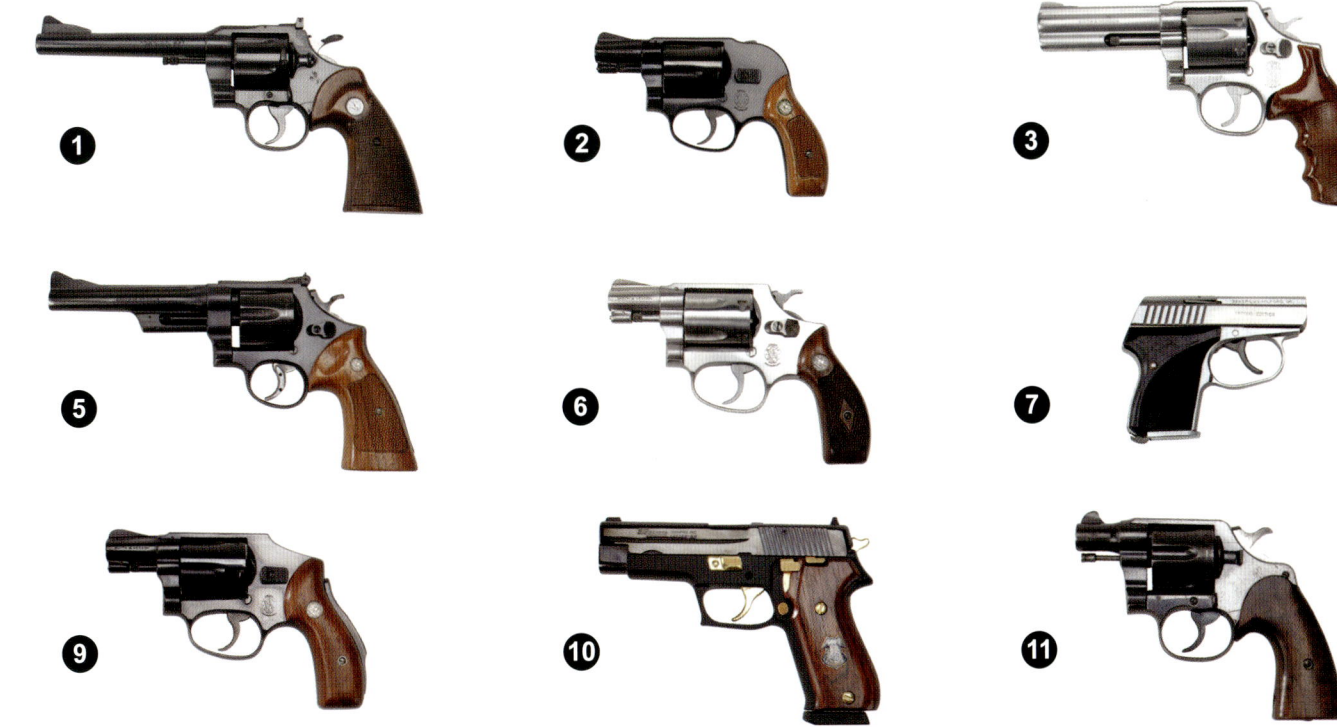

1. Colt Trooper Revolver - .38 Special - circa 1967.
2. Smith & Wesson Model 49 Bodyguard Revolver - .38 Special - circa 1969-1970 - Frame extended to conceal hammer spur, which prevents snagging on clothing during concealed carry, but allows hammer cocking for single-action firing if desired, made 1959-1996.
3. Smith & Wesson Model 681 Revolver - .357 Mag. - circa 1981-1982 - Fixed-sight double-action stainless revolver model manufactured from 1980 to 1992.
4. Colt Police Positive Special Revolver - circa 1924 - Popular police revolver, a larger version of Police Positive; one million made from 1908 to 1978, most in .38 Special.
5. Smith & Wesson Model 28 Revolver - .357 Magnum - circa 1973 - Also known as the "Highway Patrolman," a heavy N-frame revolver similar to the Model 27, but with a dull finish; it was made between 1954 and 1986.
6. Smith & Wesson Model 60 Chief's Special Revolver - .38 Special - circa 1966-1967 - Stainless-steel construction added corrosion resistance to five-shot compact concealment revolver; it has been made since 1965 to the present.
7. L.W. Seecamp LWS 32 Special Edition Semi-Automatic Pistol - .32 ACP - circa 2000-2001 - Ultracompact pocket pistol that got its start from Louis Seecamps's conversions of Colt M1911 pistols to double-action operation.
8. Remington Model 51 Semi-Automatic Pistol - .380 ACP - circa 1928-1930 - 65,000 made.
9. Smith & Wesson Centennial Model 40 Revolver - .38 Special - circa 1960-1962 - Five-shot hammerless (concealed hammer) revolver with a grip safety.
10. SIG Sauer P220 NRA Semi-Automatic Pistol - circa 2010.
11. Colt New Service Model Revolver - .45 Colt - circa 1915 - Colt's first large-frame swing-out cylinder revolver model; 365,000 were made from 1898 to 1944. This one has a bobbed barrel for concealment.
12. Smith & Wesson Model 539 Semi-Automatic Pistol - 9mm - circa 1982 - Second-generation S&W semi-auto.

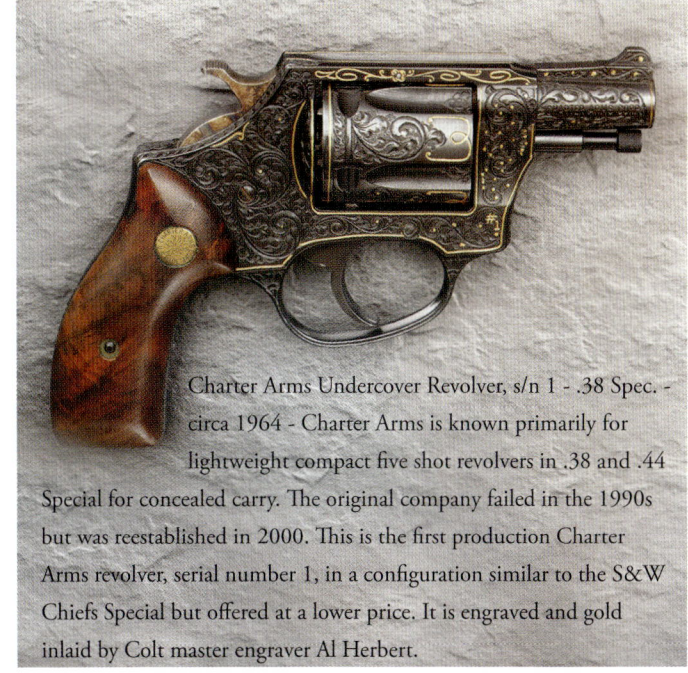

Charter Arms Undercover Revolver, s/n 1 - .38 Spec. - circa 1964 - Charter Arms is known primarily for lightweight compact five shot revolvers in .38 and .44 Special for concealed carry. The original company failed in the 1990s but was reestablished in 2000. This is the first production Charter Arms revolver, serial number 1, in a configuration similar to the S&W Chiefs Special but offered at a lower price. It is engraved and gold inlaid by Colt master engraver Al Herbert.

MODERN FIREARMS

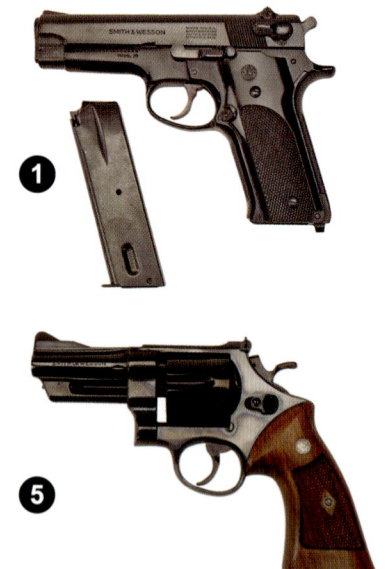
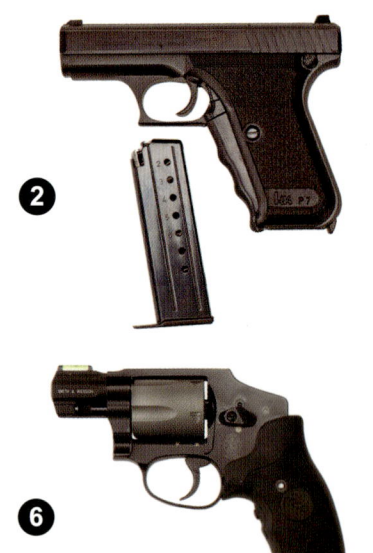

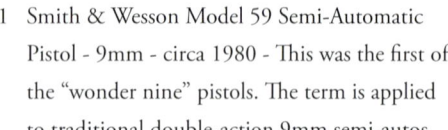

1. Smith & Wesson Model 59 Semi-Automatic Pistol - 9mm - circa 1980 - This was the first of the "wonder nine" pistols. The term is applied to traditional double-action 9mm semi-autos with double-stack high-capacity magazines; it was introduced in 1971.
2. Heckler & Koch Model PSP Semi-Automatic Pistol - 9mm - circa 1980 - With a unique squeeze-cocking action, the semi-automatic Heckler & Koch PSP and P7 pistols found little acceptance in the American law enforcement community and had only limited issue in departments including the U.S. Capitol Police.
3. AMT Backup II Semi-Automatic Pistol - .380 ACP - circa 1996 - Original model introduced in the 1980s was one of the earlier stainless steel subcompact semi-auto pistols.
4. Colt Delta Elite Semi-Automatic Pistol - 10mm - circa 1990 - Colt adapted its 1911 platform to many calibers after establishing it with the .45 ACP cartridge. The high-intensity 10mm cartridge in the Colt Delta Elite model pistol required slight modification of the frame to prevent rail cracking under recoil stresses.
5. Smith & Wesson Pre-Model 27 Revolver - .357 Magnum - circa 1956 - In the 1950s, S&W replaced model names with model numbers. The .357 Magnum became Model 27. Gun enthusiasts find it handy to refer to models made before the numbering system as Pre-Model (number).
6. Smith & Wesson Model 340PD Revolver - .357 Magnum - circa 2004 - Ultra-lightweight scandium alloy frame revolvers make for easy carry at the cost of heavy recoil when fired.
7. High Standard Model D-100 Over/Under Derringer - .22 long rifle - circa 1967-1969 - Also offered in .22 Magnum, it enjoyed brief popularity as a backup gun.
8. Kel-Tec Model P3AT Semi-Automatic Pistol - .380 ACP - circa 2003-2006 - One of the first of a new wave of ultra-compact, ultra-lightweight .380 double-action-only (DAO) pocket pistols. It is unsafe to carry a handgun in a pocket without an appropriate holster that covers the triggerguard.

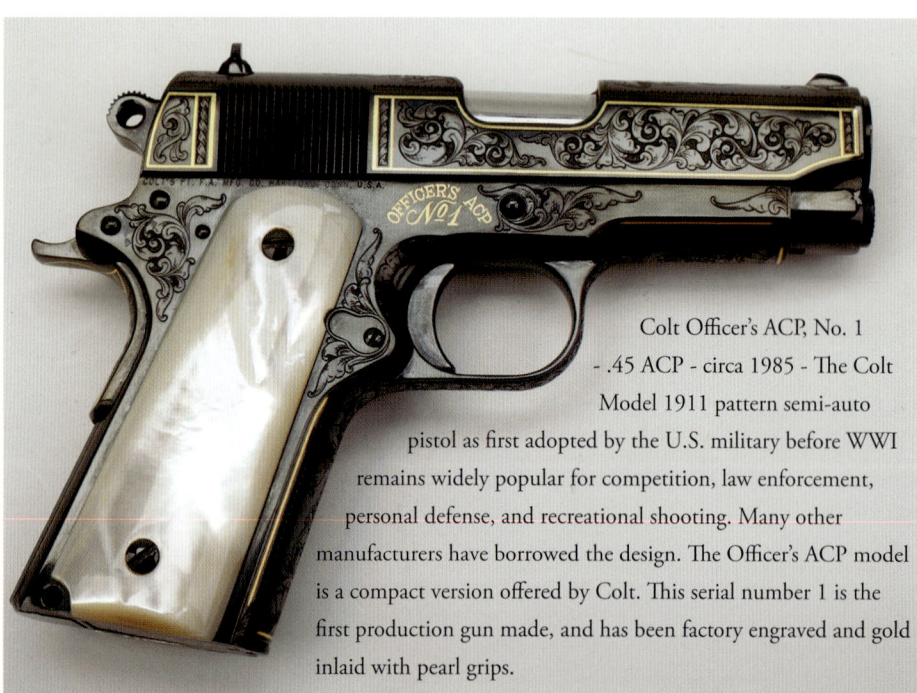

Colt Officer's ACP, No. 1 - .45 ACP - circa 1985 - The Colt Model 1911 pattern semi-auto pistol as first adopted by the U.S. military before WWI remains widely popular for competition, law enforcement, personal defense, and recreational shooting. Many other manufacturers have borrowed the design. The Officer's ACP model is a compact version offered by Colt. This serial number 1 is the first production gun made, and has been factory engraved and gold inlaid with pearl grips.

HANDGUNS

SIG Sauer P228 - 9mm - Compact version of the SIG P226. Used by U.S. military as the M11. This one was used by Matt Damon in the 2006 movie *The Departed*.

Colt Pythons, serial numbers 2, 3, and 5 - .357 Magnum - circa 1955 - The Python is renowned for its fine fit and finish with some contending it is the finest revolver ever made. Originally produced from 1955 to 2005, these are three of the first five made.

Magnumitis - Handgun power

Cartridge	Year	Muzzle Energy
.45 Colt	1873	420 ft-lbs
.45 ACP	1911	375 ft-lbs
.357 Magnum	1937	580 ft-lbs
.44 Magnum	1955	1,200 ft-lbs
.45 Win. Mag.	1999	1,200 ft-lbs
.500 Magnum	2003	2,800 ft-lbs

Wildey Pistol - .45 Win. Mag. - circa 2010. Gas operated magnum semi-auto pistol with a three lug rotating bolt.

Smith & Wesson Model 500 Revolver - .500 Magnum - circa 2009. Considered the most powerful production revolver in the world.

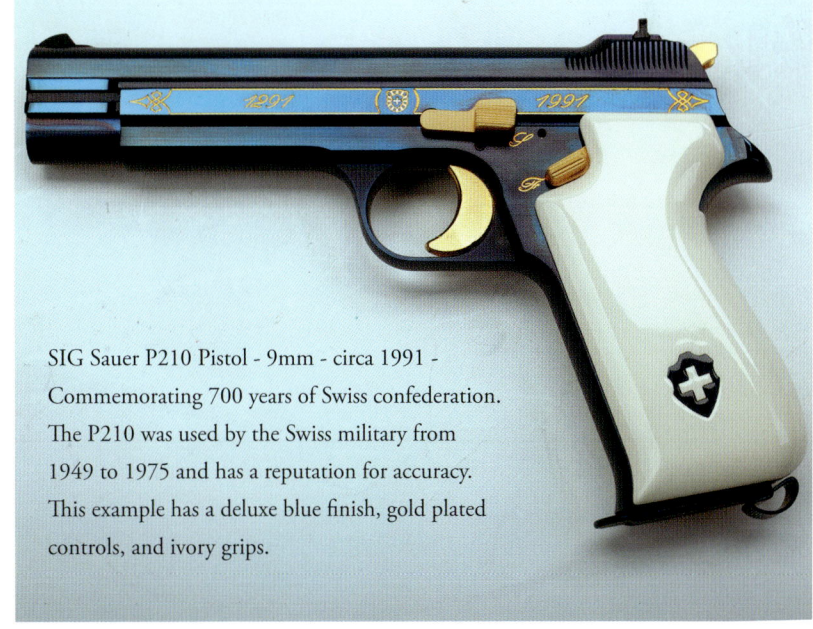

SIG Sauer P210 Pistol - 9mm - circa 1991 - Commemorating 700 years of Swiss confederation. The P210 was used by the Swiss military from 1949 to 1975 and has a reputation for accuracy. This example has a deluxe blue finish, gold plated controls, and ivory grips.

MODERN FIREARMS

Valmet M-76W Semi-Automatic Rifle - 7.62x39mm - circa 1976-1986 - Finnish Kalashnikov offered in 5.56 and 7.62 NATO variants.

Steyr AUG Semi-Automatic Rifle - 5.56mm NATO (.223) - circa 1989 - A bullpup design incorporating polymer components, the Steyr Armee Universal Gewehr (AUG) 5.56mm rifle was adopted by the Austrian army in 1977 and serves with several other military forces around the world.

Colt AR-15 Semi-Automatic Rifle - 5.56mm - circa 1979 - Semi-auto version of military M16 rifle.

Springfield Armory M-1A Semi-Automatic Rifle - .308 Win. - circa 1984 - Semi-auto version of military early Cold War era M14 rifle.

Sturm, Ruger & Co. Mini-14 Series 180 Semi-Automatic Rifle - .223 Remington - circa 1975 - Takes its "Mini-14" name from the fact that it looks like a slightly downsized semi-auto version of the U.S. M14 battle rifle.

SEMI-AUTO RIFLES

The First Remington R15 Semi-Automatic Rifle - .223 Rem., circa 2008 - s/n RA000001. The first production gun of Remington's AR pattern rifle. The modern ergonomic features, reliability, and accuracy of this type of semi-automatic have made it the most popular style of sporting rifle in America.

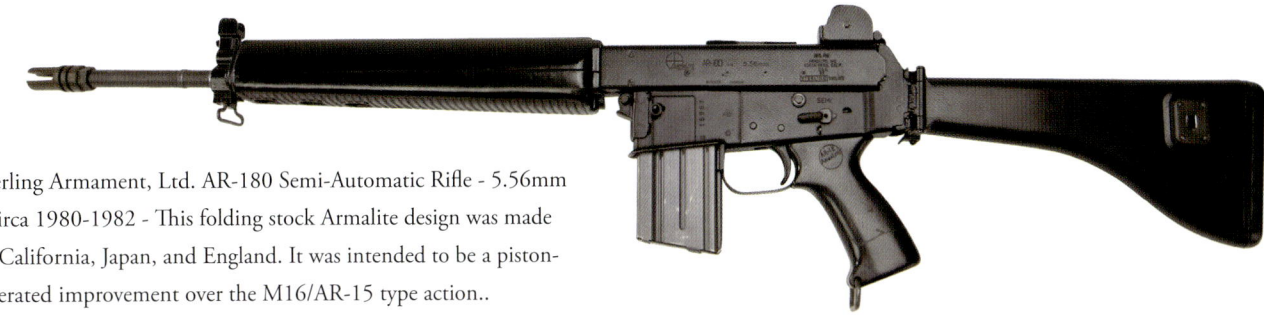

Sterling Armament, Ltd. AR-180 Semi-Automatic Rifle - 5.56mm - circa 1980-1982 - This folding stock Armalite design was made in California, Japan, and England. It was intended to be a piston-operated improvement over the M16/AR-15 type action..

Military or Sporting?

For centuries military firearms designs have adopted improvements developed in civilian firearms and vice versa. Generally these advancements improve accuracy, effectiveness, safety, and ergonomics.

It's not surprising that the returning serviceman often prefers a sporting firearm of the general pattern he or she used in the military. Semi-auto centerfire sporting rifles with detachable box magazines have been popular since the first decade of the 20th century.

The significant difference is that most military rifles have a full-auto capability, where the gun will continue firing multiple rounds when the trigger is held back, whereas sporting rifles fire only one round with each pull of the trigger.

Bushmaster Semi-Automatic Pistol - .223 Remington - circa 1986-1988 - Gwinn Arms blended AK-47 and AR-15 features into bullpup pistol. Bullpup arms, like this and the Steyr AUG on the facing page, place the trigger and grip forward of the action, resulting in a significantly shorter overall length compared to a traditional gun of the same barrel length

Calico Systems M-951 Semi-Automatic Carbine - 9mm - circa 1986 - Serial number NRA000001. This rifle uses a 100-round top-mounted magazine of an unusual helical design. The rounds are loaded into the magazine as if each is on a spiral staircase circling the internal circumference of the cylindrical housing.

MODERN FIREARMS

1. Marlin Camp Carbine Semi-Automatic Rifle - 9mm - circa 1990. Accepts S&W Model 59 14-round magazines. Up to 30-ound mags are available.

2. Uzi Model A Semi-Automatic Carbine with Scope - 9mm - circa 1982. This semi-auto version of the Israeli-designed Uzi submachine gun is functionally similar to the Marlin Camp Carbine next to it in terms of function, power, and potential ammo capacity. Other differences are mainly cosmetic. Standard magazine holds 32 rounds.

3. Sturm, Ruger & Co. Model 44 Carbine - .44 Magnum - circa 1965.

4. Browning BAR Semi-Automatic Rifle with Scope -- 7mm Remington Magnum - circa 1967.

5. Winchester Model 100 Semi-Automatic Rifle - .308 Winchester - circa 1961 - Over 262,000 produced. .

6. Heckler & Koch Model 770 Semi-Automatic Rifle with Leupold scope - .308 Winchester - circa 1984.

7. Remington Model Four Semi-Automatic Rifle - .30-06 - circa 1982 - Made for only six years.

8. Beretta BM-59 Semi-Automatic Rifle - 7.62mm NATO - circa 1960 - Based on the U.S. M1 Garand, adapted to take a detachable magazine.

SEMI-AUTO RIFLES

1. Marlin Model 88 Semi-Auto Rifle (sectionalized) - .22 long rifle - circa 1948-1956.
2. Weatherby Mark XXII semi-auto rifle - .22 LR - circa 1965-1970.
3. Sturm, Ruger & Co. Model 10/22 International Semi-Automatic Rifle - .22 long rifle - circa 1968. Over 6 million Ruger 10/22's have been sold since its introduction in 1964, making it one of the most popular .22s of all time. This one has a full-length Mannlicher-style stock.
4. Marlin Model 60 Glenfield Semi-Automatic Rifle - .22 rimfire - circa 1982. Serial number 2,000,000. Semi-auto Marlin .22s have enjoyed wide popularity for decades.
5. Heckler & Koch Model 300 Semi-Automatic Rifle with Scope - .22 Winchester Magnum Rimfire - circa 1980.
6. Norinco Chinese MAK-90 Semi-Automatic Rifle - 7.62x39mm - circa 1993. Function, power, and ammo capacity is the same as any semi-auto AK variant, but this was cosmetically redesigned with a wood stock to avoid federal ban during the so-called Clinton assault-weapon ban years.
7. Heckler & Koch Model 91 Semi-Automatic Rifle - .308 Winchester - circa 1988. Semi-auto version of the H&K G3 which was based on the CETME Model 58.,
8. CETME Spanish Model 58 Semi-Automatic Rifle - 7.62mm CETME - circa 1958.

Semi-auto rifles with box magazines have been offered in the sporting market since the first decade of the 20th century, as illustrated in this N.C. Wyeth painting "Dangerous Bend" for period advertising or outdoor magazine cover art.

MODERN FIREARMS

Remington Model 40, Serial Number One - .22 LR - circa 1956 - This s/n 0001 is the first made of this precision target rifle.

1. Remington Model 788 Bolt-Action Rifle - .222 Remington - circa 1967-1983. Offered in nine calibers, but it has less features than Model 700 rifle.
2. Steyr-Mannlicher Austrian Model M-Luxus Bolt-Action Carbine - .270 Winchester - circa 1972.
3. Remington Model 600 Magnum Bolt-Action Carbine - 6.5mm Remington Magnum - circa 1965-1968. Laminated walnut/beech stock.
4. Browning BBR Bolt-Action Rifle with Bausch & Lomb Scope - .270 Winchester - circa 1978. Mauser-style sporter built by Miroku in Japan. Earlier Brownings were built in Belgium.
5. Smith & Wesson Model 1500 Bolt-Action Rifle with Leupold Scope - 7mm Remington Magnum - circa 1983. Made for only two years.
6. Remington Model 722(A) Bolt-Action Rifle - .244 Remington - circa 1948-1958. Short-action model offered in choice of seven calibers.
7. Oester Waffenfabrik Ges. Steyr Austrian Sporter Bolt-Action Rifle - 9 x 56mm Mannlicher/Schoenaue - circa 1968.
8. Colt-Sauer Bolt-Action Rifle with Leupold Scope - .30-06 - circa 1971.

BOLT-ACTION RIFLES

Modern Bolt-Action Sporting Rifles

Since the introduction of the Model 1898 Mauser, most commercial companies have attempted to create similar actions in the sporting arms field. Weatherby, Winchester, Savage, Ruger, Remington, and others have all refined the bolt-action to varying degrees. These classic blue steel and walnut rifles remain a popular choice for hunting and precision shooting

At right:
The Winchester Model 70 was offered in 18 standard chamberings from .22 Hornet to .458 Win. Mag. and many configurations. It was introduced in 1936 and sometimes called "The Rifleman's Rifle." Collectors pay a premium for guns made before 1964 when manufacturing techniques changed.

1. Sturm, Ruger & Co. Model 77 Bolt-Action Rifle - 6mm Remington - circa 1968.
2. Weatherby Mark V Bolt-Action Rifle - .300 Weatherby Magnum - circa 1959-1973.
3. Remington Model 700 Left-Hand Bolt-Action Rifle - 7mm Remington Magnum - circa 1990.

MODERN FIREARMS

1. Browning FN High Power Bolt-Action Rifle with Browning scope - .458 Winchester Magnum - circa 1959. Safari Grade.
2. Griffin & Howe Custom Rifle - .416 Rigby - circa 1980.
3. Steyr-Mannlicher Mannlicher/Schoenauer Model 1961 MCA Rifle - .338 Winchester Magnum - circa 1961. Mannlichers Collectors Association edition.
4. Waffenfabrik Steyr Austrian Mannlicher-Schoenauer Model 1905 Rifle - 9 x 56mm Mannlicher/Schoenaue - circa 1970.
5. Ranger Arms NRA Centennial Rifle - circa 1971. Ranger Arms in Gainesville, TX, was a manufacturer of fine-quality bolt-action rifles in the 1970s. This rifle was produced in 1971 for advertising in the American Rifleman magazine.
6. American Masters Series Custom Mauser Rifle - .30-06 - circa 1988. Roberts American Masters Award rifle.
7. U.S. Springfield Model 1903 Rifle (sporterized by Paul Jager) - .30-06 - circa 1946-1950. Military rifles were popular as the starting point for custom sporters in the 1950s through 1970s.
8. Winchester Model 54 Rifle - .30-06 - circa 1934. First high-velocity bolt gun the company made.
9. Remington Model 725 Rifle - .270 Winchester - circa 1959. About 16,635 made.
10. Kimber Model 82 Custom Classic Rifle with Scope - .22 rimfire - circa 1982.
11. Newton Arms Co. First-Type Standard Rifle - .256 Newton - circa 1917. Made in Buffalo, NY.
12. Winchester Model 52-B Rifle - .22 long rifle - circa 1948.
13. Kleingunther K15 Bolt-Action Rifle with Scope - .30-06 - circa 1999. Built to offer extreme accuracy, this commercial rifle is sold with a guaranteed 100-yard accuracy level for the original purchaser.

BOLT-ACTION RIFLES

Hartmann and Weiss interchangeable barrel takedown bolt-action rifle - .338 & .300 calibers - circa 1980-2000, with Pachmayr logo.

Dubiel Classic Sporter Rifles - *Top:* .270 Win. *Bottom:* 7mm Rem Mag left-hand model - both circa 1975-1990.

Savage Model 45 Bullpup Configuration Bolt-Action Rifle - .257 Roberts - circa 1935. Action mounted in buttstock behind trigger.

1. Weatherby FN Mauser Rifle with Scope - .300 Weatherby Magnum - circa 1971. Author Erle Stanley Gardner, creator of Perry Mason, owned this early sporter.
2. Sako Finnish L461 Rifle with Scope - .17/222 centerfire - circa 1971.
3. Weatherby Vanguard VGX Rifle - .25-06 - circa 1989-1993. Started in 1945, Weatherby is noted for development of proprietary high-velocity cartridges, strong accurate rifles, and the distinctive post-WWII modernistic aesthetics of their stock designs. This example has inlaid 1976 NRA Patriot Army medallions in the stock.
4. U.S. Springfield Krag-Jorgensen Model 1898 Rifle (sporterized) - .30-40 Krag - circa 1940-1950. Home-gunsmithed sporter.
5. Remington Model 720A Rifle - .30-06 - circa 1942.

MODERN FIREARMS

One Millionth Savage Model 99 - .300 Savage - circa 1960 - Ornately engraved and gold inlaid and presented to the NRA. The six round rotary magazines of the Savage Models 1895 and 1899 permitted the use of ballistically efficient pointed spitzer bullet in lever-action repeaters with the risk of accidental detonation poised by spitzers in tubular magazines common to most earlier lever-actions. The box magazines of the Winchester Model 1895 and the much later Browning BLR also permitted the use of spitzer bullets.

1. Browning Model 81 BLR Lever-Action Rifle - .308 Winchester - circa 1970-1980.
2. Winchester Model 71 Lever-Action Rifle - .348 Winchester - circa 1951 - About 47,000 made.
3. Browning BL-22 Grade I Lever-Action Rifle - .22 rimfire - circa 1969.
4. Marlin Model 336 Presentation-Grade Lever-Action Rifle - .30-30 - circa 1979 - Serial number 3,000,000.
5. Henry Repeating Arms Golden Boy Lever-Action Rifle - .22 LR - circa 2010 - Boy Scout Centennial commemorative. Founded in 1996 in Brooklyn, NY, by Anthony Imperato, Henry produces a popular line of lever-action and other firearms.
6. Remington Model 6 Slide-Action Rifle - .308 Winchester - circa 1981-1987.

LEVER, PUMP & DOUBLE RIFLES

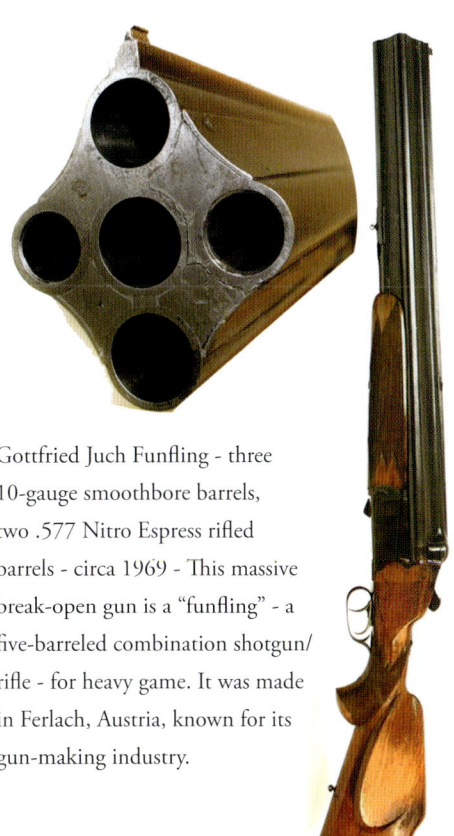

Gottfried Juch Funfling - three 10-gauge smoothbore barrels, two .577 Nitro Espress rifled barrels - circa 1969 - This massive break-open gun is a "funfling" - a five-barreled combination shotgun/rifle - for heavy game. It was made in Ferlach, Austria, known for its gun-making industry.

Double rifles. *Upper* - Holland & Holland .700 Nitro Express, circa 1988. *Lower* - Purdey .600 Nitro Express, circa 1997 - Both engraved by Phillipe Grifnee. The .600 NE cartridge was introduced in 1900 and was the most powerful hunting. cartridge until the introduction of the .700 Nitro Express round in 1988. Heavy game rifles including the .600 NE were used in WWI by the British to effectively engage German snipers who had been shielded from standard .303 British rounds by steel plates.

Elephant Guns

Large dangerous African game such the Elephant, Cape Buffalo, and Rhinoceros require powerful cartridges. Traditionally, these have been chambered in double rifles. For comparison, some cartridges are pictured at right, actual size. The .223 is the U.S. service round, and a popular light hunting and target round. The .30-06 is widely used for most North American big game, and was the U.S. WWII service cartridge. Cartridge power is expressed in muzzle energy measued in foot-pounds. This will vary depending on the powder charge used and bullet weight.

Cartridge - Muzzle energy in foot pounds
- .223 Rem - 1,300 ft-lbs
- .30-06 - 2,900 ft-lbs
- .458 Win Mag - 5,570 ft-lbs
- .600 H&H Nitro Express - 7,600 ft-lbs
- .700 H&H Nitro Express - 8,900 ft-lbs

MODERN FIREARMS

Flaig's Vierling Combination Gun - 20 gauge x 20 gauge x .22WMR x .243 Winchester - circa 1968. Multiple barrel combination guns allow hunters to take advantage of mixed-bag hunting where legal, ready for birds, small game or large game. Three barrels are "drillings." Four barrels are "vierlings."

1. Browning Model 78 Single-Shot Rifle with Leupold scope - .30-06 - circa 1973-1982 - Modern version of Winchester Hi-Wall.
2. Colt/Sharps Falling Block Sporting Rifle with telescopic sight - .22-250 Remington - circa 1971 - About 500 made.
3. Paul Jaeger Custom Falling-Block Sporter Rifle with Scope - .270 Winchester - circa 2000-2001 - Engraved by Claus Willig.
4. Sturm, Ruger & Co. No. 1-H Tropical Falling-Block Rifle - .458 Winchester Magnum - circa 1976.
5. Shiloh Products Model 1874 Sharps Single-Shot Falling-Block Rifle - .45-70 - circa 1986 - Reproduction sidehammer Sharps made in Farmingdale, NY.
6. Knight MK 85-1 Prototype In-line Percussion Muzzleloading Rifle - .50 caliber - circa 1985 - In-line muzzleloaders like this were the first blackpowder arms to utilize regular centerfire primers for ignition. The hot ignition allowed usage of synthetic blackpowder materials like Pyrodex.
7. Michigan Arms Wolverine In-Line Black Powder Rifle .50 caliber percussion.
8. Savage Model 24J-SL Over/Under Combination Gun - .22 rimfire /20 gauge - circa 1974 - Versatile double-barrel rifle/shotgun.
9. Ludwig Borovnik Austrian Vierling Four-Barrel Combination Gun - 12 gauge/12 gauge/.22 Hornet/.308 - circa 1900-1920.

SINGLE-SHOT RIFLES & DOUBLE-BARREL SHOTGUNS

John Olin's King Buck Winchester Model 21 Grand Royal - 20 gauge - circa 1955 - In the world of Winchesters, the Model 21 is without argument, the finest quality gun produced by the venerable arms making firm. The highest grade offered by the factory was the "Grand Royal," and only five were made in this pattern. In the world of Model 21s, this gun, John Olin's "King Buck" 21, is considered to be the finest Model 21, and thereby the finest Winchester, ever produced. Features include a unique scalloped boxlock action, with engraving and gold inlay by Alvin White and Andrew Bourbon. In addition to a portrait of Olin himself, the featured theme is Olin's favorite hunting dog, a Champion black lab named "King Buck." Images of King Buck were used in numerous advertising campaigns. He was the only dog ever pictured on a federal duck stamp.

Pair of Purdey Over/Under Shotguns - 12 gauge - circa 1978 - This exquisite pair of J. Purdey & Sons over-and-unders are vent-ribbed guns with single triggers and two sets of barrels for each gun for a total of four barrels. The pair has highly figured stocks and are engraved by Purdey master engraver Ken Hunt.

MODERN FIREARMS

1. Rigby Hammer Side-by-Side Shotgun. 12 gauge - circa 1973. Ornate floral scroll engraving.
2. Parker VHE Grade Skeet Side-by-Side Shotgun - 20 gauge - circa 1937-1938.
3. Parker DHE Grade Side-by-Side Shotgun - 28 gauge - circa 1937-1938.
4. Sturm, Ruger & Co. Stainless Red Label Skeet Over/Under Shotgun - 20 gauge - circa 1985 - Engraved by Neil Hartliep.
5. Remington Model 32 TC Over/Under Shotgun - 12 gauge - circa 1932-1942.
6. L.C. Smith Eagle-Grade Single-Barrel Trap Shotgun - 12 gauge - circa 1921.
7. Browning Broadway Trap Presentation 3 Superposed Shotgun - 12 gauge - circa 1961-1976.
8. James Purdey Shotgun - 12 gauge - circa 1967 - Rose and scroll engraving.
9. Kreighoff Four-Barrel Shotgun Set - circa 1996.
10. Ithaca 7E Single-Barrel Trap Shotgun - 12 gauge - circa 1930 - Engraved by William McGraw.
11. James Purdey & Sons Single-Barrel Trap Shotgun - 12 gauge - circa 1924 - Restocked with Monte Carlo.

DOUBLE-BARREL SHOTGUNS

1. Remington Prototype Parker Shotgun - 20 gauge - circa 1987 - Original production of Remington's Parker shotguns ended in 1942. After a limited run of prototypes, including this example, a new line of Parker shotguns was announced in 2006. These new shotguns are manufactured at the Connecticut Shotgun Company.
2. Winchester Model 21 Trap Grade Shotgun - 12 gauge - circa 1951.
3. James Purdey & Sons British Best-Grade Side-by-Side Shotgun - 10 gauge - circa 1908.
4. Katsenes Custom Side-by-Side Shotgun - .410 gauge - circa 1956.
5. Laurona Spanish Model 153 Over/Under Shotgun - 12 gauge - circa 1983.
6. Tate Vintager Side-by-Side Shotgun - 12 gauge - circa 2004.
7. Winchester Model 101 Over/Under Shotgun - 20 gauge - circa 1966.
8. James Purdey & Sons British Over/Under Shotgun - 12 gauge - circa 1953 - Presented to Thomas B. Walton by Purdey CEO Tom Purdey.
9. Hopkins & Allen Forehand Single-Shot Shotgun - circa 1940.
10. Eduard Kettner Koln-Suhler German Gewehr-Fabrik Drilling - 16 gauge/.32 caliber - circa 1890.

MODERN FIREARMS

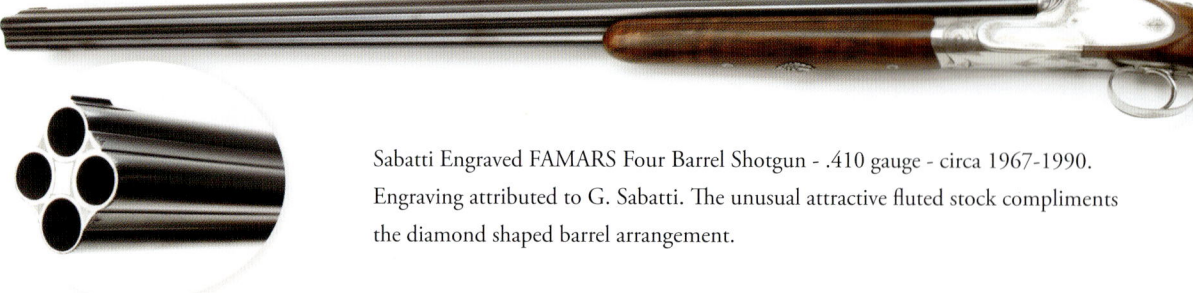

Sabatti Engraved FAMARS Four Barrel Shotgun - .410 gauge - circa 1967-1990. Engraving attributed to G. Sabatti. The unusual attractive fluted stock compliments the diamond shaped barrel arrangement.

Princess Diana's Wedding Westley Richards Side-by-Side Shotgun - 12 circa - circa 1981 - Made for the wedding of Lady Diana Spencer and HRH Prince Charles, engraved by the Brown Brothers with the British royal seal and other heraldic emblems of the couple.

1. Browning Euromarket Superposed Shotgun - 20 gauge - circa 1982.
2. Pietro Beretta Premium-Grade Side-by-Side Shotgun - 12 gauge - circa 1990 - Presentation given to Beretta VP.
3. Winchester Model 23 XTR Side-by-Side Shotgun - 20 gauge - circa 1979.

REPEATING SHOTGUNS

Above: The First Remington Model 870 Pump Shotgun - 12 gauge - circa 1948 - s/n 000. This is believed to the the first production Mod. 870.

At right: The pump-action Remington Model 870 and Mossberg Model 500 are the most popular smoothbores in America. These are the ten-millionth made specimens of each.

The Remington 870 is the most manufactured shotgun in history. Introduced in 1951, this s/n 10,000,000 was made in 2009 and is on loan from Remington Arms Company.

The Mossberg 500 was introduced in 1961, and reached the ten million milestone faster than any other shotgun, with this s/n U500,000 made in 2013 and donated to the NRA by Mossberg Arms.

MODERN FIREARMS

1. Prototype Remington Model 11-48 semi-auto shotgun - .410 bore - circa 1948, s/n 000000.
2. Browning Auto-5 Light Twelve Semi-Automatic Shotgun - 12 gauge - circa 1981.
3. Browning B-80 Semi-Automatic Shotgun - 20 gauge - circa 1980.
4. Savage Stevens 30-D Slide-Action Shotgun - 12 gauge - circa 1971.
5. Remington Model 870 Slide-Action Shotgun. Rifle sights allow the use of solid slugs for big game hunting.- 12 gauge - circa 1980-1982.
6. Benelli Nova Pump Shotgun - 20 gauge Current production. Synthetic stock.
7. Winchester Model 12 Black Diamond Trap Slide-Action Shotgun - 12 gauge - circa 1950.
8. Winchester Model 25 Slide-Action Shotgun - 12 gauge - circa 1951 - About 88,000 were made.

REPEATING SHOTGUNS

1. Seitz Serial Number 1 Engraved Single-Barrel Trap Shotgun - 12 gauge - circa 1985-1993 - Serial number 1 engraved by Jack West.
2. Winchester Model 42 Slide-Action Shotgun - .410 gauge - circa 1949.
3. Ithaca Model 37 Trap Slide-Action Shotgun - 12 gauge - circa 1937-1955.
4. Winchester Model 12 Pigeon Grade Shotgun - 12 gauge - circa 1957.
5. Remington Model 1100 Trap Semi-Automatic Shotgun - 12 gauge - circa 1987-1999.
6. Luigi Franchi Semi-Automatic Shotgun - circa 1968.

Rabbit Hunting - Collins

MODERN FIREARMS

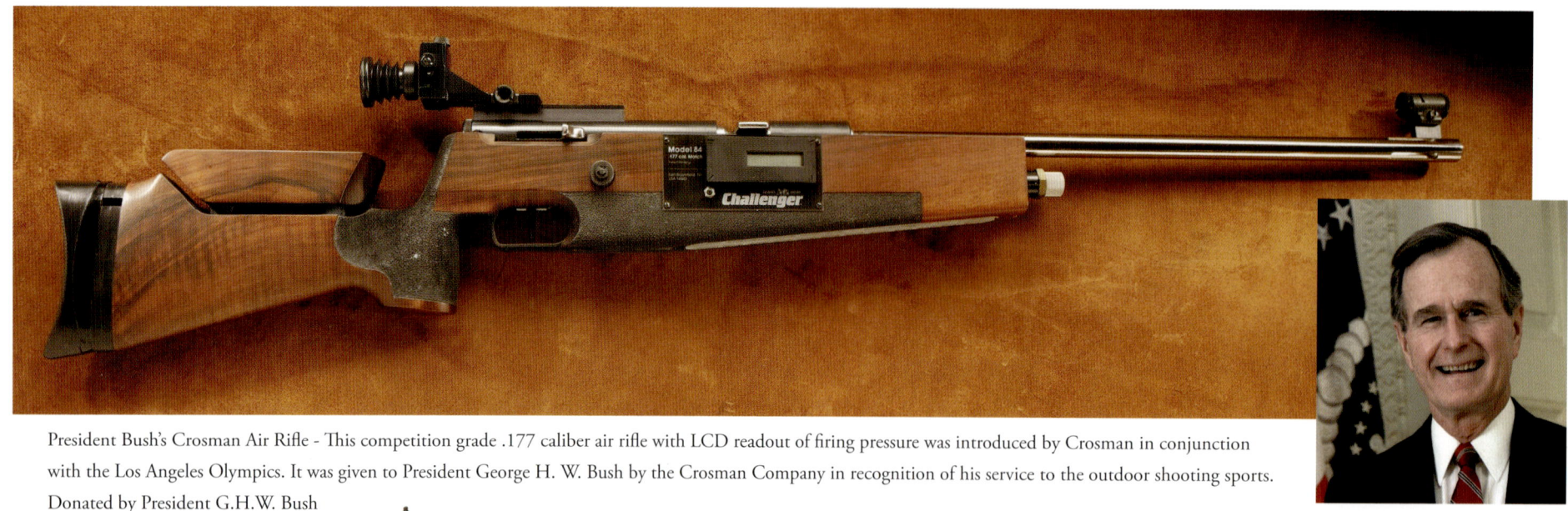

President Bush's Crosman Air Rifle - This competition grade .177 caliber air rifle with LCD readout of firing pressure was introduced by Crosman in conjunction with the Los Angeles Olympics. It was given to President George H. W. Bush by the Crosman Company in recognition of his service to the outdoor shooting sports. Donated by President G.H.W. Bush

Kaiser Wilhelm's Spandau M1888 Sporter Rifle - 8x57mm - circa 1910 - Created for Kaiser Wilhelm I from a military rifle, this custom takedown sporter Mauser is engraved in gold on the rifle's chamber with the imperial German family crest.

HRH Prince Charles' Omega Air Rifle - This presentation .177 caliber air gun was crafted for the Prince of Wales by Don Robinson of Halifax, England and bears serial number 42042 as well as an inlaid House of Windsor crest. Donated by HRH Prince Charles.

PRESIDENTS AND ROYALTY

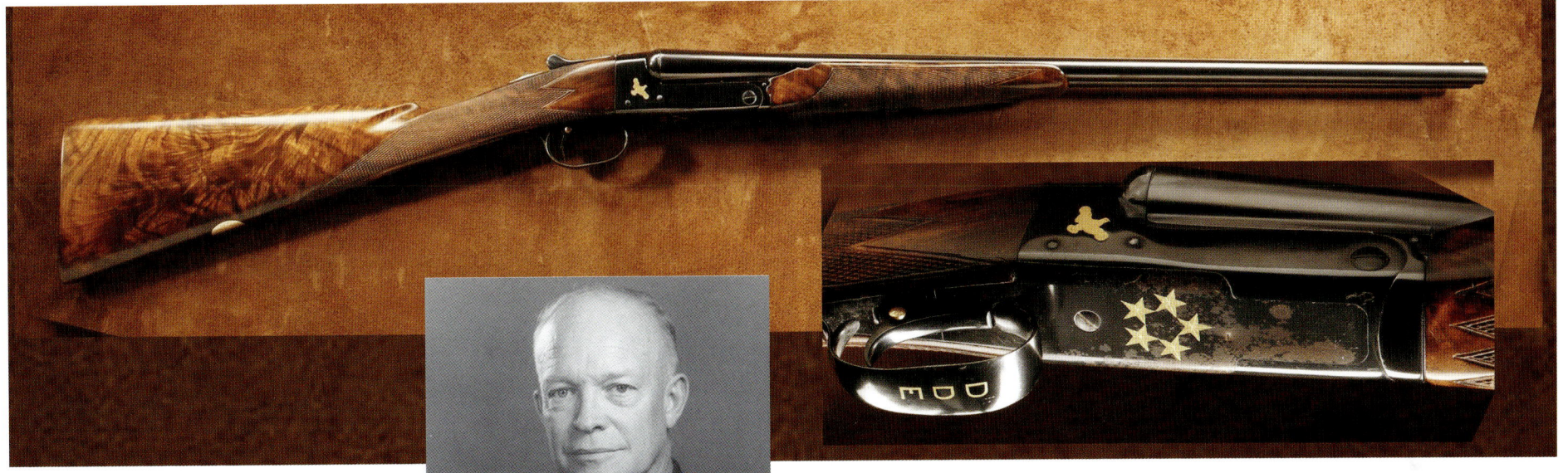

Engraved Presentation Winchester Model 21 Shotgun - 20 gauge This engraved side-by-side double, fitted with two sets of barrels, was presented to General Dwight D. Eisenhower from Robert Woodruff, President of Coca-Cola. It was a favorite of Ike's for bird hunting.

Colt New Frontier Revolver - .45 Colt, 1963. Made by Colt as gift for President John Fitzgerald Kennedy. The elaborate engraving motifs include a JFK monogram, the presidential seal, the White House, and a gold PT boat inlay. Appropriately, the serial number is PT-109. Alvin White engraving. Colt had intended this gift to honor Kennedy's choice of the words "New Frontier" to represent America's space program's dedication to visiting the moon, and Colt's decision to re-issue the traditional Colt Single Action Army revolver with a new adjustable rear sight as the "New Frontier" model. The President's assassination in late November 1963 prevented this handgun from being presented.

MODERN FIREARMS

Above and below - Angelo Galeazzi bulino engraving, Beretta Set of Five double shotguns depicting the history of hunting

Manrico Torcoli bulino engraving of nudes and big cats on Peter Hofer single-shot rifle.

Modern Engraving

Despite the masterpieces of earlier eras, the most beautiful firearms engraving of all time is being done in the modern era. Master artisans still carve beautiful works by hand. The relatively new technique called "bulino" expanded the possibilities of engraving. Bulino uses hundreds of thousands, or even millions, of hand-punched dots of varying diameter and depth to create almost photo-realistic images on metal.

Machine or laser-cut engraving has made attractively decorated firearms accessible to the mass market, but the works made with a machine process can never compare to the handwork that created the pieces shown here.

Facing page, top to bottom:

Alfredo Bregoili swan & vine engraving on Rizzini side-by-side shotgun.

Brown Brothers high-relief quail engraving on Westley Richards double.

Rodolfo Balneari bulino engraved game scene on Piotti side-by-side.

Facing page, far right:

Phillipe Grifnee gold inlaid lion and high relief scroll engraving on Holland & Holland double rifle.

ENGRAVING MASTERPIECES

MODERN FIREARMS

Brown Brothers engraved Holland & Holland shotgun with gold relief mythological scenes. Titled "The Empire Gun" and awarded H&H "Product of Excellence" for 1983.

Ken Hunt floral scroll engraved Boss & Co. shotgun marked in gold "75th Anniversary Model."

ENGRAVING MASTERPIECES

Rodolfo Balneari bulino game scene with fine scroll borders, Piotti side-by-side, circa 1986.

Firmo Fracassi bulino game scene, Famars side-by-side shotgun.

Phil Coggan bulino engraved game birds, Purdey .410 over/under shotgun.

MODERN FIREARMS

ENGRAVING MASTERPIECES

Facing page: Firmo Fracassi bulino engraved Rizzini sshotgun, circa 1989. Fracassi is generally considered the finest bulino engraver in the world.

Below: Leonard Francolini engraved Colt Single Action Army, circa 1973. Reportedly commissioned for Horace Greeley IV for his wife whose nickname was "Punkin," as reflected in the engraving.

At right: "Vampire Hunter's Kit" by Colt Master Engraveer Leonardo Francolini, circa1977. Colt Detective Special engraved with bats in the flutes, a cross over the muzzle, and a rampant colt on a coffin. It is in a coffin shaped case with silver bullets with carved vampire faces, an oiler labeled "Holy Water," and a wooden stake attachment for the cleaning rod. It has been called "One of the most unusual guns Colt ever made," and "Francolini's greatest masterpiece."

MODERN FIREARMS

At left, top and bottom:
Richard Roy engraved Ansley H. Fox elegant small double-barreled guns by Connecticut Shotgun. Top is a .410 gauge shotgun and bottom is a .22 LR double rifle.

At left, middle:
Phillipe Grifnee engraved Holland & Holland .577 Nitro Express Double Rifle.

Below:
Acanthus leaf engraving on Purdey shotgun.

ENGRAVING MASTERPIECES

Above and below: Manrico Torcoli bulino engravings of cape buffalo and elephants in the mist engraving on Beretta EEGS double rifle.

At right: Giancarlo Pedretti bulino hunting dog scene on Connecticut Shotgun over/under.

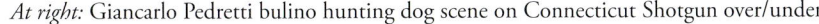

MODERN FIREARMS

ENGRAVING MASTERPIECES

Lee Griffiths engraving.

At left: A military-themed cone-hammer broomhandle Mauser and a nautical-themed Bergmann Bayard pistol.

Above: A multi-generational plinking scene on a Winchester Model 63 .22 semi-auto rifle.

Below: Browning Auto .22 rifle with Old West scenes.

TO KEEP AND BEAR ARMS

GUNS OF THE NRA

"FROM MY COLD DEAD HANDS"
Sharps Model 1874 Rifle - .44-90 - circa 1877 -

This is the rifle that NRA President Charlton Heston held aloft when he made this famous statement. Donated by the Estate of Charlton Heston. Heston served in the US Army Air Corps in WWII. His acting career spanned six decades with over 130 film and television credits. He was awarded two Oscars and two Golden Globes. He was active in the Civil Rights movement of the 1960s. He served as President of the NRA for an unprecedented five terms (1998-2003) and was present at the grand opening of the National Firearms Museum in Fairfax, Virginia in May of 1998.

Firearms retain a unique place in American history and contemporary society because America is a unique country. It is ultimately up to the people to decide who will govern. Nowhere else on earth has a constitutional government been established that guarantees the people a right to keep and bear arms for personal defense and as a balance against a tyrannical government or the invasion by a foreign foe.

Charlton Heston, in a speech before the National Press Club in September 1997, said:
" ...[the] doorway to freedom is framed by the muskets that stood between a vision of liberty and absolute anarchy at a place called Concord Bridge. ... go forth and tell the truth. There can be no free speech, no freedom of the press, no freedom to protest, no freedom to worship your god, no freedom to speak your mind, no freedom from fear, no freedom for your children and for theirs, for anybody, anywhere, without the Second Amendment freedom to fight for it."

These selected firearms represent parts of the myriad stories told within the NRA Museums galleries that encompass the story of firearms, freedom, and the American experience. Each of these firearms represents a chapter or story in the history of the National Rifle Association of America. For over 140 years the members of the NRA have striven to keep America strong as a nation of marksmen, sportsmen, hunters, competitors, and above all, patriots, able to answer the call at a moment's notice, much like on the morning of April 19, 1775, when tyranny and oppression were faced with armed resistance so that all Americans could live free.

TO KEEP AND BEAR ARMS

U.S. Springfield Presentation-Grade M14 Semi-Automatic Rifle, serial number 6 (deactivated) - 7.62mm NATO - circa 1957 - The M14 selective-fire rifle, chosen to replace the semi-automatic M1 Garand rifle, was the U.S. Army's primary issue rifle from 1957 to 1958. Presented by CJCS General Lyman Lemnitzer at the NRA Annual Meetings in 1961, he related the significance of this gun's serial number 6. "Got your six" was Army radio code for "having someone's back," a tribute to the membership of the NRA who so generously support and participate in Army marksmanship programs.

U.S. Springfield Model 1911 Semi-Automatic Pistol - .45 ACP - circa 1914-1915 - In 1915 and 1916, National Rifle Association life members and members of affiliated clubs could purchase a military Colt or Springfield Armory Model 1911 pistol for $16, nearly $6 cheaper than the commercial equivalent, the Colt Government pistol. Less than 300 of these pistols were sold through this program. They were marked "N.R.A." under the serial number of the pistol to distinguish it from other M1911 handguns still in military inventory. Today, the Civilian Marksmanship Program offers members of affiliated shooting clubs the opportunity to purchase surplus U.S. military rifles.

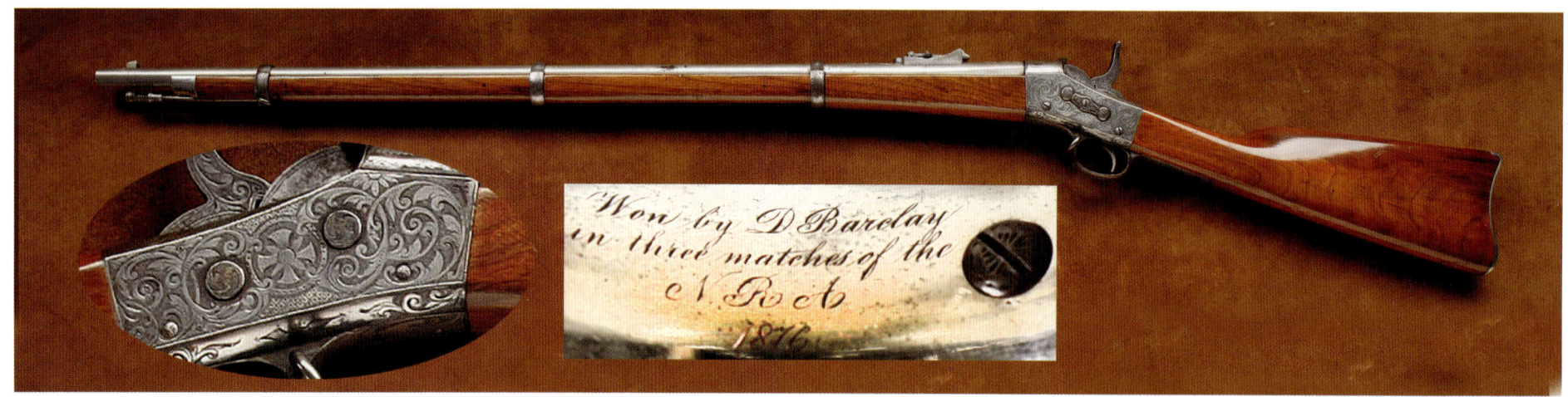

Remington Rolling Block Rifle - .45-70 caliber - This No. 1-sized action model of the rolling block was presented to D. Barclay of the NRA for winning one of the International Matches in 1876 at the Creedmoor range. This gun is recorded as one of the first guns presented to the NRA for its collection, which eventually became the National Firearms Museum. The engraving is attributed to L.D. Nimschke. The No. 1-sized rolling-block action was one of Remington's most popular models with over one million produced between 1867 and 1888.

GUNS OF THE NRA

French Model 1886/93 Presentation-Grade Rifle - 8mm Lebel - circa 1920 - The National Rifle Association offered marksmanship training to military personnel of other countries. After World War I concluded, France presented this bolt-action Lebel rifle to the NRA in appreciation for the assistance it rendered in training French soldiers.

Swinburn Presentation-Grade Peabody/Martini-Henry Single-Shot Rifle - .577 caliber - circa 1874 - In 1874. Major Arthur Blennerhasset Leech, on behalf of the Irish Rifle Association, issued a challenge to the Riflemen of the World to compete in a long-range rifle match with the American team using American-made rifles. The Irish team used the finest Rigby muzzleloading target rifles. The American team won the match with a close score of 934 to 931. In token of the American victory, Major Leech presented this Martini-action single-shot rifle to the captain of the American team, Colonel George Wingate, later to become an NRA President. The presentation of this rifle symbolized the arrival of the National Rifle Association of America on the world stage of international competition. It was also one of the earliest guns donated to the NRA collection.

Wingate's NRA Life Member badge

Burnside 5th Model Percussion Carbine - .54 caliber - circa 1865 - The first president of the National Rifle Association was Major General Ambrose E. Burnside. His invention of a breechloading carbine prior to the American Civil War and its subsequent manufacture were among the reasons Burnside was asked to serve as the Association's first chief officer. He also served as Governor of Rhode Island, and as a U.S. Senator. His distinctive facial hair added the word "sideburns" to the English language. By oral tradition, it is believed that this presentation carbine was given to the NRA by Burnside upon his retirement.

YOU, YOUR GUNS, & THE NRA MUSEUM

NRA Firearms For Freedom: A program that assists individuals in the Patriotic Disposition of firearms that are no longer needed or wanted. Firearms may be donated to the NRA National Firearms Museum and/or sold by an auction company to provide funding to the NRA, NRA-ILA, or one of the NRA 501 (c) (3) charitable non-profit affiliates as a current donation, a planned gift or to fund a charitable gift annuity for the lives of you and or your spouse. See the program website at www.nrafff.com for information on the program or to access the auctions of firearms where 100% of the bid price comes back to the NRA beneficiary the donor designates. You can support your NRA by purchasing quality firearms at eGunner.com (Click on the home page NRA Firearms For Freedom banner). To learn more about donating firearms today, in the near future or making a provision for their disposition in a will or trust, call 855-4NRAFFF (855-467-2333) or use the formatted email at the program web site. This program is especially advantageous to collectors whose life style changes in old age require collection downsizing or to insure a surviving spouse, heirs or estate executors are not burdened with handling the disposition of your collection. The program is first a service to members and non-member supporters of the 2nd Amendment that happens to also support the NRA Museum, the NRA, and the NRA's charitable non-profit affiliates (The NRA Foundation, The NRA Civil Rights Defense Fund, The NRA Special Contribution Fund and The NRA Freedom Action Fund Foundation).

- **Donations for display.** The Museum is always interested in rare, historic, and important guns for display. The Museum staff are glad to discuss with collectors whether their special guns would be put on display if donated. Occasionally, the Museum will display extraordinary guns on loan. To discuss donation for display, call 703-267-1602.

- **The collectors before you.** Remember, if not for the generosity and foresight of collectors before you, the Museum would not exist. Of the more than 10,000 guns in the Museum system, 99.9% have been donated or are on loan.

The Museum offers a glimpse into the firearms that built our nation, helped forge our freedom, and captured our imagination. The Museum was built by NRA members, and its future depends on NRA members. This is YOUR National Firearms Museum.

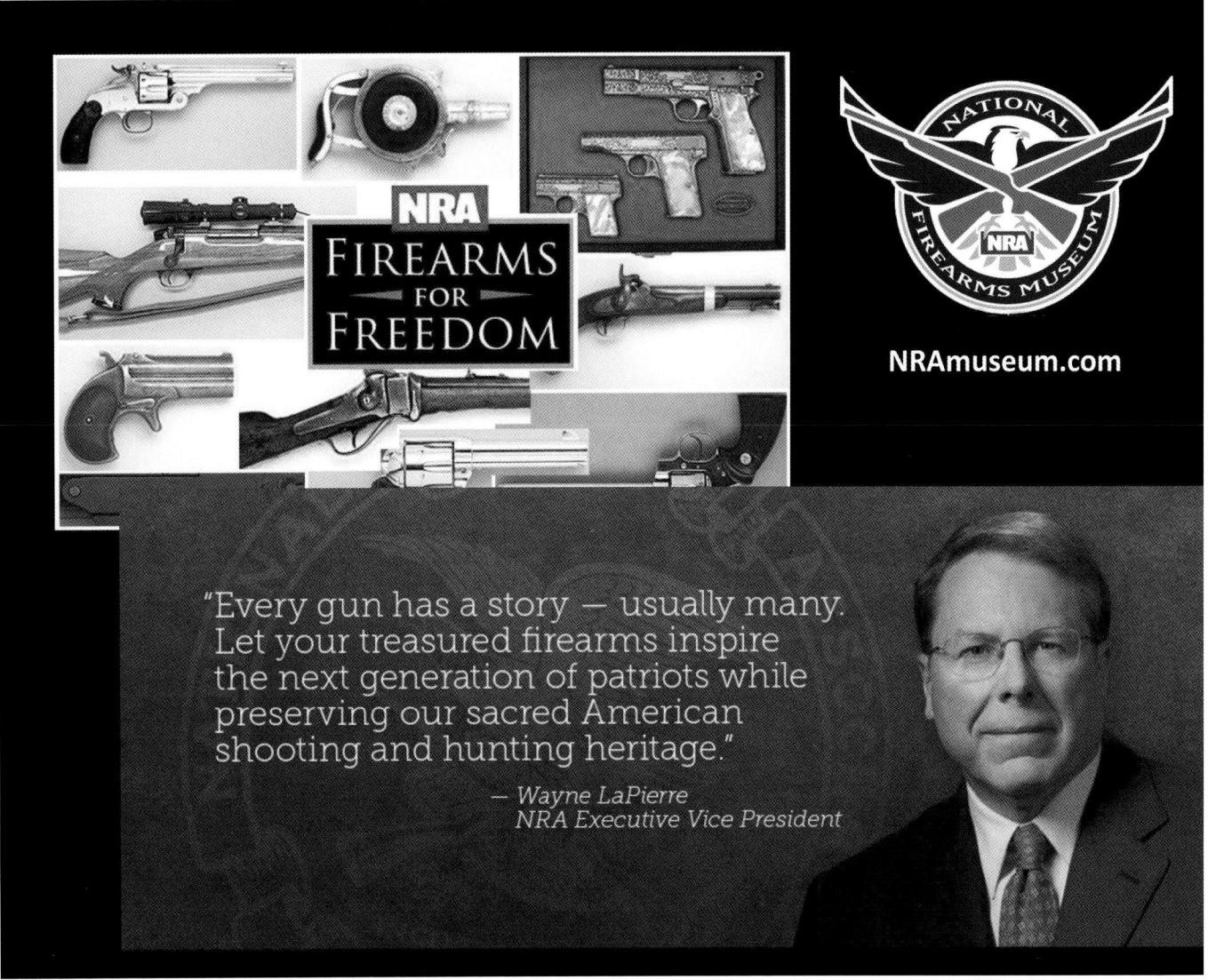

THE NATIONAL RIFLE ASSOCIATION'S PROGRAMS: The Core of Our Mission

NRA GENERAL OPERATIONS: ROOTED IN EDUCATION, TRAINING & MARKSMANSHIP

The NRA is every bit as invested today in the core mission and principles it was founded to achieve in 1871—a commitment to training, education and marksmanship. While widely recognized as a major political force and as America's foremost defender of Second Amendment rights, the NRA has, since its inception, been the premier firearms education organization in the world. NRA General Operations (G.O.) continues those traditions today through the numerous and diverse programs, events and resources it provides.

Our education, safety, training, and marksmanship programs, events and resources feature offerings for everyone, from the gun safety lessons of the Eddie Eagle GunSafe® Program taught to school children, to the legendary training programs that empower gun owners young and old. From hunter safety and training, youth gun safety, basic marksmanship and self-defense courses, to elite competition shooting and gunsmithing schools, the NRA invests in Americans who want to become better, safer and smarter gun owners. The programs offered by NRA G.O. are at the heart of the National Rifle Association—training Americans to be responsible, safe and well-educated firearms owners and users. To learn more about NRA programs, **visit explore.nra.org**.

FIREARMS TRAINING

With roughly 150,000 people attending NRA training courses annually, the NRA is recognized nationally as the gold standard for firearm safety training. Whether you're a new or prospective gun owner or hunter in search of training, whatever your age or level of expertise, whatever type of firearm you're interested in, the NRA has the course for you—from gunsmith schools and courses, to become certified Instructors, Counselors, Coaches, and Range Safety Officers (RSOs), to expert-led concealed carry training. From beginner to serious competitor, the NRA Training Department develops safe, ethical, responsible shooters through a network of over 125,000 RSOs, instructors who teach NRA's basic firearm courses, and coaches who develop competitors at the club, high school, collegiate and national levels. **Visit firearmtraining.nra.org**.

COMPETITIVE SHOOTING

The NRA sanctions more than 11,000 shooting tournaments and sponsors more than 15 national championships each year. The NRA and the Competitive Shooting Division offers a wide range of activities in all types of shooting from the Collegiate Shooting Program serving student athletes at more than 300 colleges and universities in the U.S., the annual NRA World Shooting Championship which gathers the top shooters in the world to compete in virtually every type of major firearms shooting sport, to the America's Rifle Challenge competition events and more. There is something for everyone from the novice to the world-class competitor. Visit **competitions.nra.org** to find out more near you.

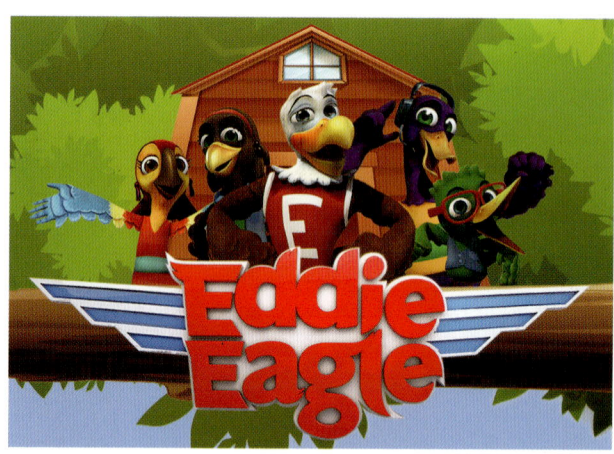

SAFETY & EDUCATION

Safety is not only critical in handling firearms but in everyday life, and the NRA offers resources and training to ensure personal safety and protection inside and outside the home. The Eddie Eagle GunSafe® program has taught more than 32 million children in pre-K through third grade the four important steps to take if they find a gun: STOP! Don't touch. Run Away. Tell a Grown-up. The Refuse To Be A Victim® program provides tips and techniques to help men and women of all ages avoid dangerous situations and develop a pesonal safety strategy. And the NRA School Shield program addresses the many facets of school security, including best practices in security infrastructure, technology, personnel, training and policy. **Visit eddieeagle.nra.org, rtbav.nra.org** and **nraschoolshield.org**.

THE NATIONAL RIFLE ASSOCIATION'S PROGRAMS: The Core of Our Mission

YOUTH PROGRAMS

The NRA has been actively involved in promoting the shooting sports to youth since 1903. Today, youth programs are still a cornerstone of the NRA, with more than 1 million youth participating in NRA shooting sports events and affiliated programs. A wide variety of youth programs, including competitions, awards and contests, training and safety courses, scholarships and more, help instill firearm safety and introduce shooting sports to the next generation of gun owners. From NRA's Youth Hunter Education Challenge (YHEC) and the NRA Marksmanship Qualification Program, to the National Junior Shooting Camps, National Youth Shooting Sports Ambassadors program, NRA Day presented by Brownells, and more, NRA provides opportunities for youth to learn, share, and grow in appreciation of the shooting sports in a safe environment. **Visit youth.nra.org**.

AFFILIATED CLUBS, RANGES & BUSINESSES

The NRA Clubs & Associations Department provides services and assistance to a network of more than 15,000 NRA-affiliated clubs, associations and businesses, offering access to benefits including grants, awards, discounts on products, software and more. NRA Range Services offers resources to public and private ranges across the country, including on-site assistance, educational seminars, and grants. The NRA Business Alliance provides NRA member businesses with a marketplace to sell goods and services to fellow NRA members while receiving many member benefits. **Visit clubs.nra.org**.

LAW ENFORCEMENT, MILITARY & SECURITY

The NRA has been offering the best in law enforcement and military firearms instruction training since 1960, with the primary mission of providing the law enforcement community with a means to certify law enforcement firearm instructors. For almost 60 years, the NRA has trained more than 55,000 law enforcement firearm instructors and currently has over 11,000 active certified instructors. The NRA Law Enforcement division also offers law enforcement firearm competitions, including the National Police Shooting Championships and Police Pistol Combat events, as well as a multi-gun competition called the Tactical Police Competition (TPC). Plus, the NRA provides scholarships, life insurance policies, instructor liability and self-defense insurance, opportunities for affiliation and more for active and retired law enforcement officers, including information on the Law Enforcement Officers Safety Act (LEOSA). Visit **le.nra.org**.

WOMEN'S INTERESTS

With the number of women shooters on the rise, the NRA is dedicated to providing programs and resources to female gun enthusiasts. Women can receive firearms training by certified instructors through Women On Target®, get involved in clubs and competitions, receive awards and scholarships, experience an array of firearms education and hunting activities at a Women's Wilderness Escape and much more. The NRA has opportunities for brand new and experienced shooters to share their passion for the outdoors and shooting sports with like-minded women. Visit **explore.nra.org/interests/womens-interests/** to learn more or go to **nrainstructors.org/Search.aspx** to register for any NRA training course near you.

HUNTING PROGRAMS

For more than 60 years, America's millions of hunters have depended on the NRA's support. The NRA built the first-ever hunter education program in 1949, and now it has developed a state-of-the-art, 100% free NRA Hunter Education course to be the most comprehensive online hunter education instruction in the United States. NRA's YHEC provides a fun environment for kids to improve their hunting marksmanship and safety skills through simulated hunting situations, live fire exercises, and educational and responsibility events. Plus, from Hunters for the Hungry's hunger relief efforts to the Hunter Clinic Instructor Program's instruction of advanced hunting skills and more hunting resources, the NRA is working to preserve this treasured tradition for present and future generations. **Visit hunting.nra.org**.

EVENTS & PRODUCTS

The NRA holds our Annual Meetings each spring and the Great American Outdoor show each winter, providing members and supporters of the shooting sports lifestyle opportunities to come together with fellow gun enthusiasts and connect with the NRA. The official NRA store has the gear and accessories Second Amendment enthusiasts need to show their support—and 100% of the profits go directly to support vital NRA programs—while the NRA Program Materials Center provides training resources for instructors, coaches, programs and law enforcement officers. **Visit nraam.org, greatamericanoutdoorshow.org, nrastore.com** and **materials.nrahq.org**.

Preserve the Right to Keep and Bear Arms for this and future generations - JOIN THE NRA

The Institute for Legislative Action (ILA) is the political arm of the NRA. Established in 1975, ILA is committed to preserving the right of all law abiding individuals to purchase, possess, carry and use firearms for legitimate purposes as guaranteed by the Second Amendment to the U.S. Constitution. ILA's ability to fight successfully for the rights of America's law-abiding gun owners directly reflects the support of NRA's 5 million members-a number that has more than tripled since 1978. When restrictive "gun control" legislation is proposed at the local, state or federal level, NRA members and supporters are alerted and respond with individual letters, e-mails and calls to their elected representatives to make their views known.

Combined with the strong grassroots efforts of NRA members and NRA affiliated state associations and local gun clubs, ILA has worked vigorously to pass pro-gun reform legislation at the state level.

These efforts include enacting laws that recognize the right of honest citizens to carry firearms for self-protection; preemption bills to prevent attacks on gun owner rights by local anti-gun politicians, and fighting for legislation to prevent the bankrupting of America's firearms industry through reckless lawsuits.

In 1975 when ILA was formed, only four states had right-to-carry laws. In 2019, 42 states have right-to-carry laws. These laws would be meaningless if every local government in the country could come up with a different set of rules, but due to the hard work of NRA members, 45 states prohibit local governments from enacting gun ordinances that are more restrictive than state law.

And, in 2005, NRA achieved an incredible victory for gun owners with passage of the Protection of Lawful Commerce in Arms Act. That law prevents frivolous lawsuits that would shut down the gun industry, and with it, law-abiding Americans' ability to exercise their right to acquire firearms.

ILA is also involved in educating the public about the facts concerning the many facets of firearms ownership in America. Through the distribution of fact sheets, brochures and articles and the posting of information daily on its website (www.nraila.org) and social media platforms, ILA provides facts about responsible firearms ownership, the Second Amendment and other topics of interest.

At NRA Headquarters in Fairfax, Va. and in offices in Washington , D.C. ILA employs a staff of more than 90, with a team of full-time lobbyists, lawyers, and support staff protecting and expanding gun rights on Capitol Hill, in state and local government bodies, and in the courts.

While NRA is a single-issue organization, ILA is involved in any issue that directly or indirectly affects the firearm rights of NRA's members and America's 100 million gun owners. These involve such topics as hunting and access to hunting lands, wilderness and wildlife conservation, civilian marksmanship training and ranges for public use, law enforcement-related issues, product liability, and criminal justice reform.

JOIN NRA TODAY

Make NRA one member stronger and join Freedom's Safest Place!

NRA Membership Benefits:

24/7 Defense of Your Gun Rights • Official Membership Card and Decal • Exclusive Access to the NRA Travel Center
Your Choice of Magazine • Savings and Special Offers from Trusted NRA Partners • more at Benefits.NRA.org

---

☐ NEW MEMBER   ☐ RENEWAL # _____

FIRST NAME: _____   LAST NAME: _____   SUFFIX: _____

ADDRESS: _____

PHONE: (____) _____   D.O.B: ___/___/_____   E-MAIL: _____

SELECT MEMBERSHIP TYPE:
☐ *ONE-YEAR: $35 (reg. $45)*   ☐ *THREE-YEAR: $85 (reg. $100)*   ☐ *FIVE-YEAR: $125 (reg. $150)*   ☐ *LIFE: $1,000 (reg. $1,500)*

SELECT ONE MAGAZINE:
DELIVERY METHOD: ☐ PRINT   ☐ DIGITAL (E-MAIL ADDRESS REQUIRED)
☐ *AMERICAN RIFLEMAN*   ☐ *AMERICAN HUNTER*   ☐ *AMERICA'S 1ST FREEDOM*   ☐ *SHOOTING ILLUSTRATED*

PAYMENT TYPE: ☐ **CHECK** OR **MONEY ORDER** *(PAYABLE TO NRA)*   ☐ CREDIT CARD
CARD TYPE: ☐ VISA   ☐ MASTERCARD   ☐ AMEX   ☐ DISCOVER

SIGNATURE (CC# only): _____

XR025732

Flip over for mailing instructions and more information

XR025732

MAIL YOUR COMPLETE APPLICATION TO:

NATIONAL RIFLE ASSOCIATION
C/O RECRUITING PROGRAMS
11250 WAPLES MILL RD
FAIRFAX, VA 22030

JOIN INSTANTLY
800-672-0004
www.NRA.org/MuseumOffer

Contributions, gifts or membership dues made or paid to the National Rifle Association of America are not refundable or transferable and are not deductible as charitable contributions for Federal income tax purposes. $3.75 of the membership dues are designated for magazine subscription. **Foreign postage add $5 for Canada, $10 for all other countries.**

Membership starts the day of processing of dues payments by NRA. The moving discount is off the Interstate Commerce Commission approved tariff rate. For specific state-by-state disclosures, please visit http://www.nra.org/NRA-UniformDisclosureStatement.pdf

ACKNOWLEDGEMENTS

ACKNOWLEDGEMENTS - DONORS and LENDERS

The collection of the NRA National Firearms Museum has been built over the past eighty-five years from donations by individuals, businesses, and organizations with the foresight to preserve America's firearms heritage and to ensure that future generations are educated on the history of Americans and their firearms.

Today, donors are supporting the NRA and the National Firearms Museum through gifts or bequests of guns to the Firearms for Freedom program, nrafff@nrahq.org or (877) NRA GIVE.

The NRA Museums would like to acknowledge those who donated or loaned firearms that appear in this book. In an effort of this scale, with additions, deletions, and changes, some donors and lenders may have been overlooked, and to them we offer our sincere apologies. While we do not list donors and lenders here whose guns are not pictured, we wish to extend our sincere gratitude to them as well.

MAJOR COLLECTION DONATIONS:

ROBERT E. PETERSEN GALLERY

The 2010 opening of the Petersen Gallery marked the largest value gift in NRA history. Robert E. Petersen was the head of Petersen Publishing. With more than 400 guns donated by the Petersen Estate through Mrs. Margie Petersen, the museum is able to present an exceptional gallery of the finest engraved and historic firearms on display in the country, along with historic guns such Annie Oakley guns and a dozen Gatling guns including the one used by the Rough Riders. The Parker Invincible Shotguns and the Engraving Masterpieces on pages 142-144, 270 and 287- 293 are among the Petersen arms included in this book

AMERICAN LIBERTY and ARTISTRY IN ARMS COLLECTIONS

In 1993 Dr. William L. Roberts and Mrs. Collette N. Roberts donated a large and wide-ranging collection that provided a core for the new museum location in Fairfax, VA. The American Liberty Collection includes significant models throughout history, with illustrations spread throughout the book. The Artistry in Arms collection features engraved guns.

DOC J. THURSTON III COLLECTION

With nearly 3,000 guns, blades, and related artifacts bequeathed to the NRA Foundation in 2019, the Thurston Collection is the largest donation to the NRA Museums in terms of numbers of items. Over 850 of these have been retained in the NRA Museums' permanent collection. This broad collection includes arms from all eras, but especially the Civil War and Old West, with an emphasis on historically inscribed guns. There is also an emphasis of firearms oddities, including some of the items on pages 52-53, 102-107, and 258.

RAYMOND SUCKLING ESTATE

Raymond Suckling left the NRA Foundation an impressive collection of 700 guns and 400 firearms locks in 2018. The collection is strong in early guns, along with firearms curiosa, some of which are shown in this book with the Thurston oddities.

DONORS OF COLLECTIONS:

Taz and Bailey Brower
Donations of U.S. military trials pistols including some of those on pages 155 & 156, and donations and loans of exceptional Savage semi-auto pistols.

Family of Bruce Stern
20th century military long arms.

Randle Goetz
Thompson submachine guns.

Horace Greeley IV
General Officers Pistols

Melvin Gordon
Winchester Model 70 rifles.

Mrs. Walter Groff
Ed McGivern handguns.

Tom Selleck
Former NRA Board member Selleck's donations have included guns used by him in movies.

Joel Gross
Prototypes of W.H.B. Smith

Philip R. Lichtman
Semmerling Pistols

Collection of Paul Chapman
Texas Ranger guns

Dr. Harold Cottle
Harmon Leonard
Estate of Max Shaefer
Maj. Gen. Julian S. Hatcher, U.S. Army
Leon C. "Red" Jackson
Lt. Gen. Milton A. Reckord, U.S. Army
Ruth Strader
The Thomas W. Sefton Trust
The Stanley Kellert Trust
Estate of Alan T. Schemm
Johnny Reavis
Rev. J.B.M. Frederick in memory of his father, Karl T. Frederick

THANKS TO THE FOLLOWING WHO DONATED ONE OR MORE FIREARMS PICTURED IN THIS BOOK:

Col. Wallace Weber
Michael Carrick
Eldon J. Owens
Estate of Lt., Col. William McMillan
Dr. William F. Farr
Mrs. John W. Hession
Mossberg
Helen Malloy
Ron Adolphi
John Ying
Doris Thompson
Mark Caldwell
John and Barbara Rumpel
Bruce Staud and Anita Berns

ACKNOWLEDGEMENTS

Colt Manufacturing Co.
Estate of Charlton Heston
Lt. Philip Hemphill, Mississippi Highway Patrol
Beretta U.S.A.
Sturm, Ruger & Co.
U.S. Army
E. Kiimalehto
Estate of Maj. Gordon Bess, U.S. Army
Joseph S. Kasaveach
Estate of Will Hoffeld
Lee L. Coleman
Harold G. Cheetham
C. Thomas Clagett, Jr.
National Park Service
Gary Fisher in memory of his father, Clay Fisher
Estate of Kenneth Tiny Miller
Family of Morgan Vance
Estate of Frank J. Woodworth
Hunter's Lodge
R. Alexander Montgomery
Dorothy A. Briggs in memory of her husband, Alfred Briggs
Estate of John F. Forsyth
Gen. Bryce Poe II, U.S.A.F.
William A. M. Burden IV
Earl Copeland
Val Forgett, Jr.
Colt
United States Department of State
Col. Nguyen Thanh Chuan, Special Forces, A.R.V.N
General P.X. Kelley, U.S.M.C., Ret.
Smith & Wesson
Estate of Lt. Col. William McMillan, U.S.M.C.
Estate of Clifford E. Bjornson
Dwight D. Van Horn

Barbara Agnew Maloney
U.S. Post Office Department
Remington Arms
Savage Arms
Winchester-Western
Daisy
President George Herbert Walker Bush
His Royal Highness Charles, Prince of Wales
Crosman Arms Co.
Virginia Military Institute Museum
P.C. Dorsey
Karl Rankin
Robert Phelps
Alden Family in care of William Alden
Delmar Weigel
James E. Serven
Duncan Persons
Michael Zomber
Robert N. Luke in dedication to Ruth E. Dressel
Daisy Ligon
C.R. Gutermuth
Clifford Wetzel
Charlotte Gollobin in memory of Leonard P. Gollobin
Wilson I. Domer
Bertha Herrmann
John W. Johnston
Michael Davenport
Malcolm Colby
Anna McCleaft
G. W. Wilcox
L. R. Johnson
Richard Ellis
Melvin Gordon
James David Burney & Barry Lee Burney
Henry D. Palmer
John P. Sowle

Roger J. Muckerheide, Jr., in memory of his friend, Leon C. "Red" Jackson
Ernest Bell
Ruth Traxel
John D. Flayderman
William R. Barnhart
Heckler & Koch
Tom Bennett
Henry Blumberg in dedication to Glen B. Payne
Merrill W. Wright
Mrs. V.R. Mueller
Raymond E. Dirkin
Archie Walker
Albert C. Ross
George Martian
Max Sweet
Marv Adams
Vernon Berning
Garner D. Hook
Helen Hansen
Estate of Harvey M. Aungst, Jr.
Francis Parker, Jr.
Joseph Cervenka
Mary McDonough in memory of her husband, John P. McDonough
Dr. Pierce MacKenzie
Bruce Albert Gustafson
John H. Wesson
L.W.J. Reinger
Estate of Buford McCurry
Eugene A. Ferrand
Gerard Whitmore in memory of John J. McGurk
K. W. Warner, Sr.
E. W. Griffin in memory of G. Carlyle Cooke
William Camp in memory of Mary Catherine Camp

Robert A. Yard
Margaret Greeley
Island Gun Club
John Paty
William Payne
Eva C. (Kay) Tyler in memory of her husband, Maj. Donald J. Tyler, U.S.A.F.
Ned Choate
Frank Bulawa
William C. Thum
Estate of Charles F. Seitz, Jr.
Eugene Kjellander
Robert John Hart
Hildalgo Trading Company
James Adams
James Ritchie and Charles Taylor
John J. O'Hara
C. H. Olson
Harry Abernathy
James Murphy
John Macrae
Terry J. Popkin
Lt. Col. F.L. Greaves
Welton M. Modisette
F. Russek
Loma O'Allen
William Frayseth
Col. Townsend Whelen, U.S. Army
A. Mattson
Charles D. Brooks in memory of his father, Robert D. Brooks
Estate of Wayne B. McGinnis
Farrel Owen
Herbert Bishop
Robert Topham
Roland Scheffler
David Savadyga
Paul Sokolovsky
Sheldon Grant

ACKNOWLEDGEMENTS

Ruby Fox
Edson W. Hall
Winfield Arms Co.
Chauncey Williams
David Welch
Donald D. Carruth
Michael Scanlan
Raven E. Corn
Edward Raymond Clark
Franz Schager
Gene Taylor
George F. Steeg
Murray A. Popple
Richard E. Morrell
Robert A. Rolli
Wallace Walford
LCDR Robert D. Hatcher, U.S. Navy
Ronald A. Kosin
Gordon Baxter
Nelson Shultis
Robert Hall
George R. and N. Butonne Repaire Estate and Trust
Nelson Otto Klaner
A. F. Elwell
Alex Brown
Mrs. Calvin Goddard
Charles Stroudt
Charles W. Retz
Stephen W. Popple
Northwest Montana Arms Collectors
Don and Donna Norton
Kenneth E. Harte
Barbara C. Stoller
Edward J. Holba
Edward L. Gruber
Estate of Joseph W. Bell
Page Hufty
Rupert Andrews
J. H. DeFrees
Alan Osbourne in memory of his bird dog, Inky Dot
Fred T. Huntington
N.E. Thompson
Adrian Peters
Estate of Ralph Scott
Frank W. Jones
Otto J. Lindo and J.N. Perkins
Fred Rowan
William Salem
Cornelius V.S. Roosevelt
Owen Albert
R.C. Wright
J. Wagram
Clifford Ackerson
Harold E. Johnson
Edith Lauren
J. Cantor
M. Solimene
Willis Bledsoe
F. Bob Chow
J. R. Maxwell
Northwest Montana Arms Collectors Association
B. Beers
David Anderson
Dr. J.A. Smith, Jr.
Mrs. Donald Lewin
Commander Marvin O. Register, U.S. Navy, Ret.
Estate of Glen B. Payne
Mr. and Mrs. August Vander Ley
Thadeus L. Hartman with the assistance of Tris Barry
Francis Meyer in dedication to Robert N. Newton
Col. Ralph V. Strauss, U.S. Army
Century Arms Co.
Titus Crow
Nevylle L. Smith
Winchester
Rueben Brown
Robert L. Baird
Springfield Armory, Inc.
Michael Marcus
Douglas Terrel and CWO4 Allen F. Manley, USN Ret.
John Reichwein
Robert Cox
Joseph L. O. Rubbio
William Boatman
C.E. Gregg
R.J. Buckwald
Estate of Heer Dohrman
H.P. Abbott
Ida M. Younger
N. Ischkum
W. R. Warner
David Silk
Gordon Hill
John W. Lindberg
William C. Arthur, Jr.
Karl Funkhouser
Capt. Samuel G. Green, Jr., U.S. Navy
Robert Standish
Estate of Ruth E. Dressel
Dietrich Apel
Maurice A. Long
Ralph DeMarco
Raymond Landgren
Tom Hamon
James W. Davis
Robert Cornell Harriss
Capt. John T. Trussell, Metropolitan Police Dept., Washington, DC
Walter Bud Fisher
Charles S. Taylor in memory of his father,
Charles L. Taylor
H. Dunkle
Paul Wahl
John H. Wesson
Mrs. Eric E. Anschütz
William A. Frederick
Jess C. Steinhauer
Golden State Arms Co.
Burton Brenner
Inter Ordnance
John Hayslip
Bruce Clark
Capt. Montgomery B. Graves
George Arbones
George B. Skidmore
Irv Benzion
J.H. Cosner
Ben Petree
James Beck Estate
B.Gen. Robert M. Gaynor, U.S. Army
James Brown
Malcolm J. MacCallum
Mrs. Francis A. Den Outer
Forest Brooks
Allan Cors
John Finn
Robert Joerg
Carl Hornberger
Lt. Gen. Willis D. Crittenberger, U.S. Army
Susan Nielsen in memory of Peter Nielsen
Frank D. Taylor
Jo Lynn Mohr in memory of her husband, Dr. Richard J. Mohr
Tom Caceci
Pacific Coast Stainless Steel German
WWII U-Boat Flare Pistol Collectors
Edgar Rice Burroughs
Edward A. Baldwin

ACKNOWLEDGEMENTS

Estate of George H. Measley, Jr.
Fletcher Williams
Harris Johnson
Doris J. Kramer, with the assistance of Bill Pace
Gail Brophy Barry and William S. Brophy III
Ernestine Bellmore
Fairchild Engine and Airplane Co.
Charles E. Hunt
Col. James C. Jewel, U.S. Army, Ret.
Estate of Terrence Hoffman
John Walter Moser
Gertrude B. Meyer
Phyllis Hall
John Fust in memory of Major General Donn R. Pepke
Jeannine M. Harvey
Arsenal, Inc.
Barrett Firearms Manufacturing Co.
Defense Procurement Manufacturing Services, Inc.
Bill J. Boyce
Bruce M. Wincentsen
Bernard Rieck
Donald Keefer
James Frisque
R. Hatcher
Rosco L. Slick
Otto Demplewolf
John Davis
NRA Technical Division
Jack Strader
John Pevear
Leo Manville
Raymond L. Sargent
Estate of Jane R. Taylor
Katherine Lee
Alan Aman

Dan W. Schlernitzauer
Francis Cason Estate
Merchantville Police Department on behalf of Glen Steely
Estate of Seymour R. Magee
Firearms International
Hämmerli
Lance Olson
William and Virginia Waterman Estate
Interarms
J. R. Cowman
Mr. Rogers
Edward Conrow
Eric R. England
Evelyn Baldwin in memory of Roy Ivan Baldwin
Francis W. Parker III
Thurman Randle
C. Suydam
David W. Arliss, Jr.
National Rifle Association of Great Britain
Wallace Beinfeld
Estate of Art Blatt
G. David Tubb
Richard Martin Ornburn
Anschütz
Jim Carmichel
Dieter Anschütz
Mrs. Frank C. Hoppe
Frank Lege III
Lt. Col. T.D. Smith, U.S.A.F.
Don Nissen
Drs. Lynn and Jerry Parson
Frank E. White
Norman George
Bill Jordan
Estate of David C. Ritchie
George A. Whitehead

Heckler & Koch, Inc.
W.O. Francis A. Higginson, U.S.M.C.
Bradley W. Taylor Collection
Richard Beckman
Family of Michael E. Garbarino
John DiStephano
Penguin Industries in memory of Frank A. Hoppe
W.T. Atkinson
Col. Theodore Shook, U.S. Army
Melvin Gordon
G. Norman Albree
John R. Lucas
Herbert T. Randall
Stockton Rush
Walter Howe
John W. Loosemore
Karel Michalek
Sommer & Ockenfuss
Halton Henderson
Harvey Leibowitz
Ralf E. Dieckmann
Robert Inness
Browning
Dr. William Saunders
James Keller
Noble
B. J. McCausey
H. W. Budd Schroeder
James Cassada, Jr.
Marlin
Armalite Corp.
Edward Hill
Gene's Sporting Center, Inc.
Kenneth L. Martin
Paul B. Miller
R.A. DeByle
W.T. Genetti
Allen Aman

Diamantis Demetriadis
E.P. Burlew
Estate of Harold W. Glassen
Louis F. Klusmeyer
Philip Y. Hahn, Sr.
Robert Hoelscher
Daniel Szatkowski
George H. McDaniel
Glen E. Liddy
Hy-Score
Merlin V. Fox
Sheridan Products, Inc.
Frank Wallace
Gen. Sydney Hinds, U.S. Army
Benjamin Air Rifle Co.
Elliott Jones
Thomas L. Stoughton
Ed Thompson
High Standard
John Kozina Estate
Leonard Cole
Milburn E. (Mel) Estes
Olan W. Christie
Sam Frank
Calico
Harry B. Andree, Jr.
Marlin Firearms Company
Constantine Vontsolos
Estate of Erle Stanley Gardner
Gordon Treharne in dedication to Jesse C. Hartzell
Sharps Arms Company
William A. Knight
Sandy Cushman
Weatherby
Michael Silbernagel
Richard Martin Ornburn
Gordon B. Rogers
Bradley W. Taylor Collection

ACKNOWLEDGEMENTS

Estate of Alan T. Schemm
Alabama State Trooper Jim Collins (ret.)
A.D. Bissel in the name of Mrs. Charles Newton
Orvis C. Hoffman
Sam Friedman
Eileen Cumming
William L. Davies
Estate of Bertha A. Baier
Harold Christensen
Herbert Cox
Col. Jeff Cooper
Gen. John S.D. Eisenhower
Josephine W. Snyder
Peter W. Duvall, Jr.
Robert L. Harper
Sheppard Kelly
Edward Finch
Mrs. Ernie Ford
Art Wheaton in honor of the efforts of Richard E. Heckert
Estate of Thomas Wang
Gabilondo y Cia
Joseph V. Falcon
George Whitehead
Robert E. Perry in memory of his mother, Elizabeth Jane Perry
Arthur B. Leech
James O. Adams
Mrs. John W. Hessian
Melissa Scott Smith
Savage Arms Company
Union of Shooting Societies of France
D. Phillips
Estate of Leslie P. Drew

LOANS OF COLLECTIONS

REMINGTON ARMS COMPANY
Arms and art from the Remington factory collection fill a gallery at the NRA National Sporting Arms Museum at Bass Pro Shops. They include factory prototypes, factory engraved pieces, historic milestones in firearms production, and factory cutaways, among others. The paintings in this book from the Remington collection are classic illustration of outdoor adventure and shooting, most of them prepared for advertising or outdoor magazine art in the early 20th century.

F.L. Starbuck Collection
    – U.S. Martial pistols, 1799-1898
Kurt House
    – Guns of old west outlaws & lawmen.
Frank and Nanita Pachmayr Foundation
    – Custom firearms
The Smithsonian Institution, National Museum of American History
Mike Papac – Hollywood guns
Al Frisch – Hollywood Guns & Props
Chris Hearn – Hollywood guns
Peter Dowd – Antique American arms
Paul Stefanye – Early Mauser prototypes

THANKS TO THE FOLLOWING WHO HAVE LOANED ONE OR MORE FIREARMS PICTURED IN THIS BOOK:

Johnny Morris
Wanenmacher Arms Show
U.S. Marshals Museum
Dick Burdick
Arnold Duke
Lt. Col. Brian Ross, USMC
Leroy Merz
Larry Jones
Dr. Frederick Novy
Daniel D'Allara
Lanny Bassham
Ellis Joubert
Michael Tatham
William Kelley
Anthony Sapienza
National Park Service Sagamore Hill Theodore Roosevelt Birthplace
Robert S. Jepson, Jr.
Aquaviva Productions
Beretta U.S.A.
Robert Bonaventure
David Stefanye, loaned in his memory by his wife and children
John Milius
Norman Hall
H. Wayne Sheets
Dr. Frederick G. Novy
Cletus Klein
Art Cook
Launi Meili
Valmore Forgett III
Robert H. Plimpton, Edith P. Reynolds Fleeman, William P. Reynolds, and Katie P. Reynolds
Norman B. Tomlinson Collection courtesy of the Paterson Museum
Woody Matthews
Micky Reilly Collection
Jacob Yost
Logan Reed
Bill Miller
David W Bunn
Director of Civilian Marksmanship
Norm White
Tom Bass
Jessica Sparks
Jason Hill
Doug Kelley
Philip Schreier
Doug Wicklund
Jim Supica
Anonymous

THANKS TO THE FOLLOWING FOR SPONSORSHIP OF MAJOR GALLERIES IN THE MUSEUM:

Estate of Robert E. Petersen
Eldon J. and Edith W. Owens
Estate of Doc J. Thurston III
Beretta USA Corporation and Benelli USA Corporation
Dr. William L. and Collette N. Roberts
Friends of Charlton Heston
William B. Ruger
Col. Wallace Weber

INDEX

SYMBOLS

2nd U.S. Dragoons	55
5.56mm NATO	19
5mm Velo-dog	99
6mm XC	230
9mm Luger (or 9mm Parabellum)	16
13.2mm projectile	167
.38 Dardick Tround	257
.44 Automag caliber	261
.44 Magnum	20
.44 rimfire	12
.45 ACP (Automatic Colt Pistol)	17
.223 Remington	19
.303 British	275
.357 Magnum cartridge	20
.454 Casull	262
.458 Win Mag	275
.500 Magnum	262
.600 H&H Nitro Express	275
.700 H&H Nitro Express	275
1768 Flintlock Cavalry Carbine - .80 caliber	35
1769 Short Land Pattern Musket	36
1777 Short Land Pattern Flintlock Musket	35
1849 Pocket Model	11
1851 Navy Model	11
1860 Army Model	11

A

Abbott, C & G, all metal pistol	75
Adams Patent Small Arms Co. Percussion Revolver	89
Adolph, Fred R. Hammerless Double Rifle	141
African Rifles, general	143
Air Guns, general	244
AK74	19, 199, 207
AK47S Polytech/KFS Rifle	203
Alexander Henry Howdah Pistol	142
Allen & Thurber Double-Barrel Single-Trigger Pistol	62
Allen & Wheelock Double-Action Bar Hammer Pistol	75
Allen & Wheelock Sidehammer Rimfire Single-Action Revolver, 2nd Model	85
Amberg Arsenal German Model 71/84 Bolt-Action	152
American Arms Derringer .22/32 rimfire	101
American Arms New Safety Hammerless Revolver	99
American Flintlock Long Rifle	39
American Long Rifle	43
American Masters Series Custom Mauser Rifle	272
American Rifleman Magazine	4, 247
America's Rifle Challenge	300
AMT Backup II Semi-Automatic Pistol	264
An Age of Elegance, general	142
Anschütz Model 54 Super Match Bolt-Action Rifle	231
Anschütz Model 380 Air Gun	231
Anschütz Model 1811 Bolt-Action Rifle	231
Anschütz Model 1813 Bolt-Action Rifle	227
Anschütz Model 1827 Fortner Biathlon Rifle	231
Anschütz Woodchucker Bolt-Action Rifle	242
AR-15	19
Arcadia Machine Tool AutoMag Semi-Auto Pistol	261
Argentine Mannlicher Model 1905 Semi-Auto Pistol	168
Armalite AR-7 Explorer Semi-Automatic Rifle	242
Armalite AR-10 Semi-Automatic Rifle	201
Armalite Golden Gun Semi-Automatic Shotgun	256
Armee Universal Gewehr (AUG)	266
Armel, Detective Vicky	215
Ashton Underhammer Percussion Pistol - .28 caliber	75
Askins, Col. Charles	239
assault rifle, general	19
Aston Model 1842 Army - .54 caliber	78
Atlas Single-Shot Air Rifle	246
Atlas Single-Shot Rifle	242
Austrian Cape Gun - 16 gauge/6.5mm rimmed	146
Austrian Percussion Pistol - .70 caliber	89
Austrian Steyr Daimler Puch A.G. Model 1907 Roth Steyr Semi-Automatic Pistol	168
Austrian Steyr Oester Waffenfabrik Ges. Model 1909 Semi-Automatic Pistol - 7.65mm	169
Austrian Tube-Primed Percussion Military Pistol	56
Austrian Waffenfabrik Steyr Model 1895 Bolt-Action Carbine - 8x57mm	166
Austrian Waffenfabrik Steyr Steyr-Mannlicher Model 1890 Bolt-Action Rifle	169
Austrian Werder Single-Shot Pistol - 11mm Werder	168
Austro-Hungarian Model 1867 Werndl Rifle	166
avtomat kalashnikova	199

B

Ballard action	221
Ballard No. 5 Pacific Falling Block Single-Shot Rifle	118
Banks, Texas Ranger Captain Jay	218
Barclay, D.	4
Bardem, Javier	251
Barnett English Model 1853 Enfield Percussion Musket	89
Barnett Northwest Trade Gun - 20 gauge	122
Barrett Light .50	209
Barrett M82A1 Semi-Automatic Sniper Rifle	209
Barrett/Remington XP-100 Rail Gun	239
Bassham, Lanny	234
Bass Pro Shops	5, 72, 320
Belgian Anciens Etablissements Pieper Model 1908 Bergmann-Bayard Semi-Automatic Pistol	169
Belgian Brevet Counet Revolver - 11mm centerfire	164
Belgian British Bulldog Revolver - .38 S&W	99
Belgian Bulldog Revolver - .32 cartridge	99
Belgian Charles Clement 1910 Semi-Automatic Pistol	168
Belgian Hopkins & Allen Contract Mauser Model 1889 Bolt-Action Rifle - 7.65mm Mauser	162
Belgian Montenegrin Single-Action Revolver	163
Belgian Nagant Brevet Revolver - 7.5mm Nagant	164
Belgian Pinfire Revolver - 7mm pinfire	67
Belgian Revolver - .45 caliber	96
Belgian Screw-barrel Percussion Pistol - .46 caliber	75
belt buckle pistol	184
Benelli Model 90	20
Benelli Nova Pump Shotgun	282
Benjamin Model 30/30 Carbine	247
Benjamin Model 362 CO2 Carbine	246
Bennett & Haviland Many-Chambered Revolving Percussion Rifle - .40 caliber	61
Bentley English Percussion Plains Rifle - .44 caliber	77
Berdon, A.E.	223
Beretta, Bartolomeo	26
Beretta BM-59 Semi-Automatic Rifle	268
Beretta, Giovanni, Italian Folding Snaphaunce Pistol	26
Beretta Model 92	20
Beretta Model 92 SB Texas Ranger-Issue Pistol - 9mm	214
Beretta Model 1934 Semi-Automatic Pistol - 9mm Kurz	194
Beretta Tipo Olimpionico Semi-Automatic Pistol	226
Beretta XM9 Semi-Automatic Pistol - 9mm	207
Bergmann M18 submachine gun	18
Berliner-Luebecker Maschinenfabrik Gewehr 41	187
Billy the Kid	92
Birmingham Small Arms (BSA)	196
Black Magic finish	177
Blade-barrel Pinfire Revolver	106
Blake Bolt-Action Repeating Rifle - .30-40 Krag	154
blow-forward recoil system	169
Blunderbuss, general	40
Blunderbuss, Oval Bore Percussion	40
Blunderbuss, Pape & Christian Flintlock - .80 caliber	40
Blunderbuss Pistol, Alexander Wilson British Muzzleloading Flintlock, 1.00 caliber	40
Blunderbuss, T. Henshaw British Sea Service Flintlock	40
Bolt-Action Rifles, general	136, 137
Bonaparte, Napoleon, Flintlock Double Fowler - 20 gauge	31
Book of Eli	250
Borchardt C-93 Semi-Automatic Pistol - 7.65x25	134
Bouton British Militia Pattern 1760 Light Infantry Flintlock Carbine - .75 caliber	36
Brackley Double-Barrel Tap-action Flintlock Pistol	58
Breechloaders, general	54
breechloading system	10
Bresnahan, Major General Richard Anthony	204
Bridgeport Firearms Co. Prototype P66 Pistol	259
British Ballester-Molina British Contract Pistol	180
British B.S.A./Holland & Holland No. 4 Mk I (T) Bolt-Action Sniper Rifle - .303 British	181
British BSA Sparkbrook Model 1893 Mk II Magazine Lee-Metford Bolt-Action Rifle - .303 British	161
British East India Co. Pattern Flintlock Carbine	49
British Enfield No. 1 Mk VI Revolver - .455 Webley	180
British Enfield No. 2 Mk I Revolver - .38 S&W	180
British Enfield No. 3 Mk I Bolt-Action Rifle - .303 Brit.	161
British Enfield No. 5 Mk I Bolt-Action Jungle Carbine with No. 5 Mk I Bayonet - .303 British	178
British Enfield SMLE Mk III Bolt-Action Rifle	178
British Farquhar-Hill Model 1909 Experimental Semi-Automatic Rifle - .303 British	160
British Lee Metford bolt-action	15
British Long Land Pattern Brown Bess Musket	38
British Model 1838 Land Pattern Percussion Musket	77
British P. Webley & Sons Pryse Revolver - .455 Webley	163
British Short Land Pattern Second Model Brown Bess	38
British SMLE Mk III Bolt-Action Rifle - .303 British	161
British Webley Mk I Revolver - .455 Webley	163
British Webley Mk IV Revolver - .455 Webley	163
British Webley Mk VI Revolver - .455 Webley	163
British Webley No. 1 Mk 1 Flare Pistol - 26mm	163
British Webley & Scott Model 1912 Mk I Semi-Automatic Pistol - .455 W&S Self-Loader	163
Brooklyn Arms Company Slocum Revolver - .32 rimfire	99
Brophy .50 BMG Korea Sniper Rifle	200
Brown, Arlayne	238
Brown Bess	9, 35
Brownell Museum of the Southwest	5, 320
Browning Auto-5 Light Twelve Semi-Auto Shotgun	282
Browning B-80 Semi-Automatic Shotgun	282
Browning BAR Semi-Automatic Rifle	18, 268
Browning BBR Bolt-Action Rifle	270
Browning BL-22 Rifle	242, 274
Browning Broadway Trap Presentation 3 Superposed	278
Browning Euromarket Superposed Shotgun	280
Browning FN High Power Bolt-Action Rifle	272
Browning Grade 1 Semi-Automatic Takedown Rifle	139
Browning High Power	20
Browning, John Moses	16, 138
Browning Model 78 Single-Shot Rifle	276
Browning Model 1878 Standard Single-Shot Rifle	139
Browning .50-caliber machine gun	18
Browning T-Bolt T-2 Straight-Pull Bolt-Action Rifle	243
Brugsmueller Drilling - 16x16 gauge & 9mm	119
BSA Sten Mark II Submachine Gun	196
B. Tyler Henry	66
Buffalo Bill Cody	92

INDEX

Buffalo Bills Wild West Show	126
Burgess Slide-Action Folding Gun - 12 gauge	121
Burnside 5th Model Percussion Carbine	297
Burnside, Major General Ambrose E.	297
Burroughs, Edgar Rice	195
Bushmaster Semi-Automatic Pistol	267
Bush, President George H. W.	284
Butterfield Army Model Percussion Revolver	85

C

Calamity Jane	92
Calico Systems M-951 Semi-Automatic Carbine	267
Callahan, Inspector Harry	251
Camp Atterbury	224
Camp Perry	224, 235
Camp Perry National Matches	229
Canadian Ross Model 1905 Straight-Pull Rifle	178
Canadian Ross Rifle Co. Model 1905 Straight-Pull Rifle	161
Canadian Ross Rifle Co. Model 1910 Straight-Pull Rifle	161
Cane guns	105
Carl Gustafs Stads Gevarsfaktori Model 96 Sniper Bolt-Action Rifle with Telescopic Sight - 6.5mm	187
Carl Gustafs Stads Gevarsfaktori Swedish Model 1894 Mauser Bolt-Action Carbine - 6.5mm Swedish	152
Carl Gustafs Stads Gevarsfaktori Swedish Model 1896 Mauser Bolt-Action Rifle - 6.5x55mm	153
Carmichel, Jim	239
Caron French Single-Action Pinfire Revolver	89
Cartridge Conversions	90
Carver, Frank "Deadshot Doc"	126
Cash, Johnny	240
Caswell Trophy	228
Cemetery gun	53
Centerfire cartridge, general	67
Central and Northside Railroad	222
Ceskoslovenska Zbrojovka Brno Czech Copy of Kar 98K Bolt-Action Rifle - 7mm Mauser	197
Ceskoslovenska Zbrojovka Brno Model 98/29 Persian Contract Bolt-Action Rifle - 8mm Mauser	197
CETME Spanish Model 58 Semi-Automatic Rifle	269
Chameleon Czechoslovakian Epoxy Revolver	259
Champlin Firearms Left-Hand Bolt-Action Rifle	227
Charles Daly Side-by-Side Shotgun - 10 gauge	149
Charleville French Model 1774 Flintlock Musket	39
Charleville Percussion Conversion Musket - .70 caliber	88
Charter Arms Undercover Revolver, s/n 1	263
Chassepot single-shot rifle	15
Chatelerault French Model 1874 Gras Bolt-Action	152
Chiang Kai-Shek Short Model Bolt-Action Rifle	203
Chief's Grade Trade Gun	122
Chinese Chiang Kai-Shek Short Model Mauser-Pattern Bolt-Action Rifle - 8mm Mauser	191
Chinese Liu Prototype Semi-Automatic Rifle - 7.92mm	173
Chinese Mukden Arsenal Manchurian Mauser 98	197
Chinese SKS Type 56 Semi-Automatic Carbine	202
Civilian Marksmanship Program	296
Cleveland, Grover	145
Cochran Revolving Turret Rifle - .45 caliber	64
Cogswell & Harrison British Side-by-Side Shotgun	146
Collette System Gravity Feed Repeater - 11mm	102
Collier, Elisha	62
Colt 3rd Model Derringer - .41 rimfire	101
Colt .44 Walker Model	73
Colt Agent Revolver	262
Colt AR15A3 Tactical Semi-Automatic Carbine	217
Colt AR-15 Automatic Rifle	201
Colt AR-15 Semi-Automatic Rifle	266
Colt Bisley Flat-top Target Model - .32-20	92
Colt-Burgess Lever-action Rifle - .44-40	114
Colt Camp Perry Double-Action Single-Shot Pistol	223
Colt Delta Elite Semi-Automatic Pistol	264
Colt Dragoon Revolving Rifle - .44 caliber	77
Colt First and Second Model derringers	100
Colt First Model Dragoon Revolver - .44 caliber	73
Colt Frontier Six Shooter - .44-40	92
Colt Gatling Gun - .30-40 Krag	151
Colt Government Model Semi-Automatic Pistol	225
Colt House Model Revolver - .41 rimfire	97
Colt Lightning Rifle	126
Colt Lightning Slide-Action Rifle, Large Frame - .38-55	114
Colt Lightning Slide-Action Rifle, Medium Frame	114
Colt Lightning Slide-Action Rifle, Small Frame	114
Colt M1921 Thompson Submachine Gun	217
Colt Mark IV Series 70 Gold Cup National Match Pistol	225
Colt Marshal - .38 Special	214
Colt Marshal Model Revolver	262
Colt Model 1848 Baby Dragoon Revolver - .31 caliber	73
Colt Model 1849 Pocket Percussion Revolver - .31 caliber	73
Colt Model 1849 Pocket Revolver	73
Colt Model 1851 Percussion Revolvers - .36 caliber	83
Colt Model 1855 Percussion Revolving Carbine	82
Colt Model 1855 Revolving Percussion Military Rifle	79
Colt Model 1855 Root Sidehammer Pocket Percussion Revolver, Model 2 - .28 caliber	85
Colt Model 1860 Percussion Revolver - .44 caliber	83
Colt Model 1861 Navy gunsmith conversion - .38 rimfire	90
Colt Model 1861 Navy Percussion Revolver - .36 caliber	84
Colt Model 1871-1872 Open-Top Revolver - .44 Henry	92
Colt Model 1877 Double Action Revolver	93
Colt Model 1878 Double Action Revolver	93
Colt Model 1883 Shotgun - 12 gauge	121
Colt Model 1892 New Army Revolver - .38 Colt	155
Colt Model 1900 Automatic	17
Colt Model 1902 Military Semi-Automatic Pistol	138
Colt Model 1902 Sporting Semi-Automatic Pistol	138
Colt Model 1903 Hammerless Type III Pocket Semi-Automatic Pistol	138
Colt Model 1905 .45 Semi-Automatic Pistol	138
Colt Model 1905 Machine Gun, aka "Potato Digger"	151
Colt Model 1907 - .45 ACP	155
Colt Model 1911A1 National Match Pistol	224
Colt Model 1911 Semi-Automatic Pistol	223, 224
Colt Model 1914 Machine Gun	157
Colt New Frontier Revolver	285
Colt New Line Revolvers	97
Colt New Police	14
Colt New Service Model Revolver	263
Colt Open-Top Pocket Model - .22 rimfire	97
Colt Paterson	10
Colt Paterson Holster Model No. 5 Revolver - .36 caliber	63
Colt Paterson Revolvers	73
Colt Pocket Model factory conversion - .38 rimfire	90
Colt Pocket Navy Model factory conversion	90
Colt Police Positive Special - .32-20	214
Colt Police Positive Special Revolver	263
Colt Prototype Pistols	258
Colt Python	265
Colt SAA U.S. Military "Artillery" Model - .45 Colt	92
Colt SAA U.S. Military "Cavalry" Model - .45 Colt	92
Colt, Samuel	10, 63
Colt-Sauer Bolt-Action Rifle	270
Colt/Sharps Falling Block Sporting Rifle	276
Colt "Sheriff's Model" SAA - .38-40	92
Colt Single Action Army	12, 13, 92
Colt Single Action Army Revolver - .45 Colt	151, 155
Colt Sporter Target Model AR-15 Semi-Automatic Rifle	230
Colt Third Model English Dragoon Percussion Revolver	73
Colt Trooper Revolver	263
Colt U.S. Model 1902 Army Revolver - .45 Colt	155
Colt Walker Revolver - .44 caliber	63
Colt Woodsman Semi-Automatic Pistol	224
Columbus Firearms Manufacturing Company Confederate Revolver - .36 caliber	86
Committee of Safety Flintlock Musket - .80 caliber	39
Committee of Safety Musket - .78 caliber	38
Committee of Safety Musket - .80 caliber	36
Compact Off-Duty Police	262
Competitive Shooting Division	300
Coney Island Shooting Gallery	241
Connecticut Arms Hammond Bulldog - .44 rimfire	100
Continental Arms Co. Pepperbox	102
Cook, Art	233
Coonan Arms, Inc. .357 Magnum Semi-Automatic	262
Cooper, James Fenimore	42
Cooper Patent English Pepperbox Pistol - .44 caliber	75
COP Four-Barrel Derringer	262
Creedmoor	222
Critchfield, Ammon B.	224
Crosman Company	284
Crosman CO2 Rifle	247
Crosman Experimental Air Rifle	246
Crosman Hahn 45 Single-Action Air Pistol	245
Crosman M1 Carbine Air Rifle	246
Crosman Marksman BB Pistol	245
Crosman Model 116 Air Pistol	245
Crosman Model 130 Single-Shot Air Pistol	245
Crosman Model 140 Single-Shot Air Rifle	247
Crosman Model 150 CO2 Pistol	245
Crosman Model 700 Pellmaster Air Rifle	246
Crosman Powermaster 760 Air Rifle	247
Crosman Single-Action 6 CO2 Pistol	245
Crosman V-350 Air Rifle	246
Crown City/Kart .22 Conversion Pistol	223
C.S.A. Fayetteville Armory Percussion Rifle-Musket	88
C.S.A. Richmond Arsenal Percussion Rifle-Musket	88
C.S. Shattuck Single-Action Revolver	99
Cugir Arsenal SAR-2 semi-automatic rifle 5.45x39mm	207
Custer, Gen. George Armstrong	92
Czech VZ-52 Semi-Automatic Carbine - 7.62mm x 45	198
Czech VZ54 Sniper Bolt-Action Rifle - 7.62x54R	202
CZ Model 1924 Semi-Automatic Pistol - 9mm Kurz	193

D

Dagger Pistol - .48 caliber	75
Daisy Buck Jones Special BB Gun	246
Daisy-Heddon V/L Single-Shot Caseless Cartridge Rifle	256
Daisy Manufacturing Company	244
Daisy Model 25 Slide-Action Air Rifle	246, 247
Daisy Model 99 Lever-Action Air Rifle	247
Daisy Model 104 Double-Barrel Air Gun	246
Daisy Model 118 Target Special Air Pistol	245
Daisy Model 188 Air Pistol	245
Daisy Model 300 CO2 Rifle	246
Daisy Model 917 Powerline Air Rifle	247
Daisy Model 1894 Lever-Matic Repeating Air Rifle	247
Daisy Model 2201 Bolt-Action Single-Shot Rifle	242
Daisy NRA Centennial Commemorative Peacemaker Repeating Air Pistol	245
Daisy Red Ryder No. 111 Model 40 Lever-Action	247
D'Allara, Sgt. John	215

INDEX

Danish Model 1889 Krag-Jorgensen Carbine - 8mm 152
Danish Rifle Syndicate Schouboe Semi-Auto 259
Dan Wesson Model 12 Revolver 261
Dan Wesson Model 15 Revolver 262
Danzig Arsenal German Gewehr 98 Bolt-Action Rifle 154
Darby, Kim 250
Dardick Series 1500 Pistol 257
Darne Sliding Breech Side-by-Side Shotgun 254
da Vinci, Leonardo 24
Day's Patent Truncheon Pistol 106
de Coubertin, Baron Pierre 232
De La Sota, Juan Manuel 34
Depfer, Samuel German Cheek-Stock Doglock Musket 27
Deringer, Henry 9, 74
Deringer Model 1842 Navy - .54 caliber 78
Derringers 74, 100
Detroit Rifle Co. No. 11 Rifle 242
Diana German Model No. 1 Air Pistol 245
Die Hard 249
Director of Civilian Marksmanship 223
Dirty Harry 20, 251
doglock flintlock 27
Dolne "Apache" 7.6mm 103
Dornaus and Dixon Bren Ten Semi-Automatic Pistol 259
Double-Barrel Percussion Pistol - .58 caliber 75
Double rifles, general 275
DPMS M160 Selective-Fire Rifle - 5.56mm 208
Drepperd Percussion Long Rifle - .54 caliber 70
Dreyse needle gun 10
drillings, general 276
Dubiel Classic Sporter Rifles 273
Duckfoot pistols 59
Duke of York Flintlock Fowler 30
Dunlap Custom Bolt-Action Rifle 227
Dutch Musket - .79 caliber 38
DWM Model 1902 Luger Semi-Automatic Carbine 146
DWM P.08 Luger Semi-Automatic Pistol - 9mm 185

E

Eagle, Chief Ed 128
E. Allen & Co. Vest Pocket Derringer - .22 rimfire 101
Eastwood, Clint 250, 251
Eclipse Single-Shot Pistol - .22 rimfire 101
Eddie Eagle GunSafe 300
Eduard Kettner Koln-Suhler German Gewehr-Fabrik Drilling 279
Edwinson, Green and Sons Triple Barrel Shotgun 119
Egg English Percussion Shotgun 76
eGunner.com 299
Eisenhower, General Dwight D. 285
Eisenhower, Mamie 4
Elephant Guns, general 275
Elgin Cutlass Pistol - .53 cal. 78
Eller, Walton 232
Emmons, Matthew 232
Enfield Model 1884 Revolver - .476 Enfield 96
English Barnett Model 1853 Rifle - .58 Berdan 124
English Double-Action Bar-Hammer Percussion Revolver - .44 caliber 89
English Enfield Snider Rotating Block Conversion Rifle 124
English Matchlock Musket 22
English Saw-Handle Single-Shot Percussion Pistol 75
Engraving 129
Eprouvettes 53
E. Remington & Sons Side-by-Side Hammer Shotgun 120
Essex Arms M1911 Race Gun 224
European Bar Magazine Harmonica Pistol - 9mm pinfire 61
European Hand Cannon 22
Evans Lever-Action Repeating Carbine - .44 Evans 114
Evans Pocket Percussion Pistol - .44 caliber 75

F

Fabbrica d'Armi Pietro Beretta S.p.A 26
Fabrica Nacional de Arms Mauser Model 1936 Bolt-Action Rifle - 7mm Mauser 197
Fabrica Nacional de Arms Mexican Model 1910 Mauser Bolt-Action Rifle - 7mm 153
Fabrica Reale Italian Flintlock Pistol - .69 caliber 28
Fabrique Nationale 138
Fabrique Nationale Belgian Mauser Model 1916 Bolt-Action Carbine - 7.65mm Mauser 154
Fabrique Nationale/Browning P-35 Hi-Power Semi-Automatic Pistol - 9mm Parabellum 192
Fabrique Nationale Contract Model 1924/30 Bolt-Action Rifle - 7mm Mauser 197
Fabrique Nationale FAL Semi-Automatic Rifle 208
Fabrique Nationale GP Competition pistol 224
Fabrique Nationale/Inglis P-35 Hi-Power Pistol 180
Fabrique Nationale Model 1924/30 Bolt-Action Rifle 197
Fabrique Nationale Model FN-49 Semi-Automatic 198
Farr, George 229
F. B. Radom WZ-29 Bolt-Action Short Rifle 187
Feinwerkbau Model 65 Air Pistol 225
Ferdi Furwith Austrian Tube-Lock Percussion Rifle 56
Finnish Mosin Nagant Model 27 Bolt-Action Rifle 179
Fisher, Morris 232
Fjestad, S. P. 5
Flaig Vierling Combination Gun 276
flintlock 7, 8, 34
Flintlock .53 caliber dueling pistols 39
Flintlock Double Rifle, John Palm #192 Swivel-Breech 44
Flintlock Fowler - .72 caliber 43
Flintlock Fowler - .75 caliber 34
Flintlock Fusil - .61 caliber 34
Flintlock Fusil - .65 caliber 34
Flintlock Fusil, Swedish - .63 caliber 35
Flintlock Jaeger Rifle - .52 caliber 42
Flintlock Long Rifle, Jacob Albright - .50 caliber 44
Flintlock Long Rifle, John Hagy - .52 caliber 47
Flintlock Long Rifle, Mathias Miller - .50 caliber 44
Flintlock Musket, Dutch English Club Butt - .65 caliber 42
Flintlock Musket, French/Persian Repeating - .65 caliber 61
Flintlock Musket, Spanish Model 1803 - .69 caliber 33
Flintlock Pistol, Bissell Scottish Metal Frame - .56 caliber 41
Flintlock Pistol, Royet French - .59 caliber 41
Flintlock Pistols, general 41
Flintlock Rifle, John Miles - .52 caliber 47
Flintlock Rifle, J.P. Beck/Wolfgang Hagy - .58 caliber 47
Flintlock Rifle, Ketland & Allport - .60 caliber 34
Flintlock Rifle, Lancaster - .60 caliber 46
Flintlock Rifle, Melchior Fordney - .54 caliber 47
Flintlock Rifle, P. Quattlebuw - .36 caliber 46
flintlock sword pistols 52
Flobert Belgian Model 5 Rifle 240
Flobert, Nicolas 67
folding knife pistols 104
Ford Brothers Percussion Target Rifle 219
Ford, Tennessee Ernie 239
Forehand & Wadsworth Model 1890 Hammerless Top-Break Double-Action Pocket Revolver - .38 S&W 97
Forehand & Wadsworth Swamp Angel - .41 rimfire 97
Forsyth, Dr. Alexander 57
Forsyth Scent-bottle Priming Fowler 56
Foss, Joe 183
Four-Barrel Flintlock Pistol - .36 caliber 58
Frankenau Patent Purse Gun 102
Frank Wesson No. 2 Mid-Range Underlever Falling-Block Single-Shot Rifle 222
Frank Wesson Superposed - .41 rimfire 101
Franz Jager Herold Three-Barrel Shotgun - 16 gauge 149
Freedom Arms Model 83 Premier-Grade Revolver 262
French Berthier Model 1907/15 Bolt-Action Rifle 162
French Berthier Model 1916/27 Bolt-Action Carbine 162
French Charleville Musket 9
French Chassepot Model 1866 rifle - 11mm 152
French Lebel Model 1907/15 Bolt-Action Rifle - 7.5mm 178
French Lebel Model 1907-15 Bolt-Action Rifle 162
French MAS 1949 Semi-Automatic Rifle - 7.5mm M29 203
French MAS 1936 Bolt-Action Rifle - 7.5mm M29 178
French MAS 1938 Submachine Gun - 7.65mm 203
French Model 1746 Charleville Musket - .69 caliber 38
French Model 1766 Charleville Musket - .69 caliber 38
French Model 1886/93 Presentation-Grade Rifle 297
French St. Etienne French Model 1917 Rifle 162
French St. Etienne French Nagant Model 1892 Double-Action Ordnance Revolver - 8mm 180
French St. Etienne MAS 1936 Bolt-Action Rifle 203
French St. Etienne Model 1886/93 (R-35) Carbine 178
French St. Etienne Model 1892 Service Revolver 164
French Sutterlin Lipmann & Co. St. Etienne Model 1873 Revolver - 11mm French Service 164
French Tulle Model 1886/93 Lebel Bolt-Action Rifle 162
Freres Superposed Charge Shotgun. 12 gauge 60
Freund Sharps Rifles 117
frizzen 7
Frye, Tom 238
Ft. Sumter 80
funfling 275
Fusil 34

G

Gage, General Thomas 37
Gaither, Lt. General Ridgely 204
Galand Revolver - .38 Galand 96
Gal, Uziel 18
Garand, John C. 172
Garand Semi-Automatic Rifle 172
Garbarino, Master Police Officer Michael E. 215
Gardone Fascist Youth Bolt-Action Carbine 188
Gardone Model 1891 Mannlicher Carcano Rifle 188
Garrett Colt Model 1877 Double Action 91
Gatling Gun 17, 151
Gatling Gun Model 1883 250
Gaulois 8mm cigarette case pistol 103
General Officer Pistols, general 204
German 1888 Commission rifle 15
German Ball-Butt Dag Wheellock Pistol - .51 caliber 29
German Bergmann Model 1896 Semi-Automatic Pistol 168
German Crank-Action Air Rifle 247
German CS CGH Suhl Single-Action Model 1883 Commission Reichsrevolver 167
German Deutsche Waffen & Munitions Fabriken P.04 Naval Luger Semi-Automatic Pistol - 9mm Parabellum 169
German Deutsche Waffen und Munitionsfabriken Model 1914 Artillery Luger Semi-Automatic Pistol 168
German Deutsche Waffen und Munitionsfabriken Model 1917 Artillery Luger Semi-Automatic Pistol 165
German Dreyse Model 1879 Commission Single-Action Reichsrevolver - 10.6mm German Service 167

INDEX

German Erfurt Arsenal German Karabiner 98a Bolt-Action Carbine - 8mm Mauser	166
German Erfurt Arsenal Model 1891 Commission Bolt-Action Carbine - 8mm Mauser	166
German Erfurt Luger LP-08 Artillery Pistol	165
German Flare Pistol - 26mm	195
German Gebruder Mauser und Cie Model 1879 Double-Action Reichsrevolver - 10.6mm German Service	167
German Jager Waffenfabrik Semi-Automatic Pistol	169
German J.P. Sauer & Sohn Gew98 Sniper Rifle - 8mm	165
German Langenhan FL Selbstlader Pistol - 7.65mm	169
German Lever-Action Single-Shot Air Rifle	247
German Matchlock Musket	23
German Mauser (byf) K98k Sniper Rifle - 8mm Mauser	185
German Mauser G41 (m) rifle - 8mm	185
German Mauser Gew 98 Bolt-Action Sniper Rifle	166
German Mauser Model 1888 Commission Bolt-Action	165
German Mauser Model 1896 Broomhandle Export Semi-Automatic Pistol - 9mm Mauser	168
German Mauser Model 1896 Broomhandle Semi-Automatic Pistol - 7.63 Mauser	168
German Mauser Model 1896 Broomhandle Semi-Automatic Pistol - 9mm Mauser	169
German Mauser Model 1896 Broomhandle Semi-Automatic Pistol - .30 Mauser	167
German Mauser Model 1896 Broomhandle Semi-Automatic Pistol with shoulder stock - 7.63 Mauser	169
German Mauser Waffen Munitionsfabrik Single-Shot Bolt-Action Anti-Tank Rifle - 13mm	167
U.S. M3 submachine gun	18
German Multi-shot Wheellock/matchlock	25
German Schwarzlose Gmbh Model 1908 Pistol	169
German Velo-Dog Revolver - 5mm Velo-Dog	99
German Waffenwerke Oberspree Kornbusch Gew98 Bolt-Action Rifle - 8mm Mauser	165
German Zimmershutzen Rifle	220
Gevaerfabriken Kjobenhaven Danish Model 1899 Krag-Jorgensen Bolt-Action Rifle - .30-40 Krag	153
Girardoni, Bartolomeo	68
Girardoni Repeating Air Rifle - .46 caliber	68
G. Knaak German Vierling Combination Gun	148
Glisenti Model 1910 Semi-Automatic Pistol	194
Glock, Gaston	20, 261
Glock Model 17	261
Glock Model 17 Semi-Automatic Pistol	214
Grant Hammond .45 ACP	156
Grant Hammond Serial Number 1 - .45 ACP	156
Gran Torino	251
Grapeshot revolver	87
Gray, Jamie Lynn	232
Great American Outdoor show	301
Griffin English Breechloading Flintlock Musket	54
Griffin & Howe Custom Rifle	272
Grifnee, Phillipe	275
Griswold and Gunnison Navy Percussion Revolver -	86
Gunga Din	250
gunpowder	6
Gun Stories television show	320
Gyro Jet	257

H

Hahn Model 45 Single-Action CO2 Pistol	245
Half-Stock Percussion Rifle - .44 caliber	71
Hall, John H.	55
Hall North system	10
Hall Revolving Rifle - .38 caliber	64
Hall's Breechloader	55
Hamilton, Clarence	244
Hamilton No. 27 Single-Shot Rifle	242
Hämmerli Master Air Pistol	226
Hämmerli Model 103 Free Pistol	225
Hämmerli Model 150 Single-Shot Free Pistol	225
Hämmerli Model 200 Olympia Semi-Automatic Pistol	226
Hämmerli Model 208 Standard Semi-Automatic Pistol	225
Hämmerli Single Shot Air Pistol	225
Hancock, Vincent	232
Hand Cannon, general	22
Hand Firing Mechanism Mk II	184
Hardin Colt Model 1877 Double Action	91
Harmon, Sheriff "Bus"	214
Harrington & Richardson 1920 Single-Shot Shotgun	240
Harrington & Richardson Pocket Revolver	97
Harrington & Richardson Model USRA Target Pistol	223
Harrington & Richardson T48 Selective Fire Rifle	208
Harrington & Richardson Young America Revolver	99
Harris, General Hugh Pate	204
Hartliep, Neil	278
Hartmann and Weiss takedown bolt-action rifle	273
Hatcher, Julian	239
Hawken, Christian Sr.	69
Hawken Percussion Plains Rifle - .50 caliber	71
Hawken Percussion Rifle - .43 caliber	70
Hawken Rifle, general	69
Healthways Model 175 Plainsman CO2 Pistol	245
Heckler & Koch Mark 23 Offensive Handgun System	208
Heckler & Koch Model 91 Semi-Automatic Rifle	269
Heckler & Koch Model 300 Semi-Automatic Rifle	269
Heckler & Koch Model 770 Semi-Automatic Rifle	268
Heckler & Koch Model PSP Semi-Automatic Pistol	264
Heckler & Koch MP-5 9mm submachine gun	18
Heckler & Koch MP5A3 Submachine Gun	216
Heineman Prototype Semi-Automatic Carbine	254
Helfricht, Cuno	130
Henry Lever-Action Rifle by New Haven Arms Co.	108
Henry M. Kolb Baby Hammerless Revolver - .22 rimfire	99
Henry Repeating Arms Golden Boy Lever-Action Rifle	274
Henry Repeating Rifle	66, 67
Herbert, Al	263
Herman English Double-Action Percussion Revolver	89
Hession Musket - .79 caliber	38
Hession U.S. Springfield Model 1903 Bolt-Action Rifle	182
Heston, Charlton	295
Hickock, Wild Bill	127
High Standard Military Model 106 Pistol	224
High Standard Model 10B Semi-Auto Tactical Shotgun	216
High Standard Model D-100 Over/Under Derringer	264
High Standard Trophy Semi-Automatic Pistol	223
Holland & Holland .700 Nitro Express	275
Holland & Holland Maharaja Grade Double Rifle	142
Holland & Holland Royal Ejector Double Rifle	143
Hollis English Percussion Pistols - .50 caliber	75
Hollywood Guns, general	248
Hollywood Guns Gallery	5
Hooker, Marshal Ralph	128
Hopkins & Allen Falling Block Rifle	240
Hopkins & Allen Forehand Single-Shot Shotgun	279
Hopkins & Allen Junior Repeater Rifle	242
Hopkins & Allen Junior Rifle	242
Hopkins & Allen Vest Pocket Derringer - .22 rimfire	100
Hopkins & Allen XL No. 8 Single Action Revolver	96
Harrington & Richardson Pocket Revolver	
H. Sauer German Percussion Target Rifle	219
H. Stotzer Single-Shot Target Pistol	225
Hungarian Fegyvergyar Model 37 Pistol - 7.65mm	193
Hungarian Mosin Nagant Model 1891/30 Bolt-Action	202
H. V. Perry Three-Barrel Percussion Rifle - .45 caliber	58
Hy-Score Model 800 Air Pistol	245
Hy-Score Model 808 Single-Shot Air Rifle	246

I

IBM	175
I Have This Old Gun	320
Indian Matchlock Gun	23
Inglis Mk I Semi-Automatic Pistol - 9mm Parabellum	198
Ingram English Volunteer Pattern Percussion Rifle	89
Inland Division General Motors	175
In-line muzzleloader	276
Institute for Legislative Action (ILA)	302
Ishapore Arsenal SMLE No. 1 Mk III Bolt-Action Rifle	198
Israeli Military Industries Galil Sniper Rifle - 5.56mm	208
Israel Military Industries Desert Eagle Pistol	262
Italian Castelli G.A. Model 1889 Service Revolver	164
Ithaca 7E Single-Barrel Trap Shotgun	278
Ithaca Engraved Hammerless Shotgun	148
Ithaca Model 37 Trap Slide-Action Shotgun	283
Iver Johnson Model 1879 Revolver	99
Iver Johnson Safety Hammer Revolver	99

J

Jager, Paul	272
James & Ferris Half-Stock Percussion Target Rifle	77
James Purdey & Sons Shotgun, general	277, 278
James Purdey & Sons British Best-Grade Side-by-Side	279
James Purdey & Sons British Over/Under Shotgun	279
James Purdey & Sons British Best Grade Side-by-Side	120
James Purdey & Sons Side-by-Side Hammer Shotgun	120
James Purdey & Sons Side-by-Side Shotgun - 12 gauge	146
James Purdey & Sons Single-Barrel Trap Shotgun	278
James Purdey & Sons .600 Nitro Express	275
James Purdey & Sons Side-by-Side Shotgun - 12 gauge	142
Japanese Kokura Army Arsenal Type 99 Arisaka	190
Japanese Baby Nambu Semi-Automatic Pistol	195
Japanese Ceskoslovenska Zbrojovka Brno Contract VZ-24 Bolt-Action Rifle - 8mm Mauser	191
Japanese Koishikawa Arsenal Type 30 Arisaka	190
Japanese Koishikawa Arsenal Type 35 Arisaka	190
Japanese Kokura Army Arsenal Type 38 Arisaka	190
Japanese Kokura Army Arsenal Type 99 Arisaka	190
Japanese Matchlock Temple Gun	23
Japanese Model 1922 Light Machine Gun Trainer	191
Japanese Nagoya Army Arsenal Type 2 Arisaka	190
Japanese Nagoya Army Arsenal Type 14 Nambu Semi-Automatic Pistol - 8mm Nambu	195
Japanese Nagoya Army Arsenal Type 94 Semi-Automatic Pistol - 8mm Nambu	195
Japanese Nagoya Army Arsenal Type 97 Arisaka	181
Japanese Nagoya Army Arsenal Type 99 Arisaka	191
Japanese Tokyo Artillery Arsenal Model 1902	195
Japanese Tokyo Artillery Arsenal Type 26 Revolver	195
Japanese Tokyo Juki Kogyo Type 99 Arisaka	189
Japanese Toyo Kogyo Type 99 Arisaka	189
Japanese Type 1 Folding Stock Paratrooper rifle	185
Japanese Type 5 Semi-Automatic Rifle - 7.7mm	173
Japanese Type 14 Nambu pistol - 8mm Nambu	195
Japanese Type 20 Murata Bolt-Action Carbine - 8mm	189
Japanese Type 38 Arisaka Bolt-Action Rifle - 6.5mm	189
Japanese Type 44 Bolt-Action Carbine - 6.5mm	189
Japanese Type 90 3-Barrel Flare Pistol - 28mm	195
Japanese Type 99 Bolt-Action Sniper Rifle	181
Japanese Type I Bolt-Action Rifle - 6.5mm	189
J. Baker English Flintlock Rifle - .69 caliber	49

INDEX

J. Blattman Peabody-Martini Free Rifle	220
J.C.A. Brun Percussion Shotgun - 16 gauge	133
Jennings by Robbins & Lawrence Rifle - .54 rocket ball	108
Jennings Multi-Shot Flintlock Rifle	60
J. G. Anschütz Wehrsportkarabiner Bolt-Action Carbine	186
J. Henry & Son Percussion Plains Rifle - .36 caliber	71
John Evans & Son	62
Johnson, Nancy	232
Jordan, Bill	211
Jorgensen, Erik	150
Joseph Manton English Tube-Lock Percussion Fowler	56
Joslyn-Tomes Model 1870 Straight-Pull Rifle	124
J. P. Sauer & Sohn M30 Luftwaffe survival drilling	184
J. P. Sauer & Sohn Model 38H Double-Action Pistol	193
JJ. Richards English pistols - .63 caliber	51

K

Kaiser Wilhelm	284
Kalashnikov, Mikhail	199
Katsenes Custom Side-by-Side Shotgun	279
Keith, Elmer	239
Kelley, USMC Commandant P.X.	205
Kel-Tec Model P3AT Semi-Automatic Pistol	264
Kendall Underhammer Percussion Rifle - .50 caliber	70
Kennedy, President John Fitzgerald	285
Kentucky rifle	43
Kentucky Style Combination Gun	59
Kerr Revolver - .44 caliber	87
Ketchum Colt Single Action Army	91
Kettle Hill	151
Kimber Model 82 Custom Classic Rifle	272
King James II Flintlock Fowler	30
Kleingunther K15 Bolt-Action Rifle	272
Kleszczewski Excelsior Drilling	148
Knife pistols	52, 104
Knight MK 85-1 Prototype In-line Percussion Rifle	276
Kollner, Gaspard	34
Kotter, August	34
Krag Jorgensen	15
Krag, Ole Hermann Johannes	150
Kreighoff Four-Barrel Shotgun Set	278
Kreighoff P.08 Luger Semi-Automatic Pistol - 9mm	192
Kropatschek bolt-action repeater	15

L

Lancaster Four-Barrel Pistol - .455 centerfire	102
Lancaster Four Barrel Shotgun - 28 gauge	119
Lancaster Over/under Double-barrel Percussion Pistol	58
Lane, A.P., "The Pistol Wizard"	232
Lane & Read New England Flintlock Militia Musket	49
Lange Pistole 08	165
Laurona Spanish Model 153 Over/Under Shotgun	279
Law Enforcement Officers Safety Act (LEOSA)	301
Law Enforcement Revolvers	211
L. B. Taylor & Co. Single-Shot Pocket Pistol .32 rimfire	101
L. C. Smith Drilling - 12 gauge/.44 caliber	120
L.C. Smith Eagle-Grade Single-Barrel Trap Shotgun	278
Lee, Admiral Willis Augustus	183
Lee, Colonel John	223
LeFaucheux, Casimir	89
Lefever G Grade Side-by-Side Shotgun - 12 gauge	148
LeMat First Model Percussion Revolver	87
LeMat system	66
Lever-Action Rifle, general	108
Lewis & Clark	68
Lewis Machine & Tool Defender 2000 rifle 5.56x45mm	207
Liberator Single-Shot Pistol	184
Lindsay Young America Superposed Charge Pistol	60
Little Bighorn U.S. Springfield 1868 Trapdoor Rifle	123
Ljutic Industries Space Gun	230
Long Rifle, Anstate - .45 caliber	46
Long Rifle, D. Christ - .45 caliber	46
Long Rifle, J.P. Beck - .54 caliber	47
Long Rifle, Percussion	46
Loosemore Destroyer Pistol/Carbine Prototype	256
Loosemore Prototype Open Bolt Rifle	256
Lorenz Austrian Model 1855 Percussion Rifle	89
Ludwig Borovnik Austrian Vierling Gun	276
Ludwig Loewe & Co. German Argentine Contract Model 1891 Bolt-Action Carbine - 7.65mm Mauser	153
Ludwig Loewe Waffenfabrik German Model 1895 Chilean Contract Bolt-Action Rifle - 7mm Mauser	153
Ludwig Loewe Waffenfabrik Model 1895 Spanish Contract Mauser Bolt-Action Rifle - 7mm Mauser	153
Luger, Georg	16
Luger Model 1901 U.S. military purchase 7.65mm	155
Luger P.04	169
Luger Pistole 09 (P-09)	16
Luigi Franchi Semi-Automatic Shotgun	283
L.W. Seecamp LWS 32 Special Edition Pistol	263
Lyles, Ernie	5

M

M1 Garand Training Model	172
M16	19, 199
M16A1	201
M24	209
M33/40 carbine	186
MacArthur, General Douglas	205
Madsen G1A Bolt-Action Rifle - .30-06	197
Manhattan Pepperbox Revolver - .31 caliber	75
Manhattan Pocket Model Percussion Revolver - .31 caliber	85
Mannlicher Carcano Model 41 Bolt-Action Rifle	188
Mannlicher Carcano Model 91/24 Bolt-Action Rifle	188
Mannlicher Carcano Model 1938 Bolt-Action Rifle	188
Mannlichers Collectors Association	272
Mantegna, Joe	249
Manton & Co. Double Rifle - .500 Express	120
Manton, John, English Flintlock Duelling Pistol	28
Markham Air Rifle Company Model 1886 Air Rifle	244
Markham King Model D Air Rifle	246
Marlin Ballard Hunter's Rifle - .44 caliber	118
Marlin-Ballard Lever-Action Schuetzen Rifle	220
Marlin-Ballard No. 4 A-1 Mid-Range Single-Shot Rifle	222
Marlin Camp Carbine Semi-Automatic Rifle	268
Marlin Firearms Company	112
Marlin, John Mahlon	112
Marlin Model 19 Slide-Action Shotgun	121
Marlin Model 20S Slide-Action Rifle	243
Marlin Model 60 Glenfield Semi-Automatic Rifle	269
Marlin Model 88 Semi-Auto Rifle	269
Marlin Model 336 Presentation-Grade Lever-Action	274
Marlin Model 1881 Lever-Action Rifle, Second Style	112
Marlin Model 1892 Lever-Action Rifle	112
Marlin Model 1893 Lever-Action Rifle	112
Marlin Model 1894 Lever-Action Rifle	112
Marlin Model 1897 Lever-Action Rifle	112
Marlin XX Standard 1873 Pocket Revolver - .22 rimfire	97
Marlin XXX Standard 1872 Pocket Revolver	97
Marquis, Louis	184
Marston Three Barrel Derringer - .32 rimfire	101
Marston Union Pocket Model Revolver - .31 caliber	85
Martini action	297
MAS French FAMAS Bullpup Carbine - 5.56mm	208
Massachusetts Arms Co. Double-barrel Fowler	57
Massachusetts Arms Co. Maynard Falling-Block Rifle	219
Massachusetts Arms Maynard Model 1873 Rifle	221
Masterson Colt Single Action Army	91
matchlock	6, 8, 22, 23
Matchlock Musket, Spanish - .78 caliber	32
Matson, Thomas English Doglock Musket - .75 caliber	27
Maus, Brig. Gen. Marion P.	205
Mauser Bolt-Action Rifles	16, 135
Mauser/Deutsche Waffen und Munitions Fabriken P.08 Luger Semi-Automatic Pistol - 9mm Parabellum	192
Mauser German Karabiner 98A Bolt-Action Rifle	154
Mauser German Model 1871 Bolt-Action Carbine	152
Mauser German Type B Bolt-Action Rifle	149
Mauser HSc Pistol - .32 ACP	193
Mauser Model 712 Schnellfeuer Machine Pistol with Detachable Shoulder Stock - 7.63 Mauser	194
Mauser Model 1896 Broomhandle Military Semi-Automatic Pistol	16, 146, 192, 195
Mauser Model 1896 Spanish Contract Bolt-Action	153
Mauser Model 1934 Semi-Automatic Pistol	193
Mauser P.08 Luger Black Widow Pistol	192
Mauser P.38 Semi-Automatic Pistol	192
Mauser, Peter and Paul	15
Mauser Spanish Contract M1893 rifle	150
Mauser-Werke K98k/ZF-41 Bolt-Action Sniper Rifle	186
Mauser, Wilhelm and Paul	135
Maxim, Hiram	17
Mayer & Grammelspacher Diana Model 27 Air Rifle	247
Mayflower Gun	32
Maynard Tape-Priming System	57
MB Associates Gyrojet Mark I Pistol - 13mm Gyrojet	257
MB Associates Gyrojet Mk I Model B 007 Carbine	257
McGivern, Ed	236, 237
McMillan, Lt. Colonel William	225
Meili, Launi	232, 233
Meriden Arms Co. Single-Shot Rifle	243
Merwin Hulbert & Co. Revolvers	13, 95
Merwin Hulbert & Co. Single-Action Pocket Revolver	97
Metallwaren Budapest Model 98/40 Bolt-Action Rifle	186
Mexican Fabrica de Armas Obregon Pistol - .45 caliber	180
Mexican Percussion Target Rifle	219
Meyer, Lt. General Richard	204
MG42 Machine Gun	196
Michigan Arms Wolverine In-Line Black Powder Rifle	276
Miculek, Jerry	236
Mikkenger Arms Grizzly Single-Action Revolver	259
Mildren, General Frank Thomas	204
MIL, Inc., Thunder Five Revolver	262
Minie, Francois	67
Minneapolis Firearms Co. Palm Pistol	103
Miquelet	7
Miquelet Fusil, Ramon Zuloaga - .54 caliber	34
Miquelet, Persian .58 caliber	26
Miquelet Pistol, Spanish .70 caliber	26
Miquelet, Sardinian - .44 caliber	30
Miquelet, Spanish 16 gauge	26
Miquelet, Spanish Blunderbuss	33
Miquelet, Spanish Escopeta - .72 caliber	33
Mississippi Rifle	78
Mix, Tom	128
Model 1752 Flintlock Musket	35
Model 1765 Cassagnard Flintlock Fusil	35
Model 1777 Flintlock Musketoon .69 caliber	35
Model 1803 Flintlock Musket - .69 caliber	28
Model 1816 Flintlock Musket	50

INDEX

Model 1816 Percussion Conversion Musket - .69 caliber	88
Model 1817 Common Rifle	50
Model 1842 Musket	78
Model 1866 lever-action	12
Model 1873 lever-action	12
Model 1887 Lever-Action Shotgun	121
Model 1903 Springfield	150
Model 1921 Thompson, .45 ACP,	171
Modern Engraving, general	286
Moll Percussion Long Rifle - .36 caliber	70
Montlahuc & de Bastid Palm Pistol	104
moon clips	177
Moore's Patent Firearms Co. Front-Loading Single-Action Revolver - .32 teatfire	67
Moore's Patent Firearms Co. No. 1 Derringer	101
Moore's Patent Single-Action Belt Revolver	85
Moses Brothers Self-Defense Engine Frontier Model B	251
Mosin Nagant bolt-action	16
Mosin Nagant Model 1891/30 Bolt-Action Rifle	202
Mosin Nagant Type 53 Bolt-Action Rifle	203
Mossberg Model 500	281
Mossberg Model L Single-Shot Rifle	242
Murdock, Margaret Thompson	232

N

National Firearms Museum	4, 295
National Junior Shooting Camps	301
National Police Shooting Championships	301
National Smallbore and National Pistol Championships	224
National Youth Shooting Sports Ambassadors	301
Nederlandishe Wapenmagaieijn Haarlem Dutch Double-Action Service Revolver - 9.4mm Dutch	164
New Haven Arms Company Volcanic Rifle	108
New Jersey State Rifle Association	222
Newton Arms Co. First-Type Standard Rifle	272
Newton Double-barrel Percussion Shotgun - 12 gauge	76
New York City Fire Department	215
New York Sun	222
Nimschke, L.D.	129, 296
Noble Model 70 Slide-Action Shotgun	243
Nock Volley Gun	59
No Country for Old Men	251
Noel Pill-lock Twelve-Shot Pill Lock Turret Pistol	102
Norinco Chinese MAK-90 Semi-Automatic Rifle	269
North American Arms Company	159
Norwegian Model 1914 Pistol - .45 ACP	163
Novo folding revolver	106
NRA Affiliated Gun Collector Clubs	320
NRA Annual Meetings	301
NRA Business Alliance	301
NRA Civil Rights Defense Fund	299
NRA Clubs & Associations Department	301
NRA Firearms For Freedom	4, 299
NRA Foundation	299
NRA Freedom Action Fund Foundation	299
NRA General Operations	300
NRA Gun Gurus television series	320
NRA Hunter Education	301
NRA Law Enforcement division	301
NRA Marksmanship Qualification Program	301
NRA Military Heritage Museum	224
NRA Museums	4, 299, 320
NRA National Gun Show	320
NRA National Sporting Arms Museum	5, 156, 320
NRA Program Materials Center	301
NRA Range Services	301
NRA Special Contribution Fund	299
NRA World Shooting Championship	300
NRA Youth Hunter Education Challenge	301

O

Oakley, Annie	126, 127
Oester Waffenfabrik Ges. Steyr Austrian Sporter Rifle	270
Olin King Buck Winchester Model 21	277
Omega Air Rifle	284
Omohundro, Texas Jack	127
Osburn, Carl	232

P

Palma Match	228
Palmer, General Bruce, Jr.	204
Palmetto Armory Percussion Pistol - .54 caliber	87
Pancost Percussion Long Rifle - .40 caliber	70
Parker A-1 Special Side-by-Side Shotgun - 20 gauge	146
Parker AAHE-Grade Side-by-Side Shotgun - 12 gauge	146
Parker Brothers BH Grade Side-by-Side - 12 gauge	148
Parker Brothers Lifter Action Side-by-Side - 10 gauge	120
Parker DHE Grade Side-by-Side	278
Parker Invincibles	147
Parkers Snow Co. Rifle-Musket, Miller Model 1861	124
Parker VHE Grade Skeet Side-by-Side Shotgun	278
Parsons, Herb	238
Patrick English Percussion Double Rifle - .70 caliber	77
Patton, General George S., Jr.	172
Paul Giffard French Single-Shot CO2 Rifle	247
Paul Jaeger Custom Falling-Block Sporter Rifle	276
Paul Jung Drilling	148
Pedersen device	157
Pendrill English Flintlock Breechloading Rifle	54
Pennsylvania rifle	43
Pennsylvania Rifle Works Percussion Over/Under Combination Gun - .45 over .50 caliber	70
Pepke, Major General Donn Royce	206
pepperboxes	62
Percussion Benchrest Rifle - .50 caliber	77
Percussion Long Rifles	70
Percussion Pistol - 44 caliber	75
percussion system	10, 57
Perkins English Flintlock Pistols	28
Perry, Oliver Hazard	224
Petersen, Robert E.	4
Pettengill Army Percussion Revolver	85
Petty Half-Stocked Percussion Rifle - .45 caliber	71
Philippine Resistance Revolver - .38 cartridge	180
Pieper Mexican Military Revolving Carbine	114
Pietro Beretta Premium-Grade Side-by-Side Shotgun	280
Pinfire Sword Pistol	106
Pinfire System	11, 67
Plains Rifle	12, 69
Plant's Mfg. Co. Eagle Arms Front Loading Revolver	85
Plate Double-barrel Percussion Shotgun - 12 gauge	76
Plate Percussion Side-by-Side Shotgun - 10 gauge	77
Plinking	240
Poe, General Bryce	205
Polytech/KFS AK-47S Legend Folding-Stock Rifle	203
Pond Front-Loading Revolver - .32 rimfire	85
Pond Single-Action Belt Revolver - .32 rimfire	85
Prescott Pistol Co. Crescent Revolver - .30 rimfire	99
Prince Charles	284
Princess Diana	280
Providence Tool Co. Peabody Lever-Action Carbine	124
P. Webley & Son British Metropolitan Police Revolver	96
P.W. Porter Revolving Turret Military Carbine	64
Pyrodex	276

Q

Quackenbush Convertible Air Rifle	240
Quackenbush, Henry M.	244
Quackenbush Model 1886 Bicycle Pump Rifle	242
Quackenbush Single-Shot Air Rifle	247
Quality Hardware	175
Quigley Down Under	248
Quirt Pistol	106

R

Raaen, Maj. Gen. John Carpenter	206
Radom P-35 VIS Semi-Automatic Pistol	194
Radom Wz 29 Bolt-Action Rifle - 8mm Mauser	187
Randle, Thurman	235
Ranger Arms NRA Centennial Rifle	272
Range Safety Officers	300
Redfield Prototype Single-Shot Rifle	221
Red Jacket No. 3 Spur-Trigger Revolver - .30 rimfire	99
Red Label shotguns	252
Reeves Colt Single Action Army	91
Refuse To Be A Victim	300
Reichsrevolvers	167
Reid "My Friend" Knuckle Duster Revolver	104
Reising M50 submachine gun	196
Remington, general	9, 72
Remington 31R Slide-Action Riot Shotgun	216
Remington .41 rimfire derringers	100
Remington Arms Factory Collection	5, 72
Remington Beals Army and Beals Navy Revolvers	84
Remington Combination Rifle-Shotgun	72
Remington Cook Rifle - .40 centerfire	154
Remington Creedmoor Long-Range Rifle	222
Remington Double Derringer - .41 rimfire	101
Remington-Elliot Derringer	102
Remington Elliott Rifle - .45 centerfire	154
Remington Factory Collection	156
Remington-Hepburn No. 3 Mid-Range Creedmoor Rifle	221
Remington Hepburn Single-Shot rifle	118
Remington Keene Rifle - .45 centerfire	154
Remington Lee rifle, 6mm	154
Remington M24 Sniper Bolt-Action Rifle	209
Remington Model 6 Single-Shot Rifle	240
Remington Model 6 Slide-Action Rifle	274
Remington Model 10 Slide-Action Shotgun - 12 gauge	149
Remington Model 11-48 semi-auto shotgun, Prototype	282
Remington Model 11 Autoloader Shotgun - 12 gauge	139
Remington Model 11-87 Police Semi-Automatic	217
Remington Model 17 Slide-Action Shotgun - 20 gauge	139
Remington Model 25 Slide-Action Rifle	241
Remington Model 32 TC Over/Under Shotgun	278
Remington Model 37 Rangemaster Bolt-Action Rifle	233
Remington Model 40 Serial Number One	270
Remington Model 51 Semi-Automatic Pistol	263
Remington Model 53	156
Remington Model 81 Police Semi-Automatic Rifle	216
Remington Model 81 Woodmaster Rifle	149
Remington Model 512 Sportmaster Bolt-Action Rifle	243
Remington Model 600 Magnum Bolt-Action Carbine	270
Remington Model 700 Left-Hand Bolt-Action Rifle	271
Remington Model 720A Rifle	273
Remington Model 722(A) Bolt-Action Rifle	270
Remington Model 725 Rifle	272
Remington Model 788 Bolt-Action Rifle	270
Remington Model 870	20
Remington Model 870 Pump Shotgun, First	281

INDEX

Remington Model 870 Slide-Action Shotgun	282
Remington Model 1100 Semi-Automatic Shotgun	20
Remington Model 1100 Trap Semi-Automatic Shotgun	283
Remington Model 1861 Army	84
Remington Model 1861 Navy Revolver	84
Remington Model 1867 Rolling Block Single-Shot Pistol	96
Remington Model 1875	93
Remington Model 1890	93
Remington Model Four Semi-Automatic Rifle	268
Remington Model No. 4S "Military Model"	240
Remington Mosin Nagant Model 1891 Bolt-Action	161
Remington New Model Army	84
Remington New Model Army factory conversion	90
Remington New Model Navy factory conversion	90
Remington New Model Navy Revolvers	84
Remington New Model Pocket Conversion revolver	93
Remington Nylon 76 Lever-Action Rifle	243
Remington Old Model Army conversion - .44 centerfire	90
Remington Percussion Target Rifle - .42 caliber	72
Remington Prototype Parker Shotgun	279
Remington R15 Semi-Automatic Rifle s/n RA000001	267
Remington Rand	175
Remington-Rider Magazine Pistol	102
Remington Rolling Block Rifle	12, 115, 296
Remington-Smoot New Model No. 1 Revolver	97
Remington-Smoot New Model No. 3 Revolver	97
Remington M40A1 Bolt-Action Scout/Sniper Rifle	210
Remington Vest Pocket Pistol - .22 rimfire	101
Remington XM24 Sniper Bolt-Action Rifle	209
Remington XP-100 Bolt-Action Pistol	261
R. E. Terni Mannlicher Carcano Model 38 Bolt-Action	188
revolving rifle	64
Reynolds, Captain Malcolm "Mal"	251
Rhode, Kim	232
Richards Colt factory conversion of 1860 Army Model	90
Richards Mason Colt factory conversion of 1861 Navy	90
rifling, rifled muskets, rifles	8
Rigby English Percussion Pistol - .54 caliber	75
Rigby Farquharson Single-Shot Lever-Action Rifle	146
Rigby Hammer Side-by-Side Shotgun	278
Rimfire cartridge	67
Robert E. Petersen Gallery	5
Roberts, Dr. William L. and Collette N.	4
Robinson, Don	284
Rock-Ola Manufacturing	175
Rodda Double Rifle - 15 bore	142
Rollin White Arms Co. Single-Action Pocket Revolver	67
Roos and Sohn Percussion Side-by-Side Shotgun	120
Roosevelt, Cornelius V.S.	4
Roosevelt, Theodore	5, 14, 141, 142, 151, 211
Roper Repeating Shotgun - 16 gauge	121
Ross Rifle Co. Canadian Bolt-Action Sporting Rifle	149
Rough Riders	151
Ruger, William B.	20, 252
Russell, Charles	128
Russia America Fur Co. Model 1838 Percussion Musket	77
Russian Contract Winchester Model 1895 Lever-Action	162
Russian Mosin Nagant Model 1891 Bolt-Action	161, 179
Russian Mosin Nagant Model 1944 Bolt-Action Carbine	179
Russian MU-55 Target Pistol	226
Russian Nagant Model 1895 Revolver - 7.62mm Nagant	180
Russian SVD Dragunov Sniper Semi-Automatic Rifle	207
Russian SVT-40 Semi-Automatic Sniper Rifle	179
Russian Tokarev Model 1933 Semi-Automatic Pistol	180
Russian Tokarev Model 1938 SVT Semi-Automatic Rifle	179
Russian TOZ 8 Bolt-Action Target Rifle	226

S

Sabatini, Erin	5
Sabatti Engraved FAMARS Four Barrel Shotgun	280
Saive, Dieudonné	138
Sako Finnish L461 Rifle	273
Sako Finnmaster Pistol	225
Samuel Walker	63
San Juan ridge	151
Sauer Model 1930 Berhorden Semi-Automatic Pistol	193
Savage Albree Prototype Model 7 Semi-Automatic Rifle	256
Savage Model 24J-SL Over/Under Combination Gun	276
Savage Model 45 Bullpup Bolt-Action Rifle	273
Savage Model 99 Lever-Action Rifle	149
Savage Model 99, One Millionth	274
Savage Model 1895 Lever-Action Carbine - .303 British	149
Savage Model 1911 - .45 ACP	155
Savage No. 4 Mk I Bolt-Action Rifle w Folding Bayonet	178
Savage & North Figure 8 Percussion Revolver, Second Model - .36 caliber	85
Savage Revolving Firearms Co. Figure 8 Navy Revolver	85
Savage SMLE No. 4 Mk I/3 Bolt-Action Rifle	198
Savage Stevens 30-D Slide-Action Shotgun	282
Savage Stevens Model 87 Semi-Automatic Rifle	243
Schaerff Buffalo Rifle - .58 caliber	69
scheutzenbund, *scheutzenfest*, *scheutzen* match	219
Schmidt Rubin bolt-action	16
Swiss Schmidt-Rubin Swiss K-31/43 Straight-Pull Rifle	181
Schoyen heavy target barrel	219
Schreier, Philip	5
Schwarzkopf, General Norman	207
Schwarzlose, Andreas	169
Scotti Model X Semi-Automatic Rifle - 6.5 Italian	186
S.C. Robinson Sharps-Type Breechloading Percussion Carbine - .52 caliber	88
Sectionalized handguns	163
Sedgely Glove Pistol	184
Seitz Serial Number 1 Engraved Trap Shotgun	283
Selleck, Tom	248
Semmerling LM-4 and LM-3 pistols	259
Serenity	251
serpentine device	23
Shangshei Arsenal Mauser Model 1896 Broomhandle Semi-Automatic Pistol	201
Sharps "Big Fifty" Model 1874 Single-Shot Falling Block Rifle - .50-90	12, 118
Sharps-Borchardt Model 1878 Mid-Range Rifle	221
Sharps & Hankins Model 3B pistol - .32 rimfire	102
Sharps Model 1853 Percussion Carbine - .52 caliber	79
Sharps Model 1859 Single-Shot Percussion Carbine	122
Sharps Model 1874 "Old Reliable" Single-Shot Falling Block Rifle - .45 caliber	118
Sharps Model 1877 Creedmoor Falling-Block Single-Shot Target Rifle	222
Sharps New Model 1859 Percussion Carbine - .52 caliber	88
Shattuck Arms Unique Palm Pistol	104
Shaw Cookson-Type Flintlock Repeating Rifle - .57 caliber	60
S. Hawken Gemmer Rifle - .50 caliber	69
Sheridan Blue Streak Single-Shot Air Rifle	246
Sheridan VM-68 Lady Magnum Paintball Gun	247
Shiloh Products Model 1874 Sharps Single-Shot Falling-Block Rifle	276
Shiloh Sharps # 3 Rifle	248
Shooting Galleries	241
S.H. Staudenmeyer English Pistols - .59 caliber	57
SIG Sauer	20
SIG Sauer 550-2SP Counter Sniper Semi-Automatic Rifle - 5.56mm NATO	216
SIG Sauer M11 Semi-Automatic Pistol	208
SIG Sauer P210 Pistol	265
SIG Sauer P220 NRA Semi-Automatic Pistol	263
SIG Sauer P228	265
Simeon North U.S. Model 1819 Army - .54 caliber	51
Simpson Bolt-Action Rifle	243
Singer Manufacturing	175
Single shot derringers	100
Single shot Percussion Whip Pistol	106
Skelton, Skeeter	239
SKS 7.62x39mm	19
Smith-Corona	175
Smith, Horace	11
Smith, Lt. Colonel T.D.	235
Smith & Wesson	11, 20, 65, 67
Smith & Wesson 1st Model Ladysmith Revolver	214
Smith & Wesson .32 Safety Hammerless First Model Revolver - .32 S&W	98
Smith & Wesson .32 Single Action Revolver - .32 S&W	98
Smith & Wesson 38-100 British Service Revolver	177
Smith & Wesson .38 Double Action Revolver - .38 S&W	98
Smith & Wesson .38 Safety Hammerless Fifth Model Revolver - .38 S&W	98
Smith & Wesson 38 Single-Action Second Model Revolver - .38 S&W	98
Smith & Wesson .38 Single-Action Third Model Revolver - .38 S&W	98
Smith & Wesson Airweight Chiefs Special	20
Smith & Wesson American Model	12, 20
Smith & Wesson Centennial Model 40 Revolver	263
Smith & Wesson Chiefs Special	14
Smith & Wesson Chiefs Special Revolver - .38 Special	214
Smith & Wesson Fourth Model Single-Shot Pistol	223
Smith & Wesson hand ejectors	14
Smith & Wesson Military & Police revolver	14
Smith & Wesson Model 1 1/2 Second Issue Single-Action Revolver - .32 rimfire	98
Smith & Wesson Model 3 Revolver	94
Smith & Wesson Model 10 Military & Police Revolver	212
Smith & Wesson Model 14-3 Revolver	212
Smith & Wesson Model 14 K-38 Target Masterpiece	223
Smith & Wesson Model 19 Combat Magnum Revolver	262
Smith & Wesson Model 24 Revolver	223
Smith & Wesson Model 28 Revolver	263
Smith & Wesson Model 29	251
Smith & Wesson Model 41 Semi-Automatic Pistol	223
Smith & Wesson Model 46 Semi-Automatic Pistol	224
Smith & Wesson Model 49 Bodyguard Revolver	263
Smith & Wesson Model 52-1 Semi-Automatic Pistol	223
Smith & Wesson Model 59	20
Smith & Wesson Model 59 Semi-Automatic Pistol	264
Smith & Wesson Model 60 Chief's Special Revolver	263
Smith & Wesson Model 64-3 Revolver	212
Smith & Wesson Model 340PD Revolver	264
Smith & Wesson Model 342 AirLite Ti Revolver	260
Smith & Wesson Model 500 Revolver	265
Smith & Wesson Model 539 Semi-Automatic Pistol	263
Smith & Wesson Model 645 Double-Action Pistol	262
Smith & Wesson Model 681 Revolver	263
Smith & Wesson Model 1500 Bolt-Action Rifle	270
Smith & Wesson Model 1940 Light Rifle	176
Smith & Wesson Model No. 1 - .22 rimfire	65
Smith & Wesson Model Number One	83
Smith & Wesson Model Number Two Revolver	83
Smith & Wesson Model One .22 revolver	65

INDEX

Smith & Wesson Model One, Third Issue, Single-Action Revolver - .22 short   98
Smith & Wesson M&P Semi-Automatic Pistol - 9mm   214
Smith & Wesson Pre-Model 27 Revolver   264
Smith & Wesson Revolving Rifle - .320 Rev. Rif.   114
Smith & Wesson Russian model   12, 20
Smith & Wesson Schofield   12, 13, 91
Smith & Wesson Second Model Single-Shot Pistol   223
Smith & Wesson Sigma SW40F .40 S&W   261
Smith & Wesson Third Model Single-Shot Pistol   223
Smith & Wesson Volcanic Repeating Magazine Pistol   65
Smith & Wesson Chemical Co. M277 Tear Gas Pistol   214
Smokeless powder   15
snaphaunce   7, 26
Snaphaunce Pistol - .60 caliber   54
Sokolovsky .45 Automaster Semi-Automatic Pistol   262
Sommer & Ockenfuss GmbH German Tactical Rifle   256
Southern Percussion Rifle - .45 caliber   43
Spanish Mauser rifle   150
Spanish Snaphaunce Fowler   26
Spanish Unceta y Compania S.A. Astra Model 900 Semi-Automatic Pistol - .30 Mauser   195
Spencer lever-action repeater   66
Spencer Repeating Rifle Company   12
Spiller and Burr Navy Percussion Revolver - .36 caliber   86
spitzer bullet   15
Sprague & Marston Double-Action Pepperbox Pistol   75
Spreewerke GmbH Metallwarenfabrik P.38   192
Springfield Armory   21, 50
Springfield Armory 1911-A1 Semi-Automatic Pistol   212
Springfield Armory M-1A Semi-Automatic Rifle   266
Springfield M1861 Musket - .62 caliber   122
Springfield Trapdoor   125
Spurgin, Pat   232
S. S. Baird Underhammer Percussion Target Rifle   219
Standard Arms Model G Semi-Automatic Rifle   254
Standard Products Co.   175
Starr Double Action Army conversion, .45 centerfire   90
Starr Single Action Army conversion - .45 centerfire   90
St. Denis French Daudeteau/Dovitiis Conversion Single-Shot Bolt-Action Carbine - 6.5mm Daudeteau   152
Stephen Grant shotguns - 12 gauge   144
Stephen Grant & Sons Double Rifle   146
Sterling Armament, Ltd. AR-180 Semi-Automatic Rifle   267
Sterling Semi-Automatic Carbine - 9mm   203
Stevens Favorite Single-Shot Rifle   240
Stevens Ideal rifle   12
Stevens Ideal No. 49 Walnut Hill Single-Shot Rifle   221
Stevens No. 12 Marksman Single-Shot Rifle   240
Stevens No. 41 Tip-Up Single-Shot Pistol   223
Stevens No. 41 Tip-Up Single-Shot Pocket Pistol   99
Stevens No. 65 Little Krag Single-Shot Bolt-Action Rifle   243
Stevens-Pope Single-Shot Schuetzen Rifle   220
Stevens Rifle Company   220
Steyr AUG Semi-Automatic Rifle - 5.56mm NATO   266
Steyr Daimler Puch Mauser Model 98k Bolt-Action   197
Steyr-Mannlicher Austrian M-Luxus Bolt-Action   270
Steyr-Mannlicher Mannlicher/Schoenauer Model 1961 MCA Rifle   272
Steyr Mannlicher straight-pull bolt-action   15
Stoner, Eugene   199
Sturm, Alex   252
Sturm, Ruger & Co.   20, 252
Sturm, Ruger & Co. Old Model Blackhawk Revolver   261
Sturm, Ruger & Co. Redhawk Revolver   261
Sturm, Ruger & Co. KSPNY-182 DAO Revolver   262
Sturm, Ruger & Co. Mini-14 Series 180 Rifle   266
Sturm, Ruger & Co. Model 10/22   269
Sturm, Ruger & Co. Model 44 Carbine   268
Sturm, Ruger & Co. Model 77 Bolt-Action Rifle   271
Sturm, Ruger & Co. No. 1-H Tropical Falling-Block   276
Sturm, Ruger & Co. Stainless Red Label Skeet Shotgun   278
Suhler Jagd-und Sportwaffen GmbH Drilling   144
Suhl German Model 1839 Percussion Musket   89
sundial alarm clock gun   53
superposed repeaters   60
Supica, Jim   5
Swedish Cheek-Stock Snaphaunce Musket - .60 caliber   30
Swedish Husqvarna Model 1903 Semi-Automatic Pistol   180
Swedish Nagant Revolver - 7.62mm Nagant   164
Sweeney, Texas Ranger Lt. Richard   211
Swinburn Presentation-Grade Peabody/Martini-Henry Single-Shot Rifle   297
Swiss S.I.G. Mondragon Semi-Automatic Rifle   166
Swiss Waffenfabrik Bern Model 1906 Luger Semi-Automatic Pistol - 7.65 Parabellum   169
S&W Small-Frame Revolvers   98
Szecsei & Fuchs Double-Barrel Bolt-Action Rifle   253

T

Tactical Police Competition (TPC   301
Tate Vintage Side-by-Side Shotgun   279
Taurus   21
Teddy's Bear   141
Terni Arsenal Mannlicher-Carcano 91/29 Carbine   188
Texas Rangers   218
The Devil's Shotgun   133
The Horseshoe Gun   34
The Last of the Mohicans   42
The Outlaw Josey Wales   250
The Petersen Gallery   4
The Wild Bunch   250
Thomas /AJ Ordnance Semi-Automatic Pistol   262
Thompson/Center Arms Contender Single-Shot Pistol   261
Thompson Center Classic Semi-Automatic Rifle   243
Thompson, John T.   171
Thompson-LaGarde tests   155
Thompson submachine gun, Tommy Gun   18
Thompson submachine gun with 50 round drum   171
Thrasher, Ginny   232
Thuer Colt factory conversion of 1860 Army Model   90
Tokyo Arsenal Siamese Contract Mauser Model 1903/Type 45 Bolt-Action Rifle - 8mm   153
Topperwein, Ad and Plinky   238
Tranter/Adams English Patent Percussion Revolver   89
Trap and alarm guns   107
Trapdoor Springfield   13
Treeby Chain Repeating Rifle - caliber .52 percussion   61
Tribuzio Ring Trigger Pistol - 8mm   104
True Grit   250
Tschinke Muzzleloading Wheellock Rifle   29
Tubb 2000 Bolt-Action Rifle   230
Tula Arsenal Russian 1879 Berdan II Bolt-Action   152
Turkish/Balkan Rat-Tail Flintlock Pistols - .62 caliber   29
Turlock English Officer's Pistol - .69 caliber   75

U

Union Switch & Signal   175
U.S. Alfred P. Jenks & Son Model 1861 Percussion Rifle-Musket - .58 caliber   80
U.S. American Machine Works Smith Breechloading Percussion Carbine - .50 caliber   82
U.S. Amoskeag Mfg. Co. Lindner Percussion Breechloading Carbine, Second Type - .58 caliber   82
U.S. Asa Waters, Jr., Model 1808 Flintlock Militia Musket - .69 caliber   49
U.S. Auto Ordnance 1928 Thompson Submachine Gun   171
U.S. Blue Jacket No. 1 Single-Action Revolver   99
U.S. Burnside Rifle Company 5th Model Breechloading Lever-Action Percussion Carbine - .54 caliber   81
U.S. Colt Commando Revolver - .38 Special   177
U.S. Colt Model 1839 Percussion Revolving Carbine   73
U.S. Colt Model 1861 Special Musket - .58 caliber   80
U.S. Colt Model 1909 U.S. Army Revolver - .45 Colt   160
U.S. Colt Model 1911A1 Semi-Automatic Pistol   177
U.S. Colt Model 1911 Semi-Automatic Pistol   138, 156, 159
U.S. Colt Model 1917 Revolver - .45 ACP   160
U.S. Colt Model 1918A2 Browning Automatic Rifle   198
U.S. E. G. Lamson & Co. Ball Repeating Carbine   82
U.S. Elijah and Asa Waters and Nathaniel Whitmore Model 1808 Contract Flintlock Musket   49
U.S. Eli Whitney Model 1798 Contract Flintlock Musket   48
U.S. General Motors Guide Lamp M3 Submachine Gun   200
U.S. General Motors Inland Division M2 Carbine   200
U.S. General Motors - Inland Manufacturing Division M1A1 Semi-Automatic Carbine - .30 Carbine   174
U.S. Greene Breechloading Percussion Rifle   81
U.S. Hall Model 1819 Breechloading Flintlock Rifle   55
U.S. Hall Model 1819 Breechloading Percussion Rifle   55
U.S. Hall Model 1836 Breechloading Percussion Carbine   55
U.S. Harpers Ferry Armory Model 1805 - .54 caliber   51
U.S. Harpers Ferry Model 1803 Flintlock Rifle   48
U.S. Harpers Ferry Model 1816 Musket, Type II   50
U.S. Harpers Ferry Model 1816 (Type II) Musket   50
U.S. Harpers Ferry Model 1841 "Mississippi" Rifle   78
U.S. Harrington & Richardson M1 Semi-Auto Rifle   173
U.S. Harrington & Richardson Reising Model 50 Submachine Gun   196
U.S. Henry Deringer Model 1814 Flintlock Rifle   49
U.S. Ithaca Model 1911A1 Semi-Automatic Pistol   200
U.S. J. Bishop Model 1812 Flintlock Militia Musket   49
U.S. Johnson Automatics Model 1941 Semi-Automatic   174
U.S. Lemuel Pomeroy Model 1840 Contract Conversion   79
U.S. Lindsay Model 1863 Double Rifle Musket .58 caliber   81
U.S. M1A1 Thompson - .45 ACP   170
U.S. M1 Carbine   18
U.S. M1 Garand   18, 268
U.S. M14   18
U.S. Massachusetts Arms Co. Maynard Second Model Breechloading Carbine - .50 caliber   82
U.S. Military Pistol Trials   155
U.S. Model 1836 Flintlock Pistol by Asa Waters   57
U.S. Model 1836 Percussion Conversion Pistol   57
U.S. Model 1841 Rifle   78
U.S. M. T. Wickham Model 1816 Contract Musket   50
U.S. Navy Colt Model 1911 Semi-Automatic Pistol   159
U.S. New Haven Arms Co. Henry Lever-Action   81
U.S. North American Arms Model 1911 Pistol .45 ACP   159
U.S. North and Cheney First Model 1799 - .69 caliber   51
U.S. N.P. Ames Jenks "Mule Ear" Carbine - .54 caliber   82
U.S. Ordnance Department   92
U.S. Remington Mk III Flare Pistol - 10 gauge   160
U.S. Remington Model 11 Shotgun - 12 gauge   175
U.S. Remington Model 1863 Percussion Contract (Zouave) Rifle - .58 caliber   81
U.S. Remington Model 1903A1 Bolt-Action Rifle - .30-06   174
U.S. Remington Model 1903A4 Bolt-Action Rifle   176, 203
U.S. Remington Model 1917 Bolt-Action Rifle - .30-06   158
U.S. Remington Rand M1911A1 Pistol   201, 224
U.S. Remington-UMC Model 1911 Pistol   159
U.S. Richardson & Overman Gallager Carbine   82
U.S. Rifle, Caliber .30, M1   172
U.S. Robert & J. D. Johnson Model 1817 "Common" Rifle   50

INDEX

U.S. Sharps & Hankins Model 1862 Single-Shot Breechloading Percussion Carbine - .52 rimfire	82
U.S. Sharps New Model 1859 Breechloading Rifle	79
U.S. Sharps New Model 1859 Percussion Carbine	82
U.S. Smith-Corona Model 1903A3 Bolt-Action Rifle	174
U.S. Smith & Wesson 2nd Model Hand Ejector Revolver	160
U.S. Smith & Wesson Model 1917 Revolver	160, 177
U.S. Spencer Lever-Action Repeating Carbine	81
U.S. Spencer Model 1860 Army Repeating Rifle	81
U.S. Springfield Armory M1D Sniper Rifle - .30-06	198
U.S. Springfield Joslyn Breechloading Rifle	124
U.S. Springfield Krag-Jorgensen Model 1898 Rifle	273
U.S. Springfield Krag Jorgensen Rifle with Pope Barrel	228
U.S. Springfield M1 Garand National Match Rifle	228
U.S. Springfield M1 Garand Semi-Automatic Rifle	173
U.S. Springfield M1816 Percussion Conversion Musket	123
U.S. Springfield Model 1795 Flintlock Musket, Type I	48
U.S. Springfield Model 1816 Musket - .69 caliber	50
U.S. Springfield Model 1817 Type I - .69 caliber	51
U.S. Springfield Model 1842 Percussion Musket	78
U.S. Springfield Model 1855 Percussion Pistol/Carbine	79
U.S. Springfield Model 1855 Percussion Rifle-Musket	78
U.S. Springfield Model 1863 Type II Rifle Musket	80
U.S. Springfield Model 1875 Lee Vertical-Action Rifle	124
U.S. Springfield Model 1882 Chaffee-Reese Bolt-Action	152
U.S. Springfield Model 1884 Trapdoor Rifle - .45-70	150
U.S. Springfield Model 1896 Krag-Jorgensen Bolt-Action	150
U.S. Springfield Model 1898 Gallery Practice Rifle	154
U.S. Springfield Model 1903	150
U.S. Springfield Model 1903 Bolt-Action Rifle	227
U.S. Springfield Model 1903 Bolt-Action Rifle	157, 158
U.S. Springfield Model 1903 Bolt-Action Sniper Rifle	160
U.S. Springfield Model 1903 Gallery Bolt-Action	158
U.S. Springfield Model 1903 National Match Rifle	228
U.S. Springfield Model 1903 NRA/NBA President's Match Presentation Bolt-Action Rifle	228
U.S. Springfield Model 1903 Rifle	272
U.S. Springfield Model 1911 .22 Caliber Prototype Pistol	159
U.S. Springfield Model T44 E4 Selective Fire Rifle	201
U.S. Springfield Presentation-Grade M14 Semi-Automatic Rifle, serial number 6	296
U.S. Springfield T3E2 Semi-Automatic Rifle	172
U.S. Starr Arms Co. Model 1858 Army Double-Action Percussion Revolver - .44 caliber	84
U.S. Starr Arms Co. Model 1863 Single Action Army Revolver - .44 caliber	84
U.S. Stevens Model 620 Slide-Action Shotgun	175
U.S. T. French Model 1808 Flintlock Militia Musket	49
U.S. Underwood-Elliot-Fisher M1 Carbine	176
U.S. Union Switch & Signal Model 1911A1 Pistol	177
U.S. Victory Training Rifle	175
U.S. Waters Model 1816 Type III Contract Musket	50
U.S. Whitney Arms Co. Model 1861 Navy Percussion Rifle - .69 caliber	80
U.S. Winchester Model 12 Slide-Action Riot Shotgun	175
U.S. Winchester Model 1897 Slide-Action Trench Shotgun - 12 gauge	158
U.S. Winchester Model of 1918 Browning Automatic Rifle (BAR) - .30-06	174
U.S. Winchester Prototype Model 1917 Bolt-Action Magazine Rifle - .30-06	158
Uzi 9mm submachine gun	18
Uzi Model A Semi-Automatic Carbine with Scope	268

V

Valmet M-76W Semi-Automatic Rifle	266
Van Horn, Dwight	214
Vickers Armstrong Ltd. Vickers-Pederson Semi-Automatic Rifle - .276 Pedersen	172
vierlings	276
Viet Cong Bolt-Action Carbine - 7.62x39mm	202
Viet Cong Muzzleloading Thumb-Trigger Rifle	202
Viet Cong Semi-Automatic Pistol - .45 ACP	203
Viet Cong Slam-Fire Blow-Back Rifle - 7.62x39mm	202
Vietnamese 1911 Pattern Pistol - .45 ACP	203
Viller Persoa 9mm submachine gun	18
Virginia Manufactory of Arms	50
Virginia Manufactory of Arms 2nd Model Rifle	51
Virginia Manufactory of Arms Model 1795/1808 Percussion Musket	88
VK Belgian Single-Action Revolver - .44 S&W	96
VMT State Metal Works Finnish Lion Bolt-Action Single-Shot Target Rifle	227
Volcanic lever-action repeating magazine pistols	65
Vollmer, August	212

W

Waffenfabrik Brunn AG DOT Karabiner 98k Rifle	186
Waffenfabrik Brunn AG Mauser Model 33/40 Carbine	186
Waffenfabrik Steyr Austrian Gewehr 88 Commission Bolt-Action Rifle - 8mm Mauser	152
Waffenfabrik Steyr Austrian Mannlicher Model 1893 Bolt-Action Rifle	228
Waffenfabrik Steyr Austrian Mannlicher-Schoenauer Model 1905 Rifle	272
Waffenfabrik Steyr Austrian Model 1874 Gras Bolt-Action Rifle - 11mm Gras	152
Waffenfabrik Steyr Norwegian Contract Model 1894 Krag-Jorgensen Bolt-Action Rifle - 6.5x55mm	153
Walch Pocket Model Percussion Revolver - .31 caliber	85
Walker, Captain Samuel	10, 63
Walker Model	11
Walther Free Pistol	226
Walther Gewehr 43 Semi-Automatic Rifle with Telescopic Sight - 8mm Mauser	185
Walther GX-1 Bolt-Action Rifle	234
Walther K43 Semi-Automatic Rifle - 8mm Mauser	187
Walther Model 41W Semi-Automatic Rifle	187
Walther Model LP 2 Air Pistol	226
Walther Model PP Semi-Automatic Pistol - 7.65mm	193
Walther OSP Semi-Automatic Target Pistol	226
Walther PPK Semi-Automatic Pistol - 7.65mm	193
Walther SLE Stainless Steel Flare Pistol - 26mm	195
Walther Volksturm Gewehr VG1 Rifle - 8mm Mauser	186
Washington, Denzel	250
Wayne, John	250
Weatherby FN Mauser Rifle	273
Weatherby Mark V Bolt-Action Rifle	271
Weatherby Mark XXII semi-auto rifle	269
Weatherby Vanguard VGX Rifle	273
Weaver, Walter	215
Webley Junior Air Pistol	245
Webley Mk V Revolver - .455 Webley	163
Webley & Scott Single-Shot Falling-Block Rifle	146
Webley Tempest Air Pistol	245
Wesson, Daniel	11
Wesson & Harrington No. 3 Rod Ejection SA Revolver	99
Westley Richards Side-by-Side Shotgun	280
Westley Richards Super Magnum Paradox Side-by-Side Shotgun - 12 gauge	148
Weston, A. B., English Flintlock Turn-barrel Pistol	28
Weston, A & E, Side-by-Side Flintlock Fowler	28
W.H.B. Smith Prototype Lever-Action Rifle	254
W.H.B. Smith Prototype Semi-Automatic Rifle	254
W.H.B. Smith Prototype Single-Shot Shotgun	254
wheellock musket	6, 8, 24
wheellock pistol with battle-axe	52
Whelen, Townsend	239
White, General Issac Davis	204
White, Rollin	65
Whitney Arms	9
Whitney-Burgess-Kennedy Repeating Musket	113
Whitney-Burgess-Morse Lever-Action Repeating Rifle	113
Whitney conversion for U.S. Navy, .38 rimfire	90
Whitney, Eli	9, 48
Whitney Firearms Corp. Wolverine Pistol	261
Whitney-Kennedy Lever-Action Repeating Rifle .38-40, .40-60, .44-40	113
Whitney Navy & Eagle Co. Percussion Revolver, 1st Model, 2nd Type - .36 caliber	84
Whitney Phoenix Single-Shot Breechloading Rifle	118
Whitney Repeating Rifles	113
Whittington Center	5
Wicklund, Doug	5
Wildey Pistol	265
Wilhelm Collath German Over/Under Combination Gun - 12 gauge/9.3 x 65mmR	148
William B. Ruger Gallery	5
William Evans Cast Stock Shotgun - 12 gauge	144
Wilmont Percussion Double Shotgun - 12 gauge	69
Winchester 1885	16
Winchester Accuracy Test Fixture - .50 Browning	176
Winchester-Lee Straight-Pull U.S. Navy Rifle	150
Winchester Lever-actions	109
Winchester Low Wall	12
Winchester Model 12	20
Winchester Model 12 Black Diamond Trap Shotgun	282
Winchester Model 12 Pigeon Grade Shotgun	283
Winchester Model 21 Grand Royal	277
Winchester Model 21 Shotgun	285
Winchester Model 21 Trap Grade Shotgun	279
Winchester Model 23 XTR Side-by-Side Shotgun	280
Winchester Model 25 Slide-Action Shotgun	282
Winchester Model 36 Single-Shot Shotgun	242
Winchester Model 42 Slide-Action Shotgun	283
Winchester Model 52 Bolt-Action Rifle	228
Winchester Model 52-B Rifle	272
Winchester Model 52C Bolt-Action Rifle	256
Winchester Model 54 Rifle	272
Winchester Model 59 single-shot bolt-action rifle	242
Winchester Model 62A Slide-Action Rifle	241
Winchester Model 67 Bolt-Action Rifle	243
Winchester Model 69 Bolt-Action Rifle	175
Winchester Model 70 Bolt-Action Rifle	227, 271
Winchester Model 70 Bolt-Action Rifle Radio Stock	253
Winchester Model 70 Bolt-Action Sniper Rifle	210
Winchester Model 70 Palma Bolt-Action Rifle	231
Winchester Model 71 Lever-Action Rifle	274
Winchester Model 99 Thumb Trigger Rifle	254
Winchester Model 100 Semi-Automatic Rifle	268
Winchester Model 101 Over/Under Shotgun	279
Winchester Model 190 Semi-Automatic Rifle	243
Winchester Model 290 Deluxe Semi-Automatic Rifle	242
Winchester Model 1866 Lever-Action	109
Winchester Model 1866 Third Model Lever-Action	108
Winchester Model 1873 Lever-Action	109
Winchester Model 1876 Lever-Action	109
Winchester Model 1885 Falling Block	220
Winchester Model 1885 Falling-Block Schuetzen Rifle	221
Winchester Model 1885 High Wall	12

INDEX

Winchester Model 1885 High Wall Falling-Block Rifle	222
Winchester Model 1886 Lever-Action	109
Winchester Model 1890 Slide-Action Rifle	17, 241
Winchester Model 1892 Lever-Action	16, 109
Winchester Model 1894 Lever-Action	16, 109
Winchester Model 1895 Lever-Action	16, 109, 274
Winchester Model 1897 Slide-Action Shotgun	121, 217
Winchester Model 1906 Slide-Action Rifle	241
Winchester Model 1907 Police Semi-Automatic Rifle	217
Winchester Model 1907 Semi-Automatic Rifle	139
Winchester Model 1911 SL Autoloader Shotgun	139
Winchester, Oliver	11
Winchester Repeating Arms Company	138
Winchester/Schoyen Model 1885 Falling Block Single-Shot Target Rifle	219
Winchester Winder Single-Shot Musket	139
Wingate, Colonel George	222, 297
W.J. Jeffery & Co. Double Rifle	143
Women On Target	301
Women's Wilderness Escape	301
wonder nines	20, 264
Wood, Colonel Leonard	151
Woodward James Over/Under Shotgun	144
World Trade Center	215
W. R. Pape Double-Barrel Percussion Pistols	58
Wurfflein Percussion Plains Rifle	71
Wurfflein Single-Shot Pistol	223
W. W. Greener Double Rifle	120
W. W. Greener Ltd. British Peabody-Martini	148
Wyatt Earp	92

Y

Yeager, Chuck	206
Yeomanry Carbine by Henry Nock	38
Young, Gustave	129

X

Zanotti, Cassiano, Italian Snaphaunce Pistol - .60 caliber	30
Zelner, Caspar	25
Zuloaga, Ramon	34

MORE FROM THE NRA MUSEUMS

THE NRA MUSEUMS

Free admission.

Open every day of the week.

NRA National Firearms Museum

at NRA Headquarters, 11480 Waples Mill Rd.

Fairfax VA 22030

NRA National Sporting Arms Museum

at Bass Pro Shops, 1935 S. Campbell Ave.

Springfield, MO 65807

Brownell Museum of the Southwest

at NRA Whittington Center

34025 Hwy 64 West, Raton NM 87440

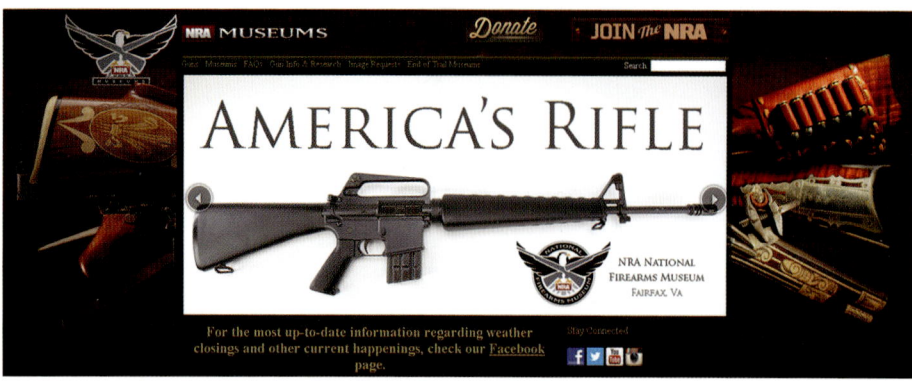

NRAmuseums.com website

Over 10,000 photos of firearms from the NRA collection. Articles by Museum Staff.

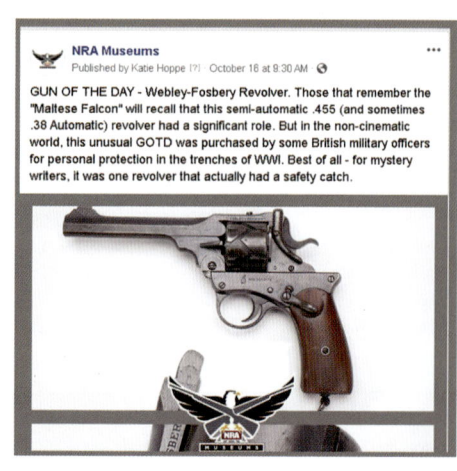

NRA Museums Facebook page

Gun-of-the-day, firearms info, museum updates.

NRA Museums guns, staff, and locations are featured on most episodes of Gun Stories.

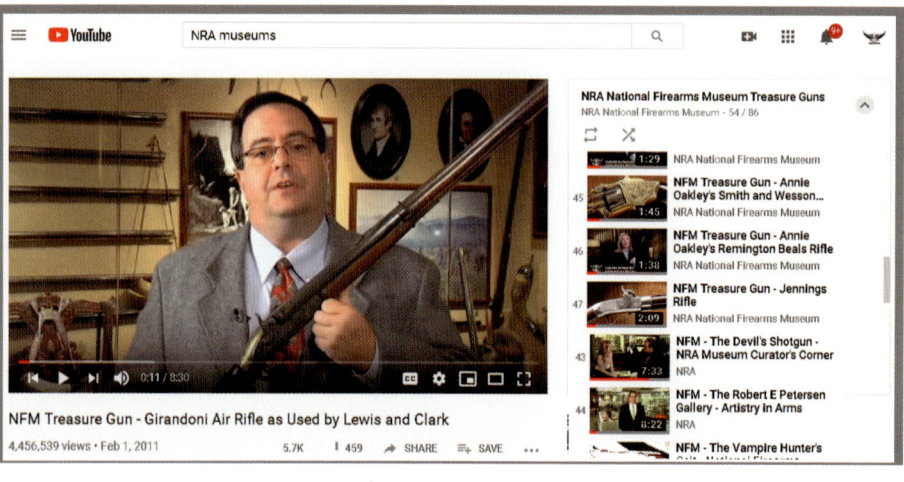

NRA National Firearms Museum YouTube Channel - over 400 gun videos on demand.

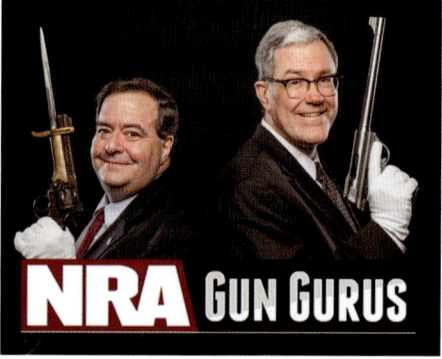

NRA Gun Gurus television series

Educational Display Competitions featuring exceptional firearms from private collections.

The NRA Museums conduct two competitions each year and recognize outstanding educational displays with special awards. NRA Affiliated Gun Collector Clubs present displays at the NRA Annual Meeting of Members at a different location each year. The NRA National Gun Show, hosted by a different NRA affiliate each year, presents awards for displays by individual collectors.

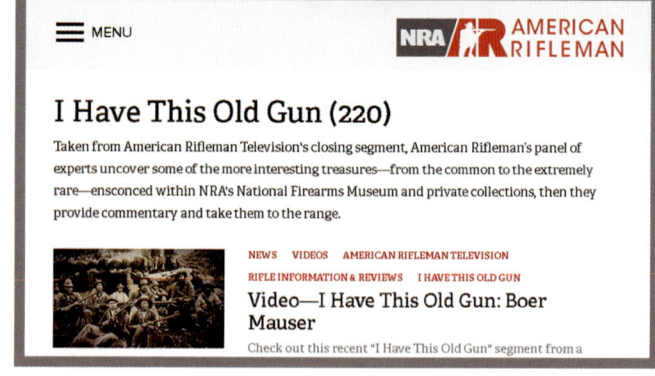

"I Have This Old Gun"

Featured segment on every episode of American Rifleman Television.